APPLETON-CENTURY-CROFTS SOCIOLOGY SERIES

Edited by *John F. Cuber,* The Ohio State University

SOCIAL MOVEMENTS

SOCIAL MOVEMENTS

An Introduction to Political Sociology

by

RUDOLF HEBERLE

Professor of Sociology
Louisiana State University

New York

APPLETON-CENTURY-CROFTS, INC.

HN
15
.H47

Editor's Foreword

Professor Heberle is eminently qualified by experience as well as training for his ambitious task. He is acquainted at first hand with the panorama of social movements and counter movements in Germany and elsewhere on the Continent, both before and after the Second World War. The American analyst of social movements has, through him, access to sources of information and interpretation not common among American-trained sociologists. This makes the mode of analysis found in this book fresh as well as challenging.

Professor Heberle has added a thoroughly scholarly volume to a slowly growing literature on social movements. This book replaces none, competes with none—it is singular in its problem, its method, and its contributions.

JOHN F. CUBER

Ohio State University

Preface

The intention of this book and its plan are explained in detail in the introduction. Its main objective is to present a general sociological theory of social and political movements. If we regard sociology as the study of social action, then the study of political action should be an important field of sociology. The more or less accidental and arbitrary departmentalization of the social sciences in our universities should not prevent us from realizing the fact that each of them deals merely with particular aspects of the same object; never should we forget the unity and wholeness of society. The study of those forms of social action with which we shall deal in this book is, perhaps, the most suitable introduction to political sociology.

The subject certainly is vast, and the only way to cope with it in a book of moderate scope is to select those aspects which are of foremost relevance to a general system of sociology. Even so, many interesting problems had to be left untouched; many important movements have not even been mentioned. We beg the reader to keep in mind that this is not a history of social movements but a systematic and comparative treatise; the references to any particular movements should be regarded as "cases." In teaching, I have found it expedient to assign papers and book reports on particular social movements or on political behavior in certain geographic areas in order to give the student an opportunity to apply the concepts and principles presented in the text.

The author of a book is likely to be most acutely aware of its shortcomings; but I am not going to deprive my critics of their fun. I merely ask that the book be taken for what it intends to be. There are certainly omissions in the literature cited, partly because some recent publications were not available to me at the time of writing, partly because I thought it advisable not to overload the book with citations of literature in foreign languages not accessible to the American student.

My interest in this field developed about thirty years ago, when I wrote my doctoral dissertation on the labor movement in Sweden. It was then that I first felt the need for a general systematic theory of social movements and political parties. Some years later, during a sojourn in the United States as a Fellow of the Rockefeller Foundation, my interest in the sectional aspects of American parties was aroused by Professor Charles E. Merriam. He also drew my attention to the work of André Siegfried on the geography of political "climates" in France.

After my return to Germany, I offered courses on the Sociology of Political Parties at the University of Kiel. Publication of a book on this subject had to be cancelled when the Hitler régime was established. Also, a study of political movements and elections in rural Schleswig-Holstein which I undertook during the years 1932 to 1934 had to be shelved until 1945 when I wrote a condensed translation under the title, *From Democracy to Nazism*. Soon after the publication of this study by the Louisiana State University Press the plan for the present book began to take shape. A major concern was to present the subject in a form which would be intelligible to upper-class and graduate students without committing the blunder of oversimplification. The book in its present form is very largely an outgrowth of teaching experience; in fact, a first draft prepared from my own and some students' class notes has served for a textbook through several semesters.

I was fortunate in receiving encouragement and assistance from the Louisiana State University through the Institute of Population Research and the University Council on Research. I am also indebted to the Social Science Research Council for a grant-in-aid which matched the grants received from Louisiana State University. These grants enabled me to work in the Library of Congress, the libraries of Harvard, Princeton, and the University of Michigan; also to utilize the Library of the Institute of Advanced Studies at Princeton and the archives of the Office of Opinion Research at Princeton. To these institutions and the many persons on their staffs who were kind enough to advise me, I want to express my gratitude. Acknowledgements are due to the following journals and publishers for permission to use copyrighted material as indicated in the footnotes: American Sociological Review, The Macmillan Company, International Publishers Company, Inc., American Psychological Association, Inc., *The Washington Post*, The University of Chicago Press, Louisiana State University Press, *The New Republic, Political Science Quarterly*, McGraw-Hill Book Company, Inc., Yale University Press, Philosophical Library, *The New York Times, Social Forces*, University of Pennsylvania Press and Rinehart and Company, Inc.

To several colleagues and former students, I am indebted for advice and aid in the preparation of this book; in particular to Marion T. Loftin for assistance in preparation of a first draft; to Sten Sparre Nilson of Chr. Michelsens Institutt at Bergen for helpful suggestions made during his visit at Louisiana State University; to Eric Voegelin for valuable references to literature; to Page Dees, George Hillery, and Perry Howard for editing the manuscript; to Jenelle Lounsberry and Beverly Burris for untiring clerical aid; and to Mrs. Augusta Bradsher for expert and circumspect typing.

R. H.

Louisiana State University

Contents

Part I

THE IDEAS IN SOCIAL MOVEMENTS

Part II

THE SOCIAL PSYCHOLOGY OF SOCIAL MOVEMENTS AND POLITICAL PARTIES

xii CONTENTS

CONTENTS

SOCIAL MOVEMENTS

1

Introduction *

* Adapted from R. Heberle, "Observations on the Sociology of Social Movements," *American Sociological Review*, Vol. XIV, No. 3 (June, 1949).

GENERAL ORIENTATION

Purpose of This Book

THE EXPERIENCE OF two world wars, the revolutions in Russia and Germany thirty years ago, the rise and fall of Mussolini and Hitler, the Civil War in China, the expansion of the Soviet sphere of influence into the very heart of Europe, and the ensuing tensions between the partisans of capitalism, socialism, and communism have aroused an intensified interest in the study of those forces and factors which have contributed to the present crisis of Western society. Of foremost importance among these are patterns of concerted social action and more or less organized groups which are commonly referred to as social and political "movements."

The conventional approach to the study of these phenomena has been a historical and philosophical study of their ideas or theories. These were interpreted and analyzed as if they were systems of philosophy; they were submitted to critical evaluation in terms of empirical truth, logical consistency, and ethical standards. Not much attention was paid to the meaning of these ideas to the masses of people who made up the movement or party, nor to the social structure

of these groups, nor to other problems of sociological relevance.

In more recent years, however, these neglected aspects
have received more attention. This, I believe, is due, apart
from the influence of mass and crowd psychology, to the
example of the sociology of political parties, which began
with the study of the caucus and boss rule and seems to have
been stimulated by the discovery of oligarchic tendencies
even in parties standing for democracy, and by the observation of similarities in structure and in tactics between the
Communist and the Fascist parties and régimes. The methods
which have been used in these studies can also be applied
in the study of social movements. In doing this we are aiming at the development of a comparative, systematic theory
of social movements within a more comprehensive system
of political sociology.

The main justification for this undertaking is that movements with very different aims and doctrines have in common many characteristics of organization, structure, and tactics, just as modern political parties, irrespective of their
programs, share certain traits. Furthermore, it is also well
recognized that movements which aim at comprehensive
and radical changes in the order of a society spring up in
certain typical situations, a fact which permits certain generalizations concerning their causation.

The Study of Social Movements in Early Sociology

Little systematic theoretical work has been done in the
study of social movements.[1] And yet this is a field in which

[1] The present state of sociological literature on this matter in this country
may be indicated by the fact that there are, so far as I know, only three or
four recent books which attempt a more or less comprehensive treatment of
social movements.

About twenty years ago Professor Jerome Davis of Yale wrote what he
thought was "the first textbook on modern social movements to be published

we can lean not only on a vast literature but also on one of the oldest traditions in our science. In fact, it may be claimed that the study of social movements was one of the origins of sociology.

---

in America"—*Contemporary Social Movements* (New York, D. Appleton-Century, Inc., 1930), p. ix.

It was and still is a very useful collection of documents, sources, and readings on socialism, communism, fascism, the coöperative movement, and the British labor movement, with side glances at the labor movement in the United States; but it begins with six chapters on Utopias and concludes with several chapters on the peace movement—a somewhat incongruous selection.

There is also an introduction in which the author develops some general principles concerning the origin and development of social movements, leadership, and social control, and a great deal of connecting text between the readings. Davis does not intend to give a comprehensive, methodical, comparative sociological analysis of social movements.

Harry W. Laidler's *Social-Economic Movements* (New York, Thomas Y. Crowell Company, 1946) is a useful reference book on socialism and the socialist movement, including syndicalism and communism, but it contains very little information on organization, structure, tactics, leadership, and other sociologically relevant aspects; Laidler does not attempt an analysis of the societal origins and the socio-psychological foundations of those movements.

The latter are the central subject in Hadley Cantril's *Psychology of Social Movements* (New York, John Wiley & Sons, Inc., 1941). This, however, is a series of case studies rather than a systematic comparative theory of social movements. The selection of cases (the Lynching Mob, the Kingdom of Father Divine, the Oxford group, the Townsend Plan, and the Nazi Party) while useful for the author's purposes, is inadequate from a sociological point of view; there is not enough on the organization and structure of the movements, and there is no methodical consideration of their relations to political parties.

The book that comes closest to the type of approach I have in mind is Sigmund Neumann's *Permanent Revolution* (New York, Harper and Brothers, 1942)—an excellent study of fascism and Nazism with side-glances at Russian communism and Western democracy. It deals with the institutions of régimes as well as with the dynamics of the political movements.

For a survey of American Ph.D. theses on social movements, see Paul Meadows, "Theses on Social Movements," *Social Forces,* Vol. 24 (May, 1946), pp. 408-412; for references to articles by Meadows, *ibid.*

A report on undergraduate studies in this field is given in J. Stewart Burgess, "The Study of Modern Social Movements as a Means for Clarifying the Process of Social Action," *Social Forces,* Vol. 22 (March, 1944).

See also Herbert Blumer, "Social Movements," in Robert E. Park, ed., *An Outline of the Principles of Sociology* (New York, Barnes & Noble, Inc., 1939), and in A. M. Lee, ed., *New Outline of Principles of Sociology* (New York, Barnes & Noble, Inc., 1946).

France has been the classical field for the study of social movements. The Great Revolution itself in its various phases and the subsequent revolutions and counter-revolutions, each accompanied by a change in the form of government, inevitably gave incentive to inquiries into the causes of such changes and therefore led to the development of general theories on the structure and change of society. But France also had become, by 1830, the breeding ground of socialistic and communistic theories. A century ago a German scholar, Lorenz von Stein,[2] expressed the idea that these social theories were no longer of significance, except as "indications and forerunners of impending greater developments." What really matters will, from now on, be the actual movements of the proletariat, which Stein calls the Social Movement. The purpose of Stein's work is to analyze the causation and development of this movement and to show that ways and means of integrating the proletariat into society must be found, if a social revolution much more catastrophic than the previous political revolution of the bourgeoisie is to be forestalled. Reform and revolution are thus presented as alternative ways of adjusting the form of government and the legal order to the changing order of society. The Social Movement, in other words, need not culminate in a revolution.[3]

[2] Lorenz von Stein, *Geschichte der Socialen Bewegung Frankreichs von 1789 bis auf unsere Tage* (1st ed. 1850), edition of 1855, p. vi.

[3] *Ibid.*, p. lxxii, also pp. cxxiv ff. This is not the place to discuss Stein's critique of socialism and communism or his own program of social reform, although it would be interesting enough in the light of later developments in Germany and in regard to the present situation in the United States. See Heinz Nitzschke, *Die Geschichtsphilosophie Lorenz von Stein's,* (Munich and Berlin, 1932), and Gottfried Salomon's "Vorwort," *Lorenz von Stein, Geschichte der Socialen Bewegung Frankreichs* (Munich, 1921). Stein was already well known as the author of the first comprehensive work on socialism and communism in France (*Der Socialismus und Communismus des heutigen Frankreichs,* 2d ed. Leipzig, 1848), which was published in 1842 and must have had influence upon Karl Marx. (For Marx's relation to Stein, see Heinz Nitzschke, *op. cit.,* pp. 135 ff.) Stein treated the doctrines of socialism and communism in the conventional way, analyzing them like systems of philosophy. But already in the second edition, which

The significance of Stein's ideas for our discussion lies in two points: (1) he makes a clear conceptual distinction between the theoretical systems or doctrines on the one hand, and the actual social movement on the other hand; and (2) he ascribes to the study of the social movement a central place in his system of sociology. Not only is the emergence of the social movement given as the reason why a science of society is needed, but Stein's entire system is really built around the analysis of the origin and movements of the social classes and their influence upon the forms of government.[4] In developing these principles, Stein set the pattern which all the outstanding sociological treatises on socialism and communism were to follow. Karl Marx's designation as "Utopian" of all those systems which did not relate the ideal of a communistic society to the emancipation of the proletariat is very likely also a fruit of Stein's work. As late as 1919 Werner Sombart, who in the past fifty years has been one of the prominent authorities in this field, defined socialism and communism as intellectual-spiritual expressions of the modern social movement; the latter he described as the synthesis (*Inbegriff*) of all emancipation efforts of the proletariat—the practical attempts to realize the ideal goal of socialism.[5]

---

appeared in the fateful year of 1848, Stein made the remarkable statement that the real significance of socialism and communism is to induce inquiries into the concept and nature of society (p. vii). Consequently, the later work begins with an introduction entitled, "The Concept of Society and the Law of Its Movement," which is a small book in itself. Here we find a theory of revolution, as distinguished from other anti-authoritarian actions, and a distinction between various types of revolution. Here we also find a very realistic analysis of the class structure of modern Western society and the struggle of classes for power.

[4] *Ibid.*, p. cxxx.

[5] Werner Sombart, *Sozialismus und Soziale Bewegung* (1919), pp. 1, 11.

THE CONCEPT "SOCIAL MOVEMENT"

The main criterion of a social movement, then, is that it aims to bring about fundamental changes in the social order, especially in the basic institutions of property and labor relationships. But no longer can we identify the concept of *social movement* with the proletarian movement. The very existence of fascism and its derivations precludes it; and there are also the nativistic movements in the colonial possessions of European powers, the peasant movements in eastern Europe and the farmers' movements in this country to take into account. Further, we need a concept that can be applied to social movements in pre-capitalistic societies and periods.

We are not concerned, however, with a hard and fast taxonomic classification of patterns of concerted social action into "movements" and "non-movements." Our concern is to find those characteristics essential in social movements of major importance which serve us as prototypes; our concern is to develop, rather than define, a type concept.

All Western languages use the metaphoric term *movement* or its equivalent for the phenomenon we want to define: *Soziale Bewegung* in German, *mouvement social* in French, *sociala roerelse* in Swedish, *bevegelse* in Danish, *movimento sociale* in Italian, and so forth.

The connotation in all these languages is that of a commotion, a stirring among the people, an unrest, a collective attempt to reach a visualized goal, especially a change in certain social institutions. Assuming that intention to change the patterns of human relations and social institutions is the essential characteristic of a social movement, we can exclude a large number of phenomena which have some similarity to social movements, but have little immediate social relevance. In other words, we shall focus our attention on social movements of more profound historical significance.

It is true, however, that movements of minor significance which aim at a partial reform in the social order, and even movements limited to a local community, may show traits of general sociological significance. One can learn from such movements a good deal that is helpful for the understanding of major social movements and they may therefore contribute to a theory of social movements, just as one can learn much about political parties by observing factions within a college faculty or a student body.

Short-lived, more or less spontaneous mass actions, such as wild-cat strikes or riots, while not regarded as social movements in the strict sense of our concept, are nevertheless worthy of study because they do occur within the framework of genuine social movements; in fact they are usually among the first symptoms of social unrest, and they also form part of the tactical devices of a movement. Furthermore, their relative simplicity facilitates the understanding of many aspects of the more complex movements.

We further maintain that mere similarity of sentiments occurring independently among a large number of people does not constitute a movement, nor does mere imitative mass action. A sense of group identity and solidarity is required, for only when the acting individuals have become aware of the fact that they have sentiments and goals in common—when they think of themselves as being united with each other in action through these sentiments and for these goals—do we acknowledge the existence of a social movement. The theoretical problem is very similar to that of determining the characteristics of a fully developed social class: the consciousness of class among people in like class position is what really constitutes a class as a social entity. Or, to use another example, a nation is not merely a multitude of people who have similar ethnic and linguistic characteristics—what constitutes a nation are the sentiments, the attitudes, and the goals which unite the people.

Social Movements Treated as Groups

It is in this sense that we propose to treat social movements as a special kind of social group. They are groups of a peculiar structure, not easy to grasp. Although containing among their members certain groups that are formally organized, the movements *as such* are not organized groups. On the other hand, they are, as a rule, large enough to continue their existence even if there should be a change in the composition of the membership. Such groups we shall call "social collectives" (Tönnies). Social movements then are conceptually defined as a kind of social collective. This definition may cause some difficulty for those who are accustomed to think of movements in social life as processes rather than groups.

Trends and Tendencies Are Not Movements

The difficulty seems to arise from the fact that the term *movement* is sometimes used in reference to *trends* or *tendencies*. Thus we speak, for example, of the movement toward industrial democracy, meaning certain changes in the institutional relations between employers and employees, and perhaps also in attitudes which are the result of many uncoördinated actions of single employers and employees, as well as of certain groups. In this sense, what we call a movement is really a tendency. The League for Industrial Democracy, on the other hand, is part of a social movement in the sense of our concept.

The conceptual distinction between *social movement* and *social trend,* or tendency, will perhaps help to clarify the issue. Social movements are, of course, very important factors in producing tendencies or trends of social change, but not all social change is a result of that kind of concerted social action which we call social movement. Many trends and tendencies are merely the aggregate effect of many individual actions. For example, urbanization is the effect of millions of individual moves from country to city; mechanization of agriculture is possible without any collective action whatsoever, merely through adoption of certain technical methods by a sufficiently large number of individual farmers.

On the other hand, a social movement is often the *response* to changes which have been brought about in the form of trends or tendencies: the labor union movement was originally a reaction of industrial wage earners against the changes in labor relations which had been brought about by industrialization. Thus, both trends or tendencies as well as social movements are related to the general phenomenon of social change; trends are to be considered as processes, social movements as a kind of social collective.

Movements Distinguished From Pressure Groups and Parties

Social movements should be conceptually distinguished from two types of action groups with which they have much contact and often even closer relations in actual life. These are pressure groups and political parties. By *pressure group* we mean an organized group formed for the pursuit of a particular, limited political goal, usually a special interest; it attempts to create a favorable public opinion and to impose its policy upon one or more of the political parties. A pressure group is distinguished from a genuine social movement by the limitedness of its goal—it does not aim at a general change in the social order—and by the fact that it is an organized group. *Political parties* are bound to have a more or less comprehensive political program or platform which gives consideration to all important political issues. It is true that groups have been formed under the name of a party which really represented only very particular interests—for example, those of real estate owners or of retail merchants—but no successful and lasting political party has ever been formed on such limited basis. The same is true of all major and historically more important social movements. One might say that a direct relation exists between the durability of a social movement and the comprehensiveness of its program.

What, then, is it that distinguishes a social movement from a political party? The distinction, we are inclined to say, lies in the fact that the latter has a formal organization. And indeed this line has actually been drawn. The National Socialists, for example, distinguished between the party, which was an incorporated association with the status of a *persona juris,* and the movement, which included all followers of Adolf Hitler, whether members of the party or not. However, if we consider that formal organization in political parties is, as we shall see, a fairly recent development, and if we further take into consideration that the organized membership of a party is often only a small fraction of the people who identify themselves with that party, we have to abandon this criterion. We cannot escape our difficulty by calling the unorganized adherents or sympathizers a movement because not every party intends to move, that is, to change, the existing social order. Apparently no clear-cut distinction between *movement* and *party* can be made by this method of searching for a single distinguishing trait. More promising seems to be an approach which takes into consideration the function or rôle of the two kinds of groups in the larger society in which they operate. A political party is not necessarily, as Burke assumed, "a body of men united, for promoting by their joint endeavours the national interest, upon some particular principal in which they are all agreed." [6]

By this definition the two major parties in the United States, and many parties in Latin American countries would not qualify as political parties at all. It is more realistic to

[6] Edmund Burke, *Thoughts on the Cause of the Present Discontents, 1770* (Cambridge, Cambridge University Press, 1930), p. 96.

define a political party as a group of people who "propose to act in concert in the competitive struggle for political power." [7] This definition leaves open the question of whether the main uniting bond in a party is a principle, a complex of common and similar interests, an emotional attachment to a leader, or simply the desire to secure offices and patronage for members of the group. A genuine social movement, on the other hand, is always integrated by a set of constitutive ideas, or an ideology, although bonds of other nature may not be absent.

Furthermore, a party is by definition related to a larger group, within which it operates against at least one partial group of similar character. Parties can appear in all kinds of corporate groups, but a political party by definition can occur only within a body politic, that is, only within a state. A social movement, on the other hand, need not be restricted to a particular state or to a national society. [8] In fact, all major social movements have extended over the entire sphere of Western civilization and even beyond.

Finally, without intent to belittle the need for precise conceptual distinctions, we shall be more concerned with the relations between social movements and other action groups than with the differences.

THE SOCIOLOGICAL APPROACH

As mentioned before, the prevailing approach to the study of social movements has taken the form of histories of social thought, theories, or ideas. For instance, the study of socialism, in the conventional approach, would be a historical or perhaps a systematic presentation of the various kinds of

[7] Joseph Schumpeter, *Capitalism, Socialism, and Democracy* (New York, Harper and Brothers, 1942), p. 283.

[8] The problems which arise from the appearance of political parties that are part of a supra-national federation or corporate body will be discussed in Chap. 16.

socialistic theories, not a study of the socialist movements in various countries. These theories or doctrines are treated very much in the same way in which one might treat systems of philosophy. If they are critically analyzed, the critique usually applies standards of logic, of empirical validity, and eventually of ethics.

Justified as this approach is for certain purposes, it is inadequate for an understanding of social movements as action groups. For it concerns itself with only one aspect of the movements, and it is likely to lead to erroneous conclusions. Social theories which seem not to be sound according to scholarly standards are likely to be under-rated in their power of appeal to human beings whose sentiments, desires, and interests happen to be in harmony with them, and who consequently can be aroused by those ideas. In studying the ideas in social movements we shall take them as proclamations of aims and as expressions of will, rather than as statements of economic or political truth. In other words, we shall regard them as ideologies which have definite functions within social collectives.

Ideologies

In the study of ideologies considerable refinement of methods has been attained during the past half-century, largely through the sociology of knowledge and the theory of the political myth.[9] No longer do we judge the social ef-

[9] In view of the tendency among contemporary writers to use the term *myth* indiscriminately in reference to various kinds of beliefs concerning social and political matters, it seems advisable to draw attention to Sorel's original theory. In *Reflexions sur la violence* (ed. 1907, pp. 32-33), Sorel says: "The men who participate in the great social movements represent to themselves their future action in the form of visions of battle (*images de batailles*), assuring themselves of the triumph of their cause. I proposed to give the name 'myths' to these constructions, the knowledge of which offers so much of importance to the historian: the general strike of the syndicalists and the catastrophic revolution of Marx are myths...."

The full meaning of the concept can of course only be understood by knowing Sorel's use of it in his critique of democratic socialism and of bourgeois society.

fectiveness of ideas by standards of logical consistency or empirical truthfulness. We have learned through bitter experience that even absurd and scientifically refutable ideas can become immensely effective tools in arousing men into action and in building up sentiments of solidarity and loyalty.[10]

As sociologists, we are primarily interested in studying the ways in which ideas are accepted by the masses and in the extent to which they become *constitutive values* [11] in social movements. The more important social movements tend to absorb a great deal of the social thought of their time and their ideologies therefore tend to become rather complex aggregates of ideas. Some of these may be regarded as specific and essential to the movement; they are the really integrating ideas. Others may be of mere accidental significance for this particular movement. The former may be called the *constitutive* ideas, since they form the spiritual-intellectual foundation of group cohesion or solidarity.

Having thus isolated and analyzed the integrating ideology of a movement, we will want to know what kind of people adhere to it and why.

Social Psychology

The first step will be an inquiry into the attitudes and motivations which are typical of participants in social movements, and which determine the socio-psychological *texture* of various types of movements. We are using the term *texture*

[10] We are in our day of social psychology and propaganda technique confronted with the experience of purposively manufactured ideologies of the Fascist and Nazi type, consisting of ideas which are often not believed in by those who propagate them, nor shared by all who call themselves members or followers of the movement in question.

In a case like this, the simple device of asking members of the movement what they see in it, and what induced them to join, may result merely in the reproduction of the official propaganda line of the movement.

[11] I owe this concept to Ernst Jurkat, "Das Soziologische Wertproblem," *Phil. Diss. Kiel* (ca. 1930).

to denote the characteristic quality of socio-psychic inter-relations between members of a group, as distinguished from its formal organization and social structure. From the socio-psychological level we pass on to the sociological plane of analysis by studying the relations between social movements and other social collectives which furnish members, leaders, and followers of the movement.

Social Foundations

It is generally recognized, as mentioned before, that the chances of an idea's becoming part of the creed of a mass movement depend not so much upon its intrinsic value as upon its appeal to the interests, sentiments, and resentments of certain social strata and other groups. The strength of the appeal will depend largely on constellations of several factors which may vary greatly in the course of time and from place to place. Consequently, the carriers of social movements range very widely from primary groups to ethnic groups and social classes.

The particular significance of an appeal to a certain social class or classes is now generally recognized. It has its explanation in the fact that major social and political changes will always affect the distribution of the societal income and wealth and thereby induce changes in the relative power position of the classes to one another.

Social movements, even if they are not primarily concerned with the welfare of a particular class, are therefore as a rule closely bound to certain social classes and opposed by others.

The founders of modern socialism, Karl Marx and Friedrich Engels, as well as the conservative advocate of social reform, Lorenz von Stein, deserve credit for having demonstrated that ideologies are linked with the social situation of certain classes—expressing the socio-political interests or needs of these classes; and that, if they are not linked in this way to the actual social situation of certain classes, the ideas will remain without practical effect.

The principle of this theory was not new. Earlier thinkers, like Montesquieu and Ferguson, had pointed out that forms of government cannot be arbitrarily instituted, but that they are conditioned by a variety of natural, human, and social factors. What Stein and the socialists contributed was the theorem that political ideas and social philosophies are the expressions of the group consciousness of social classes, and that the class structure of a society is primarily conditioned by the conditions of production of goods and services. These conditions of production are subject to evolutionary change, each new system evolving from the preceding one. Consequently the political and social ideas of an epoch or a society are an expression of the class structure and the state of economic development of that society.

This theory has proved to be a very valuable hypothesis, but it needs verification in concrete cases. The participation of people in social movements and particularly their adherence to political parties is conditioned by a variety of factors which require careful study in each particular situation. Wherever it is possible, quantitative analysis is desirable. We shall therefore devote a special chapter to the discussion of quantitative studies of social movements and political behavior.

Structure

Sociology, whether defined as the study of social interaction or as the study of the forms of association or of social entities, is concerned with the structural-functional aspects of human relationships. By *structure* in reference to social movements we mean in the first place the differentiation of rôles and the distribution of power, influence, and authority within the movement; in the second place we mean the relation of the movement to political parties, the structure and organization of the latter, and the inter-relation between parties and other organized groups within the movement. A close inter-relation exists between the goal of a movement, its structure, and its strategy and tactics. The composition of the supporting social groups is also of consequence for the structure as well as for the strategy and tactics.

Strategy and Tactics

Whether admission to the organized groups and activities of the movement is restricted or not, whether authority within the movement is centralized or not—these and other structure traits depend largely on the revolutionary or evolutionistic strategy of the movement. The size and structure of its organized units are largely determined by tactical considerations. In order to illustrate this point we need merely to refer to the structural differences between the older political parties in Western democracies and the new type of fascistic and communistic political orders.

Functions

Apart from these aspects of structure in their relation to the internal functioning of social movements and in particular to the organized groups which they comprise, we shall have to study the *functions* of these groups in the larger society in which they exist. The intended functions are of course to be determined from the ideology, from the programs and other declarations of goals. But the actual functions are not identical with the intended functions. The proclaimed goals may not be reached, or they may change during the course of action, or the unforeseen and unwanted effects may be more important. Besides, certain objective functions of all social movements, as of all political parties, can be discerned, which aid in the understanding of these phenomena. As such objective functions, we distinguish first, the contribution to the formation of the common will or political group will on various levels of integration; and second, the contribution to the selection and training of the political élite. The term *élite* as used in this connection is to be taken in a neutral, technical sense, free of any judgment as to the moral or intellectual quality of the persons concerned.

MEANING AND VALUE OF A GENERAL THEORY OF SOCIAL MOVEMENTS AND POLITICAL PARTIES

To attempt a systematic treatise of the scope indicated in the preceding discussion may seem to be an almost impossible task. How is the study to be limited in terms of time and space? How can any degree of thoroughness be attained in so vast a subject? It is not surprising that most of the literature in this field has dealt with only one or the other of the various aspects indicated or with one particular movement only. A comprehensive, empirical treatment of the major social movements at all times and in all countries would certainly require several volumes. But our intention is different. The purpose of a general theoretical study of social movements is not to convey information about every one of the more significant social movements past and present; that would be the objective of a sociological *history* of social movements. The purpose of this treatise is to enable the student to analyze and understand *any* social movement—even new movements which may spring up in the future. In other words, *we intend to provide the theoretical tools for the study of concrete social movements.*

In a theoretical treatise of this kind all references to particular social movements serve as illustrations, examples, or cases which demonstrate a particular general principle or problem. It follows from this premise that no definite limitations of the material covered are required in terms of time and space. Theoretical systematization, not historical completeness, is our aim. Material is therefore selected for its theoretical relevance rather than its historical or empirical comprehensiveness.

Certain limitations are suggested by the very nature of our subject. The social phenomena which we are going to study had their origin very largely in the area of Western civilization and in relatively recent times. Certainly we will not be limited to the American scene. The history of Great Britain, France, and Germany—countries which have so fundamentally and copiously contributed to American society and culture—is a rich source of case material. Furthermore, the use of "foreign" material has educational advantages: it enables the student to acquire a *detached* view of certain social phenomena which would easily arouse his emotions when treated in connection with his homeland, and at the same time it helps to overcome the students' ethnocentrism.

A treatise of this kind should of course be oriented towards a general system of sociological theory. In fact, it ought to be a step towards the building of such a system. If sociology is the study of social action, the systematic study of certain types of political action undertaken in this book may be regarded as an important and significant branch of general systematic sociology. The author, to be sure, is aware that whatever contribution this book may offer is only a beginning.

One question may arise in the mind of the reader: Is this the proper time for such an undertaking? In a world full of tensions, conflicts, and uncertainty, in an age of great instability in the power relations between nation-states, and in a period of rather rapid changes in political tendencies within the national societies, it may seem imprudent to attempt the elaboration of general principles concerning some of these elements of change.

On the other hand, perhaps there has never been a greater, more pressing need for the kind of work we have undertaken. The involvement of the United States in close political relations—friendly as well as hostile—with other powers has increased the need for an understanding of the moving forces within modern societies, our own as well as those of foreign countries. It seems that these considerations ought to have more weight than the fear that some of our findings may soon become obsolete. As a matter of fact, the probability that this may occur is much less in the case of a general theoretical treatise than in the case of a comprehensive descriptive study. This may be illustrated by a reference to the now defunct Hitler movement. Although Nazism is no longer a political force, many insights into the nature of totalitarian movements and régimes remain valid and can be applied in the study of other movements and régimes—past, present, and future.

It is fairly safe to say that the validity of a sociological principle increases with abstraction; the more general a principle, the greater its independence from any particular historical situation. For these reasons we believe that a theoretical systematic treatment of our subject is likely to retain its validity and utility even in an age of rapid social change—at least for some time. In this field, as in the social sciences in general, theory is never intended as a final statement of truth; it is subject to testing through application in the study of concrete social phenomena, and to revision in the light of new empirical evidence.

I

THE IDEAS IN SOCIAL MOVEMENTS

2

General Principles and Survey of
Social Movements

GENERAL PRINCIPLES

THE FIRST STEP towards an understanding of a social movement suggests itself by common sense: we want to know
what it is all about. We ask: What is it that these people
want? What is their program? What do they demand? What
do they propose to do? We want to know the end or goal, the
objectives of the movement.

Even if we can get an answer to this question, we may not
be satisfied. The goal may appear to us very strange or repulsive. We then want to know the reasons by which those
people justify their objectives. What is it that they dislike in
the present order of our society and why do they think the
order which they propose would be more satisfactory? What
is their general idea of a good society, of the relation of the
individual to society, and of human nature?

In addition, we may also want to know what immediate
steps they intend to take in order to achieve their goal. Do
they believe in gradual reform, or in a sudden and violent
revolution? Do they believe that the time for achievement of
their goal will come soon, or do they reckon on a long period
of preparation?

In short, we want to know the entire complex of ideas,
theories, doctrines, values, and strategic and tactical principles that is characteristic of the movement. We call this

complex the *ideology* of the movement, using the term in a broad, nontechnical sense.[1]

The ideas of which we are speaking are to a social movement what a program or platform is to a political party: they are the principles and action programs on which the members have reached a general agreement. They define the movement in terms of its aims.

The existence of such a set of ideas is not peculiar to the groups mentioned. It is a general phenomenon in all social groups. Every social group, whether large or small, can exist only if and insofar as the members agree on certain aims and principles of action and on certain basic value-conceptions. Without such a set of aims, values, and rules of conduct, no truly social group is possible. It is their presence which distinguishes human society from animal societies. However, in many social groups these ideas are never clearly formulated and expressed. In others they are very definitely fixed by formal agreements and resolutions; for example, the dogma of a church or sect. In social movements one finds great variations in this respect.

Constitutive Ideas

Constitutive ideas are those ideas considered most essential to the movement. They form the basis of its solidarity.

These ideas usually concern three main problems: (1) the final goals or ends of the movement, (2) the ways and means by which the goal is to be attained, and (3) the reasons for the endeavors of the movement—that is, the justification of the movement or, as one might say, its social philosophy.

In addition, there are found in most social movements ideas which are not essential and not generally agreed upon, although in some cases they may be derived from certain constitutive ideas. For example, there was at one time among socialists in continental Europe a strong and organized

[1] On the restricted, technical use of the term, see below, p. 28.

movement for cremation, which had no essential connection with socialism; however, since the established churches opposed cremation, the socialists, who were quite generally anti-clerical, favored it.

Problems in Studying Ideologies

We are here concerned only with the constitutive ideas. Research in this field is often difficult because of the way in which these ideas are presented. One rarely finds a well organized, systematic presentation. Ideologies are usually formulated in proclamations, resolutions, speeches, programs, platforms, pamphlets, essays, and newspaper articles. They are also contained in autobiographies of leaders and influential members of the movement, and in letters and diaries. In some cases, the founder or one of the outstanding leaders in the movement has expressed his ideas in a book or in a series of writings which become the authoritative sources of the movement's doctrine. This has been the case in the Marxist branch of the socialist movement, where the works of Friedrich Engels and Karl Marx—especially the *Manifesto* of the Communist Party—and the works of Lenin have become the infallible sources of ideology.

As a rule, one has to reconstruct the thought system of a movement from many different sources. In some cases one has to study the actual behavior or conduct of the leaders, the representatives, and the rank and file of a movement in significant situations; further, one must investigate their attitude with regard to essential issues in order to find out what they really intend. For instance, how they vote on certain bills may be significant.

The publicly proclaimed goals and ideas are not always the true and real aims of a movement. Sometimes the goals are intentionally formulated in a very vague way, so as to unite masses of members who would not be able to agree on a more definite formulation. The Nazi movement offers a good case. Political parties often follow this practice in order to attract the largest possible number of voters. A too specific program or platform would repel certain groups of voters which could be won if the program was vague enough to permit an interpretation that would dispel their objections. Sometimes the ideology of a movement is not even quite clear to the members themselves; they may be still searching for a formulation of their ideals and for a theoretical support of their actions and intentions. A good example of this situation is the German youth movement in the years before the First World War. The movement was at that time widespread and vigorous, and a sense of belonging together permeated all its branches; but when, in 1913, at the Hohe Meissner meeting an attempt was made to formulate a declaration of principles, agreement could be obtained only on a few very general and indefinite theses.[2] In some movements, the true and ultimate aims are concealed and kept secret within a small circle of the initiated. To some extent this was true of the Nazi movement; it was a characteristic trait of the early phases of the Masonic movement.

The systematic presentation of the constitutive ideas of a movement is but the first step; it has to be followed by analysis and interpretation. The methods of analyzing the ideologies and action programs of social movements have been greatly refined in the past thirty or forty years. The Marxists, as well as Pareto, Scheler, Mannheim, and others, working in the "sociology of knowledge" have shown that in the realm of political and social ideas the expressed thoughts are not always to be taken at their face values, and that social theories and doctrines are likely to be conditioned by their authors' position in the social stratification of their society and by the historical situation in which the ideas were conceived. Sometimes we find statements which were true at the

[2] Howard Becker, *German Youth: Bond or Free* (New York, Oxford University Press, 1946).

time when the document was composed, but no longer fit the facts. The Communist Manifesto of 1848 is full of such statements, but the orthodox Marxists still accept it as absolute scientific truth.

The interpretation of such thought systems has to start from an inquiry into the practical intentions of their authors: What did these men want, and against whom are these proclamations directed? The next step, then, is to inquire into the actual function of the ideas in the social movement under consideration. In this connection, it is important to remember, as Eduard Spranger points out,

that certain social theories are justifiable and understandable not because they truthfully describe objective facts and bring them into logical relations, but because they create a higher will to life and victory. Marxism, for instance, is such a militant doctrine. . . . Political theories, as well as constructions in the philosophy of history are often rooted more in the will to live than in mere historico-social facts and the will to pure objectivity.[3]

Karl Mannheim has suggested a conceptual distinction between different types of ideologies, basing the distinction upon a functional difference. He maintains that in general those social groups which strive for recognition and power tend to express their social ideas in forms of a Utopia—a logically consistent system, proposing a new social order, usually of a rational nature. Those groups, on the other hand, which are attempting to defend a position of power and prestige, tend to express their ideology in form of a complex of principles which appear logically inconsistent but prove to be related to each other through their common function as arguments in defense of the interests of the group.[4] In Mannheim's terminology, socialism would be called a Utopia,

---

[3] Eduard Spranger, *Types of Men*, trans. by P. J. W. Pigors (Halle, M. Niemeyer, 1928), p. 93. The remark about Marxism is questionable, as we shall see.

[4] Karl Mannheim, *Ideology and Utopia* (New York, Harcourt, Brace & Company, 1936). See also "Sociology of Knowledge" in *Encyclopedia of the Social Sciences* (New York, The Macmillan Company, 1942).

whereas conservatism would be called an ideology. The distinction is useful for certain purposes, but we shall continue to use the term *ideology* whenever we speak of a complex of ideas characteristic for a social movement or political party.

In popular language the term *ideology* is often used in a derogatory sense, as if the political opponents were intentionally dishonest in their proclamations of purposes, creeds, and beliefs. In sociological terminology, *ideology* has no such derogatory connotation; it designates merely a type of thought structure.

Typically, the defensive ideologies, in Mannheim's restricted sense of the term, do not attempt to justify a social order on account of reason; they tend to emphasize the organic growth of all social institutions, the desirability of an undisturbed evolution, the futility of any attempt at reorganization of society according to rational, thought-out schemes. They may even deny the rational nature of man and posit a theory of man based on biological conceptions such as race.

The theories which explain social stratification in terms of social selection (social Darwinism) have become, in many instances, part of the ideology of the ruling classes. On the other hand, the idea that human beings can be improved morally by improving the social environment seems to be a utopian element in present-day socialism and communism.

Whenever one encounters in a social movement a set of ideas which are untenable on the ground of scientific knowledge and irreconcilable with logic and reason, one may find the clue to an understanding by inquiring into the group interests which these ideas serve to propagate and defend. Ideological thinking in the specific sense of Mannheim's theory is quite frequent in the propaganda of certain pressure groups. One may find, in one and the same pamphlet or speech, an emphatic defense of free enterprise, free competition, freedom of contract, and opposition to government interference with private property; and on the other hand, demands for tax exemptions, protective tariffs, direct government subsidies for shipping, and opposition to anti-trust laws.

In concrete historical cases, it is difficult to distinguish beyond doubt between utopian and ideological thought and the attempt can easily lead to biased conclusions. Be it, therefore, sufficient to state that in many cases a seemingly inconsistent ideology reveals its inner consistency when one recognizes the ultimate aim. In our days, the most striking example of this has been German National Socialism, as we shall see later.

That ideologies are largely determined by group interests is now quite generally recognized, in principle. To prove it in concrete cases may be a very difficult task. The main difficulty consists in relating certain ideas to certain social groups, such as socio-economic classes; classes are not easily defined, and on certain issues disagreements occur within a certain class. The problem will be discussed later in detail (Chapter 8). Further complications arise from the fact that the leading thinkers in a social movement quite often come from other social classes than those whose cause they serve. Neither Marx nor Lenin was of working-class origin; many of the leaders in early liberalism came from the nobility, and the theoretical formulation of conservatism was largely the work of middle-class intellectuals. Burke, the great British conservative,[5] was a commoner, and Stahl, the philosopher of Prussian conservatism, was a university professor of middle-class origin.

The Inter-Relations Between Ideologies

The ideologies of social movements stand to each other in a twofold relationship: first, as the integrating creeds and

[5] B. Guttmann, *England im Zeitalter der buergerlichen Reform* (1923), p. 101.

immaterial weapons of social groups in conflict with one another; in this sense we may observe that socialism, being the ideology mainly of the working-class movement, is the antagonist of liberalism, the ideology primarily of the middle classes. But there is a second kind of relationship between ideologies; that is the relationship between ideas in the realm of intellectual endeavor.

The best way to reach an understanding of the intellectual relationship between the ideas of social movements is through their history. The history of ideas is made most understandable if one regards it as a conversation between great minds: a debate which extends over the centuries. One set of ideas is attacked by another, which emerges victoriously only to arouse new arguments from a third theory, and so forth. Every new social theory is influenced by its forerunners. We find, for instance, that socialism, although it is essentially a social creed of the proletariat, has incorporated many elements of the social philosophy of liberalism, which was the creed of its adversary, the bourgeoisie. We shall see also that the ideology of any counter-revolutionary movement contains certain ideas which are adopted from its revolutionary antagonist.[6] From this point of view, it matters little whether a particular idea has taken hold among the masses or not, as long as it has had any effect on other thinkers. Even forgotten ideas may become relevant for the intellectual history of thought if they have anticipated what later was propagated with more success.

Steps in the Analysis of Ideologies

We may now summarize the various steps which have to be taken in the analysis of an ideology (using the term in the broad sense); these steps represent different levels or planes of inquiry:

[6] See A. Meusel, "Revolution and Counter-Revolution" in *Encyclopedia of the Social Sciences.*

1. We begin with the systematic presentation of the proclaimed content of the ideology.

2. This may be followed by an inquiry into the historical
origin of the various ideas which compose the ideology; in
this connection the influences of other ideologies may have
to be traced.

3. We then inquire into the underlying assumptions concerning the nature of man and of society on which the
proclaimed program or ideology is based; this means, in
philosophical language, an inquiry into the anthropology and
social philosophy of the movement.

4. Finally, the question may be raised as to what made
this ideology appealing to the people who participate in the
movement. This question we may try to answer in terms of
group interests and socio-psychological categories.

On the first level of analysis we are primarily concerned
with problems of selection and systematization; the essential
and characteristic ideas have to be isolated from the non-
essential, more or less incidental notions that may have been
received into the movement's arsenal of propaganda in order
to increase its sphere of attraction. Incoherently publicized
ideas have to be brought together in a systematic order. The
discovery of this order is, however, often impossible before
the second and third steps have been taken.

In particular, the third level of analysis will often present
us with those ideas that enable us to bring order into the
whole. Here we will encounter such propositions as that the
community is more important than the individual and that
therefore the welfare of the individual is subordinated to the
welfare of the community—or the opposite position.

It is on this third level of analysis that we will most likely
be concerned with the ultimate values of the movement's
ideology, which are beyond empirical proof or disproof. Such
transcendental quality of ultimate values has to be accepted
as a fact; it should not, per se, mislead us into unfavorable

value judgments about the movement in question. And yet, ultimate values of a movement may be in harmony with the value system of our own Western society or they may be opposed to it or irreconcilable with it. This we can prove by rational analysis, and on the basis of a careful rational critique we may arrive at a value judgment, approving or rejecting the goals of the particular movement under consideration. In saying that it is theoretically possible to do this, we do not mean to say that everybody can do it, nor that the result would be entirely beyond controversy.

On the fourth level we will be confronted with problems of causality which may turn out to be very complicated. Why a certain complex of ideas arises at a given time and place and not at another one, and why this particular set of ideas finds acceptance among certain categories of people remains often a matter of conjecture. This is particularly true in cases where we have no evidence that the people in question did not have any other choice. For example, we can make it appear very plausible why the ideology of Nazism appealed to certain types of people in Germany, but the question, why these people did not turn to communism or evolve some other ideology remains still open. Finally, when we attempt to explain the conversions or choices of particular individuals, we are very often left without really conclusive evidence.

THE GREAT SOCIAL MOVEMENTS IN THE WEST SINCE THE END OF THE EIGHTEENTH CENTURY

Our contemporary Western society is largely the creation of the *bourgeoisie*. This term is often used synonymously with the term *middle class*. However, the two terms do not have identical meanings: middle class (or middle classes) may, at least in the United States, include farmers and skilled workers as well as businessmen and clerical workers; bourgeoisie on the other hand, as used in technical social science terminology, refers to the various kinds of capitalistic entrepreneurs, especially in commerce, banking, and manufacturing.

The essential characteristic of the bourgeoisie is that its income is derived from investment of capital in continuously operating establishments or enterprises in a competitive market-economy. The income of the bourgeoisie consists of interest and profit—the latter being the real objective purpose of capitalistic enterprise. To discover and to utilize opportunities for profitable investment of capital is the characteristic function of the entrepreneur. To make profit, to acquire wealth, is by no means the strongest personal motive with every entrepreneur; the desire of power, or recognition, or pride in achievement may be even stronger motives. But profit-making is the regulative principle in modern capitalistic business; a private business enterprise that fails to show profits will sooner or later end in bankruptcy. The entrepreneur therefore cannot afford to disregard this principle. The second characteristic of the bourgeois is his total devotion to the operation of his business. Modern business, especially manufacturing, is carried on continuously, contrasting to the intermittent and often casual transactions which were characteristic of early capitalism.

The bourgeoisie has come into existence gradually since the end of the Middle Ages (fifteenth century) and reached its full development in the nineteenth century. Modern manufacturing industry was created by this class and became its main field of operation.

Liberalism and the Rise of the Bourgeoisie

As the bourgeoisie gained in economic strength and influence, it began to demand a corresponding share in political power and higher social prestige than it enjoyed under the *ancien régime*. The movement began in England—the country most rapidly advancing economically—in the seventeenth century, and led to the movement for independence in the American colonies, and eventually to the American Revolution. The movement of the bourgeoisie led also to the various revolutions in France and other continental countries from the end of the eighteenth to the middle of the nineteenth centuries.

The main objectives of the bourgeoisie were (1) freedom from the many restrictions on economic activity which had been instituted in the medieval solidaristic society by the urban craftsmen and later by the governments of the new territorial states (mercantilism); (2) protection against arbitrary interference of government with private property and business enterprise; (3) a legal system adapted to the needs of the entrepreneur; a reliable administration of justice; and (4) political institutions which would guarantee the preservation of these attainments.

These objectives, together with the philosophical arguments for their justification, make up the thought system of liberalism. The image of society which liberalism proposes is characterized by equal chances of acquisition in unrestricted competition and by participation of all qualified citizens in the formation of the political group. Liberalism can therefore be sociologically defined as the constitutive idea of the movement of the bourgeoisie. It was the creed and battle cry of the bourgeoisie during the period of its struggle for political power and social recognition. This is not to say that liberalism was an invention of the bourgeoisie —many of its elements are of much older origin. But the objective class interests of the bourgeoisie found a particularly fitting expression in the combination of these ideas.

The Labor Movement

The most important change in the structure of Western society which resulted from the rise of manufacturing industry was the growth of a legally free but economically dependent class of wage workers which makes up a very large proportion of the population in all industrialized countries and regions. In this class, the bourgeoisie created its antagonist. The workers in capitalistic enterprises were no longer owners of the means of production. They did not own the machines or materials or buildings required for manufacturing, nor did they as a rule have a share in the capital invested in the factories, mines, and other enterprises in which they were employed. Being without property in this sense, they could live only if employed by a property owner for wages. On the other hand, the wages which they received were to the entrepreneur an item in the cost of production which he had to hold down, whereas to the workers they were the indispensable basis of their existence, which they tried to raise as far as possible.

In this position, the workers could have no strong interest in the preservation of an economic system based upon private property controlling the means of production. At first they attempted to improve their economic condition within the capitalistic system. When these efforts met with resistance from the employers, and when the latter used their newly acquired political power to suppress and destroy the workers' organizations, trade unions, and consumers' coöperatives, the workers began to wonder whether an entirely different socio-economic order might not be needed in order to give the wage earner full access to the accomplishments of Western civilization.

The labor movement became the other great social movement of the nineteenth and early twentieth centuries. Like the movement of the bourgeoisie, it began in England, the most highly industrialized country. It spread to the United States, though here it was retarded by the simultaneous dynamic expansion of the American economy, and it spread all over the continent of Europe. Sharing much of the liberal ideology in its beginnings, the labor movement has turned more and more to a different ideology.

Socialism

The poor and underprivileged had at all times been attracted by schemes for the establishment of an entirely different, better social order, in which there would be no poverty and no great wealth, where the drudgery of making a living would be reduced and more evenly distributed, where a spirit of brotherhood would prevail, and mutual aid and coöperation would take the place of competition and exploitation. The abolition of private property and the introduction of communal ownership and use of land, factories, and other means of production, were often proposed as the solution. Perhaps then one might even do without kings and princes, or without any kind of government at all. In short, communistic, socialistic, and anarchistic schemes had always been popular among the poor workmen.

The variety and the influence of such ideas have increased rapidly with the rise of modern industry, especially in France and England since the end of the eighteenth century. From these countries the socialistic, communistic, and anarchistic movements spread all over Europe and into the United States in the course of little more than a century. Since the middle of the nineteenth century, one particular kind of socialism, that which Marx and Engels regarded as the only scientific (and therefore true) socialism, became the ideology of the major and most vigorous branches of the labor movement in various countries.

Conservatism

The picture would not be complete, and the course of movements and ideas not intelligible, unless we took cognizance of the reaction of the old ruling classes. Since the main attack on the pre-capitalistic social order came from the bourgeoisie, the supporters and adherents of the *ancien régime* (the gentry and its associates in church, bureaucracy and the professions) developed an anti-capitalistic but at the same time anti-liberal ideology which, probably through French usage, acquired the label of *conservatism*. The old ruling classes rallied their forces in various kinds of groups and proceeded to the counter-attack in every field of social action. To speak of conservatism as a social movement is therefore not at all so paradoxical and contradictory as it would seem. In the course of time, the conservative movement received reinforcement from those elements of the bourgeoisie which found themselves content with the socio-political positions which they had reached.

Fascism

The last thirty years have seen the rise and fall of a new mass movement: Italian Fascism and its German form, National Socialism. This is a complex phenomenon which would require very careful analysis. Its relation to the class structure of our society is not so clear as that of the other movements. Tentatively we may say that Fascism and National Socialism arose among the disillusioned and uprooted elements of the urban middle classes (we use this rather vague term intentionally), found support among the economically insecure farmers, and came into power through an alliance with certain elements among the bourgeoisie who hoped to use the Fascist forces against the Socialist-Communist labor movement.

In eastern Europe and in the United States there have arisen farmers' movements of considerable importance, but their ideologies were in all essential points derived from those other movements; therefore they do not require separate consideration.

We shall now proceed to discuss briefly some of the ideologies of these major social movements.

3

Liberalism and Conservatism

~~~~~~

LIBERALISM

The Meaning of the Term

LIBERALISM IN THE broader sense according to the great Italian historian of liberalism, Guido de Ruggiero, is "a deep-lying mental attitude; its primary postulate, the spiritual freedom of mankind, posits a free individual, conscious of his capacity for unfettered development and self-expression"—an idea derived from Christianity and Greek philosophy.

> It follows therefore ... that any attempt on the part of constituted authorities to exert artificial pressure or regulation on the individual ... is an unjustifiable interference, a stultification of his personality and initiative. Against such coercive interference, whether in the moral, the religious, the intellectual, the economic, or the political sphere, liberalism has constantly arrayed its forces.

As an attitude, liberalism is not related to any particular historical period or to any particular social groups.

Liberalism in the more precise sense of political liberalism aims at political liberty as the prerequisite for the attainment of liberty in the broader sense. The basic aim in early liberalism was to limit the interference of the state in the private life of the citizens, and to transform "state policy into a vehicle for promoting the liberties of individuals and groups." [1]

[1] G. de Ruggiero, "Liberalism," in *Encyclopedia of the Social Sciences* (New York, The Macmillan Company, 1942).

Historical Origin

In order to understand the problem rightly, it is necessary to realize that the medieval kings were not absolute rulers. They were restricted in their power by ancient customs and tradition, by the dualism of secular and spiritual power (emperor and pope), and by rights and privileges which they granted to the nobles and the communes (cities), as the price for support received. As the power of the kings increased through standing armies, through the creation of a royal administration staffed with experts, through the decline of the power of the church in certain countries, and through the submission of the nobility, they began to encroach upon the ancient rights of their subjects. Absolute monarchy became identical with unlimited and arbitrary use of the power of government to the advantage of the monarch and his favorites and retainers. The fight for liberty therefore became a fight for restrictions of the power of the government, or rather of the new territorial state with its unprecedented centralization of power in the hands of the monarch.

Constitutive Ideas and National Variations

The concrete demands which were made by the bourgeoisie varied from country to country. If we may take British liberalism as the prototype,[2] we find the following essential postulates:

1. Foremost is the claim for civil liberty or "the right to be dealt with in accordance with the law" by the state. In other words, freedom from and security against the arbitrary use of state power by the king or any of his officers is the first demand of the new middle class. Incidentally, in this move for the limitation of the power of the crown, the bour-

---

[2] The following presentation follows closely L. T. Hobhouse, *Liberalism* (New York, Henry Holt & Company, Inc., 1911). Professor Hobhouse's ideas may be taken as a mature expression of British liberalism.

geoisie is often supported by parts of the nobility and the clergy. The "rule of law" means the establishment of the government's obligation to observe, in its dealings with the subjects, certain general norms known to everybody in the commonwealth and applicable by the courts of justice. This was important especially to the merchants and manufacturers, because the nature of their business required certainty of the legal consequences of any transaction, and also required rational impartiality of the administration and of the courts.

2. The freedom from arbitrary imposition of taxes (fiscal liberty) and the claim that only such taxes may be levied as have been approved in advance by the representatives of the people is really a derivation from the first postulate.

3. Since in England large parts of the new middle classes adhered to the nonconformist sects and churches, and found themselves therefore in danger of persecution or discrimination by the combined powers of state and established church, "the right to worship in any form which does not inflict injury on others or involves a breach of public order" became one of their most urgent demands. Gradually the more general principle of freedom of thought, or rather the right to express one's opinion in public, became part of the liberal credo. After the religious struggle subsided and religious toleration became established as a principle of government in the Western countries, the freedom of political opinion became more important, in particular with the spreading of anti-capitalistic ideas.

The postulate of freedom of opinion follows from the belief in the dignity of the individual and the right to seek spiritual salvation in his own way; it is supported by the supposition that new and unorthodox ideas and beliefs which are based upon truth cannot be crushed by forcible measures but can be fought only through rational discussion. Forcible suppression may give momentary results, but in the long run the oppressed opinions will emerge again and create much greater difficulties.[3]

4. Of greatest immediate importance to the bourgeoisie was the abolition of restrictions on economic activity. This involved: (*a*) The right to choose any occupation, unrestrained by the social rank or status of one's parents. The abolition of privileges and discriminatory institutions which limited the various ranks or status groups in their choice of occupation was prerequisite to the creation of a competitive market economy in which everybody had, at least in principle, equal chances. It also was a condition without which the modern manufacturing industries with their need of a freely movable labor force could not have been created. (*b*) Freedom of economic enterprise, that is, freedom from the many restrictions which the guilds had imposed upon the crafts in order to secure for each master a fair and decent living; and also abolition of the policy of mercantilism with its granting of privileges or monopolies to individual entrepreneurs and companies, its internal and external tariffs and subsidies to shipping companies and other enterprises. The new bourgeoisie had reached the stage—at least in Great Britain—where the protective and nursing hand of the state was no longer needed. Freedom to invest one's capital in the most profitable way, freedom to sell throughout the territory of the state, freedom of trading with foreigners and in foreign markets were now the most urgent demands of the new middle classes. (*c*) Freedom of contract between buyers and sellers as well as between employers and workers, and finally, freedom of association for business enterprise and for the promotion of common interests. In other words, economic freedom meant freedom from state and corporational (communal and guild) restrictions.

5. These personal and group rights had to be secured and

[3] Bennigsen, quoted after H. Oncken, *Rudolf von Bennigsen*, Vol. I (1910), p. 300.

guaranteed by active participation of the middle classes in the legislative and executive functions of government. Political liberty and popular sovereignty became therefore an essential element of the liberal ideology. Only a government which is responsible to the people as a whole could be expected to respect the entire complex of liberties. A legislature based upon extended or universal suffrage is assumed to be the only institutional device by which this kind of government can be established.

It is at this point that liberalism and the democratic idea merge: "I venture to say that every man who is not presumably incapacitated by some consideration of personal unfitness or of political danger is morally entitled to come within the pale of the Constitution," said Gladstone in 1864, professing thereby his sympathy with the impending democratic reform of the British election system.[4] However, the liberals were much more inclined than the democrats to draw the line between those who were considered fit to have the right of voting and those who were regarded as incapable or dangerous elements. For a long time, the liberals, being largely men of property or of higher education, considered it right to exclude the unpropertied and uneducated masses from the right to vote.

German and Italian liberalism assumed a peculiar character through the coincidence and combination of the middle classes' fight for these liberties with the movement for national unity.[5] Both countries were in a state of political disintegration, split up into small principalities and kingdoms. This was the very time when the rising bourgeoisie needed a uniform régime within the boundaries of the national market and needed as well the protection of a mighty national

[4] See Hamilton Fyfe, *The British Liberal Party* (London, George Allen & Unwin, Ltd., 1928).

[5] G. de Ruggiero, *op. cit.*

government in foreign markets. The movement found strong support from scholars, intellectuals, and from the free professions and students; in other words, it found support from all those groups who took a lively interest in the advancement of a national culture and whose professional interests were hampered by the multiplicity of régimes.

For Germany, tragic consequences resulted from the fact that the attempt at resurrecting the German Empire by a popular movement in 1848 was thwarted, and that the unification was achieved, in 1871, through a federation of the German princes under Bismarck's impulse and direction. As soon as this aim of German liberalism was realized, the fight for political liberties lost much of its momentum. It is true that in Germany the more progressive liberals carried on the fight for parliamentary government. This was true in other continental European countries where the powers of the legislatures were rather restricted under the form of constitutional monarchy. But it is quite safe to say that the lack of real understanding of the meaning of liberty, so characteristic of German middle-class thinking since Bismarck, was largely due to the fact that the German liberals had never carried the fight for civil rights to the finish.

Towards the end of the nineteenth century, liberalism in most European countries began to show signs of decadence. The very class which had been its main standard-bearer began to desert it. The bourgeoisie, having attained controlling positions in the state, and having realized its most immediate objectives, became increasingly apprehensive of the political and economic aspirations of the new industrial working classes, to whom they did not intend to grant equality of legal and political status. At the same time, the upper strata of the middle classes, the high bourgeoisie, who had succeeded in building up extremely powerful business concerns in industry, banking, and commerce, ceased to be genuinely interested in freedom of enterprise.[6] They advocated protective tariffs and other forms of state subvention and shifted politically towards conservatism.

On the other hand, as the economic and political power of the entrepreneurial classes grew and the actual economic and political dependence of the employed classes became quite obvious, many liberals began to realize that the political and cultural aims of liberalism could not be attained under an economic policy of laissez-faire; in order to protect the economically weaker elements in society, regulative interference by the state with private enterprise appeared necessary. By advocating such measures of a social policy, the liberals began to approach certain positions of the socialists.[7] The result was that since the end of the nineteenth century the liberal parties have crumbled, losing supporters both to the conservatives and to the socialists.

Assumptions Concerning the Nature of Man and Society

The theoretical arguments by which the liberals supported their fight were based upon two charges: (1) that the crown had acquired through usurpation certain powers which rightfully and traditionally belonged to the people—and (2) that the institutions of government had been shaped in contradiction to human nature and in violation of the natural rights

[6] The saturation of the dominant strata of the bourgeoisie is well characterized in a German progressive liberal politician's statement at the time of the first great schism of German liberalism:

"It is quite natural that the two elements which formed the *National-Verein* from its beginning, should separate again, now that the common purpose has been attained [the unification of the Reich]. . . . What objections can a liberal bourgeois have against the present state of affairs? If the parliamentary forms were observed a little stricter, if the anti-usuary laws were repealed, and some other manchesterly reforms were made, the Eldorado would be perfect."

(L. Reickert, in a letter to Nagel, September 28, 1867, quoted after Oncken, *Bennigsen*, Vol. II, p. 80.)

[7] In England, John Stuart Mill may be considered as the most influential representative of the new liberalism.

of human beings. Depending on the predominance of one or the other set of ideas, we can discern a conservative, or more correctly, traditionalistic strain, as well as a progressive and rationalistic strain of liberalism. The former is characteristic of early English, the latter of early French liberalism. "British liberalism up to the eighteenth century was concerned primarily with conservation, while French liberalism . . . proceeded rationalistically, indifferent, on the whole, to its political heritage." [8]

American liberalism followed the English pattern in its earlier phases, whereas later, after Jefferson's return from France, French ideas became more influential. [9]

The rationalistic type of liberalism rests on the assumption that man is essentially good; that he is a being endowed with reason, which he is capable of applying to the affairs of his community. Men are able to perceive what is needed for their own good, and they are therefore also able to establish and operate those social institutions that are necessary in the "pursuit of happiness." In this respect all men are equal; none are by nature particularly qualified to rule over others. The government and the state are perceived as man's work and therefore subject to change according to man's reasonable judgment.

As long as men regard the social order in which they live as ordained by the will of God, or as long as they do not question its goodness at all, there can be no movement aiming at fundamental changes in the social order. Only when the idea arises that there is another, original order, a natural order which has been distorted by human government, can a movement arise that aims at fundamental changes in the

---

[8] G. de Ruggiero, *op. cit.*

[9] The essentially traditionalistic nature of the American Revolution aroused the sympathy of men like Edmund Burke, who became the most vocal opponent to the French Revolution. See Otto Vossler, "Die Amerikanischen Revolutionsideale in ihrem Verhaeltnis zu den Europaeischen," *Beiheft 17 der Historischen Zeitschrift* (Berlin, Muenchen, 1929).

social order. All progressive movements within Western civilization therefore were based on the natural-rights philosophy or the theory of natural law. There have been many variations of this theory. In modern times its main proponents are Hobbes, Locke, Rousseau, and Paine. The one principle which these thinkers have in common is that the state is a creation of human will and reason. Governments are the result of an agreement among the citizens to establish a superior authority which shall safeguard their rights and to which everyone owes obedience. In Hobbes' construction this agreement is a covenant of everybody with everybody, by which is created a political commonwealth or, as we would say today, a state. Once political power has been transferred to the sovereign, the power is absolute and irrevocable.

Rousseau's theory is quite similar, except that in his construction the people retain their sovereignty, the government becoming an organ of the general will of the people. If particular wills obtain control of the government, the people would have the right to reaffirm their general will against the authority in power. Locke, being more realistic and closer to the historical development of the British Constitution, held that the state was "founded upon a contract between the king and the people, a contract which was brought to an end if either party violated its terms." [10]

From this premise follows the second principle, that the government itself is bound by the law. The individual, in giving up his natural rights, receives in return civil rights. There is, theoretically, no longer a sphere, free from custom and law, in which the monarch can do what he thinks is required in the interest of the state. Government becomes rule of law or constitutional government.

This idea of rule of law is not a specific liberal doctrine. It has been adopted by the conservatives as well. But ac-

[10] Hobhouse, *op. cit.*, p. 54.

cording to liberal theory, "civil rights should agree as nearly
as possible with natural rights." [11] In other words, the positive law, which is created by legislation and enforced by the
state, should interfere as little as possible with the natural
rights of the individuals.

Third, if the law is the expression of the general will, it
follows that all citizens have a right to take part, personally
or through their representatives, in its creation.[12] But how
are the citizens to know whether the laws which they are
making are good? Suppose the people, through their representatives, make laws which abridge certain rights of the
individual. Ought such laws be obeyed in the name of popular sovereignty, or be disobeyed in the name of individual
rights?

The theoretical solution to this problem is found in the
fourth theoretical principle of liberalism—the greatest happiness principle. According to this principle, which was developed by Bentham, any action is good which tends to
promote the greatest possible happiness of the greatest possible number of those affected by it.[13] This is, of course,
merely a general directive.

Concretely, it has to be implemented by collective decisions reached through discussion. This is a very important
point. Confidence in the efficacy of free and public debate
and deliberation is an essential element in liberal theory.
The idea of popular sovereignty rests upon it. Liberal theory
assumes that valid insight as to what is right and wrong for
a society can be gained by a contest of opinions which eventually will result in a universally acceptable compromise.[14]
The acceptability of compromise presupposes the assump-

[11] Hobhouse, *op. cit.*, p. 57.
[12] Article VI of the Declaration of the French Assembly in 1789. See
Hobhouse, *op. cit.*, p. 61.
[13] Hobhouse, *op. cit.*, p. 68.
[14] Hobhouse, *op. cit.*, pp. 116 ff. See also A. D. Lindsay, *The Essentials
of Democracy* (Philadelphia, University of Pennsylvania Press, 1929).

tion of the existence of a true will of the group (the "sense of the meeting"), which may be discovered by rational discussion and debate. As we shall see later, this assumption is important for the understanding of the functions of political parties in a democratic society. (See Chapter 17.)

Finally the demand for economic liberty or the doctrine of laissez-faire, which became the most distinctive idea in nineteenth-century liberalism, rests upon the basic idea of a natural harmony between individual and group interests. Applied to the sphere of economic action, this idea leads to the presumption that the greatest possible aggregate wealth will be obtained if the production and distribution of goods is regulated by nothing else but the free decisions of the individual economic agents. Give every man the right to buy in the cheapest and sell in the dearest market, let every man use his property in the most profitable way, give complete freedom of contract to employers and employees, then capitalists will make the highest profits; wage earners, the highest possible real wages. In other words, the economic order is seen as a self-regulating system in which each individual, by intelligently pursuing his own particular interest, contributes to the greatest total output of goods and services and contributes also to their most rational economic distribution.

As mentioned before, this economic doctrine proved to be the most vulnerable element in the ideology of liberalism. It rested on the assumption of an economic system in which a large number of independent entrepreneurs compete with each other under conditions of near equality of chance. With the development of corporations and with the domination of local labor markets by one or a few employers, the very premises of laissez-faire became invalid. The interests of the economically weak were obviously not identical with those of the strong, and the growth of a class of undernourished, poorly housed, and uneducated industrial wage earners was obviously not to the good of the community.

The Interests of the Middle Class

We can see now quite clearly why the new middle classes of commercial, industrial, and other entrepreneurs turned to these ideas as an adequate expression of their own interests and social and political aspirations. Harold Laski states the relation as follows:

> The middle class needed exactly the central principles of liberal doctrine if it was to prosper. It required religious tolerance because the establishment of this principle was inextricably intertwined with the rights of property. It required limitation upon monarchical prerogative lest it be ruined by arbitrary taxation. It required a controlled aristocracy because the establishment of internal peace was the essential condition of commercial prosperity. It required the abrogation of the medieval theories of restrictive regulation in the interest of morality because in such terms individual enterprise could not reach its maximum fruition. The new economic order, in a word, required a secular state; and a secular state in its turn required a liberalizing doctrine if politics was to be more than a branch of theology.... A state was built which corresponded to the wants of the new men to whom power had flowed.[15]

The new type of capitalistic enterprise required a large market; hence, the demand for the abolition of internal and external tariffs. It required an ample supply of labor which could move freely from one place to another and from one occupation to another; therefore, the abolition of serfdom and of guild restrictions. It required the greatest possible freedom of disposition over any kind of property, whether land or movable capital; thus, the abolition of restrictions on the sale and purchase of land; thus, the demand for freedom of association for purposes of business and for the advancement of the interest of the bourgeoisie.

Finally, the new type of capitalistic enterprise needed a system of law which was not only in agreement with the needs of commerce and industry but also one which was uniform over large territories and which permitted a citizen to foresee

[15] Harold J. Laski, "The Rise of Liberalism," *Encyclopedia of the Social Sciences*, Vol. I.

the legal implications and consequences of business transactions—in other words, a rational, calculable system of law
binding all citizens without distinction of rank and enforce-
able in all courts of the country.[16] This need resulted (1) in
the gradual displacement of customary law by legislative
law, (2) in the movement for codification which was supported by the liberals on the continent of Europe, and (3)
in the insistence in England and America on "due process
of law"—a safeguard against administrative and legislative
encroachments on the rights of individuals, in particular on
property rights.

CONSERVATISM

The Meaning of the Term

Against the social theories of liberalism and democracy
there arose a twofold opposition: the conservatism of the
old ruling classes, and the socialistic and communistic movement of the new industrial proletariat.

The word *conservatism* has two different meanings: First,
it means the tendency to maintain the status quo, regardless
of what it may be. In this sense the word is devoid of philosophical content. It does not denote a specific set of political
ideas. In this sense, any group in power tends to become
conservative. Second, it means a particular view of society,
a specific theory of the state and of politics.[17] However, if one
is taking the word in the first sense, one could scarcely
speak of a conservative movement; that would be a contradiction in itself. In this sense, conservatism is an attitude
of opposition to change rather than a movement. It is the

[16] See Max Weber, *General Economic History*, trans. by F. H. Knight
(New York, Greenberg, Publisher, Inc., 1927), Part Four, Chap. XXIX,
pp. 338-343.

[17] Karl Mannheim, "Das Konservative Denken," *Archiv für Sozialwissen-
schaften und Sozialpolitik*, Vol. 57 (1927). See also R. Michels, "Conservatism," in *Encyclopedia of the Social Sciences*.

second meaning which we have in mind if we refer to conservatism as a movement.

Historical Origin

The historical origin of conservatism in this sense lay in the opposition of the old ruling classes to the liberal and democratic movements. Their leaders—mostly members of the nobility, the clergy and the bureaucracy—very soon took collective action to oppose the new middle classes in their aspiration to political power and social recognition. Since the ruling classes were opposing a well-founded rational social theory, they had to find a theoretical justification for their own standpoint; thus they developed a new social and political philosophy, which came to be called conservatism. The name is probably derived from a French journal *Le Conservateur* edited by Chateaubriand and Lammenais. The term became generally accepted in Europe by 1835. Conservatism in this sense is thus not to be confused with mere traditionalism. It is a definite social theory of modern origin.

The Ideology

The conservative ideology arose in both England and France out of opposition to the ideas of the French Revolution, and the ideas of enlightenment and rationalism. Significantly enough, Burke, the founder of English conservative theory,[18] was in sympathy with the American Revolution because of its conservative nature, as mentioned before. He saw in it a movement for the reassurance of inherited rights of the people, while the French Revolution appeared to him to be an attempt to construct a radically new society without regard to the past.

[18] Burke was a Whig, but his political philosophy became the foundation of conservatism. Compare B. Guttmann, *England im Zeitalter der buergerlichen Reform* (1923), and R. Lennox, *Edmund Burke und sein Politisches Arbeitsfeld, 1760-1790* (München and Berlin, 1930), pp. 101 f.

Genuine conservatism in Germany developed mainly in Prussia, particularly in its old, eastern parts; here it came into existence as a political party in reaction against the revolution of 1848. Here it was a real movement initiated by a few aristocrats and intellectuals and supported by many organized groups.

In all three countries, conservatism was supported mainly by the land-owning nobility, its retainers among the clergy and free professions, and by the wealthier farmers. The urban merchants, manufacturers, artisans, and small farmers were at that time not much in sympathy with this movement. Later, towards the end of the nineteenth century, large blocs of the middle classes began to break away from the liberal parties and join the conservatives, thereby changing the very nature of the conservative thought.

Unfortunately for the student of political theory, the main supporters of conservatism were not given much to public writing. Thus we have but few records of their thinking. The theoretical formulation of conservative thought has been largely the work of outsiders like Burke and Stahl, who belonged to the intelligentsia of middle-class origin.

Conservatism has little or no confidence in man's ability to improve the social order by the power of reason. It is this pessimistic conception of man's rôle in society which distinguishes the "anthropology" of conservatism from that of liberalism.

Conservative thinking rejects the liberal conception of the state as an institution which men set up for their security and convenience and which they can reorganize at will. Conservatives also deny the subserviency of the state to the welfare of the individuals. The state, according to conservative thought, has value in itself, independent of the individual, or the state has come into existence without the conscious efforts of the people who compose it. It is regarded either as a creation of divine will, or as a result of slow or-

ganic growth, not dependent on human will. It has, therefore, a will and consciousness of its own. Likewise, law and
property in particular are the products of a slow evolution
through many generations. Therefore a deep respect for the
common law is characteristic of British conservatism, and
distrust of legislation and codification of law characteristic
of conservative thinking in general.

Consequently, conservative thinking opposes any attempt
to improve the existing social order by rationally constructed
schemes and by radical renovation of social institutions. "The
very idea of completely wrecking the existing structure of
society in order to start it all over again is absolutely wrong
and foolish," says F. J. Stahl, the theoretician of Prussian
conservatism.[19]

This denial of the voluntaristic nature of the state, the
fundamental position of all progressive social theory, is
based upon a conception of human nature which may be
called pessimistic insofar as it tends to emphasize the limitations of the mind, and the imperfections of man rather than
his perfectibility. "Man can apply his small mind usefully
only in seeking to understand and adapt his life to the inherited institutions; if he attempts to change them substantially,
he will destroy them and will be unable to reconstruct
them." [20]

Therefore conservatism puts its confidence in the tested
institutions of the past rather than in experimentation with
new legal and political institutions. "When ancient . . . rules
of life are taken away, we have no compass to govern us,
nor can we know distinctly to what port we steer." [21] This
conservative distrust of premeditated, intentional social
change is founded in the belief that any tampering with existing institutions will result in unforeseen and unwanted

[19] F. J. Stahl, *Die gegenwaertigen Parteien* (1863), pp. 63 f.
[20] F. W. Coker, *Recent Political Thought* (New York, Appleton-Century-
Crofts, Inc., 1934), pp. 26-27.
[21] Burke, quoted by Coker, *op. cit.*, p. 27.

consequences. Any change which is not the result of slow, organic evolution is considered dangerous, for such intentional innovation is likely to disregard the influence of the past which determines the possibilities of change.[22] This conception of organic growth involves also the idea that a mere change in institutions cannot relieve the world of social evils. This can be accomplished only through a change of heart.[23]

Conservatism also denies the principle of spontaneous harmony of the individual interests and the welfare of the community. It insists therefore on the necessity of an authoritative moral order, which derives its legitimation not from reason, but, lastly, from God. To this moral order, the economic and political spheres of action are subordinated. Therefore, the conservative rejects the idea of absolute freedom of contract—all contractual relations, including those between employer and employee, involve moral obligations.

Consequently, the conservatives acknowledge a responsibility of the ruling groups towards the ruled; it is a paternalistic conception of the relations between masters and servants which leads true conservatives to advocate protective labor legislation, social insurance, and other measures for the protection of the economically weaker classes. But this principle of responsibility of the ruling groups has a reverse side: the duty of loyalty on the part of the ruled. From this duty is derived the insistence on the employer's authority in labor relations of any kind, and the denial of the worker's right to strike.

In the political sphere, conservatism rejects the liberal idea of the social contract, although in some types of conservative theory, especially in England, we find the assumption of a contract between king and people; the people are,

---

[22] Coker, *op. cit.*, p. 29.
[23] In this connection it is significant that the founders of Prussian conservatism belonged to the pietistic circles of the nobility.

however, in conservative thought, not a mass of independent and equal individuals but a hierarchy of organic groups or corporations, each of which enjoys its own particular rights or liberties. There is no general liberty, but only the liberties of organic groups such as local communities and occupational groups. Therefore, conservatism opposes the centralizing tendency of the modern state, which threatens to destroy all autonomy of local communities and corporate groups, and to level out all the colorful variety of organically grown institutions.

In particular, conservatism is opposed to the liberal conception of property which does not recognize any fundamental qualitative differences between various kinds of property. It denies that land should be treated, legally, in the same way as mobile goods—that is, as a commodity which can be sold or inherited according to the whim of the owner. Conservatism has therefore maintained the institution of entailed farms, as well as restrictions on the mortgaging of land, state control over the stock exchange, and similar restrictions on the freedom of capitalistic enterprise.

National Variations: Germany

The national variations of conservatism are even more striking than those of liberalism. This is understandable if one realizes that the quality or composition and social position of the pre-capitalistic ruling classes varied greatly from one country to the other. And again one has to distinguish between various phases in the development of conservative thought.

German conservatism had its origin and main support among the smaller land-owning nobility—the *Junkers*—especially in the eastern parts of northern Germany. It was essentially a Protestant movement, the Catholic conservatives being comprised within the Catholic Center party (*Zentrumspartei*). The high nobility of very large land owners, particularly in Silesia and other mining areas, who had industrial interests formed the *Freikonservative* or *Reichspartei*, which also found support among the agrarian and heavy industry interests in the western regions (for example, in Schleswig-Holstein and Oldenburg). In addition to the land owners, the conservative party was supported by the higher bureaucracy, who came largely from the small nobility or had acquired titles in the civil service, and by the army officers, who also were largely younger sons of the *Junker* families. Originally these classes which made up the main strength of the conservative party had no very pronounced economic interests; they were concerned mainly with their position as the political élite.

The beginnings of conservatism in Germany are to be found in the reaction of the nobility and of parts of the intelligentsia against the Napoleonic régime. This reaction was much sharper in the agrarian eastern parts of Germany than in the west, where Napoleon's reforms were widely welcomed by the powerful middle classes as a step towards a more adequate social-political order. In the east, resistance against Napoleon meant resistance not only against the conqueror but also against the ideas of the French Revolution.

The budding conservative movement, however, subsided during the period of reaction after the wars of liberation when there was no need for a militant fight against liberalism.

As a continuous and politically organized movement, conservatism dates from the revolution of 1848. The revolution, which aimed at the unification of the Reich under a constitutional monarch or eventually as a republic, was suppressed by force of arms; but the king of Prussia, like other monarchs, conceded the establishment of a diet, the lower house of which was to be elected. It was in preparation for the first elections (to the Prussian Constitutional Assembly) that a group of country gentlemen under the leadership of Count Otto von Bismarck founded the first conservative party. They acquired control of a newspaper, the *Neue Preussische Zeitung*, also called the *Kreuzzeitung* on account of the iron cross which was carried in the masthead. The iron cross served as a symbol with manifold meanings: it had the connotation of piety and of valiance, since it recalled the glorious order of the Teutonic Knights, founders of the Prussian state, and at the same time evoked memories of 1813, the rise of the Prussian people against the oppressor. The full significance of this symbolism appears when one considers that most of the founders were Pietists; they belonged to "that small circle which, being tied together by neighborhood and kinship, was firmly united through religious ideals, like economic pursuits and like political aims." [24]

Contact with the masses of voters, in the first line the farmers, was established through the numerous agricultural associations. The purpose of these groups was the improvement of agricultural techniques and farm management. Since the pietistic *Junkers* were as a rule also outstanding agriculturists, they could easily use these associations for the propaganda of their political ideas. [25] In addition, numerous clubs or associations of purely political nature were founded, some of these surrounded with much secrecy. The veterans' (of 1813) associations also proved useful instruments for the control of voters. [26]

From their religious convictions these leading conservatives derived a highly idealistic conception of the landowner's social responsibilities. "To serve one's neighbor in true love while maintaining oneself in the victorious habit of ruling" became one of their slogans. [27] It expresses an attitude of Christian paternalism. However, another, more utilitarian

[24] Erich Jordan, *Die Entstehung der Konservativen Partei und die preussischen Agrarverhaeltnisse von 1848* (Muenchen, Leipzig, 1914), p. 132.
[25] *Ibid.*, pp. 200 ff.
[26] *Ibid.*, pp. 246 ff.
[27] *Ibid.*, p. 140.

and opportunistic, group soon showed itself within the ranks of the party; its main aim, the protection of the economic interests of the large land owner, was indicated in the name of the association formed by this group.[28]

These two tendencies continued to determine the policy of the Conservative Party throughout its history.[29] In the latter part of the nineteenth century, the agrarian interests, organized in the *Bund der Landwirte* (Agrarian League) gained control of the party and led it into a policy of agrarian protectionism.

After 1918 a rejuvenation of German conservatism seemed to be possible. New elements of non-agrarian classes had joined the party, the most important among them consisting of salaried employees and professional workers (*Deutsch-nationaler Handlungsgehilfen Verband*). Theirs was a strongly nationalistic and to a certain extent anti-capitalistic political ideology. This combination of nationalism and anti-capitalistic sentiments among the clerical and managerial groups, as well as among the younger civil servants, is not surprising; these groups resented the fact that political leaders like Walther Rathenau and Gustav Stresemann initiated a policy of reconciliation with the former enemies, and they ascribed this to the absence of patriotism in the circles of big business with whom these politicians were closely associated.

However, at the same time the party received reinforcements from heavy industry (mining, iron and steel manufacturing) and other big business interests. When these, under the guidance of Hugenberg, gained complete control of the party organization in 1928, the party began to split along

---

[28] V. Bülow-Kummerow's "Verein zur Wahrung der Interessen des Grundbesitzes und zur Aufrechterhaltung des Wohlstandes aller Klassen des Volkes," translated: "Association for the Promotion of Interests of Land Owners and for the Maintenance of the Welfare of All Classes of the People" —probably the association with the longest name ever invented.

[29] Jordan, *op. cit.*, p. 261.

the old friction lines. This disintegration of the conservative party helped to pave the way for the Nazis.

The Hugenberg wing of the party entered upon an alliance with Hitler in the expectation that they could use the Nazis for their purposes, but was crushed. The other wing, the Christian-idealistic group, formed the nucleus of the heroic underground movement which after years of conspiracy against the Hitler régime found its tragic end in the miscarried *coup d'état* of July 20, 1944.[30]

National Variations: The United States

In the United States of America no genuine conservative movement has ever developed. The nearest approach to true conservatism may be found among the planters of the Old South. A small number of them developed a style of life and a social philosophy and attitude which may be called truly aristocratic. While they were wealthy and made money through the sale of surplus products—staple goods like rice, indigo, tobacco, and cotton—making money was not their only concern. They assumed the rôle of a ruling class with all its responsibilities towards the community and towards their subordinates. They did not like to sell their slaves; they did not overwork them; they cared for them in sickness and old age; they served in the armed forces when need arose, and they kept themselves fit for such service by hunting and other gentlemanly sports. Most of the planters, however, were simply large-scale agriculturists, bent upon making money; they had to, because coming from the poorer white classes, without inherited wealth, they could not afford the style of life of true gentry. The development of a broader class of real aristocrats was cut short first, through the civil war, as W. J. Cash has shown,[31] and second, through

[30] Hans Rothfels, *The German Opposition to Hitler* (Hinsdale, Ill., Henry Regnery Company, 1948).

[31] W. J. Cash, *The Mind of the South* (New York, Alfred A. Knopf, Inc., 1941).

post-war developments. The war destroyed the flower of their youth, and the post-war period forced many of the survivors into commercial and industrial activities. In addition, there began the period of general commercialization of life in the South, which did not leave agriculture in the plantation areas untouched. Today, very little is left of the old gentry and gone with it is the conservative outlook on society. William Percy's recollections may be considered as a late document of Southern conservatism.[32]

Apart from the South, American society from its very beginning has been predominantly a middle-class society. Unlike the European agrarians, the leading groups among American farmers and planters were not at all opposed to the new capitalistic society; on the contrary, they were its very backbone. The political conflict between the Federalists and the Republicans, or the Hamiltonians and the Jeffersonians, arose over the distribution of the national income, or rather over measures affecting it, not over fundamental questions of the economic order. But there was another more basic issue involved: the fear of the ruling commercial and planters' classes that the broad masses of poorer farmers and laborers might rise to power. Furthermore, the ideas of 1776 were so closely related to those of 1789 that no reaction against the latter could be of broad and permanent effect. The very fact that the American Revolution had anticipated, in a different and more conservative spirit, the main ends of the French Revolution, precluded the ideas of 1789 from making a great and dangerous inroad upon American society.

The French Revolution aroused, of course, both sympathy and antipathy in America. The rich and well-born feared the spread of radical democratic ideas. They attacked and tried to suppress as "Jacobinistic" the democratic societies which the anti-Federalists were organizing all over the country.

---

[32] William Alexander Percy, *Lanterns on the Levee, Recollections of a Planter's Son* (New York, Alfred A. Knopf, Inc., 1941).

They were particularly afraid of movements among the poor backwoods farmers and the rabble of the cities which might result in repudiation of private and public debts and in legislation damaging to the interests of the property-owning classes. But this controversy between the wealthy and the poor, an old and almost universal phenomenon in any stratified society, was not the only factor in the formation of the two parties. The other, and more important factor, was the antagonism between agrarian and commercial interests, and in this conflict the Southern planters took sides with the poor in opposing Federalist policies.[33]

Clearly, the entire dispute was one within the ranks of the middle classes, for in America even the farmers were, with few exceptions, supporters of the new economic order of capitalism and therefore not, like English and French country nobility and Prussian *Junkers,* opposed to the political and economic ideals of the bourgeoisie. Thus there was no need for a conservative ideology, and the absence of social strata which could have carried it made a conservative movement impossible.[34]

Conservative attitudes, in the more general sense of the word, have of course been present among all those social

[33] Charles and Mary Beard, *The Rise of American Civilization,* Vol. I (New York, The Macmillan Company, 1927), pp. 364-369.

[34] The absence of a conservative party in the United States was noticed and explained by a German historian who wrote one of the earliest and most comprehensive historical treatises on political parties. Apart from the conflict about states' rights, he says,

"There was never any conflict over the Constitution as such ... and never in such a way that [the senate] might have presented itself as the aristocratic, [the house] as the democratic part of the nation. Nobility there was none; money aristocracy was, owing to the general hustling of the money-makers, on too mobile and changing a foundation as that it could have formed a steady layer of society."

Wachsmuth continues with a description of the struggle for offices and seats in the legislatures and the general drive for westward expansion, which he thinks became a dominating principle of American politics—"There was no standstill party,"—no party which wanted to preserve the *status quo,* no party opposed to progress. Wilhelm Wachsmuth, *Geschichte der Politischen Parteiungen alter und neuer Zeit,* Vol. III (1853-1856), p. 338.

strata which at one time or other were content with the existing conditions and desirous of preserving them. In the last forty years, conservative political attitudes have become increasingly frequent among big business men and large farmers. The arguments of these groups, however, are taken largely from the arsenal of laissez-faire, and from the political doctrines of early liberalism.

4

Socialism

~~~~~~

WE SHALL NOW turn to those complexes of ideas which for the last century and a half have gained practical significance as the ideology of the movement of the working class.

MEANINGS OF SOCIALISM AND COMMUNISM

The first to point out the essential relationship between these thought-systems and the rising movement of the industrial proletariat was probably Lorenz von Stein. Having made a comprehensive and penetrating study of the numerous varieties of communism and socialism in France, he came to realize later that from then on any meaningful discussion of these theories would have to treat them as ideologies of the revolutionary proletarian movement. A few years later, Karl Marx and Friedrich Engels appealed to the proletarians in all countries to rally under the guidance of the communist league. About two generations later, Werner Sombart in his book, *Socialism and the Social Movement,* defined socialism as the ideological manifestation of the labor movement. This identification is not quite correct,[1] as we shall see later, but the immense political significance of the socialistic and communistic doctrines lies in the fact that they have become the constitutive ideas of the more mili-

[1] Sombart later revoked it in the introduction to a selection of readings on socialism, *Grundlagen und Kritik des Sozialismus,* Vol. I (Berlin, 1919), pp. viii-xi.

tant branches of the working-class movement in all parts of the globe, and the state doctrine in the U.S.S.R. and its sphere of influence, as well as recently in the major portion of China. This phenomenal spread of the ideology has occurred in the short period of a hundred years and mostly in the last fifty years. Each of two world wars has been followed by a wave of expansion of the domain and following of these creeds. There must be in these ideas a great convincing power, an appeal to emotions and sentiments as well as to reason and interest; otherwise their tremendous spread would be inexplicable.

The terms *socialism* and *communism* have been used more or less synonymously in the past. In many cases communism is regarded as a particular branch of socialism. Both terms have several meanings. Sometimes they are used to designate a future order of society, sometimes they refer to the movements which aim at the creation of this new society, and sometimes they mean the ideologies of these movements. There are many varieties of communistic and socialistic ideologies. All of them have in common a conception of an economic order in which the guiding principle would be, not the acquisition of wealth by individuals, but the coöperative production of goods and their just distribution among the members of the community. To achieve such an economy for use (as opposed to an economy for profitable exchange), socialists and communists advocate the abolition of private property, at least private ownership of the means of production, and its replacement by public ownership.

As a rule, the difference between socialism and communism is seen in the method of income distribution. Socialism means a system in which each worker (and all able adults would work in a socialistic society) is compensated according to the value of his services to the community—that is, according to his contribution to the total income of society; communism means a system in which each worker receives income according to his needs. In present-day orthodox communist terminology, socialism is a period of transition from capitalism to communism.

If used to designate social movements, socialism today means the social-democratic movement (and parties), whereas communism refers to the movements and parties which are, with a few exceptions, organized under the supreme direction of the Russian Communist Party or Bolsheviks.

Although both of these major movements derive their ideologies from the theories of Karl Marx and Friedrich Engels, it should be remembered that not all socialists and communists are Marxists. There are at least three important forms of non-Marxist socialism: Christian, or religious socialism; state socialism; and utopian socialism.

Christian Socialism

Christian socialism has its origin in the teachings of Christ and in the communistic institutions of some of the early Christian communities. Attempts to establish a new kind of society by application of Christian ethics to economic activities have been made again and again by groups within the Christian churches and particularly by sectarian groups since the Reformation. All these experiments were based upon the Christian principles of brotherly love instead of self-interest and on coöperation instead of competition; their guiding principle in economic relations within the community was a sharing of wealth rather than the individual pursuit of profits.[2]

Modern Christian socialism (and communism) began as a reaction of the old ruling classes against the social evils of modern industrial capitalism. In particular, many clergymen who were shocked by the inhuman aspects of the new

[2] H. W. Laidler, *Social-Economic Movements* (New York, Thomas Y. Crowell Company, 1946) pp. 720 f. See also "Christian Socialism," (Great Britain by M. B. Reckitt, United States by V. D. Scudder), *Encyclopedia of Social Sciences* (New York, The Macmillan Company, 1942).

economic order began to advocate legislation for the physical and moral protection of workers, their women and children. Very important in the rise of Christian socialism has been the experience that under the unmitigated form of capitalistic industry the working-class youth would often grow up virtually without any religious instruction. It has been especially influential in England, where many of the industrial wage earners belonged to nonconformist denominations. In the United States, Christian socialism is closely related to the rise and spread of the "social gospel" in the Protestant churches.

Whether certain tendencies among the Catholic clergy and laymen which are referred to as Christian socialism can properly be so named appears doubtful in view of the definite rejection of any kind of socialism by the Church. Catholic doctrine pertaining to the socio-economic problems of our age is proclaimed in the encyclical *Rerum Novarum* of 1891 and in the encyclical *Quadragesimo Anno* of 1931. In these papal letters private property is upheld as an institution of natural and divine law, although restrictions on the use and abuse of property may be imposed upon the individual owner in order to safeguard the social and public aspects of ownership.[3] The Church therefore advocates policies which would enable the wage earner to acquire "a certain moderate ownership"; instead of abolishing the wage system, the Church advocates the principle of a just wage.[4]

On the other hand, it is admitted that the position of the more moderate socialists with regard to property and other questions of social order is changing, and that if these changes continue, their program may no longer be different from that of the Church.[5] However, the main objections of

[3] *Quadragesimo Anno*, Arts. 42, 43.
[4] *Ibid.*, Arts. 69, 71.
[5] *Ibid.*, Art. 123.

Catholic doctrine to socialism are based upon the socialists' secular conception of man and society, which is irreconcilable with the spiritual destiny of man and with the relation of human society to God. The Church maintains that man "is placed here on earth in order that he may spend his life in society, and under an authority ordained by God, that he may develop and evolve to the full all his faculties to the praise and glory of his Creator." Of this "sublime end of individuals and society," socialism is "entirely ignorant." The socialists are solely concerned with ways and means of increasing the production of "temporal goods" and for this aim they are willing to sacrifice man's higher goods, including liberty. Therefore, the encyclical reaches the conclusion that "religious socialism" and "Christian socialism" are contradictions in terms; "no one can be at the same time a sincere Catholic and a true socialist."[6]

State Socialism

State socialism involves a group of social reform schemes which propose state or municipal ownership and operation of public utilities, means of transportation, and basic industries in combination with protective labor legislation and nationwide social insurance (social security).

State socialists were quite influential in Germany from about 1870 to 1918, both in practical politics and in the universities, where many of the outstanding economists belonged to the "school" of *Kathedersozialisten* (professorial socialists). The older generation of American economists who received their graduate training in Germany came under their influence (for example, Richard T. Ely) and the social legislation in some states, like Wisconsin, seems to have been indirectly influenced by them.

If any generalization as to the theories of these thinkers is permissible, one may say that they regretted the fact of

[6] *Ibid.*, Arts. 130, 131.

the class struggle and desired a reintegration of the proletariat into the national society. This they believed was impossible under a system of unregulated economic competition. An appeal to private entrepreneurs, on Christian or humanitarian principles, to live up to their social responsibilities as property owners and employers must remain ineffective under the conditions of a purely capitalistic economy. Consequently, the state has to create such conditions of competition among entrepreneurs and such working conditions for the proletarians as would be compatible with Christian and humanitarian ethics as well as with the national interest.

In addition, it was believed that certain economic functions hitherto provided by private enterprise would have to be assumed by the state, either because the magnitude of the tasks to be performed would surpass the power of private business, or because if they remained in the hands of private enterprises, there would result positions of economic power which were regarded as politically undesirable. It was also found that certain essential goods and services under a system of profit economy could not be provided at a cost which made them available to all in need. Such services as health insurance and medical care therefore would have to be provided by public institutions. Some of the state socialists, like Adolf Wagner, believed that for these reasons the sphere of state activity would be continuously expanded until all of the basic economic activities would come under state control.

Commenting on this "law," the American economist Richard T. Ely observed that its operation would result in the establishment of the socialistic state, since in the end all business would be state owned and controlled. There would be in the end only one employer, the state, which would reign over a hierarchy of employees of various ranks.[7]

7 After Laidler, *op. cit., p.* 739.

It seems doubtful whether these tendencies and schemes of social reform should really be called socialism—even if hyphenated, for none of them proposes a society in which *all* private property of means of production would be abolished. Many of the professorial socialists were, like Gustav Schmoller, conservatives at heart who wanted to save as much as possible of the existing social order by social reforms.

Utopian Socialism

Quite different from the philosophical premises of Christian and state socialism are those schemes of a radically new order which Marx contemptuously called "utopian" and which Sombart, with greater detachment, designates as "rationalistic" socialism or communism.

All these schemes are characterized by the rationalism of their underlying ideas of man and society and by their disregard for social evolution. Man is assumed to be by nature a rational, sociable being, capable of creating through his power of reason a perfect society by abolishing the present corrupted social order and by restoring the principles of a natural order of social life. The organization of the new society is to be rational and it is described in great detail in most of these schemes (Fourier). Reason also will induce men to accept the idea of the new social order. Not only the poor, the wage earners, but also the rich, especially the industrial entrepreneurs and the engineers, will eventually become converted to the new social philosophy and will take the initiative to institute the new society (Saint-Simon).

Socialistic and communistic communities can be established within the capitalistic society as experiments and as models which will help to win more followers.[8] The pattern for the schemes of the new society is Thomas More's (1478-1535) *Utopia;* therefore the name given to them by Karl

[8] W. Sombart, *Sozialismus und Soziale Bewegung,* 8th ed. (1919), p. 43.

Marx. Plato's idea of a ruling élite is found in some of these constructions—for example, in that of Saint-Simon, who expects the technological and scientific experts to become the ruling group. All of these thinkers reject the use of violence: "not by force, but by reason shall the victory be won; . . . force is not conviction and is extremely unworthy of the cause of justice." [9] Most decided in rejection of force and compulsion are the anarchists. Their goal is the creation of a decentralized society consisting of more or less autonomous communities based entirely on sympathy and concord, on voluntary coöperation without any compulsive authority.[10] Consequently the utopian socialists emphasize, not the antagonism, but the fundamental harmony of interests between the social classes.[11]

Utopian socialists and communists have established numerous "pilot" communities, most of them short-lived, and they have also exerted considerable influence upon present-day socialism and communism. America, especially the United States, became a favorite testing ground for communistic experiments. However, they did not create a real mass movement.[12]

MARXISM

The Theories of Marx and Engels

All present-day socialism and communism has come under the overwhelming influence of Marxism. This is a very complex view of society and is by no means restricted to the field of economic and political action. It incorporates a great deal of the ideas of earlier socialistic and communistic

[9] Godwin, quoted by Sombart, *ibid.*, p. 43.
[10] See Godwin, Proudhon, Krapotkin. The use of violence for purposes of propaganda among certain anarchists in tsarist Russia is a special case.
[11] See Laidler on Owen, *op. cit.*, p. 93.
[12] For a contemporary account of these communities, see Charles Nordhoff, *The Communistic Societies of the United States* (New York, Harper and Brothers, 1875), with interesting illustrations.

movements; its main efforts—as a theory—are, however, directed at a critical analysis of capitalistic society. This analysis is performed with the methods of historical materialism or, as it is sometimes called, dialectic materialism.[13]

To attempt anything like a comprehensive presentation even of the main tenets of Marxism would go beyond the scope of this book. We can do no more than treat briefly those elements of Marxism which seem to have had the strongest and broadest influence. In this endeavor we are confronted with a paradoxical situation: the most influential socialist ideology contains no plan for the future society. While Marxism is by no means free of utopian ideas concerning the future of human society, it is in the first place a theory of capitalistic society and its development. We may say it is a theory of social change which involves at the same time an action program for its followers. In reading

[13] See Sidney Hook, "Materialism," in *Encyclopedia of the Social Sciences*. The principles of this philosophy of history were developed by Karl Marx and Friedrich Engels when they undertook a critique of Hegel's philosophy and of various tendencies in German philosophy which were influenced by Hegel. The earliest source for the study of Marxism is the *German Ideology* which Marx and Engels wrote "for purposes of self-clarification" in 1845. This work had never been completely published until 1931. There is now available an English translation of the most important parts of this work. (New York, International Publishing Co., Inc., 1939).

The critique of Hegel was followed by a critique of the classical political economy. Main sources: *Critique of Political Economy*, 1859, Karl Marx, *Das Kapital,* and several historical studies dealing with the social movements in France, England, and Germany. However, by far the greatest influence upon the socialist and communist movement has been a short pamphlet, which Marx and Engels wrote in winter 1847 for the Communist League in London—a small, originally secret, society consisting mostly of German artisans and craftsmen—and which was published in January 1848 in London under the title *Manifesto of the Communist Party* (*Manifest der Kommunistischen Partei*). The original edition was written in German; there are now numerous English translations. The Communist Manifesto has been translated into every important language and it is estimated that the total editions amount to several million copies.

Another widely read source is Friedrich Engels' *Socialism, Utopian and Scientific* (Die Entwicklung des Sozialismus von der Utopie zur Wissenschaft) trans. by E. Aveling (Chicago, Charles H. Kerr and Company, 1914).

Marx and Engels, we look in vain for a detailed description of the future communistic social order as we find it in the works of the utopian socialists. The very vagueness of the Marxian picture of the future may have been one element which explains the mass influence of Marxism; it is a common experience that vague programs can rally more support than very definite and detailed schemes of social reorganization.

On the other hand, Marx and Engels mean to leave no doubt that the communistic society is bound to come as a necessary result and culmination of the development of the capitalistic economic system. Contrary to utopian and state socialists, Marx and Engels deny that a new social order can be established by an appeal to reason or to the sense of social justice. It is therefore futile to expect the initiation of a radical reorganization of capitalistic society either from the bourgeoisie or from the state. No ruling class has ever abdicated voluntarily, and why should the bourgeoisie employ the power of the state (*their* state) to abolish the very system from which the bourgeoisie benefits?

A new social order can only be created by the rise to political power of a class which is opposed to the existing order on account of its economic interest. Each social order generates in itself the class which will eventually destroy it. Thus the bourgeoisie has destroyed the pre-capitalistic social order. But in developing the new order of capitalistic economy, the bourgeoisie creates the class which will destroy this present order and, after a transitory period of socialism, establish a communistic society; this is the rôle of the proletariat, or that new social class which consists mainly of the wage earners in the employment of capitalistic entrepreneurs.[14]

These two ideas—the certainty of the emancipation from the rule of the bourgeoisie, of the delivery from the social

[14] See A. Meusel, "Proletariat," in *Encyclopedia of the Social Sciences*.

evils of capitalism, and the mission ascribed to the working class in the initiation of the new and better society—must have had a tremendous appeal to the oppressed, impoverished and exploited masses of workers. It gave them hope and filled them with a new kind of self-respect.

On the other hand, Marx's warning against premature proletarian insurrection made his ideas acceptable even to workers who by temperament or conviction would have shied from a conspiratory revolutionary movement. It is one of the principles of Marxism that a revolutionary action cannot be successful unless the socio-economic system which is attacked has run its course of development; every social order will continue until it has exhausted its possibilities. This is a principle the form of which has been adopted from Hegel; but with Hegel the historical process is identical with the unfolding and dialectic succession of ideas, whereas Marx and Engels see the moving force or the independent variable in the social relationships which human beings create in the course of the development of the techniques of production and distribution of material goods.

In an early critical study of Hegel's philosophy of law,[15] Marx and Engels had come to the conclusion that

institutions of law as well as forms of state could neither be understood by themselves, nor explained by the so-called general development of the human mind, but that they are rooted in the material conditions of life, which are summed up by Hegel, after the fashion of the English and French of the 18th century, under the name 'civil society' (*Buergerliche Gesellschaft*); the anatomy of that civil society is to be sought in political economy.[16]

In analyzing the latter, Marx arrived at the following "general result" which furnished the "guiding principle" for his further writings:

[15] Published in part in *Deutsch-Franzoesische Jahrbuecher*, (1844).
[16] Karl Marx, *A Contribution to the Critique of Political Economy*, trans. by N. I. Stone (New York, International Library Publishing Co., 1904) p. 11.

In producing socially the material substance of their lives, men enter into definite, inevitable relationships which are independent of their will; these relationships of production correspond to a definite stage of development of their material powers of production (*ihrer materiellen Produktivkraefte*). The totality of these production-relationships forms the economic structure of society, the real foundation on which rises a juristic (*juristischer*) and political superstructure, and to which correspond certain forms of social consciousness (*gesellschaftliche Bewusstseinsformen*). The method of producing the material of life conditions the social, political, and spiritual process of life. It is not the consciousness of men that determines their existence, but, on the contrary, their social existence determines their consciousness.[17]

It is important to notice that Marx understands by the material conditions of life not merely the physical environment or the technology but also the social relationships which are formed between human beings in the course of their efforts to produce, in society, the material means of subsistence. The material conditions are thus the work of man, and Marx emphasizes again and again the idea that men make their history; however, at each stage of development of the productive capacities of society men are limited in their possibilities of action—they have only a limited number of choices.

On the other hand, the unfolding of the productive capacities will force them to make changes in the superstructure, because the potential capacity of society for production will now be greater than the conditions of private property will permit.

At a certain stage of their evolution, the powers of society for material production come in contradiction to the relationships of production, or—what is merely a juristic term for it—to the property relations within which they had hitherto operated. From forms that aided the unfolding of productive capacities these institutions now turn into restraints. Then begins a period of social revolution. With the change of the economic foundation the entire immense superstructure begins to revolve more or less rapidly.

Marx observes that in order to understand such periods of social revolution one has to distinguish

[17] *Ibid.*, p. 11. German phrases added by present writer.

between the "material" transformation in the economic conditions of production—which can be observed with scientific accuracy—and "the juristic, political, religious, artistic or philosophical"—in short, ideological forms in which men become conscious of this conflict and fight it out.[18]

This is the essence of Marx's and Engel's realistic interpretation of history. It is a theory of social evolution in which the structure of economic action is regarded as the prime mover, as the causal factor. There is no chance of a sudden overthrow of a social order by premature insurrection. Revolutions occur when the time has come where the new production forces burst the fetters of the old legal, political institutions. For, as Marx emphasizes, no social order ever declines before all productive capacities "for which there is room in it" have been developed; and "new and higher relationships of production do never take their place before the material conditions of their existence have been hatched in the womb of the old society." Marx assumes, in other words, that within each social order the technological and economic-institutional foundation of a new order has to be prepared before the revolution in the superstructure can take place.

The birth of a new order is indicated by antagonisms within the old, antagonisms between social classes, which have their real foundation in the contradictions between the productive capacities of the society and the actual institutions of production. These antagonisms within a society are not motivated by personal animosities between the individuals, but by the social conditions of their existence.[19] This is important for the understanding of Marx's idea that all history is the history of class struggles. Far from advocating or praising the struggle between classes or ascribing it to individual motivation, Marx regards it as an inevitable conflict of objective political and legal interests which have their

[18] *Ibid.*, p. 12.
[19] *Ibid.*, p. 13.

roots in the economic relationships. The conflicts between capital and labor are thus raised from the psychological level of hard feelings between workers and bosses to a sociological level of group conflict. This, too, is important because it enables the worker who is on good terms personally with his employer, or the trade unionist who negotiates collective agreements, to reconcile their short-run rôles with their long-run belief in socialism.

The antagonisms within the capitalistic society are a consequence of the inherent contradictions in the economic organization upon which it is built. The institution of private ownership of the instruments or means of production—land and capital—enables the owner, the entrepreneur, or capitalist to appropriate the product of the labor of his employees. He returns to them in the form of wages only as much as is necessary to maintain and reproduce the physical labor force in the society. The surplus value created by the workers is appropriated by the capitalist—the property owner—in spite of the fact that the entire product was created, not by the proprietor, but by the combined labor of the workers. Engels remarks that this "contradiction between socialized production and capitalistic appropriation manifests itself as the antagonism of proletariat and bourgeoisie." [20]

Technological progress under conditions of competition results in further concentration of ownership of capital and in the proletarization of the great majority of the people. Small craftsmen and artisans, small traders and businessmen, even small farmers lose their economic independence and are transformed into wage-laborers in the employment of capitalistic entrepreneurs, thus swelling the ranks of the proletariat. The growth of the proletariat involves, Marx and

[20] Friedrich Engels, *Socialism, Utopian and Scientific,* E. Aveling, ed. (Chicago, Charles H. Kerr and Company, 1903), p. 55.

Engels believed, the impoverishment of the broad masses of workers.

The economic crises which recur at fairly regular intervals are the consequence of the enormous increase in productive capacity on one side and the impossibility for the impoverished masses to purchase the commodities produced on the other side. The anarchy which reigns in the capitalistic economy as a whole—in contrast to the organization within each enterprise—thus results in periodic breakdowns of the entire circulation of commodities.[21] An outlet is sought in the conquest of new markets and more intensive exploitation of old markets—leading to new and even more disastrous crises. The bourgeoisie is no longer capable of solving its self-created troubles.

> The arms with which the bourgeoisie once threw feudalism to the ground (free enterprise, private property) now aim at the bourgeoisie itself. . . . But the bourgeoisie has already created the men who will use these arms—the modern workers, the proletarians.[22]

In the attempt to defend their wage levels, the workers begin to form coalitions or associations against the capitalists; or, as we would say, trade unions. First formed on a local level, these organizations become nationwide class organizations. The class struggle becomes a political struggle, because the workers, who have no property, are bound to strive for the abolition of the present institutions of property and the present forms of appropriation.

In this struggle the proletariat represents the overwhelming majority; in this respect the proletarian movement distinguishes itself from all past movements which have always been minority movements. Within the proletarian movement, the communists have a particular mission. They are the most enlightened part of the proletariat, they have the

[21] *Ibid.*, pp. 105-117.
[22] Marx and Engels, *Communist Manifesto.*

best insight into the conditions, the course, and the general results of the proletarian movement.[23]

Since the institution of wage-labor is the basis for the suppression of the proletariat, it has to be abolished, and it can be abolished only through abolition of private property. For the great majority of individuals, private property has already been abolished; it remains to abolish the highly concentrated ownership of means of production or capital and to convert it into public ownership. Since classes, according to Marx, are distinguished by the sources of their income (rent, profit, wages) which are in turn the result of differences in property relations—whether a person owns land or capital or has nothing to rely upon but labor [24]—the abolition of differences in property through the institution of community property (except for personal belongings) will result in the abolition of social classes, and thus put an end to the class struggles.

At this point a surprising idea occurs in Marx's own statement.

In broad outline, [he says], we can designate the asiatic, the ancient, the feudal, and the modern bourgeois methods of production as so many epochs in the progress of the economic organization of society. The bourgeois relations of production are the last antagonistic form of the social process of production;

the productive capacities which unfold themselves within this society create the material conditions for the solution of that antagonism. "With this formation of society the prehistory of human society comes to an end." [25] This is clearly an eschatological idea, which stands in a strange contrast to the preceding arguments.

Does the transition from capitalism to communism involve a violent political revolution? Did Marx and Engels assume

[23] *Ibid.*
[24] Karl Marx, *Das Kapital,* Dritter Band, 2. Teil, Buch III, ed. Fr. Engels, (Hamburg, 1894), Ch. 52.
[25] Marx, *A Contribution to the Critique of Political Economy,* p. 13.

that an armed insurrection of the proletariat would be necessary? No definite answer can be given to these questions. The controversies which they have caused among the Marxists are largely responsible for the splits within the movement particularly between the Social Democrats and the present-day Communists.

It is certain, however, that Marx and Engels foresaw a period during which the proletariat in the possession of political power would have to use it in order to crush all resistance against the transformation of private into public ownership. Lenin, in elaborating Marx's and Engels' ideas on this point, refers to this phase as the dictatorship of the proletariat. The term indicates that the proletarian régime will have to use extralegal means and that it is not meant to last forever. It will become superfluous when the resistance has been broken and when the productive forces of society, freed from the fetters of bourgeois economy, have been developed to full capacity. When these conditions have been reached, there will be an abundance of goods. The socialistic mode of distribution—to everybody according to his contribution—will give way to the communistic mode of distribution—to everybody according to his needs. The amount of daily (or weekly) labor required from each worker will become so small that the division of labor will virtually disappear: in the morning a ditch digger, in the evening, a critical philosopher. In this order of society, the state, the instrument of the ruling class, is no longer needed, the dictatorship of the proletariat will "wither away." [26]

Influence of Marxism

The combination of such utopian ideas with the detached, seemingly scientific analysis of the capitalistic economy made a strong impression on the better-educated and intel-

[26] Friedrich Engels, *Anti-Duehring* (New York, International Publishing Co., Inc., 1939)

lectually alert industrial workers, many of whom were voracious readers. However, the extent to which Marxism became the predominant ideology of the labor movement varied from one country to the other.[27] Central and eastern Europe were the areas of greatest influence of Marxism—especially Germany and Austria; it was weaker in Italy, France, and Spain, where syndicalistic and anarchistic traditions were strong, and where the development of large-scale manufacturing was lagging behind.

In Great Britain, Marxism had little influence on the labor movement; the early rise and great strength of trade unions probably was one factor, the strong religious bonds between workers and the smaller manufacturers another factor which delayed the spread of Marxism. Finally, the peculiarly English form of socialism which emanated from the Fabian Society contributed to the limitation of Marxian socialism in the British labor movement.

In the Scandinavian countries a very strong labor movement developed, comprising trade unions, coöperative societies, and social democratic parties; ideologically it was oriented towards Marxism, but its policies were primarily concerned with immediate goals.[28]

In the United States, Marxistic ideas remained for a long time mainly an ideology of immigrant workers and intellectuals from central and eastern Europe.[29]

On the other hand, the action programs and policies of the labor movements in all countries, whether Marxist or not,

[27] W. Sombart, *Socialism and the Social Movement*, trans. by M. Epstein (New York, E. P. Dutton & Co., Inc. 1909). There is also an excellent survey in Joseph Schumpeter, *Capitalism, Socialism, and Democracy* (New York, Harper and Brothers, 1942).

[28] R. Heberle, *Zur Ideengeschichte der Arbeiterbewegung in Schweden* (Jena, 1925). See also R. Heberle, "Trade Unions—Scandinavian Countries," in *Encyclopedia of the Social Sciences*.

[29] See M. Hillquit, *Loose Leaves from a Busy Life* (New York, The Macmillan Company, 1934), and *History of Socialism in the United States* (New York, Funk & Wagnalls Company, 1903). For a detailed discussion of American workers' political attitudes, see Chap. 9, below.

have become increasingly socialistic. But it was reformistic, gradual socialism, not revolutionary socialism, which gained mass adherence in the period before the First World War. The critique of Marxism by the "revisionists," of whom Eduard Bernstein was the most outstanding representative, together with the increasing power of trade unions and parliamentary socialist parties, were the main factors in bringing about the decline of revolutionary socialism.

LENINISM

The Background of Bolshevism

The rebirth of revolutionary Marxism began with the Russian Revolution and the foundation of the third or Communist International (Comintern) in 1921. In Russia, the Social Democratic Party had split into two organizations, the Bolsheviks and the Mensheviks. While the latter continued the strategy of the Social Democrats, the former began to prepare themselves for a violent revolution. The division was, at first, not over aims but over strategy and tactics as well as over the form of party organization (see Chapters 15 and 17).[30]

This is not the place to narrate the history of Bolshevik theory and the spread of communism. We can only point out the main tenets of communist ideology. We shall limit the discussion to those principles which have particular significance for the understanding of the Bolshevist movement

[30] *Bolshevik* means "a member of the majority." At a meeting of Russian socialist leaders in exile in 1903, the revolutionary group constituted a majority, although it cannot be said that the Bolsheviks controlled a majority in the socialist movement. Besides the Marxistic Social Democrats there were the non-Marxist Social Revolutionaries, who worked mainly among the peasantry. But *bolshe* in Russian means "more," so that Bolshevik has also the connotation of "all-outer." See Sir Bernard Pares, *Russia* (New York, Mentor Book, the New American Library of World Literature, Inc., 1949), pp. 51-53.

up to the Russian Revolution and of the present-day communist movements outside the Soviet Union.[31]

If one wants to understand the peculiar development of Marxism to Bolshevism, it is necessary to consider at least very briefly the cultural heritage of the Russian people and the structure of pre-revolutionary Russian society. The Russian (Greek) Orthodox Church has never integrated into its theological doctrine the philosophical heritage of the Greeks; there is no equivalent to the great synthesis of Thomas Aquinas. The Renaissance also did not touch Russia, and there has been no Reformation. The great schism within the Greek Orthodox Church was caused by controversies about symbolic ritual, not by dissent about essential points of dogma.

Consequently, intellectual and spiritual life in old Russia was free of the controversies, tensions, and stimuli which enriched Western culture and, after fierce and often violent conflicts, resulted in a new spirit of toleration. It seems that in Russia the masses of the people have never questioned the ideals of conformity and group solidarity which prevail in archaic societies. Just as the Russian village community even in the nineteenth century did not recognize the majority principle, but insisted on unanimous decisions, so the broad masses, including the intellectuals, seem to have been fundamentally untouched by Western individualism. The modern virtue of independence of conviction in religious or political matters, which we Westerners owe to the Renaissance and the Reformation, seems to have remained quite foreign to the Russian mind. The Russian, whether commu-

---

[31] See Martin Ebon, *World Communism Today* (New York, McGraw-Hill Book Company, Inc., 1948). The essential doctrines of communism (Bolshevism) are contained as in a nutshell in relatively few writings of Lenin and Stalin: V. I. Lenin, *State and Revolution*, (1917) (New York, International Publishing Co., Inc., 1935); The Program of the Communist International adopted by the Sixth World Congress, Moscow, 1928; Joseph Stalin, *Leninism* (New York, International Publishing Co., Inc., 1933).

nist or not, has little toleration for deviating ideologies, nor the ability to stand alone by his conviction.[32]

The structure of Russian society around the turn of the nineteenth century combined strange contrasts. While the masses of the rural people were still living under pre-capitalistic conditions, there had grown in urban centers a small but highly concentrated manufacturing industry. The contrast between the wealth of the bourgeoisie and the poverty and squalor of the industrial proletariat was striking.

Social unrest was widespread among peasants and workers, but there were no open and well-organized mass movements as in western Europe. On one hand the legal and political prerequisites were lacking; freedom of association did not exist, and any kind of organized movement was likely to be persecuted; on the other hand, the masses of workers and peasants were still too immature politically. The socialist movement in Russia therefore was mainly a movement of intellectuals. The intelligentsia in tsarist Russia was a peculiar social stratum. It consisted of members of the free professions and of civil servants. Of both categories there was an overabundance. Their socio-economic position was insecure, their prospects discouraging. The result was a radicalism of resentment.[33] Coming, as a rule, from the classes of small landholders, minor civil servants, and independent artisans, they had little or no first-hand experience in industrial wage work. Being fundamentally religious even if they had broken with the Orthodox Church, many of them took to socialism as to a new religion. They embraced Marxism as

---

[32] Karl Noetzel, *Die Soziale Bewegung in Russland* (Stuttgart, 1923), pp. 56, 70, 97 and *passim*. See also Sir John Maynard, *Russia in Flux*, ed. and abridged by S. Haden Guest (New York, The Macmillan Company, 1942), p. 441:

"The religious conception of the presence of truth in the congregation and there alone passed to the Communists.... The offender, alone in an agony of isolation from the brethren, confesses all, and more than all, in the humiliation of his soul."

[33] Schumpeter, *op. cit.*, p. 325.

a revelation of absolute truth.[34] Controversies about the interpretation of Marx's and Engels' teachings assumed the form of heated, bitter disputes, comparable only to those between hostile schools of theologians. The opponent was treated as a heretic—a traitor to the cause of the revolution.[35]

All propaganda and organization work had to be carried on more or less in secret, and most of the leaders were forced to live in exile abroad for considerable periods; many of them spent years in prison or in Siberia. In short, the conditions of existence of Marxist intellectuals in Russia were quite different from those in western Europe. It is in this environment that Lenin and his early associates grew up to become the leaders, first of the Bolshevik branch of the socialist movement and later of the new Socialist Soviet Republic.

The Doctrine

The rift between Mensheviks and Bolsheviks which split the Russian Social Democratic party in 1903 was caused by Lenin's insistence upon a revolutionary course of action and his opposition to the prevailing conceptions of the organization and function of the party. As early as 1900 Lenin demanded an organization consisting of "professional revolutionaries, . . . who devote to the revolution not merely their evenings off but their entire lives." Only a party of this kind would be able to survive the relentless persecution by the political police. The majority of the socialists at that time believed that Russia would have to go through a period of bourgeois rule before the proletarian revolution could take place. In the coming revolution, the Russian socialists, therefore, would have to support the liberals. This Lenin denied. He expected that in case of a bourgeois, liberal revolution

---

[34] Noetzel, *op. cit.*, pp. 234 f. and *passim*.

[35] Lenin's earlier writings show this very clearly. They are mainly polemics, more frequently against less radical Social Democratic intellectuals than against bourgeois authors, and they try to annihilate the opponent not so much intellectually as morally and politically.

the peasants would rise against the landlords and join the bourgeoisie in the overthrow of the tsarist régime. Lenin foresaw the possibility of a combined insurrection of workers and the poorer peasants against the old ruling classes as well as against the bourgeoisie and the rich peasants. The proletariat alone would still be too small and weak to stage a successful revolution, but in alliance with the peasants it would command the vast majority of the people.

In previous revolutions the workers had fought on the barricades, and helped the bourgeoisie to overthrow the old order, only to see power pass into the hands of the bourgeoisie, who used it to oppress the workers. This Lenin wanted to prevent by telescoping two revolutions into one.[36] Lenin thus abandons the Social Democratic idea that a proletarian revolution presupposes the control of a parliamentary majority by the socialists. According to Lenin's thinking, the revolution leading to a socialist régime is no longer a proletarian revolution but an insurrection of "all the exploited masses in town and country" (as Stalin puts it) under the "hegemony" or political leadership of the proletariat.[37]

For the theoretical justification of this widening of the revolutionary front Lenin refers to certain comments by Marx in connection with the Paris commune:

In the Europe of 1871, the proletariat on the Continent did not constitute the majority of the people. A "people's" revolution (this was the expression which Marx used) actually sweeping the majority into

[36] Lenin, *What Is to Be Done?* (1902), Collected Works (New York, International Publishing Co., Inc., 1929), Vol. IV-2, and *The Proletarian Revolution and the Renegade K. Kautsky* (1919), Collected Works, (New York, International Publishing Co., Inc., 1945), Vol. XXIII, pp. 407 ff. (p. 65 of the German edition); also Stalin, *Leninism*, Vol. I, (New York, International Publishing Co., Inc., 1933), pp. 359 ff. and *passim*.

[37] Lenin, *What Is to Be Done?* The socialists must "go among all classes of the people" and arouse them against the manifestations of "capitalistic exploitation." (p. 161). "Is there a single class of the population in which no individuals, groups or circles are to be found who are discontented with the state of tyranny and therefore accessible to the propaganda of Social Democrats. . . ?" (p. 166).

its current, could be such only if it embraced both the proletariat and the peasantry. Both classes then constituted the "people." [38]

Lenin has, on the other hand, no confidence in the ability of the proletariat to establish a socialist régime under its own working-class leaders:

> The history of all countries shows that the working class, exclusively by its own efforts, is able to develop only trade-union consciousness, that is, it may itself realize the necessity of combining in unions to fight against employers and to strive to compel the government to pass necessary labor legislation. The theory of socialism, however, grew out of the philosophic, historical, and economic theories that were elaborated by the educated representatives of the propertied classes, the intellectuals. The founders of modern scientific socialism, Marx and Engels, themselves belonged to the bourgeois intelligentsia. Similarly in Russia, the theoretical doctrine of social democracy arose quite independently of the spontaneous growth of the labor movement; it arose as a natural and inevitable outcome of the development of ideas among the revolutionary socialist intelligentsia. [39]

Furthermore, the function of a revolutionary vanguard requires organization in form of a political party, a party that is guided by an advanced theory. [40] This party has to insist on strict discipline; it cannot grant its members any freedom of opinion, for it has been demonstrated in Russia and other countries "that the notorious freedom of criticism implies, not the substitution of one theory by another, but freedom from every complete and thought-out theory; it implies eclecticism and absence of principle." [41]

Marx had foreseen the possibility that in England or the United States the proletariat might seize political power by gaining control of the existing "state-machinery." Lenin states that "today, in the epoch of the first great imperialist war, this exception . . . is no longer valid." Even the Anglo-Saxon countries have created "military and bureaucratic" machineries which the people will have to "shatter," "break

[38] Lenin, *State and Revolution*, p. 35.
[39] Lenin, *What Is to Be Done?* pp. 114-115.
[40] *Ibid.*, p. 110.
[41] *Ibid.*, p. 108.

up," and replace by "something new." [42] This new form of government is to be "the dictatorship of a *single* class"—the dictatorship of the proletariat.[43] The "people's" revolution under the "hegemony of the proletariat" (Stalin) is thus to bring about a new régime in which the proletariat will be the ruling class. Now, if the proletariat in order to fulfill its revolutionary functions needs the guidance of a small and disciplined party of theoretically advanced professional revolutionaries, it may seem that the so-called dictatorship of the proletariat would turn out to be virtually a dictatorship of socialist intellectuals.

This, however, was not Lenin's intention. When on the eve of the Bolshevik revolution he developed the details of the proletarian régime—always careful to safeguard himself against the possible charge of utopianism by reference to Marx's directives, which were derived from the *experience* of the Paris commune—Lenin insisted that it would be a new and higher form of democracy. Instead of bourgeois democracy which gives the people merely a chance "to decide every few years which member of the ruling class is to repress and oppress the people through parliament," [44] Lenin visualizes a régime in which the "armed people," that is, the workers and peasants, will assume all functions of the old state and carry them out partly directly, partly through the councils (*soviets*) of their representatives.

Since the main function is the repression of the expropriated bourgeoisie, and since the latter constitutes only a small minority, no special armed forces, or officialdom, will be needed; "The majority can itself directly fulfill all these functions." [45]

The delegates to the soviets will be subject to recall, so that no new oligarchy of politicians could develop; "Repre-

[42] Lenin, *State and Revolution,* pp. 33-35.
[43] *Ibid.,* pp. 31, 35 f.
[44] *Ibid.,* p. 40.
[45] *Ibid.,* p. 37.

sentative institutions remain, but parliamentarism as a special system, as a division of labor between the legislative and executive functions, as a privileged position for the deputies, no longer exists."[46] Thus there would be no "separation of power"; the "armed workers" and the people's councils would carry out legislative, administrative, and judicial functions.

Lenin, in 1917, believed that capitalism had simplified the functions of state administration to such an extent that the proletarian state would not need an elaborate organization.

> Capitalist culture has *created* large-scale production, factories, railways, the postal service, telephones, etc., and on *this basis* the great majority of functions of the old "state power" have become so simplified and can be reduced to such simple operations of registration, filing and checking that they will be quite within the reach of every literate person, and it will be possible to perform them for "workingmen's wages" which circumstance can (and must) strip those functions of every shadow of privilege, of every appearance of "official grandeur." [47]

Towards the end of *State and Revolution* Lenin repeats this same idea:

> "In its turn, capitalism, as it develops, itself creates prerequisites for "every one" *to be able* really to take part in the administration of the state.... With such *economic* prerequisites it is perfectly possible, immediately, within twenty-four hours after the overthrow of the capitalists and bureaucrats, to replace them, in the control of production and distribution, in the business of *control* of labor and products, by the armed workers, by the whole people in arms. [As an afterthought Lenin remarks that the] staffs of engineers, agronomists and so on [who work today under the comand of the capitalists] will work even better tomorrow, obeying the armed workers.[48]

It is quite obvious that Lenin, in speaking of the establishment of a real democracy, is primarily concerned with equality and not with freedom; the latter he believes will automatically result when, after the firm establishment of

[46] *Ibid.*, p. 41.
[47] *Ibid.*, p. 38; see also p. 43.
[48] *Ibid.*, p. 83.

socialism, the next higher phase of communism can be attained and the proletarian state will become superfluous.

Only in Communist society, when the resistance of the capitalists has been completely broken . . . when there are no classes (that is, there is no difference between the members of society in their relation to the social means of production), *only then* "the state ceases to exist" and "*it becomes possible to speak of freedom.*"

When this stage has been reached, people will become capable of living in the freedom of a perfect community without supreme authority.

. . . freed from capitalist slavery, from the untold horrors, savagery, absurdities and infamies of capitalist exploitation, people will gradually *become accustomed* to the observance of the elementary rules of social life that have been known for centuries and repeated for thousands of years [!] in all school books; they will become accustomed to observing them without force, without compulsion, without subordination, without the *special apparatus* for compulsion which is called the state." [49]

Lenin does not venture to say how long the transition from socialism to communism will take, "since material for the solution of such questions is not available." [50] When, during the first year after the Bolshevik revolution, the soviet régime was attacked for being undemocratic, Lenin replied, "The revolutionary dictatorship of the proletariat is a rule which the proletariat has won in battle, which is based upon the force of the proletariat over against the bourgeoisie, and which is bound by no laws whatsoever. [51]

The last part of this statement reveals an important element in the political theory of Bolshevism: the negation of

[49] *Ibid.,* p. 73; see also p. 84.

[50] *Ibid.,* p. 79. Later, when the anticipated "withering away" of the proletarian state failed to take place in the Soviet Union, it fell to Stalin to develop the doctrine that the dictatorship would have to last as long as the socialist counry (or countries) were subject to the danger of capitalistic aggression. See Hans Kelsen, *The Political Theory of Bolshevism* (Berkeley, University of California Press, 1949).

[51] Lenin, *The Proletarian Revolution and the Renegade K. Kautsky,* p. 354.

the rule of law. Here lies the fundamental difference between present-day communism and social democracy. The latter, being a child of Western liberalism and humanism, will not, even in a period of transition, sacrifice the institutions which protect the individual against abuse of the political power.

II

THE SOCIAL PSYCHOLOGY OF SOCIAL MOVEMENTS AND POLITICAL PARTIES

5

Motivations and Attitudes

~~~~~~

IF WE OBSERVE the great mass of people in regard to participation in social movements or active work in political parties, we find that as a rule they are rather passive and indifferent unless some special event or issue arouses them. Those who are actively engaged in the service of some cause or party are only a minority. Most people seem to be quite content to pursue their own business and to watch

> how, far away in distant Turkey,
> the nations bludgeon one another.
> (Goethe, *Faust*, I.)

A few are drawn into political action by a lust for power, or by a personal sense of civic duty, or perhaps by a tradition in their family or social set. But the broad masses are likely to be activated only if their immediate personal interests are affected by some measure taken by the government. The same farmer, for example, who does not take the pains even to inform himself about such matters as national health insurance, and certainly would not write to his congressman about it, may be stirred into action if a proposed change in the tariff threatens to reduce the price of a staple crop which he produces.

The statistics on voting give a fair measure of such indifference. Participation in elections varies, of course, from one country to another (it is generally much higher in Europe than in the United States) and also in time. But in any case, very few people are willing to devote a large part of their leisure time to political activities. This fact presents one of the serious problems in all democracies and democratically organized groups. (See Chapter 13.)

We have thus to reckon with wide variations in the degree of participation in any social movement or any party. Keeping this in mind, we shall now try to understand what induces people to show preference for or to participate in a particular social movement or political party. We are going to deal here with individual motives and attitudes of more or less active participants in the kinds of groups we are studying.

TYPES OF MOTIVATION

Although we know from experience what may be the typical motives in a particular kind of social action, it is difficult and often impossible to determine accurately the motives of a particular individual in a concrete case. Even our own motives are not always easy to recognize. Thus we can distinguish certain typical motives for participation in social movements in general, but it is extremely difficult to determine exactly what motive or combination of motives made John Doe join a particular movement or why he is staying with it.

Difficulties in Studying Motives of Social Action

The difficulties in studying motives of social action are due to the following circumstances:

1. The real and true motives may be intentionally concealed by the acting individual.
2. The motives may not be clear to the acting individual; he may "persuade himself that his motives are what he declares them to be;" he may "rationalize" or "socialize" his motives "proclaiming them to be the expression of

certain simple attitudes of a kind that are socially esteemed."

3. The true motives may not be recognizable to the agent himself because they lie in his unconscious being.[1]

4. Finally, the very complexity of motives makes any accurate determination difficult.

The consequence is that it is extremely difficult to determine the exact frequency of certain motives among a multitude of individuals. Therefore it is only with great uncertainty that we can say which kind of motives prevail or predominate in a particular social movement. (See Chapter 7.) We can, however, theoretically distinguish certain types of motives of social action in general and we can apply them in order to distinguish conceptually the motives which are characteristic of participants in various kinds of social movements.

Max Weber's Typology

These types of motives are to be used merely as analytical devices; in reality, the motives will rarely be so clear-cut and simple. We may start with Max Weber's typology of motivation (orientation) of social action[2] and reduce the motives of individuals in joining and supporting a social movement to four pure types.

1. The goal of the movement as such is held to be desirable, right, and good; success of the movement is wanted for the sake of the cause which it advocates. If this conviction of the righteousness of the cause, this belief in the goodness of the goal, is based on deliberation, on careful inquiry into the validity of the ideas and the arguments used in support of them, we speak of *value-rational* motivation. This may be

[1] Robert M. MacIver, "The Imputation of Motives," *American Journal of Sociology*, Vol. XLVI, No. 1 (July, 1940), pp. 4-6.

[2] Max Weber, *The Theory of Social and Economic Organization*, trans. by A. M. Henderson and T. Parsons (New York, Oxford University Press, 1947).

considered as the ethically most desirable motivation, because it would imply the greatest clarity of mind and constitute presumably the most dependable devotion to the movement. Frequently, however, the individual will find himself only in partial agreement or sympathy with the ideals of the movement, or he may approve of the goal but may not like the tactics or policies. So long as he chooses to support this movement because he believes that its good aspects outweigh the bad ones, and so long as no other factors enter into his decision, he acts within the limits of value-rational motivation. With regard to the kind of values which the individual expects to be realized through the movement (these need not be the constitutive goals of the movement), we may distinguish political, religious, ethical, and aesthetic motivations; these may blend with one another. Thus Sombart points out that many non-proletarians became socialists out of a desire for social justice and because their aesthetic sense was offended by the squalor of the proletariat's existence.[3]

2. Often an individual is motivated to participate in a social movement, not by such rational deliberation, but by some experience which arouses his emotions against the persons and conditions which the movement attacks, or his affection for the leaders and the masses in the movement. Resentment and enthusiasm are probably much more frequent types of motivation among participants in a social movement than a clear conception of the ultimate goal and its benefits for society.

Young people especially are more often carried off their feet by the charm of a leader of great appeal than they are brought into the fold of a movement by cool, logical deliberation. This type of motivation we shall call *emotional-affectual*. It is easy to see that radical, especially revolutionary, movements are more often joined out of emotional-affectual

[3] Werner Sombart, *Der Proletarische Sozialismus*, Vol. II (Jena, 1924), p. 138.

motives than for rational reasons. The sudden conversion to a social or political cause is, like the religious conversion, a very effective way of becoming bound to a movement. "What has once entered the region of sentiment can no longer be touched by discussion."[4] It is for the emotionally-affectually oriented members of a movement in the first line that the newly embraced socio-political ideas assume the quality of a "substitute religion."

3. The third type of motivation is called *traditional.* By this term we mean that many individuals belong to a social movement because their parents or other relatives have belonged to it; because there is a tradition in the community or in the social status group or class to which the individual belongs, which demands adherence to certain ideals and support of the groups which uphold them. For example, in working-class families, especially in Europe, one finds quite often a tradition of affiliation with the socialist movement. Obviously this type of motivation presupposes that the movement has already existed for some time and that a certain amount of organization has been achieved.

We find within certain social collectives quite persistent propensities to support more or less habitually certain causes, such as liberal or progressive, and to reject others. Progressivism or liberalism often runs in families from generation to generation, while party adherence may change. These traditional tendencies may be in agreement or disagreement with new social movements and thereby become rather important factors in the success or failure of a new movement with certain classes of the population.

There are, in some countries, typical regional differences in this respect. In certain regions in France,[5] there exists a

---

[4] Gustave LeBon, *The Psychology of Socialism* (London, 1899), p. 9.

[5] Richard Peter Rohden, "Demokratie und Partei in Frankreich," in Rohden, ed. *Demokratie und Partei* (Vienna, 1932), p. 124, describes the basic political attitudes in various parts of France. "One is not *klerikal* (pro-church) in Southern France."

tradition of progressivism which induces even the small farmers to vote communist although they certainly are strongly in favor of private ownership of land. In Germany, the region of Thuringia seems to have a tradition of radicalism in religious and political matters.[6] The importance of traditional party preference in American elections is well known. A Gallup poll showed that in the 1942 presidential elections 34.4 per cent of those interviewed who voted Democratic, and 26.3 per cent of those who voted Republican, stated, "I always vote for this party."

4. Any social movement will attract individuals who join in the expectation of personal advantages. This is most likely to occur when the movement seems to have good prospects of achieving its goal or of becoming influential. The situation is analogous to that of voting for, or financially or otherwise supporting, a political party or candidate in the expectation of appointment to office or the award of public contracts. Thus we find that saloonkeepers, hotel managers, lawyers, physicians, newspaper editors and others offer their services, partly because of immediate returns, partly in the expectation of even larger future spoils. Or a farmer may join a radical farmers' movement because he hopes for a moratorium or nullification of debts. This kind of *purposive-rational* motivation is, of course, seldom frankly admitted and in the consciousness of the acting individuals it may even be hidden or rationalized by a value-rational motivation. Fear of social isolation, or of vengeance on the part of the victorious movement may, of course, also bring into the fold of a movement people who do not believe in its ideas. During the development of a social movement this kind of motivation is often fostered by deliberate propaganda tac-

[6] Albrecht Mendelssohn-Bartholdy, "The War and German Society," in *Economic and Social History of the World War* (New Haven, Yale University Press, 1937), makes an attempt to characterize the prevalent and typical attitudes in each of the major regions of Germany before 1914.

tics, appealing not so much to the convictions as to the egotistic interests and desires of the prospective followers.

After a social movement has become a political or social
power, this type of motivation tends to occur even more
frequently. We may call this the *bandwagon effect* of a suc-
ceeding social movement. If the victorious movement becomes vindictive, begins to penalize and persecute former
opponents, then "joining" becomes a means of self-protection. At this stage even opponents may take cover in one or
another of the organizations affiliated with the movement.
This was very frequent in Nazi Germany.

Modifications

These are theoretical distinctions. In reality, most men will
be motivated not in one way or the other but by a combination of motives, and any movement will contain quite a
variety of differently motivated adherents or followers. In
any social movement we find individuals who were attracted
by a fascinating leader, who fell under the spell of a great
demagogue; others who joined after suffering some personal
injustice that aroused their resentment against the present
order of things social, or whose indignation was aroused by
witnessing suffering inflicted upon others or injustice done
to some other person; and others who came to it after pro-
longed periods of reading and study, and so forth. The same
observations apply to political parties.[7]

A further complication for the analysis of motivations
arises from the fact that the motivations of an individual
member of a movement or party may change in the course of
time. Enthusiasm does not last forever. The disappointed
and disillusioned enthusiast may stay in the movement because he has become habituated to his rôle in it, or because
he finds it expedient in the interest of his business or career.

[7] Walter Sulzbach, *Die Grundlagen der Politischen Parteibildung*, (Tübingen, Mohr, 1921).

Furthermore, the socio-psychological complexion of the entire movement may change in the course of time, as it grows, as the earlier members become old or are replaced by newcomers who have not participated in the early struggles and who do not share the old guard's enthusiasm. While in the beginning emotional-affectual and value-rational motivations predominated, they may give way to traditional and opportunistic orientation.[8]

THE FACTOR OF PERSONALITY

The Older "Temperament" Theories

Motivations are quite obviously related to types of personality. Some people are emotional, easily aroused to enthusiasm for a cause or a person or both. Others are more critical, more intellectual, and still others more scheming, calculative, and so forth.

We connect personality with political attitudes in a different sense when we say, "This man looks like a typical communist," or, "Meyer does not look like a Nazi at all." We also have a mental stereotype of the political conspirator—thus Shakespeare has Julius Caesar say:

> Let me have men about me that are fat;
> Sleek-headed men and such as sleep a-nights.
> Yond Cassius has a lean and hungry look;
> He thinks too much; such men are dangerous.
>   (I. ii. 192-196)

The historian Macaulay, speaking of the origin of the two great parties which have alternately governed England since the middle of the seventeenth century, suggested that the distinction had

its origin in diversities of temper, of understanding, and of interest, which are found in all societies, and which will be found till the human mind ceases to be drawn in opposite directions by charm of

[8] See Willy Hellpach, *Sozialpsychologie* (Stuttgart, 1946), p. 101, about change of motives in social groups.

habit and by the charm of novelty. Not only in politics, but in literature, in art, in science, in surgery and mechanics, in navigation and
agriculture, nay, even in mathematics, we find this distinction. Everywhere there is a class of men who cling with fondness to whatever is
ancient, and who, even when convinced by overpowering reasons that
innovation would be beneficial, consent to it with many misgivings and
forebodings. We find also everywhere another class of men sanguine
in hope, bold in speculation, always pressing forward, quick to discern
the imperfections of whatever exists, disposed to think lightly of the
risks and inconveniences which attend improvements, and disposed
to give every change credit for being an improvement.[9]

Macaulay's explanation is thus essentially based upon a correlation of political attitudes with temperaments. Since the
temperament tends to change with the stages of life, it is
not surprising that attempts have been made to explain the
existence of parties by the diverse tempers corresponding to
the four seasons of life. Friedrich Rohmer, in his *Die Vier
Parteien* (Zurich, 1844), coördinated what he called the
radical party with boyhood, the liberal with adolescence,
the conservative with manhood, and the absolutistic with
old age.[10]

Following Macaulay and Rohmer, the Swiss political scientist Bluntschli (1808 to 1881) correlated four party types—
progressive, conservative, radical, and reactionary—with the
traditional four concepts of temperament: sanguine, phleg-
matic, choleric, and melancholic.[11]

The very fact that one's motivations in deciding for a political creed are so often quite complex lends support to these
temperament theories. Morris Hillquit, the American socialist, states in his autobiography:

I allied myself with the Social Democrats almost immediately. It
would be difficult for me at this time to define just what determined
my choice. I am inclined to believe that political creeds and philos-

[9] Thomas B. Macaulay, *The History of England*, Vol. I, Chap. I.
[10] Sulzbach, *op. cit.*, p. 28.
[11] See A. Christensen, *Politics and Crowd Morality* (London, 1915); R.
P. Rohden, *Die weltanschaulichen Grundlagen der politischen Parteien;*
Sulzbach, *op. cit.*, pp. 25 ff.

ophies of life are as a rule formed by the imponderable elements of personal temperament, predisposition, and mental affinities rather than by reasoned analysis of their merits.[12]

While this opinion contains a great deal of truth, it can hardly be maintained that a definite relation exists between a certain kind of temperament and preference for a definite political party. Not all liberals are sanguine, and so forth.

All these theories ignore the fact that abstract categories like "radical," "progressive," or "conservative" do not indicate anything about the concrete aims of a party. These really determine whether a party attracts young or old people. It is quite obvious, however, that youth is likely to be attracted to extreme, that is, radical, parties and movements rather than to moderate groups. Young people, if politically interested at all, are inclined to think in utopian terms; they are likely to be perfectionists who want an all-out solution; they are also likely to be ignorant of detailed facts and therefore inclined to think in ideas rather than in realities. Eduard Spranger, who develops these conclusions in his *Psychology of Youth and Adolescence*,[13] makes however, the modifying statement that working-class youth are more ready to think in terms of concrete aims than middle-class youth, presumably because they have more experience. This may illustrate the complexity of the problem.

Recent Personality Theories

Modern psychology, instead of operating with temperaments, constructs types of personality and relates them to the various spheres of human activity and to the basic orders of values. Thus Eduard Spranger in his *Types of Men*[14] dis-

---

[12] Morris Hillquit, *Loose Leaves from a Busy Life* (New York, The Macmillan Company, 1934), p. 9.

[13] Eduard Spranger, *Psychologie des Jugendalters* (Leipzig, 1924).

[14] Eduard Spranger, *Lebensformen* (Halle, M. Niemeyer, 1928), trans. as *Types of Men* by P. J. W. Pigors. A summary of Spranger's typology is given in Gordon W. Allport, *Personality* (New York, Henry Holt & Company, Inc., 1937), pp. 227-231. See also the discussion of Spranger's theory

tinguishes the political and the social types from the contemplative-scholarly, the economic, the aesthetic, and the religious types. Spranger's types of men are derived from types of basic "attitudes." The "political attitude" is characteristic of the more active participants in social movements and of the leaders of political parties, whereas the "social attitude" as described by Spranger seems to be more prevalent among the "joiners," or the rank and file in social movements.

The political type is motivated by a will to power for its own sake; power is for this type the highest value, to which everything else is subordinated and subservient. Even cognition (*Erkenntnis*) and truth (*Wahrheit*) are for the political type only means for the control of others. Other people interest the political man only to the extent to which they may be controlled. "For politics, man is a means to an end, in the most favorable case a means to his own good." The pure man of power is the man of self-emphasis and self-assertion. He is therefore usually not a warmhearted friend of the people, but a misanthrope.[15] The type itself is not confined to any particular kind of party or movement.

The social type, on the other hand, is motivated by sympathy, by a genuine interest in others, by the ability to take imaginatively the place of another human being, by love. The organizing principle of the mental life of this type is devotion to others, not for any ulterior aims, but for their own sake. In this the social type finds satisfaction. Politically, this attitude leads to anarchism, an anarchism of love and fraternity as Tolstoi preached it, or, eventually, to a paternalistic conservatism. One finds this type of attitude especially among the adherents of small sectarian social and political movements, in groups that do not desire power because they

in H. D. Laswell, *Psychopathology and Politics* (Chicago, University of Chicago Press, 1930), pp. 49 ff.
[15] E. Spranger, *op. cit.*, p. 196.

intend to work by the mere example of their conduct. It is essentially an apolitical type.

These types are of course constructed by a technique of "idealization" or by combining, in an image, traits which in reality rarely occur all together in the same individual—they are not supposed to be descriptions of actual human beings but ideal types which may be used in empirical studies as devices in reaching an understanding of political leaders and their followers.

Psychopathology of Social Movements

The rise of militant mass movements, in particular of Nazism, has led to much speculation about the rôle of mental diseases in the generating of social movements. These speculations have received much encouragement and support from the rapid development of abnormal psychology, especially of psychoanalysis. Attempts have been made to explain highly complex and flexible movements like Fascism or Nazism in terms of abnormal psychology. While we are highly skeptical about the value of such intellectual exercises, we believe that there are real problems of sociological importance which require the aid of abnormal psychology.

We may begin with a simple, familiar observation. A common reaction towards people who propose fundamental changes in the social order of a society is to declare them scoundrels, egotists, morally bad people, or crackpots. This may be done naïvely in perfectly good faith, or it may be done with deliberation. The imputation of morally inferior motives into the actions of an adversary [16] is a very effective weapon, and it is being used not only in international relations, but also in the struggles between religious sects and churches, between political parties, and between other action

[16] Walther Sulzbach, *op. cit.*, p. 2: "We have to know why others think otherwise and strive for other things than we do. The most simple explanation and the one which is most certain to calm all doubts is to impute inferior motives to our adversaries."

groups. But it is a rather unsophisticated weapon. In our age more crushing effects can be achieved by labeling one's adversaries as neurotics or psychopathic cases. It relieves one of the necessity of debating the merits of the adversaries' objectives. The political abuse of this device should of course be distinguished from objective, scholarly attempts at discovering abnormal traits in the personality of participants in social movements. Unfortunately, even scholars are not free from prejudices and sometimes engage in a sophisticated method of abusing fellow citizens whose ideas they do not like.

There are, however, serious and intricate problems involved, which concern the personnel of social movements. To what extent are neurotic and psychopathic individuals more frequently found in social movements than among the non-participating population? Are abnormal personalities more frequent in radical or militant movements than in moderate, gradualistic reform movements? If so, why should this be true? Under what conditions do abnormal individuals advance into leading positions in a movement? These are some of the questions that deserve investigation and discussion.

A second group of psychopathological problems concerning social movements has to do with processes of group action; here we have in mind the application of crowd psychology to the study of social movements. Two entirely different questions may be raised: first, whether and to what extent can we profit from the psychology of mobs and crowds; and second, to what extent and in what ways is deliberate use being made of crowd psychology by the founders and leaders of modern mass movements?

We shall now turn to the first complex of problems, those concerning abnormal individuals in the personnel of social movements. Many attempts have been made to explain certain kinds of political behavior and certain types of personalities in political life as psychopathological phenomena. Radicals and political activists in particular have been submitted to this kind of approach. From Lombroso and Gustave LeBon to Werner Sombart, numerous scholars have pointed out the psychopathological traits in leaders of the socialistic, anarchistic, and communistic movements and the corresponding attitudes among their followers.[17]

Leaders in the French Revolution, foremost among them Robespierre, have been made the object of psychopathological analyses.[18] Recently Harold D. Lasswell has presented a number of case studies of politically active persons in his *Psychopathology and Politics*.[19] Richard Behrend has discussed the phenomenon of political activism from a Freudian point of view, and Norman R. F. Maier has attempted to explain the "rôle of frustration in Social Movements." [20] Frederic L. Schuman's book on the rise of Nazism also belongs in this class of studies, and Allen L. Edwards' paper on "The Signs of Incipient Fascism" [21] is based upon the same principles.

The problem as seen by the psychopathologists has been well stated by Edwards.

The supporters of any social movement, it is true, tend to come from those *groups* which *are already frustrated or anticipate frustration* in some respect and which see in this particular movement a means of restoring equilibrium or obtaining relief for their anxiety.

Opposition to this same social movement, on the other hand, will tend to come from those who view this movement as a real or potential source of *frustration*—that is, a movement which will disturb accepted values and attitudes.[22]

[17] Gustave LeBon, *op. cit.;* Werner Sombart, *op. cit.*

[18] Hans von Hentig, *Robespierre, Studien zur Psycho-Pathologie des Machttriebes* (Stuttgart, 1924). Compare R. P. Rohden, *Robespierre* (Berlin, 1935), against Hentig's interpretation.

[19] See footnote 14.

[20] Norman R. F. Maier, "The Rôle of Frustration in Social Movements," *Psychological Review*, Vol. 49, (1942), pp. 586-599.

[21] Allen L. Edwards, "The Signs of Incipient Fascism," *Journal of Abnormal and Social Psychology*, Vol. 39, No. 3 (1944).

[22] *Ibid.*, p. 310. Author's italics.

Psychoanalytic Approach

The essence of the psychoanalytic theories of social movements may be summarized as follows: Individuals who are prevented—by conditions which may be beyond their control—from attaining their goals may react to this situation in two different ways: they may face the facts squarely and adjust themselves in rational ways to their misfortune and, perhaps, try to find practicable remedies for those goal-blocking conditions, or they may become frustrated, that is, develop attitudes of aggression, without having opportunity to commit aggressive actions. In the latter case, ensuing tensions may find release by participation in a social movement which may direct the aggressive tendencies at conditions or groups which are not responsible for the initial cause of frustration. The leaders of such movements may themselves be frustrated individuals or they may artfully exploit their followers' frustrations in pursuit of their own rationally perceived goals.

To illustrate: A young man whose life goal is to become a naval officer finds his goal blocked after a defeat in war, which deprives his country of its armed forces. He may then choose a constructive solution, either by taking service in a foreign country, or by choosing a civilian occupation and making this his new goal. He may also become politically active and strive for a reëstablishment of his country's position among the great powers by supporting rational methods of foreign policy. Or he may not be capable of making any of these adjustments; he will then develop that rigidity of attitude characteristic of neurotic persons; he may apparently have resigned from his former goal, but he will now develop attitudes of aggression against those individuals or categories of persons whom he holds responsible for his country's plight (and for his own bad luck). If this happens to many inidviduals, it may be the beginning of a radical or

militant movement in which aggressive (that is, noncon-
structive) attitudes serve as substitutes for rational and constructive goals. The Nazi movement, especially in its earlier
phases, contained large numbers of such frustrated individuals. It is, however, important to keep in mind that
their frustrations were the result of reaction to personal
experiences, not to the Treaty of Versailles or the depression.
And, even among the Nazis, frustrated individuals were
probably a minority. Therefore, if Norman Maier says "*The
German people* [author's italics] experienced a long period
of frustration . . ." and proceeds to explain the entire Nazi
régime by Hitler's exploitation and deliberate reinforcement
of these frustrations, we cannot agree with him. First, not
all Germans became Nazis—the real Nazis remained a minority; second, not all Nazis were frustrated; third, not all
frustrated individuals became Nazis.

Groups do not become frustrated; only individuals do. And
we may make the further limitation that only individuals
who are already frustrated will react to economic or political
adversities which befall an entire people by developing secondary frustrations and by joining a radical social movement
as a relief from their personal anxieties. It is therefore methodologically wrong to apply categories of this kind to
social entities like groups and movements as if they were
individuals. For example, to classify, as Maier does, certain
movements as "goal motivated" and others as "aggression
controlled" seems to be untenable.[23] It may be questioned
whether the theoretical distinction of two types of this kind
has any value, but certainly they should not be used as
taxonomic, that is, classifying, categories. There are plenty
of frustrated Socialists and plenty of goal motivated, well
adjusted, non-neurotic Communists. The methodological
mistake consists in the direct, unmodified application of cate-

---

[23] Maier, *op. cit.*, pp. 591-592, 595. "Socialism stresses the goals, whereas
Communism stresses the destruction of capital [sic]."

gories of personality psychology to the analysis and characterization of highly complex and flexible social groups.

In the case of concrete individuals it takes the skill of a competent psychiatrist to determine whether his attitudes and behavior are neurotic (due to frustration) or not. To discover abnormal reactions in groups is even more difficult. In dealing with groups of individuals we must realize that an aggressive attitude and militant behavior may be a perfectly sound and normal response to a challenge—for example, the violent reaction of striking workers against strike breakers or plant police. As Karen Horney points out, an individual's failure to fight back where the situation requires fighting back may very well be an essential element of a neurosis.[24]

Furthermore, the mere fact that an individual participates in a movement which proposes impracticable solutions to a social or political problem does not necessarily indicate that this individual is frustrated. If a successful businessman becomes a follower of a movement which advocates some kind of panacea for all social evils, it may merely show that he is not especially bright, or not well versed in economics, but that he has a strong sense of social justice; by no means can we be sure that his "crackpot" ideas are due to frustration.

Restatement of the Problem

Having thus cautioned the reader against too easy and too early conclusions concerning the psychopathological traits in social movements, we may now attempt a more constructive restatement of the issue. It is beyond doubt that abnormal psychology can contribute significantly to the understanding of the behavior of participants in social movements, and it is also true that certain types of social move-

[24] Karen Horney, *The Neurotic Personality of Our Time* (New York, W. W. Norton & Company, Inc., 1937), pp. 64 ff.

ments cannot be understood without the aid of abnormal psychology.

Among the founders of militant social movements, political as well as religious, we find a fair proportion of abnormal personalities; especially of neurotic and paranoiac individuals. The same is true of the early adherents of such leaders, the first disciples or followers. Although no statistical information is available, it is safe to say that, for example, among the early followers and collaborators of Adolf Hitler the proportion of abnormal individuals was probably significantly greater than in any other political movement of the time. This writer has known quite a large number of men and a few women who joined the Nazi Party before 1933 or soon after the seizure of power. In most of these cases he finds strong indications of frustration—disappointments in their careers, conflicts or frictions in marriage, absence of or unsatisfactory nature of sexual relations, and so forth. But, he also remembers similar types among members of a middle-of-the-road liberal club in Germany. After 1933, when the "bandwagon effect" came into play, the proportion of frustrated individuals among the members of the N.S.D.A.P. (National Socialist German Workers' Party) must have decreased to approximately the average proportion in the nation. The more extreme cases of Hitler, Hess, Goebbels, Streicher, Ley, and many minor figures in the Nazi hierarchy are now well known.[25] Hitler's notorious craziness and the large number of crackpots among the early Nazis were one reason why the movement in the beginning was not taken seriously by most of its opponents.

The psychoanalytic explanation of the personality of a man like Hitler is obviously a fascinating task, but a rather hopeless one for lack of reliable data. A great deal of significance has, for example, been ascribed to the childhood

[25] See for example G. M. Gilbert, *Nuremberg Diary* (New York, Farrar, Strauss & Co., Inc., 1947).

experiences of modern dictators. A stern and authoritarian father has become a standard feature in the biographies of revolutionary leaders and a welcome basis for psychoanalytic interpretations of the leader's personality. Unfortunately, and contrary to the conditions under which clinical psychoanalysis operates, there is usually no possibility of checking the accuracy of these more or less legendary childhood experiences of great men; it is even more difficult to ascertain how they were experienced by the budding dictator himself. However, it must be remembered that millions of men have had stern and strict fathers without becoming dictators or even minor figures in militant social movements.

We do not deny the possible contributions of such personality analysis towards the understanding of social behavior in mass movements, but we are skeptical about their value for the understanding of the causation of social movements. We maintain that the immediate and significant causes will be found in the conditions of society rather than in the condition of the leaders' minds or in the neuroses of their followers. Fascistic movements, for example, do not have to be created by a paranoiac leader.

There arises, then, another question, one of real sociological significance: How is it possible that under certain conditions an abnormal personality can become the successful leader of a mass movement? What conditions in German society made it possible that an obviously psychopathic man like Hitler could gather around him other neurotic and psychopathic individuals and with their aid organize a mass movement which carried him to power? Thus stated, the problem of abnormal personalities in social movements becomes a problem of social selection and social sifting. The first task would therefore be to furnish reliable evidence of the presence of an unproportionally high ratio of abnormal personalities among the members of a given social or political movement. The sociologist could then show which

ideological and institutional traits of the movement made it,
at a given time, in a given historical situation, particularly
attractive to abnormal personalities, and why these had a
particularly good chance of gaining recognition, influence,
and power in this particular movement, whereas in other
movements or parties such individuals would have been
eliminated or reduced to insignificance.

To make our point clearer, let us take the case of a socialist agitator referred to as "A" in Lasswell's book.[26] This man,
to be sure, is a psychopathic case, more likely a neurotic.
Why is it that he could attain a position of considerable
influence in the Socialist Party in the United States? Why
is it that among the great and powerful socialist leaders in
European countries types like "A" were no longer to be
found after the socialist parties had become real forces in
the political life of these countries? Why is it that apparently
perfectly normal men like Bebel and Branting took over the
leadership of the socialist parties of Germany and Sweden
after such unbalanced agitators as Lassalle [27] and Axel
Danielsson?

The answer, it seems, has to be sought in the following
direction: any social and political movement which rebels
against existing social institutions will attract individuals
who have been suffering real or imagined injustice under
these institutions.[28]

What is it that attracts these individuals? That, of course,
depends on the characteristics of the movement on the one
hand and on the personality of the individuals on the other

[26] H. D. Lasswell, *op. cit.*, pp. 79-105.

[27] Sombart, *op. cit.*, Vol. II, pp. 279 ff.

[28] Parental authority, exercised in an authoritarian, patriarchal manner,
seems to be one of the institutions of importance in this respect. See Max
Hoelz, *From White Cross to Red Flag, the Autobiography of Max Hoelz,
Waiter, Soldier, Revolutionary Leader.* Trans. from the German by F. A.
Voigt (London, Toronto, Jonathan Cape Ltd., 1930). Also, Toni Sender,
The Autobiography of a German Rebel (London, The Labour Book Service,
1940), pp. 1-10, 15-21.

hand. The neurotic, maladjusted, unbalanced or psychopathic personalities seem to be attracted not so much by the ideas as by the sense of oneness, of belonging, which appeases their feelings of insecurity, of helplessness, of isolation. It is quite obvious that militant movements which activate every member have more to offer in this respect than those in which a rank-and-file member may not have to do more than pay his dues. But the conditions of attraction to and selection within a movement tend to change as the movement develops, grows, gains in power, and becomes more complex and institutionalized in its structure.

The phenomenon which has often been observed in the growth and decline of private business firms, of visionary and creative builders, being succeeded by staid and unoriginal administrators, seems to have a parallel in the life history of social movements. The creative thinkers, the enthusiasts as well as the fanatics, the demagogues, and the crackpots, seem to have much better chances during the early phases of a movement than in its maturity. As long as the movement remains in the evolutionary phase where it resembles a sect—that is, a group or conglomeration of groups engaging primarily in protest and in the cultivation of a sense of superiority, of being holier or politically more advanced than the "ordinary" people—with *no* chance of attaining power and assuming responsibility for the political fate of the society, these types may play a very prominent rôle. Gradually, as the movement becomes influential and is confronted with concrete tasks which require practical solutions, other types of personalities will come to the fore.[29]

The history of the socialist labor movement in all Western countries has been characterized by a gradual elimination of fanatics and prophets and an increasing predominance of sober-minded, well-balanced, practical men with administrative and political ability—a fact which has often been

[29] Hellpach, *op. cit.*, pp. 168 f.

deplored by disillusioned revolutionaries. This gradual elimination process presupposes a democratic constitution of the movement, which permits replacement of office holders through elections. In an authoritarian movement such replacements are also possible through purges, as the Russian example shows. Even in the Nazi movement, the worst crackpots among the old guard—men like Gottfried Feder— were, after 1933, suspended from office or shelved in one way or another. However, if the leader of an authoritarian movement is, like Hitler, himself a pathological personality, and if he is surrounded by advisers of the same caliber, the trend towards normality in personnel may be reversed, particularly if the régime encounters a severe crisis. This seems to have happened in Germany during the later phases of the war, when many appointments to leading positions in the armed forces and in the administration were made by the *Fuehrer* solely on the basis of loyalty. In this phase apparently there occurred a counterselection of fanatics and sadists,[30] who were objectively quite incompetent for their assignments.

Enthusiasts and Fanatics

For the purposes of sociological analysis it seems useful to distinguish between two types of active participants in any kind of social movement: the enthusiast and the fanatic. The enthusiast (*Schwaermer*) is primarily inspired by the ideals of the movement, while the fanatic (*Eiferer*) is primarily concerned with action. The enthusiast has an imaginative mind; he creates the ideas, the symbols of the movement, while the fanatic is an activist, often resorting to violence in the service of ideas which have to him become a

---

[30] A related phenomenon which may be mentioned here was the deliberate training and selection of sadistic personalities for the SS guards in concentration camps. SS men who refused to beat and torture prisoners, or who broke down mentally when forced to engage in evil practices, were ruthlessly eliminated.

dogma. Many social movements have developed from enthusiasm and mysticism to fanaticism and dogmatism: Rous-
seau-Robespierre; Tolstoi-Lenin-Stalin.[31] The fanatic, as a
type, is essentially identical with the political activist who
seeks and finds fulfillment in political action as such. To
him the goals of a movement do not mean as much as the
life of combat and the experience of group action. The typical activist, therefore, can pass from one militant movement
to another, without pangs of conscience—today a Communist,
tomorrow a Fascist.

In our times, this type has become a frequent and dangerous element in Western society and probably also in some
Asiatic societies. Richard Behrend explains this phenomenon
as follows: In certain individual psychological situations, the
libido is channelled into the field of political action. A few
socially maladjusted individuals form the activistic political
élite. In normal times these are exceptional cases. The broad
masses of people remain indifferent towards the sphere of
political action. Their profounder psychic levels do not
respond in this direction; they are politically dormant. In
certain social and spiritual situations, however, larger masses
are seized with political activism. This is likely to happen
when neither their occupation nor their religious activity
offers them satisfaction and fulfillment. Under such circumstances the masses can be aroused by a minority of asocial,
disqualified individuals who come from the ruling classes,
especially among the intellectuals.[32] Economic distress may
contribute to this phenomenon, but cannot in itself explain
the phenomenon, because political activism does not pursue
economic ends in the narrow, vulgar sense. Its goals are not

---

[31] Hellpach, *op. cit.*, p. 177.

[32] Richard Behrend, *Politischer Aktivismus*, (1932), and "Psychologie et
Sociologie du Radicalisme Politique," *Revue des Sciences Politiques*, Vol. 56
(1933).

Compare also Alfred Meusel, "Die Abtruennigen," *Koelner Vierteljahrshefte für Soziologie* (3. Jahrg., Heft 2/3.)

at all of a rational kind, they can therefore neither be proved nor disproved by reason. It is action, political action as such, which is desired. This state of mind is always the consequence of a psychic conflict between the individual and his social environment, the solution of which is found in social action as such. The goals of the action assume secondary importance.

This very intriguing discourse has only a limited validity for the understanding of the motivation of those who actively participate in a militant movement. To be sure, they find the fulfillment of life in the struggle; the happiness of family life, love, contemplation—all intellectual and aesthetic values are subordinated to the one sphere of political action.[33] For example, the success of a relatively small number of Communists in gaining control in labor unions is mainly due to the fact that "they work like hell"; whereas the rank and file shows little interest in the regular, routine affairs of the union, the members of the Communist Party will give all their spare time to the advancement of their cause. They acquire a thorough knowledge of labor laws, of union procedure and of union tactics. They give up their private lives for the sake of the party.[34]

But the point where the psychoanalytic explanation fails, because of its dogmatic nature, is this: the great majority of the leaders and of the rank and file in militant movements are not political activists in the narrow, technical sense; they may behave as if they found fulfillment in action as such, but they are typically idealists in the sense that they are un-

[33] Mr. A. Upham Pope, the sympathetic and well-informed biographer of the Russian statesman, Maxime Litvinoff, relates that, on becoming a member of the underground Social Democratic Labor Party in 1898, Litvinoff "cut all ties, even the most intimate, and obliterated the past so successfully, that he has practically forgotten his younger years....He chose to be a good revolutionary rather than a good son...." A. Upham Pope, *Maxime Litvinoff* (New York, L. B. Fischer Publishing Corporation, 1943), p. 39.

[34] Alsop in *Saturday Evening Post* (Feb. 22, 1947,) on the Communists in CIO unions.

shakably convinced of the righteousness of their cause, of the validity of their philosophy and the goodness of their goals. It is this conviction, which often assumes a quasi-religious quality, that enables these men and women to endure every kind of danger, hardship, imprisonment, and torture, and to go calmly to the scaffold.

6

The Problem of Political Generations

Statement of the Problem

THE THEORIES WHICH correlate the four main types of political attitudes with the four ages of life (Chapter 5) are based on a very old and common observation: that younger people tend to differ from the older people in their outlook on life and consequently in their political views. The personality of the son is often directly opposed to that of the father; spoiled children are likely to become tyrannical parents; a conservative and intolerant king is often followed by a progressive and liberal crown prince, and so forth.[1] In modern Western society each new generation tends to attack the ideas of the older generations and to create and propagate new ideas. The sequence of schools in philosophy and in the fine arts appears to be connected with the sequence of generations. And the rhythm of changes in political ideas and institutions seems to be closely associated with the rhythm in the change of generations.

The main obstacle encountered by this theory is the difficulty of determining in concrete terms what constitutes a generation. While this is easy in a single family, it is extremely complicated in the larger society where filial generations of all ages are coexisting simultaneously. The more recent authors who have treated the problem, like F. Mentré,

[1] François Mentré, *Les Genérations Sociales* (Paris, 1920), pp. 188 ff.

Karl Mannheim, and Willy Hellpach, therefore, argue that a social generation cannot be defined in biological terms and in terms of definite age groups, but has to be defined in terms of common and joint experiences, sentiments, and ideas. "A generation is [thus] a new way of feeling and understanding of life, which is opposed to the former way or at least different from it." [2] A generation is a phenomenon of collective mentality and morality.[3] All the men of a generation feel themselves linked by a community of standpoints, of beliefs and wishes.

... have they not been witnesses of the same events, have they not read the same books and applauded the same plays, have they not received the same education and observed the same deficiencies in society? The force of facts has imposed on them a reform program which they will realize rightly or wrongly through their voluntary associations. . . .[4]

It is implied in this definition that a generation consists of contemporaries of approximately the same age, that is, of those who, on account of their age, have more in common with each other than with older or with younger people.

The individuals composing each generation tend to associate among themselves more frequently and more intimately than with the older and younger generations. While some associations intentionally or incidentally tend to span all age groups, there is a strong tendency toward the formation of clubs, circles, and associations consisting of persons of approximately the same age, the leaders sometimes being somewhat older than the rank and file. Thus the generation as a collective of mentality tends to become the basis for social groups. In this form the concept of a generation becomes a valuable tool in the study of social change. For our present purpose, this concept of a generation may be even more strictly defined as those individuals of approxi-

[2] *Ibid.*, p. 304.
[3] *Ibid.*, p. 298.
[4] *Ibid.*, p. 47.

mately the same age who have shared, at the same age, certain politically revelant experiences.[5]

Certain experiences during the most formative period of life tend to be of decisive effect on the development of the individual's social philosophy and on his political attitudes. People of approximately the same age will be influenced by the same experiences. These experiences may therefore be called the decisive experiences of a political generation.[6]

Illustrations

The American and the French revolutions, the Civil War and the reconstruction period in the South, the foundation of the German Reich by Bismarck and the unification of Italy by Cavour, the defeat of Germany in 1918 with its aftermath of internal troubles and inflation—these have been decisive experiences for certain age groups in the respective nations. The political thought of each subsequent generation in a nation is thus decisively influenced by those events of historical significance which occurred when the men and women forming a generation were in the most impressive formative period of life. This formative period cannot be defined exactly in terms of years of age. Generally speaking,

---

[5] Willy Hellpach, *Sozialpsychologie* (Stuttgart, 1946), p. 109.

[6] Hellpach, *op. cit.*, pp. 107 ff., points out that the so-called problem of generations consists first in the effects on attitudes of the age difference between parents and children, grandparents and grandchildren; second in the fact that as a rule the filial generation of a certain age will have different attitudes, objectives, prejudices, and preferences than the parent generation had when they were of the same age. However, the filial generation of brothers and sisters can have an age span of thirty-five years, and they can be up to sixty or seventy years younger than their fathers, up to forty-five years younger than their mothers. This makes the concept rather useless for purposes of the historian and social scientist. The tendency has been, therefore, to conceive of a generation as individuals of equal calendar age. But if one accepts this concept, there arises the problem of determining how many age columns and which age columns constitute a generation. This difficulty can be overcome, though not in a quantitatively exact manner, by introducing the concept of historical experience. For our purposes, it is better to narrow the concept to "politically relevant historical experiences."

it spans the period from twenty to thirty years of age, but in individual cases it may begin earlier and end later.

The Nazi movement in Germany was led by men and women who were born between 1885 and 1900 or who were between eighteen and thirty-three years old when the catastrophe of 1918 occurred. Even the older men among them were, in 1914, below thirty years of age, and therefore could not have had much political experience before the First World War interrupted their civilian life. The war and its aftermath thus became the experience which was decisive for the formation of their political views. Regardless of which party they chose, their political thinking differed in many respects from that of the pre-war generation. It is possible to detect finer differentiations within this war generation. Those who were already young men when the war began had at least some impressions of political life in Imperial Germany, perhaps already a political conviction and party affiliation. Those who were only boys when the war began received their first notions of politics from the post-war internal troubles and were inclined to think of political action in terms of conflict and combat rather than in terms of consensus and compromise.[7]

The same phenomenon can be found in the political attitudes of the various immigrant groups in the United States. Among the German element, the oldest political tradition is that of the liberal, democratic revolution of 1848. This movement was at the same time a movement for national unity. The combination of these ideas determined the political attitudes of the German elements in Wisconsin and

---

[7] E. H. Posse, *Die Politischen Kampfbünde Deutschlands* (Berlin, 1931), p. 17.

"... It has to be emphasized that not only the *Fronterlebnis* (experience of combat) contributed to the personality formation of a large part of the young people who today begin to throw themselves into political life. Much more important was the *experience of civil war*. The most active part of the young generation fought at that time in the various *Freikorps* (Corps of Irregulars). Very few had a clear idea of what they fought for."

other Mid-Western states through most of the nineteenth century.[8] Carl Schurz, friend and adviser of Lincoln, is the best-known representative of this generation. The immigrants who came over in the 1880's and 1890's were either Bismarckian nationalists or anti-Bismarckian Social Democrats, depending on whether they were of middle-class or working-class origin. It was among the middle-class immigrants of the first years after the First World War that Nazism found most of its supporters among German-Americans.

Among the political refugees from Russia, one can, in a similar way, distinguish several groups which correspond roughly to different generations. First came those who were in opposition to the tsarist régime—socialists, anarchists, nihilists (until the latter two were declared inadmissible). After the Bolshevist Revolution came the White Russians: members of the nobility and bourgeoisie, also intellectuals opposed to Lenin's régime. The most recent group contains mainly anti-Communists of various description from the satellite countries in eastern Europe, from the Soviet Union, and from China.

The "Decisive Experience"

The concept of "decisive politically relevant experience" needs further clarification. It is a complex idea, not easy to define in exact terms. Tentatively we may say it comprises the following elements:

1. The general conditions of social life during the formative period: whether it was a time of war or of peace, of prosperity or depression, of internal stability or of social unrest, of lively international relations or of national isolation from the outside world.

2. The important political issues of the period, for exam-

---

[8] The strength of liberalism and socialism in Wisconsin, in our times, is largely due to the transmission of the ideas of '48 from one generation to the other. This is an interesting example of the creation of a political tradition.

ple, controversies over constitutional or legal reforms, over the extension of civil rights to underprivileged groups, and so forth.

3. The concrete internal political and social struggles of the period: strikes, insurrections, revolution, civil war.

We have seen how the attitudes and the ideology of the founders of modern communism (Bolshevism) were conditioned by experiences which they had as young men under the tsarist régime. Similarly, the generation from which the vanguard of Nazism came received its crucial experiences in a society at war which was characterized by the disruption of normal family and community life, by the conversion of the country into a huge besieged fortress, by the suspension of normal parliamentary discussion, by military censorship of the press, and by a gradual disintegration of the Imperial régime. Later, when the war generation began to participate in political action, the nation was torn between monarchists and republicans, social democrats and communists; it was a time of internal troubles which nearly reached the dimensions of civil war. These experiences contributed to the formation of action patterns and thought-ways which made many in this generation susceptible to the appeals of Nazism.

The number of political generations will vary from period to period and from country to country. This is because the number of politically decisive experiences depends on the character of the period. Also, the decisive experiences of contemporaries can occur anywhere within a span of, roughly, sixty-five years.

A further complication is introduced by the fact that a generation enters active political life as the *ruling* generation only when it has already *passed through* the formative period of life. The politically dominating generation is composed of adults roughly between forty and sixty-five years of age. Consequently, the actual political situations and issues which confront the ruling generation are not the same as those from which it received its decisive experiences. But the issues of the day are seen, so to speak, in the light of those decisive experiences. Thus the older men and women in the politically dominant generation will tend to look upon these issues in a way different from that of younger men and women. The latter, therefore, are likely to be in the opposition.

Differentiations Within a Generation

Of course, the entire generation will not have identical objective experiences, and furthermore, subjective ways of experiencing will be quite varied—that is, rural youth and urban youth will experience the same war in different ways. But the fact that one belongs to a certain generation tends to set at least certain limits for the development of one's behavior, sentiments, and ideas.

To have the same experiences in common integrates a generation into a social collective; but a generation may include several subdivisions, if the crucial experiences are met and mastered in different ways, for example, by different class groups.[9]

These units *within* a generation are formed around concrete groups (clubs, associations, party groups) as nuclei. The actual influence of each of these groups will depend upon its ability to give adequate expression to the typical experiences of this particular generation. In what direction the political thinking and willing of a generation develops, depends on whether the present state of society seems to offer good opportunities or not. Those particular groups and units within the generation whose thinking and actions appear to be most in harmony with the prevailing experiences

[9] Karl Mannheim, "Das Problem der Generationen," *Kölner Vierteljahrshefte für Soziologie* (7 Jahrg., Heft 2, Heft 3, 1928), p. 311.

of their generation are likely to become most influential (in the generation) just as individuals whose personality and thought agree with the predominating groups in their generation are likely to become the representative and accepted types, while others will either become sidetracked or thwarted in their true strivings or form the oppressed and therefore oppositional minority (such as rationalists in a romantic period).[10] These considerations should cure us from the common fallacy of assuming that old people tend always to be conservative and young people progressive.

Differentiations Between Generations

The differentiations *between* generations are likely to be greater in periods of rapid social change than in periods of slow and gradual change. This is probably why the problem received so much attention in France during the nineteenth century. Different political régimes followed each other in that country at short intervals, a fact which naturally stimulated inquiries into the causation of social change in general.

The longer a generation stays in power politically, the sharper will be the clash with the youngest generation. Consequently, it is in the interest of a continuity of political thought that the intermediate generation—which is capable of exerting more influence on the young generation than the oldest—should in due time participate in political leadership. A society in which the politically leading group— irrespective of party affiliation—is overaged will sooner or later be faced with a revolt of youth that may assume very radical forms. Such revolt may be explained as a result of political frustration of an entire generation. It occurred in Germany after 1918 when the old political parties were led by a superannuated generation of leaders who blocked the

10 *Ibid.*, p. 325.

rise of younger men into leading positions.[11] This was the more serious since at the same time the chances of vocational advancement and business success were bad for the younger generation because of the critical condition of the national economy. Under such conditions, the more active individuals in the frustrated generation tend to seek release in radical political movements.[12] It is therefore of great significance for the relationship between political generations in the United States that young men quite frequently can gain at least a start in state politics, and that once in a while a man who has scarcely reached the age of eligibility is elected to the Congress of the United States.

Not all members of a generation have equal chances; there may be certain categories of individuals whose vocational and general social advancement is, at certain times, blocked for some reason or other. Jews and other so-called racial minorities are often found in this situation. That explains the participation of large proportions of members of such minority groups in movements aiming at a change of the existing social structure and order. In Imperial Germany many Jewish intellectuals, having no inclination for a business career and being barred from an academic or civil service career, found a field of action and a release for their resentments by entering the opposition parties, where they served as journalists and political leaders. Consequently, we find among the active progressives and socialists of that period a larger proportion of Jews than would be expected.

[11] On this subject see Hellpach, op. cit., p. 110. Hellpach is extremely critical of the entire concept of the "missing generation." See also Willy Hellpach, "Ideenwandel im Generationenwechsel," Vom Neuen Geist der Universität (Berlin and Heidelberg, Schriften der Universität Heidelberg, Heft 2, 1947), pp. 210-229. In this paper Hellpach practically discards the generation concept. "Der Begriff der Generation verfliesst in denjenigen der Epoche, das Zeitalter buendelt die Lebensalter zusammen."

[12] Frederick L. Schuman, Hitler and the Nazi Dictatorship (London, R. Hale and Company, 1936), pp. 98 ff.; also Hans Gerth, "The Nazi Party," American Journal of Sociology, Vol. XLV, No. 4 (Jan., 1940).

In the period between the two world wars, this same generation of intellectuals entered the ruling groups in all those countries which had gone through a revolution at the end of the First World War: Germany, Austria, Russia, and the eastern European states.

The theoreticians of socialism were, according to Sombart,[13] practically without exception men who had failed in their career ambitions. While this may be greatly exaggerated in its significance, it is certainly true that many of the leading figures among the older generations of socialists were middle-class people who for one reason or another had been prevented from achieving the goals of their youthful ambitions. Because the socialist movement was the most radical opposition to the existing society during their early manhood, it became the natural receptacle for these castoff middle-class individuals.

It is a matter of speculation whether the creation of an intellectual proletariat in the United States, which seems to be an inevitable byproduct of mass education on higher levels, is going to increase the ranks of a politically radical and revolutionary intelligentsia.[14]

We can see thus how the problem of generations merges with the problem of psychopathological factors in political behavior.

[13] W. Sombart, *Der Proletarische Socialismus*, Vol. I (Jena, 1924), p. 55.
[14] James B. Conant, *Education in a Divided World* (Cambridge, Harvard University Press, 1948).

7

The Social-Psychological Texture of Social Movements and Political Parties

THE QUALITY OF GROUP SOLIDARITY

ALL HUMAN GROUPS exist as *social* phenomena in the minds and through the wills of the individuals who compose them. This is a fundamental principle, but rarely clearly recognized. Society (and the groups which make it up) is often treated as if it were an ultrahuman, natural force acting upon a mass of passive human beings. This is a most distorted view, and most unrealistic.

Two individuals, in order to become socially related, have to become aware of each other, have to develop a certain amount of mutual sympathy and confidence, and have to desire a particular relationship which includes certain mutual obligations.[1] If we take as an example the social relationship of "betrothal," we can follow its development step by step from the first exchange of a glance or smile between the partners, to the final stage where the established social relationship is formally announced. The purpose of the public announcement is to demand and secure respect for the new relationship from outsiders. The relationship is then recognized by society. On the other hand, the dissolution of marriage by desertion or divorce takes place when the will

[1] Compare F. Tönnies, "Gemeinschaft und Gesellschaft," *Handwoerterbuch der Soziologie* (1931), or the translation by Loomis in *Fundamental Concepts of Sociology* (New York, American Book Company, 1940), pp. 3-29.

to maintain the relationship ceases to exist. Or, to take an example which is closer to our present field of inquiry, a number of people in a local community who believe, each for himself, in the ideas of Mr. Townsend do not form a Townsend Movement. Only when each of them becomes aware of the presence of others who hold the same views and only if they establish relations of coöperation among themselves, can one consider these people as forming a social group. In other words, the mere togetherness of individuals who have certain characteristics in common does not yet constitute a social relation. They may form, from the point of view of an outside observer, a category for statistical or administrative purposes, but they do not form a social group in the technical sense of the term. They are not even in psychic relationship and therefore not capable of acting as a unit.[2]

A *psychic* relationship is formed when individuals become aware of each other and begin to react to each other; it can be described in such terms as sympathy or antipathy, confidence or distrust, love or hatred. These categories do not refer to the purpose or function of the relationship; they fit the relations between blood relatives as well as those between parties in a business contract.

The first aspect which makes a human relationship a *social* relationship is its particular function or functions. In order to secure the function or functions of a human relationship, it is necessary that each participant have an affirmative attitude toward the relationship, a will to sustain it and to act in accordance with the mutual obligations which this particular relationship involves on account of custom, law, or morality.

The *socio-psychic* quality of the relationship depends upon

[2] Even blood relationship as such does not establish the *social* entity of "brotherhood" or "father-son" relationship, as can be clearly seen from the cases where blood relatives meet without knowing of the biological relationship that exists between them.

the quality of the volition by which it is formed and sustained. Theoretically we can distinguish two extreme cases: one in which the relationship is formed and sustained as an end in itself; the other where the relationship is formed and maintained only as a means to an end, that is, in order to realize certain compensating or like interests of the participants. An example of the first type would be a genuine intimate friendship; an example of the second type, a business contract or partnership. It is plain that in regard to social movements a close, though not rigid, correlation exists between these two types of socio-psychic texture and the typical motivations of joining which were discussed in the beginning of this section.

The motives, on the other hand, are essentially, though not rigidly, determined by the purpose or function of the relationship or group as seen by the individual members. If, in our Western society, a man marries a woman merely for her money (or vice versa), the psychic relationship between the two spouses is likely to be rather cool; normally, however, one does not enter into a relationship which involves a high degree of intimacy unless one finds his partner —or partners—congenial and sympathetic. On the other hand, in entering into a purely utilitarian, special relationship (such as a business contract) we usually do not bother about the personality of our partner so long as we have confidence that he will fulfill his obligations. There are many kinds of associations for the promotion of special purposes which we are willing to join without knowing other members personally or without regard to our attitudes toward them; the purpose is what attracts us to this kind of group.

The same principles can be applied in seeking to understand the socio-psychological quality or texture of social movements. There exists a close inter-relation between the members' conception of what the movement means to them and their motivations in becoming and remaining members;

these motivations and conceptions influence in their turn the attitudes which members of a movement develop towards each other. We have seen before that motivations vary between individuals; but here we may assume that certain types of motivations or combinations of types predominate in each social movement and that therefore each social movement has its peculiar socio-psychic texture. It is with these texture patterns that we are concerned in the present discussion.

PROTOTYPES

For purposes of analysis we may distinguish the following types:

1. The spiritual community, or fellowship of a value-oriented movement.
2. The following of a charismatic (divinely endowed) leader.
3. The utilitarian association between individuals and also the alliance between social groups.

The Spiritual Community or Fellowship

If devotion to a common cause is the prevalent motivation among the participants of a movement, an attitude of fellowship, of comradeship, or even of brotherhood will develop and prevail. In small and militant groups the resulting socio-psychic texture will be similar to that of a small and fervent religious *sect*. The members will perceive each other as part of a select minority which in its championship for a right cause stands alone against a world of unrighteous enemies. A movement of this type forms a *spiritual community:* speech forms like the brotherly "thou" or "comrade" will express symbolically this socio-psychological texture. Morris Hillquit, in speaking of the nightly gatherings of young radicals on the roofs of Cherry Street in the New York of the late nineteenth century, describes the character of these groups as follows:

> The Socialists of that period were not practical politicians. They were idealists and propagandists who clung to their social creed with religious zeal . . . few in number, misunderstood and railed by the multitude, and felt more than a mere political kinship with each other. They were *comrades in a personal and intimate way*.[3] [Author's italics.]

As the movement grows, and more and more groups are formed, and as these groups increase in membership, the attitudes and relationships between members will change; while the forms of intimate comradeship may be retained, the spirit changes. The movement will become more like a *church*. But so long as the essential bond, the devotion to the cause and ideals of the movement, lasts and functions as the main unifying factor, the movement remains a spiritual community—a fellowship of fighters for a cause.

The Following

If attachment to a charismatic leader is the predominant motivation of the members, the movement will show a different socio-psychic texture—it will be a *following*. In this case the sense of community is generated indirectly; personal attachment to the leader, who in his turn designates the goals and interprets the cause, is the intermediate link. Loyalty to a leader can, however, have varying degrees of reliability. Since in such a movement the common goal usually is not dogmatically and permanently established, but instead is subject to change through orders from the leader, there will be a constant danger of dissent and secession. Moreover, since a charismatic leader can maintain his authority only by constantly proving to his followers his extraordinary ability, his position is rather unstable and consequently the solidarity of the movement is at all times pre-

---

[3] Morris Hillquit, *Loose Leaves from a Busy Life* (New York, The Macmillan Company, 1934), p. 3.

carious.[4] Furthermore, since the degree of confidence of the leader which a member of the movement enjoys will determine the member's power and influence, there will be a fierce competition between subleaders for the favor and confidence of the leader. This was very noticeable within the Nazi movement. The result may be that a certain faction of the movement actually gains control over the leader and becomes a ruling oligarchy. Hitler seems to have avoided this danger by carefully balancing subleaders and factions against each other.

Most social movements show, at least during the earlier stages of their development, the phenomenon of the great personal leader, the great spellbinder and agitator.[5] These men create a quasi-personal following—that is, they do not intend to be personal leaders, but, to the masses, they symbolize the cause for which they are living. In these formative stages, a movement often assumes the character of a following of a quasi-charismatic leader. And just as the great religious movements have their martyrs, so have political movements and parties theirs—the persecuted leaders, the members of the rank and file who were imprisoned or lost their lives in the early struggles of the movement.

In genuinely charismatic movements there arises the problem of transforming the charismatic authority of the original leader into a more stable form, a problem of special urgency after the death of the original charisma bearer. If this transformation succeeds, the socio-psychic texture of the movement will also change, either into a fellowship or into a more rational association, the characteristics of which we shall now discuss.

[4] See Max Weber, *The Theory of Social and Economic Organization,* trans. by A. M. Henderson and T. Parsons (New York, Oxford University Press, 1947), Part III.
[5] .Willy Hellpach, *Sozialpsychologie* (Stuttgart, 1946), pp. 172 f.

The Rational Association

The third type of group corresponds to the basic sociological type of a utilitarian, purposive, and *rational association* between otherwise independent individuals; in this type, the movement itself is considered as a means to the attainment of certain immediate benefits for each of the members. Members will remain in the movement as long as their expectations of such benefits are not disappointed.

A variation of this type is the *alliance* between two or more distinct parties or movements whose objectives, though not identical, are sufficiently similar or compatible to permit at least a temporary joining of forces. A good example would be the American farmer-labor parties. They were short-lived just because they were utilitarian groups. Both farmers' organizations as well as labor unions in the United States show strong associational traits. Examples in Germany are the *Wirtschaftspartei* in pre-Nazi days and the various refugee parties that have been formed since 1945.

The larger, the more heterogeneous, the older, and the more powerful the movement becomes, the more will such purposive-rational (utilitarian) relations between its various components come into existence. In particular, the development of a large variety of organizations and institutions within the movement, the accumulation of funds and of property in which these are invested (headquarters, camps, training centers, newspapers, stores, and so forth) will favor the development from an original fellowship-like texture to a more associational texture. This is because, as the movement grows, more and more people will become tied to it by calculation rather than by conviction. Such development may of course signify the end of the movement, at least as a movement. It may have become a dominating force in society, or it may die off for lack of fighting spirit.

COMBINATIONS OF TEXTURE TYPES

In Political Parties

In the real, concrete movements and parties, we usually find combinations of all three types. A political party may be defined as an alliance of individuals and groups for the joint pursuit of their particular interests. Or, we may define a party as the result of taking sides in regard to a controversial issue of public concern. In both cases we suggest that a rational choice is being made by the party-forming individuals, so that a party might be defined as an association in the technical sense of the word. This construction would not in all cases agree with the empirical facts. Nor would it be in accordance with the conceptions of party held by many political leaders and theorists. They prefer at least to see their own party as a fellowship of fighters for a common cause.

Edmund Burke, one of the strongest defenders of parties, saw in a political party primarily a group of friends who shared the same political views, principles, and intentions. Burke thought of politics as a struggle for power, in which loyalty to one's friends was a prime virtue and disloyalty a major offense. "Public life is a situation of power and energy; he trespasses against his duty who sleeps upon his watch as well as he that goes over to the enemy." [6]

The older English political parties, led by closely knit oligarchies of politicians who in most cases had known each other since their public school days, and who in any case had grown up with each other in the service of their party, had preserved a good deal of their fellowship character. Likewise, if we read the accounts of the origin of the Prussian Conservative Party, we find that personal friendship

[6] Edmund Burke, *Thoughts on the Cause of the Present Discontents* (Cambridge, Cambridge University Press, 1931), p. 101.

among the leading founders was a very essential factor in its formation.[7]

The two major American parties are permeated with this sense of fellowship. It is at least significant that American politicians like to think of their parties as fellowships of friends rather than as associations of individuals for the pursuit of mere interests. However, the friendship among American politicians has a strong utilitarian tinge, because of the importance of patronage as a consolidating factor.

The relative weakness in American society of extra-political relations through family, school, college, or status group (which are so important in England) and the fact that American politicians are selected in other ways than English politicians, have to be considered in explaining the predominance of the associational or barter type of relationship (barter with favors) among American politicians.

There is obviously also a strong element of the "following" in the socio-psychological structure of the American parties. One may say that from the ward organization upwards, the machines consist of personal followings of professional politicians or bosses. However, the charismatic element in these followings is weak and the utilitarian element (expectation of patronage) strong.

Fascism

The Fascist and Nazi movements were primarily followings of quasi-charismatic leaders. Loyalty to the leader was the essential tie, since the goals were so indefinite and subject to change by inspiration of the leader. Smaller followings of a less charismatic character centered around local and regional leaders and around outstanding men of the inner circle around the supreme leader (such as Gregor Strasser, who, before his elimination, was a serious competi-

[7] Erich Jordan, *Die Entstehung der Konservativen Partei und die Preussischen Agrar-Verhaeltnisse von 1848* (Leipzig, Muenchen, 1914).

tor of Hitler). There were bitter animosities and feuds between these subleaders and their followers, conflicts which
were overcome merely by the authority of the supreme
leader. Loyalty to the leader thus became a matter of self-
protection against one's competitors and enemies within
the movement. Among the rank and file of the followers
there was at the same time a strong spirit of comradeship,
a sense of community which gave a feeling of security to the
individual member and lent strength to the movement.

German Youth Movement: The "Bund"

It is interesting to note that in German public life this
type of group which rested on the combination of comradeship and personal loyalty to a leader was first recognized in
the apolitical middle-class youth movement which began
about 1895 among urban middle-class youth. Here the group
type of the *bund,* as it was called, became a consciously accepted pattern in contrast to the *Verein* or associational type
of the youth guidance organizations.[8] The genuine *bund,*
however, is essentially a gang of young men and like the
latter is bound to be very unstable in its socio-psychological
ties. Secessions and schisms are frequent, and the abdication
or rejection of the leader may terminate the very existence
of the group.

Transformation in Nazism

Becker shows very clearly how the original youth movement was perverted by the Nazis. From a loose federation
of fellowships it was converted into a centralized organization, the very opposite of what the movement had been
trying to practice. From a romantic and somewhat anarchistic federation of loosely organized small groups it was con-

[8] On the transformation of the socio-psychological texture of the German
youth movement by the Nazis, see Howard Becker, *German Youth: Bond or
Free* (New York, Oxford University Press, 1946).

verted into a huge para-military organization.[9] There had
been also a good deal of transfer of youth-movement traits
to the youth organizations which after 1918 were formed
by all the major political parties. Most interesting in retro-
spect are, however, the influences which the youth movement exerted upon the Nazi movement as a whole, not
merely on the Nazi youth organizations. These influences
were manifold but subtle: the Nazis borrowed certain patterns of exterior conduct, such as the dress, the "nest," the
camp, some of the songs; but in the Hitler youth group all
this was applied in a different spirit—as a means for pre-
military and political training: the hike became an endur-
ance test, a march with full equipment, or a night march,
and so forth. The youth movement's leadership principle
most certainly influenced National Socialist thought concerning the position of the Fuehrer; also, the relations between subleaders and their men were, in theory at least,
often patterned after the youth movement model. In practice, however, subleaders were appointed from above and
derived their authority from the leader. The rank and file
had scarcely a chance to ask for the replacement of an un-
popular subleader. This was particularly true of the Hitler
Youth and the *Jungvolk*. The so-called leaders were actually
"office holders."

The highly controversial thesis of Hans Blueher that the
youth movement was held together largely by erotic relations between the young leaders and their followers was accepted as a desirable principle of social organization by
leading Nazi intellectuals like Rosenberg. These advanced
the theory that the state, instead of being an extension of
kinship and tribal groups, was essentially an outgrowth of
the *Maennerbund,* that is, the band of young warriors, who
attach themselves to a leading hero, and form a ruling élite
in the larger community. This theory, although never offici-

[9] *Ibid.*

ally adopted, had a profound influence within party circles, especially within the S.S. (élite guards).

Now that the Nazi party and the affiliated organizations have been destroyed, and the movement has gone underground, it seems to have resumed in some instances the socio-psychological characteristics of a sect. An anonymous letter to the editors of *Die Welt* expresses gratification for the publication of Dr. Goebbels' *Diary* (which apparently had induced the formation of Nazi reading circles) in the following significant words: "Imagine that now on three evenings of a week a devoted congregation somewhere listens to the reader. Beside him in candle light the pictures of the Fuehrer and of our doctor [Goebbels]."

The Communist Movement

The Communist movement has a very variable socio-psychological texture; where it is small and repressed, it tends to assume traits of a conspiracy; the units are small, the members rigidly screened and the socio-psychological relations in those small groups seem to have a sect-like quality. Where it is strong and open, centered in a large political party, the texture is likely to be quite different. But, and this is an important point, it is under all conditions a spiritual community and not a personal following of a charismatic leader. Despite all the hero worship focused upon Karl Marx, Lenin, and Stalin, the essential bond is the devotion to the common cause, the firm belief, acquired in reading circles and discussion groups through a process of intellectual training, in the absolute validity of the dogma contained in the writings of Marx, Engels, Lenin, and Stalin (the four evangelists of the communist political religion).

Labor Unions

Labor unions, while primarily utilitarian, purposive alliances of workers for the attainment of better working conditions, tend to acquire traits of a spiritual community if and insofar as their members become habituated to see in their union an instrument for the attainment of a better social order. The experience of common struggle and persecution tends to develop a feeling of comradeship, and of fellowship which becomes a value in itself. Finally we find in many labor unions a strong sense of loyalty to outstanding leaders, who are admired and venerated as unique, irreplaceable personalities, as incarnations of everything the union stands for. Certain unions, especially among the older craft unions, tend to be thought of, by their members, mainly as utilitarian pressure groups, a kind of cartel of skilled workers for the control of a local or regional labor market. The more militant industrial unions, on the other hand, show more of the non-utilitarian socio-psychological traits.

III

THE SOCIAL FOUNDATIONS

8

General Principles

~~~~~~

THE CARRIERS OF SOCIAL MOVEMENTS

ANY LARGE UNORGANIZED social group can become aroused
to concerted action aiming at social change and thus become the support or carrier of a social movement or the
basis for a political party. In the course of modern history
the following kinds of social collectives have been most important in this respect: religious groups, status groups, ethnic
groups, and social classes.

RELIGIOUS GROUPS

Religious groups often correspond to social classes or nationality groups; therefore religious movements are often at
the same time movements of social classes or national minorities. For example, the origin of political parties in England lies in the religious conflict between the Church and the
Nonconformists, which was at the same time a conflict
between social classes. This is not to say that the religious
conflict arose because of the class conflict, but it happened
to coincide. It was complicated by the fact that the urban
middle-class dissenters in their struggle against the combination of Church and gentry formed an alliance with the high
aristocracy.[1]

[1] G. M. Trevelyan, "The Two-party System in English Political History,"
Romanes lecture delivered in May, 1926 (Oxford, Oxford University Press,
1926).
"The continuity [in each of the parties] was to be found mainly in the

STATUS GROUPS

Except in slave rebellions, *status groups*, or *estates*, or
ranks as a rule aimed merely at a redistribution of power
within a social order, and not at a radically new order.[2]
Movements of status groups were the insurrections of slaves
in ancient Rome or in modern times in Haiti; the insurrections of medieval and post-medieval nobility against the
king; the revolts of medieval urban plebeians against the
patricians; the peasant revolts in the sixteenth and seventeenth centuries; the conflicts between journeymen and guild
masters.

---

unbroken connexion of the Tories with the church interest and the Whig
aristocrats with the Protestant Nonconformist voters.

"The religious division on the great political issue of the new era [the
reform of Parliament] continued to influence the course of politics until the
Reform Bills of 1832, 1867, and 1884, laid the question to rest." (p. 25.)
From the Restoration to the end of the nineteenth century "the continuity
of the two parties in English politics was very largely due to the two-party
system in religious observance, popularly known as Church and Chapel...."
This religious dualism dates from the time when the Cavalier parliament
passed the Act of Uniformity in 1662. "The dualism of the English religious
world, and the disabilities imposed on Dissenters, form a large part of the
explanation of the peculiarly English phenomenon of two continuous political parties in every shire and town of the land" surviving in spite of changes
in issues and party programs.

The Nonconformists, because of the disabilities under which they lay,
tended to act together in politics, not any longer under their own Puritan
leaders, but under the leadership of Whig aristocrats, "who conformed to
the Anglican worship, but remained anti-ecclesiastical in their general sympathies." (p. 27.)

[2] See Max Weber, *Theory of Social and Economic Organization*, trans. by
A. M. Henderson and T. Parsons (New York, Oxford University Press,
1947), pp. 424 ff. See also Max Weber, "Classes, Status Groups and Parties," *From Max Weber,* trans. and ed. by H. H. Gerth and C. Wright Mills
(New York, Oxford University Press, 1946), pp. 180 f.

ETHNIC GROUPS

Nationality Movements in Europe, Asia, and the United States

Ethnic groups create the movements of national minorities, such as the movement in Europe for political independence or cultural autonomy, and the independence movements of natives in colonial countries. Wherever the ruling classes, especially the landlords, belong to a different ethnic group, these movements are bound to coincide with class movements. Typical constellations are peasants versus landlords, or native intelligentsia in alliance with native businessmen versus the foreign bureaucracy and bourgeoisie.[3]

The independence movements of Asiatic peoples in British India, Burma, Indo-China, and the Dutch East Indies have been initiated and led by native intellectuals who often have received their education in London or Paris, or at one of the Dutch universities. Support has in some cases come from a native class of entrepreneurs—merchants and manufacturers —and from the plantation laborers and other landless peasants. The split that runs at present through these movements is a result of the diversity of class interests: the propertied classes want independence, but not at the price of a social revolution, whereas the masses of the peasants and workers, under the leadership of some intellectuals, see salvation in communism.[4]

[3] In the Baltic provinces of the Russian Empire, which later became the republics of Estonia and Latvia, the struggle of the Estonians and Latvians for national independence was directed not only against the Russian régime but at the same time against the German ruling classes of landlords, merchants and intellectuals. The Lithuanians' struggle was in the same way directed against an élite of Polish landowners and the high clergy, which was of Polish origin.

[4] See Erich H. Jacoby, *Agrarian Unrest in Southeast Asia* (New York, Columbia University Press, 1949). See also Rupert Emerson, "An Analysis of Nationalism in Southeast Asia," *The Far Eastern Quarterly*, Vol. 5, No. 2 (Feb., 1946); Nicholas Spykman, "The Social Background of Asiatic Na-

Ethnic groups have been of considerable importance in the United States in generating and spreading social and political movements. On the one hand, the various ethnic groups have carried their national sentiments, their sympathies, and antipathies with them across the ocean. The Irish, for example, have maintained enough animosity against the British to be quite opposed to any course in the United States' foreign policy which seems to them dictated by British interests. Before and during the First World War, practically every nationality group in the United States attempted to influence public opinion in favor of the particular political aims of its mother group in Europe. Poles, Lithuanians, and Czechs propagated the idea of national independence for their peoples in Europe. Generally speaking, the ideologies of these American off-shoots of the eastern European national minorities were nationalistic and at the same time democratic, for at home the struggle for national emancipation was fought against the tsarist régime and against the dynastic empire of Austria and Hungary. Russian and Polish Jews in America continued the fight for liberal political institutions in which they had been engaged in their home countries.

Besides the movements for national independence, and to some extent connected with them, there was a strong socialistic tendency among the immigrant groups. During the nineteenth century and the early twentieth century American socialism was largely a movement of workers and intellectuals from the European continent.[5]

---

tionalism," *American Journal of Sociology,* Vol. 32, No. 3 (Nov., 1926), pp. 396-399; Virginia Thompson, *Nationalism and Nationalist Movements in Southeast Asia: Government and Nationalism in Southeast Asia,* Part III (New York, Institute of Pacific Relations, Inquiry Series, 1942); A. T. Bauer, "Nationalism and Politics in Malaya," *Foreign Affairs,* Vol. 25, No. 3 (April, 1947).

[5] Morris Hillquit, *History of Socialism in the U. S.* (New York, Funk & Wagnalls Company, 1910). See also *Loose Leaves from a Busy Life* (New York, The Macmillan Company, 1934) Chap. I.

When the repercussions of the Russian Revolution of 1917-1918 reached the United States, the Slavic language groups in the socialist movement were among the first to join the new Communist Party.[6] Since then the Communist Party of America has maintained a large number of foreign language papers. The existence of large communities of Slavic, Hungarian, Finnish, and other nationalities consisting mainly of working-class people in the manufacturing cities of the Northeast, explains this. On the other hand, the Russian immigration since 1918 has been quite a considerable factor in the development of anti-Soviet opinion in the United States.[7]

The rise of Fascism and Nazism in Europe caused sharp splits within the Italian, German, Spanish, and Austrian groups in the United States. These splits were intensified when the United States was drawn into the impending conflict between the European powers, and they became very sharp after the outbreak of the Second World War. The Italian and German groups were by that time inclined to support the Democratic Party because of the New Deal; but the elections of 1940 showed a fairly strong correlation between the proportional size of these nationality groups in counties and states on the one hand, and the decline of the Democratic vote in comparison with 1936, which may be taken as an indication of a mounting anti-Roosevelt sentiment among the German and Italian voters. By way of contrast, the shifts from Roosevelt were negatively related to the size of the French-Canadian, English, Norwegian, and Swedish populations in each state.[8] The internal cleavages

[6] Laidler, *Social-Economic Movements* (New York, Thomas Y. Crowell Company, 1946).

[7] Two elements are to be distinguished in the Russian immigration: first, the counter-revolutionaries, mostly of aristocratic or bourgeois origin who fled from Russia during the early phases of the Soviet régime, and their descendants; second, the anti-Stalinists who came later and who tend to be either Trotskyites or Fascists.

[8] Louis H. Bean, Fred Mosteller, and Fred. Williams, "Nationalities and

which arose in Nazi-occupied countries during and after the Second World War were reflected within the ethnic groups in the United States. Thus the Polish groups were split in 1945 between the supporters and friends of the government in exile and the supporters of the new government in Warsaw.[9]

Generally speaking, all major phases of the political development of the European nations have had their echo among the non-Anglo-Saxon groups in the United States. Occasionally the ethnic differentiation of the American people has affected the course of domestic politics, as in the case of the repeal of prohibition, which antagonized numerous ethnic groups, whose traditions concerning the use of alcoholic beverages differed from the Anglo-Scotch-Irish pattern.

However, the importance of ethnic groups as carriers of social movements in the United States is much less important than in Europe. These groups are gradually being absorbed into American society, and they persist mainly under two conditions: as relatively isolated communities in farming or mining areas, and as large, compactly settled colonies in big cities. Furthermore, and herein lies the great difference from Europe, the ethnic differentiation in the United States does not represent definite and permanent differentiation in terms of social classes.[10] Each of the nationality groups has been able to evolve its own middle class and each group is sending increasing numbers of individuals into the higher strata of American society.

1944" in *Public Opinion Quarterly*, Vol. 8 (Fall, 1944), p. 372. A nationality group in this study comprises persons born in a foreign country and the children of foreign-born parents, that is, the first and second generations.

[9] Similarly, the Yugoslav societies are now split into Stalinists, Titoists, and anti-Communists.

[10] This is primarily because all groups have been able to acquire property in land in the United States.

The American Negroes

The case of the American Negroes is of a different nature. Culturally they are not differentiated. In language, religion, and usually in their folkways and mores, they do not stand apart. They do not strive for a Negro state. Their social values are American values, their aim is integration into American society, not the establishment of an independent, separate Negro society. They are, therefore, not a genuine ethnic group or national minority. If their fight for realization of their constitutional rights should take on the forms of a mass movement, it will most likely become closely affiliated with the labor movement, because the vast majority of Negroes belong to the working class, and because the labor unions are the largest group which advocates a program of economic fairness to Negroes.

This statement may seem surprising to those who are accustomed to think of the Southern Negroes primarily as sharecroppers and farmers. But the great mass of sharecroppers are virtually agricultural laborers, even if they are legally tenants, because if one considers the actual authority relation between landlord and tenant, and the economic function of the latter, the vast majority of sharecroppers are to be regarded as wage earners; that they receive part of their wages in kind and that they are compelled to share the risk with the landlord does not raise them to the position of genuine tenants.[11] Generally, the Negroes who are occupied in industries other than agriculture tend to be concentrated in the less skilled and less well-paid jobs. As a group they come nearer to the nineteenth-century prototype of the proletariat than any other large group in the United States.

At the present time, the Negro movement, if one may call

[11] See Karl Brandt, "Fallacious Census Terminology and Its Consequences in Agriculture," Social Research, Vol. V (1938), p. 31. Also T. Lynn Smith, *Sociology of Rural Life,* rev. ed. (New York and London, Harper and Brothers, 1947), pp. 280 ff.

the Negroes' concerted efforts to defend their rights and to improve their position a movement, shows structural traits very similar to the ethnic minority movements in other countries. The leading rôle of ministers, journalists, lawyers, teachers, and physicians, the somewhat less apparent participation of businessmen, and the relative inertia of the broad masses of farmers and workers are phenomena quite familiar to the student of nationality movements in Europe. These phenomena are characteristic of the earlier phases of such movements.[12]

Franklin Frazier's thesis [13] that Negro leadership in the United States will become more and more "functional" is in agreement with our point of view. If the American Negroes are not a caste, class, national minority, or an oppressed nation, and if their aspiration is to gain recognition as real Americans, they will have to pursue their aims in each of the major fields of socio-cultural activity, and that means their leaders will have to become leaders in these various fields. Most important from a quantitative point of view will be the Negroes' participation in the labor movement, since its aims are in harmony with the economic and social needs of the great mass of Negroes.

SOCIAL CLASSES

In contemporary society, most major social movements are movements of *social classes*, or of certain parts of classes, or of combinations of classes or parts of classes. (See Chapter 2.) In order to enter into political action, social movements

[12] The Communist Party of the United States has adopted the doctrine that the Negroes "in the black belt of the South" are "an oppressed nation," whereas the Negroes in other parts of the United States, especially in the North, are a "national minority"; consequently the party demands, for the Negroes in the black belt of the South, local self-government. For details, see Chap. 17.

[13] E. Franklin Frazier, *The Negro in the United States* (New York, The Macmillan Company, 1949).   ,

must, in the modern state, either organize themselves as political parties, or enter into a close relationship with political parties. This will be discussed in Chapter 13. Here it is sufficient to state the fact. Since the major social movements are movements of social classes, it follows that political parties must also be related in certain ways to social classes. The problem we are dealing with can thus be stated as follows: What kind of relations exist between social movements and social classes? Between social movements and political parties? And finally, between political parties and social classes?

The most difficult and also the most important part of the problem is stated in the last question. Obviously the case where a party is identical with a social movement of one class must be very rare, as the number of parties in most societies is not identical with the number of classes. But the second question is also important, since the major social movements comprise organizations other than political parties—that is, labor unions, farmers' associations, and so on. As to the first question, it has already been observed at various occasions in our discussion, that the theoreticians and the leaders of social movements quite frequently come from other classes than the rank and file of the movement. It is quite obvious, for example, that the socialist movement includes many individuals who are not workers or of working-class origin and who do not even see in socialism an exclusively proletarian movement; yet, the great social movements have very largely been the expression of class sentiments, class aspirations, and more or less class-conscious action.

OBJECTIVE CRITERIA

The popular notions of class in terms of the rich and the poor, the upper and the lower, or the upper, middle, and lower classes (and their "refinements": upper-upper, lower-upper, and so on) [14] are too vague to be useful in sociological analysis. These categories do not indicate what kinds of people make up the "upper class," and so on. The upper class in a small town is likely to consist of lawyers, physicians, retail merchants, perhaps one or two small manufacturers, and a few ministers. These same people, in a large city, would probably belong to the middle class. Skilled workers who in small towns are often regarded as part of the middle class would in large cities be ranked in the lower class, and so forth.[15] Consequently these terms do not permit any inference concerning the interests and values which might be upheld or propagated by each of these classes. Nor do they take into account the power relation that exists between classes.[16]

Classes in the sociological sense are primarily collectives of individuals in like economic positions. In a market economy, like ours, this means that the persons in question have identical or similar goods or services to offer in the market, or that they receive income from like or similar economic functions. Therefore, they will have the same or related interests concerning the acquisition and distribution of property and also concerning the political institutions which uphold the economic system. At the same time, an individual's chances of participation in the immaterial culture of the society, and his prospects of attaining prestige, influence, and

[14] Warner's "classes" are really not social classes at all, but classifications, by local people, of their fellow citizens, according to the degree of esteem and prestige that they enjoy in their town. In a plutocratic society like ours, this classification is bound to correlate to some extent with the social class positions of the inhabitants, but this is more or less accidental. W. Lloyd Warner and Paul S. Lunt, *The Social Life of a Modern Community* (New Haven, Yale University Press, 1941), and *The Status System of a Modern Community* (New Haven, Yale University Press, 1942).

[15] This has been demonstrated very neatly by Wayne Wheeler, *Social Stratification in a Plains Community* (Minneapolis, Minnesota, 1949); see also H. W. Pfautz and O. D. Duncan, "A Critical Evaluation of Warner's Work in Community Stratification," *American Sociological Review*, Vol. 15, No. 2 (April, 1950).

[16] See the excellent criticism of Warner and Lunt's first volume by C. Wright Mills in *American Sociological Review*, Vol. 7 (April, 1942).

power, all depend very largely on "economic position." In other words, the totality of one's chances in the social life of the community depends largely upon the source rather than on the size of one's income. We can say that a social class consists of people in economic classes with like or similar opportunities for social life.[17]

Size of one's income becomes a factor of social stratification only insofar as it affects the ability to attain the training, education, level of living, and other things which are the elements of a social position. The more purely capitalistic a society, the more will the plutocratic valuations be significant for one's social position in terms of prestige. However, equality of income does not necessarily constitute identity of class interests. A farmer and a skilled worker whose incomes may be equal in dollars and cents will belong to different social classes because their economic and political interests, their total prospects in society, and their opportunities for social and cultural life are different. Nor is class position determined by occupation. The same occupation may or may not be carried on independently. For example, the watchmaker who owns and operates his own small shop is in a different economic position and belongs to a different economic class than his colleague who works as a wage earner in a watch factory, even if both have the same occupations and same amount of income. The former may work all by himself, or he may employ other workers. In the latter case he would be a small capitalist; in the first case he would occupy an intermediate position between a capitalist and a wage earner. The factory worker receiving a wage income would belong to the social class of the proletariat; the independent watchmaker who works by himself and whose income consists partly of wages, partly of interest, might be

[17] See Max Weber, "Classes, Status Groups and Parties," *op. cit.*, or in *Politics* (October, 1944). See also "Class," "Class Consciousness," "Class Struggles," "Middle Class," "Proletariat," and related articles in the *Encyclopedia of the Social Sciences* (New York, The Macmillan Co., 1942).

called "proletaroid"; the watchmaker who employs a few wage-workers would be a petty bourgeois; and the factory owner (himself possibly a trained watchmaker) would be a capitalist or bourgeois whose income consists mainly of profit.

The occupation of an agriculturist can be carried on as a large-scale enterprise by a planter, rancher, or estate owner; as a family enterprise by a farmer with the aid of his wife, sons, and daughters; or as a family enterprise with the aid of a few hired hands. The planter's source of income is rent and eventually profit, whereas the small farmer's source of income is largely labor.

Agricultural tenants do not form a uniform socio-economic class, because the legal cloak of farm tenancy covers a variety of very different social relationships between landlord and tenant. Tenancy may be a device by which a farm operator who does not have enough capital to buy a farm attains the use of land; in this case it is an arrangement between a landowner and a capitalistic entrepreneur. This is the relationship which prevailed in England in the early nineteenth century and which led economists like Ricardo to develop the conceptual distinction between rent and interest. In this case, landowners and tenants form two different socioeconomic classes. But a tenancy relation may also be established between a retiring farmer and his son in order to secure an old-age rent for the parents. In this case landlord and tenant belong to the same socio-economic class. Finally, the share tenant in many regions of the world, and in particular the Southern sharecropper, although legally a tenant, is in many cases virtually an agricultural laborer who receives his wages partly in kind (the "furnishing") and partly in cash at the end of the year by an arrangement which makes him share the risk with the landlord.[18]

This scheme of social classes is based on the ownership

[18] See p. 149.

and non-ownership of the means of production: land and capital, respectively. The validity of this description of the class structure of modern society might be questioned in the light of the rise of the corporations. The modern corporation has indeed changed the meaning of ownership of the means of production. Legally, ownership in many corporations is now widely diffused among people in the most diverse economic positions, including in some cases even wage earners and other persons in the employment of a corporation. The legal relationship of a stockholder in a corporation, however, has little or no significance in the actual control of the enterprise. The broad mass of ordinary stockholders has little or no influence on the policy of the corporation. Actual control lies with a small group of large stockholders.[19] It would therefore be quite unrealistic to regard a wage or salary worker who has invested part of his modest savings in stocks and bonds as a capitalist.[20]

On the other hand, many corporations, even some of the two hundred largest non-financial corporations, are really family enterprises, owned, and in some cases operated by the descendants of the founder, whose control is secured by ownership of the voting stock, by trust funds, by family holding companies, and similar devices.[21] Furthermore one should not overlook the fact that the number of smaller, personal business enterprises is still very large. The differen-

[19] For example see *The Distribution of Ownership in the 200 Largest Nonfinancial Corporations* (Temp. Nat. Eco. Comm. for Investigation of Concentration of Economic Power, Monograph 29, Washington, D.C., 1940), pp. xvi ff. and pp. 1 ff.

[20] Incidentally, the number of persons who own stock in any kind of corporation is smaller than generally believed, probably between eight and nine million in 1940 (TNEC, *op. cit.*, p. xvii). Most of these own only small amounts. Probably three out of four stockholders do not depend on their holdings for a living. "They are not a distinct group with a predominant interest in high dividend rates or high prices of stocks." The number of persons for whom stocks constitute the major source of income and the major portion of property is estimated at about half a million (*ibid.* p. 2).

[21] *Ibid.*, pp. xv, 105 ff. on the Fords, the Rockefellers, and the Mellons.

tiation between capitalists and other classes, therefore, is not eliminated but rather emphasized by the development of the corporation.

The very large business enterprises have created a large body of managerial and administrative personnel, a business bureaucracy, whose main concern it is to serve the interests of their employers—the major stockholders (including the holding companies which control manufacturing corporations). These business bureaucrats present new problems for the sociological analysis of the class structure, since they, like all bureaucrats, are likely to seek security of financial returns rather than economic adventure and may therefore develop attitudes and ideas concerning the functions of private enterprise and its relations to government quite different from those of the genuine capitalistic entrepreneur —the old captain of industry.[22] Furthermore, there are the enormous and increasing hosts of office workers in routine clerical or technical jobs with little or no responsibility and authority. These are economically (and in the U.S. Census of Population) classified as salary workers. The terms of employment to which they are subject tend to give them a somewhat higher degree of job security than that of the wage earner but no more security than union labor enjoys under good collective agreements. This, together with the nature of their work and the ways in which they are fitted into the structure of a large business enterprise, tends to give them the characteristics of a separate class, highly stratified within itself.

Finally, there are, particularly in the United States, many individuals who pursue not one, but two or more occupations, either alternating between them seasonally or carrying them on simultaneously. The boilermaker at an oil refinery in the South who owns a dairy farm which he operates with the

[22] See Wilbert E. Moore, *Industrial Relations and the Social Order* (New York, The Macmillan Company, 1946).

aid of a Negro tenant; the government clerk who operates
a service station; the lawyer who is also a planter; the Negro
preacher who holds a janitor's job—all these individuals are
not easy to pigeonhole into a classification of economic class
positions.

We have said before that the chances or prospects of an
individual's participation in the material and non-material
culture of the society depends very largely on his economic
class position. This is also true in the sense that people tend
to maintain personal relations primarily with people in the
same or a similar economic position. Intimate social intercourse and intermarriage are actually restricted, as a rule,
to persons in one's own economic class or in classes with
similar economic position and not too different standards of
living. Membership in clubs, voluntary associations, and even
in churches and sects tends to be differentiated on account
of economic class positions.[23]

In this way, several economic classes tend to merge into
a broader social class. The resulting class stratification
extends throughout the entire society and is not limited to a
locality nor even always to a particular nation.

We may summarize our analysis as follows. Persons in like
or similar economic positions, or in similar functions with
regard to market economy, form an economic class. Economic
classes of like or similar position have like or common economic and political interests. Between economic classes of
similar positions there is social intercourse and intermarriage.

So far we have been speaking of social classes only in the
sense of objective, observable groupings of people, without
any consideration of their own consciousness.

Class Consciousness

The mere fact that a multitude of individuals are in the
same economic and social class position does not necessarily

23 Warner and Lunt, *The Status System of a Modern Community.*

mean that they also form a social group in the strict sense, that is, a group united by a common set of values and a sense of solidarity. Only insofar as individuals are aware of the fact that their socio-economic positions are alike and only insofar as they identify themselves in certain respects with their class fellows do they constitute a genuine and developed social class.

Class consciousness usually evolves gradually. Factors which tend to arouse class consciousness are (1) threats to the economic interests of certain groups of individuals, such as small farmers feeling encroached upon by planters or ranchers; (2) factory workers feeling exploited by employers; (3) large numbers of people in the same economic position living together in a local community (for example in a mining or lumber town); or (4) a manifest division of the population of the community into separate, economically determined groups, for example, in Southern textile mill towns. Class consciousness thus develops not by reasoning, but arises from repeated experiences of class differentiation, discrimination, and antagonism.

It is a common observation that individuals who belong to different economic classes tend to differ in their attitudes, opinions, and actions in regard to controversial social and political issues. In discussions concerning labor legislation, the factory owners tend to be on one side, the workers on the other. Class consciousness develops when persons in the same class position become aware of the identity of their interests and of the likeness of their attitudes and opinions concerning public affairs. At this stage there may develop ideas which express and justify their wants and wishes, anxieties and fears, resentments and ideals. These ideas may form a well-organized system or theory or merely a loosely integrated ideology.

The ruling classes are usually the first to become class conscious. When they feel that their position is endangered, they tend to develop theories which aim to prove that social stratification is inevitable, that it has its cause in the native inequality of human beings, and so on. Their theories are ideologies in the technical sense because they serve to justify and defend a social position in danger of being undermined by the rise of other classes to positions of influence and power.

A desire for social change among a rising class will lead to one of two results: (1) association of members of the class with those existing social movements and political parties which appear to be most congenial, or (2) the creation of a new party and/or other organizations to further the interests of this class such as trade unions, coöperative societies, and farmers' associations. Consequently, different classes tend to be associated with different social movements and different political parties.

Identity or similarity of economic interests alone cannot explain the relation of social classes to social movements. However, as we pointed out before, economic classes tend to become the units within which many processes of non-economic social interaction occur: social entertaining and companionship, visiting, club membership, intermarriage, and so on, are largely confined within broad socio-economic classes and combinations of classes. Communication of ideas takes place within the same groupings. Like and similar social evaluations and political attitudes and opinions therefore tend to be diffused and accepted within the confines of socio-economic classes.

Individuals often are not aware of the fact that their attitudes and opinions are conditioned by their class position even if they behave most obviously in harmony with the interests of their class. Their self-identification with their class is not reflected but naïve. Furthermore, one finds different degrees of class consciousness among individuals in the same class position. New members of a given class often refuse to identify themselves with this class. For example, factory workers who come from farm owners' families often do not understand how their social opportunities as industrial wage workers differ from those of a farmer and therefore prefer to think of themselves as middle-class rather than working-class people. This discrepancy between objective class position and class consciousness may prevent them from joining a labor union or from voting for a labor party.

Thus not all socio-economic strata are fully developed social classes. The petty bourgeoisie and the peasant farmer in some European countries, and perhaps also the Southern Negro farmer are still to some extent status groups, not clearly aware of their class position and class interests. Such people therefore hold views of society and social change which are not realistic because they are irreconcilable with the actual direction of social evolution.[24]

In times of rapid changes in the social stratification, it may happen that the political and social consciousness of a social class or subclass lags behind, so that this class or subclass continues to adhere to a political ideology and party which has long ceased to represent its interests. This has been the case particularly among the small farmers and the petty bourgeoisie in Europe. Classes or parts of classes which are declining in status, wealth, power, and prestige are especially

----

[24] See George Lukacs, *Geschichte und Klassenbewusstsein* (Berlin, 1923), for a discussion of this phenomenon. According to communistic doctrine, the consciousness of a social class is not what the individual members of the class at a given time actually think, but the "rationally adequate reaction which can be attributed to a particular typical situation (*Lage*) in the system of production." That is, the class consciousness is that consciousness concerning society as a whole, which people in a certain socio-economic position would have, if they were capable of complete rational perception and understanding of the situation and the interests which result from it.

Only two classes, the bourgeoisie and the proletariat, can (according to the communist doctrine) develop such class consciousness; the farmers and the petty bourgeoisie can not. For the bourgeoisie there arises the difficulty that a completely realistic understanding of capitalistic society would necessarily lead "to an insoluble contradiction of bourgeois class consciousness with itself...." (pp. 73 ff.)

inclined to cling to images of society no longer true and to let their social actions be guided by standards no longer applicable.

Even in a society where class consciousness is highly developed, the correlation between social classes and political parties is never perfect. It is disturbed by a variety of additional factors.

Even if they are aware of their real economic class-position, different individuals may draw different conclusions concerning proper social action. Some accept the class situation as inevitable; some believe it can be improved by gradual changes in economic and political institutions; some think it an impasse out of which only the establishment of an entirely different social system can save them; some advocate the restoration of institutions of a past age. Thus in every class conservative, progressive, revolutionary and reactionary elements can be found.

Further complications arise through the development of differentiations within social classes, for example, through the unionization of skilled workers when unskilled workers are not yet organized. Ethnic differentiations within social classes, as in the United States, particularly among the workers, tend to retard the development of class consciousness.

Finally there are certain situations where one economic class is in a position to control the voting behavior and perhaps even the opinion of another economic class. Landowners can often control the political behavior of agricultural laborers or tenants; mine operators, those of the miners; factory or mill owners in small communities, those of the workers, and so forth. In such situations, the election results will not show close correlations between class position and voting behavior.

The Causal Relation of Classes to Parties and Movements

The causal relation of social classes to political parties and social movements can be best understood if one considers that all social and political movements aim directly or indirectly at changes in the distribution of power or in the distribution of the national income, or both. The possession of power and wealth are inter-related. The social classes which hold the balance of power and wealth are likely to oppose such changes, whereas those which still have something to gain are likely to favor them.

Conflicts between political parties which are apparently caused by disagreement on problems of constitutional law or on political theory are most likely in reality conflicts over the redistribution of political power between social classes. Conflicts between political parties over principles of taxation, wage policy, labor legislation, foreign trade, social security, and other public policies and expenditures are really conflicts between classes over the redistribution of the societal income. Legislation and policies on matters like these affect the market chances and the conditions of ownership of the various classes, either directly or indirectly. Persons and groups belonging to different classes are therefore likely to disagree on such matters.

The significance of sources of income for the formation of social classes and the rôle of social classes and class antagonism in the formation of political parties has been clearly realized by English writers like Adam Ferguson, James Harrington (*The Commonwealth of Oceana,* 1656) and John Millar (*The Origin of the Distinction of Ranks,* 1793) and by American statesmen like Madison, long before Karl Marx.

Madison in his speech of Tuesday, June 26, 1787, in the convention at Philadelphia, points out that "in all civilized countries the people fall into different classes having a real

or supposed difference of interests. There will be creditors
and debtors, farmers, merchants, and manufacturers. There
will be particularly the distinction of rich and poor." Madison
foresaw and feared that as the population of the United
States increased, those "who . . . labour under all the hard-
ships of life" also increase in proportion "and secretly sigh for
a more equal distribution of its [life's] blessings." These
unruly elements he thought, might eventually outnumber
the proprietors of land, and might demand a redistribution of
land and other property. The relation between classes and
parties is masterfully demonstrated in Madison's famous
statement in *The Federalist.*[25]

[25] "The diversity in the faculties of men, from which the rights of property originate, is not less an insuperable obstacle to a uniformity of interests.
The protection of these faculties is the first object of government. From the
protection of different and unequal faculties of acquiring property, the possession of different degrees and kinds of property immediately results; and
from the influence of these on the sentiments and views of the respective
proprietors, ensues a division of the society into different interests and
parties.

"The latent causes of faction are thus sown in the nature of man; and we
see them everywhere brought into different degrees of activity, according
to the different circumstances of civil society. A zeal for different opinions
concerning religion, concerning government, and many other points, as well
of speculation as of practice; an attachment to different leaders ambitiously
contending for pre-eminence and power; or to persons of other descriptions
whose fortunes have been interesting to the human passions, have, in turn,
divided mankind into parties, inflamed them with mutual animosity, and
rendered them much more disposed to vex and oppress each other than to
co-operate for their common good. So strong is this propensity of mankind
to fall into mutual animosities, that where no substantial occasion presents
itself, the most frivolous and fanciful distinctions have been sufficient to
kindle their unfriendly passions and excite their most violent conflicts. But
the most common and durable source of factions has been the various and
unequal distribution of property. Those who hold and those who are without
property have ever formed distinct interests in society. Those who are
creditors, and those who are debtors, fall under a like discrimination. A
landed interest, a manufacturing interest, a mercantile interest, a moneyed
interest, with many lesser interests, grow up of necessity in civilized nations,
and divide them into different classes, actuated by different sentiments and
views. The regulation of these various and interfering interests forms the
principal task of modern legislation, and involves the spirit of party and faction in the necessary and ordinary operations of the government."—Alexander
Hamilton, John Jay, James Madison, *The Federalist* (New York, Random
House Inc., Modern Library Edition), No. 10, pp. 55-56.

Even issues which apparently have little bearing on politics because they seem to be merely technical questions always involve decisions concerning the spending of public funds and revenues: therefore they are likely to lead to conflicts between social classes. Some may benefit, others may feel unduly burdened by the measures to be taken, as, for instance, in the case of whether a school board should provide free luncheons to all school-children. In other cases, this conflict of interests may cause a split within one or the other of the broader socio-economic classes. Take, for example, the railroad freight rates question in the South. Producers of industrial raw materials are satisfied with the present rate structure, whereas producers of consumers' goods and other finished products demand more favorable rates for Southern shippers of such goods.

The class basis of political parties and social movements is often concealed by the fact that in order to win maximum support, these action groups present their aims not as matters of particular classes but as a national interest or a cause of humanity—they pose as spokesmen for the entire nation or society as such; yet each of the major political movements has actually been the creation of certain classes and has been drawing its main support from certain strata of society. (Chapter 2.)

Social movements which are confined to certain occupational groups such as farmers' movements and the trade union movement do not present any problem in this respect. More refined analysis is required in the case of broader movements which gather followers not on the basis of occupational or other economic interests but on the basis of political platforms, programs, or ideas.

Paradoxically, the correlation of social classes with social movements and political parties is most easily perceived in those countries where the various political parties are divided over social philosophies and political principles—as in Germany and France and also in Great Britain. In these countries we find that through the nineteenth century the politically and economically controlling classes of large landowners and big business, especially the big mining and manufacturing interests, usually associated with the conservative parties. The smaller manufacturing interests, on the other hand, with the bankers, commercial entrepreneurs, and their associates, tended to identify themselves with the liberal and progressive parties and movements. The working classes (except in strictly Catholic regions) tended to support socialistic, communistic, and syndicalistic movements. The "old" middle classes of small farmers, independent artisans, and small traders tended to support progressive liberalism—though not without some wavering towards conservatism, whereas the "new" middle classes of office workers and professional employees had not yet arrived at any definite political ideology.

However, these correlations between classes and parties were true only as long as the parties mainly represented different political theories, involving different ideals of the economic order.

However, political parties are not divided over ideals of society and state in all countries nor at all times. They may owe their existence to religious struggles, to nationalistic or sectionalistic movements that have little obvious relation to class interests. They may therefore include parts of various social classes, as in the case of the Catholic *Zentrumspartei* in pre-Nazi Germany, the English Whigs and Tories, and the Republicans and Democrats in the United States. It is also possible, on the other hand, that the same social class is represented in different political parties. For instance the German workers before Hitler were divided among the SPD (Social Democratic Party), the USPD (Indpendent Social Democratic Party), the KPD (Communist Party of Germany), and in the Center party (*Zentrum*). Farmers and workers in the United States seek representation in both major parties.

The history of the two old parties in England shows repeated secessions of middle-class groups from the liberal to the conservative party. The seceding groups were as a rule composed of those bourgeois elements whose political and economic ambitions had been satisfied. In cases like these we have to study the political tendencies within the political parties and try to recognize their correlation with the social classes. The political parties do, in these cases, obscure such affiliations rather than make them apparent.

The preceding discussion shows how important it is, for the understanding of socio-political movements and political parties, to know quite accurately the class structure of the society in which they occur.

The Persistence of Party Groupings

The great persistency of party groupings over long periods of time could not be explained unless there was a close correlation between social classes and political tendencies. In this connection it is very instructive to observe the reappearance of the old party alignments in Germany after the collapse of the monarchies in 1918 and after twelve years of interruption of party life during the Nazi régime. Among the working classes the old rivalry and antagonism between the Social Democrats and the Communists still exists in the Western zones, and the middle classes have again formed their liberal and conservative parties.[26]

The largest of these middle-class parties, the Christian Democratic Union, included not only propertied strata but also many workers who formerly belonged to the Christian trade unions, and many bombed-out people and refugees from the eastern parts of the country. The economic interests

[26] See Hans Meyerhoff, "Parties and Classes in Postwar Germany," *The South Atlantic Quarterly*, Vol. 46, No. 1 (Jan. 1947).

and political attitudes of these heterogeneous elements could hardly be harmonized, and as a result the party has lost some of its original supporters to the more militant nationalistic parties and to the new refugee parties.

The following compilation of pre-Hitler and post-war election results in Western Germany shows a remarkable stability of voting behavior which stands in strange contrast to the drastic changes in the structure of German society. The explanation lies perhaps in the fact that attitudes do not change automatically with a change in the situation.

PERSISTENCE OF PARTY GROUPS IN GERMANY

Party Groups	Percent of Total Vote	
	1928	1949 *
Labor parties	35.9	35.8
Middle-class parties	64.1	64.2
Christian and Conservative parties	32.8	34.1
Liberal parties	13.5	11.9
Splinter parties and extreme right	17.8	18.2

* Western Germany. From *U. S. State Department Bulletin* (October 17, 1949), p. 572, table 7.

The same persistence of pre-war party groupings was observed in France during the first post-war elections. Since the right-wing parties were discredited by collaboration with the Germans, the *balance* of power was shifted towards the left-wing groups. The *Mouvement Républicain Populaire,* though claiming to belong to the left, actually became a refuge for conservatives because it is essentially a Catholic party.[27]

The Importance of Class Cleavages

If we maintain that the antagonisms of political parties are based upon the antagonisms of social classes, we do not mean

[27] Alfred Cobban, "The Political Evolution of France Since Liberation," *International Affairs,* Vol. XXIV (April, 1948). Compare Meyerhoff, *op. cit.*

to say that the party system is an exact reflection of the class system, or that each class has its counterpart in a certain political party, or that each party comprises voters from one class exclusively. This would obviously contradict well-known facts. We merely maintain that *antagonism between classes has greater importance for the grouping of political parties, than any other kind of group antagonism.* This is due to the fact, already mentioned, that the modern state is constantly bound to interfere with the distribution of property and with the market chances of its citizens; so that, consequently, persons in like economic class positions are likely to be affected in the same ways by political measures and to react to them in uniform ways.

The essential point is not that economic interests, among other factors, in some way influence the political groupings, but that among the many possible groupings of economic interests those which are based on the antagonisms of economic class positions prove to be *preponderant and of decisive importance* for the alignment of parties.

Constellations

Not all classes are always in conflict with one another. Alliances between two classes against a third are not infrequent. In such situations one will find several classes or parts of several classes among the supporters of one and the same party. For example, the alliance between *Junkers* and industrial workers versus the bourgeoisie, which was responsible for protective labor legislation and the establishment of social security in nineteenth-century Germany, or the corresponding alliance of gentry with social reformers versus the bourgeoisie in early Victorian England. One may also mention the alliance between anti-slavery Western farmers and protectionist Eastern capitalists against Southern slaveholders and free-traders, which led to the formation of the two major political parties in the United States.

The following constellations and alliances between classes have been most significant in European history:

1. Bourgeoisie and industrial proletariat against the old ruling status groups (nobility, clergy, and their associates), fighting for constitutional government, religious tolerance, and separation of church and state.

2. The old ruling status groups and the industrial proletariat against the bourgeoisie, fighting for measures against the degenerating and inhuman aspects of capitalism, advocating Christian or State Socialism or social reforms.

3. The bourgeoisie combined with the old ruling status groups against the industrial proletariat for the protection of private property and the means of production. This combination is most characteristic of the social struggles during the nineteenth century. It expresses itself in the alignment of bourgeois parties against the socialist and communist movements.[28]

Additional Factors

Once a system of political parties has been established, it may show considerable resistance to any change that might be attempted by those classes or subclasses which are dissatisfied with it. The mode of electing representatives of the people may in itself make the founding of a new party by secession of a minority very difficult, as is the case in the United States, where the indirect election of the President and the composition of the electoral college constitute the strongest impediment to the rise of a third party. In Germany, on the other hand, the system of proportional representation under the Weimar constitution favored the rise of new and small parties, and this resulted in a very close coördination of social classes and political parties.

The relation between classes and parties is further com-

[28] Ferdinand Tönnies, *Die Entwicklung der sozialen Frage bis zum Weltkrieg*, 3rd ed. (Leipzig, 1919), pp. 38 f., 62 f., 133 f., 137.

plicated through the changes in the class structure of modern society on one side and the inertia of party organizations on the other side. A party, once organized, tends to perpetuate itself, and if the class position of its original supporters changes, the party may change its policy; or, if it fails to do so, the original supporters may desert it, and the party will then look for support from other social classes. A party can, therefore, in the course of some decades, change its character in regard to composition as well as in regard to political aims. The English Whigs and the later Liberals are a good example. While the politically satisfied parts of the bourgeoisie went over to the Conservatives, the party received the support of every new stratum of the petty bourgeoisie and the proletariat, which by various extensions of the franchise were admitted into the political arena. It seems that in Germany and some other European countries the Social Democratic parties now, after the Second World War, have ceased to be working-class parties and receive a great deal of support from the petite bourgeoisie and from salaried employees. This may be a reflection or result of the breakdown of the middle classes. The far-reaching physical destruction and economic devaluation of property may have caused many members of the middle class to lose interest in the preservation of the capitalistic form of property and to become sympathetic towards the ideas of planning and social security propagated by the Social Democrats.

Generally speaking, the relation between social classes and political parties is complicated by the decomposition of social classes, especially in periods of war and depression. In such times large numbers of individuals whose savings have been lost or whose vocational outlook has been spoiled, will sink from higher to lower social strata. Of course not all of these will change their political affiliations. On the other hand, some individuals will desert their class by joining political parties which are supported by the rising social classes (for example, the influx of middle-class elements into the British Labor Party).[29]

The communist parties and the fascist parties represent two extremes in the relation between party and classes. The communist parties claim to be, according to their own doctrine, the revolutionary vanguard of the proletariat; their membership embraces supposedly the most maturely class-conscious parts of the proletariat. The relation of this revolutionary élite toward the masses of the proletariat and to the peasants is one of the more intricate problems in communist theory. The communists are in close touch with the masses of workers and peasants and they assume the task of arousing them to class consciousness through revolutionary action. Later on, we shall see what consequences for organization and tactics result from this function of the party (Chapter 17). Here it is sufficient to state that the Communist Party in each country intends to be a one-class party, but that its organized membership includes only a select minority of this class.

The Fascist and Nazi parties, on the other hand, were opposed to the very idea of class struggle. The National Socialists in particular denied the existence of classes, and class organizations were not tolerated in the movement. They could not, however, eliminate the actual conditions of class conflict, but merely shifted the scene of political class conflicts into the framework of their own party and its affiliated organizations. When all other parties were abolished and the trade unions and various other class organizations were either destroyed or coördinated (*gleichgeschaltet*) with the NSDAP and its affiliated organizations, factions and tensions due to the internal heterogeneity of the party became quite apparent. Outwardly the nation was united. But the people's community (*Volksgemeinschaft*) which the Nazis instituted

[29] A. Meusel, "Die Abtrünnigen," *Kölner Vierteljahrshefte für Soziologie,* Vol. 3 (1923).

was not a genuine community. What they achieved was nothing more than a high degree of conformity of overt behavior.[30] This, however, was sufficient for their immediate purpose: the preparation for, and conduct of, a war of conquest. This artificial order collapsed as soon as the exterior controls failed to function.

[30] See R. Heberle, *From Democracy to Nazism* (Baton Rouge, Louisiana State University Press, 1945), pp. 18-21.

9

The Relations Between Social Classes, Social Movements, and Political Parties in the United States

SIMPLICITY OF STRATIFICATION

THE STRUCTURE OF American society is simpler than that of European society, therefore the constellations of social classes, social movements, and political parties also are less complicated than in Europe. The absence, in the United States, of a nobility and of pre-capitalistic economic classes reduces the number of possible class alignments in political life.

Because American society came into existence at a time when the old status-group society in Europe was already changing into a class society, the United States assumed very quickly the characteristics of a capitalistic society with power concentrated in the hands of commercial and industrial entrepreneurs. A hundred years after the founding of the United States, a leading newspaper in the South could write,

After all, business is the biggest thing in this country. When the princes of commerce and industry say to the politicians that they must let dangerous experiments alone, they will be heard and obeyed. ... Politicians may talk, but businessmen will act, control and dominate the destinies of this common-sense country....[1]

[1] From *Atlanta Constitution,* January 4, 1890, quoted in C. Vann Woodward, *Tom Watson, Agrarian Rebel* (New York, The Macmillan Company, 1938), p. 145.

In America more than anywhere else, society tended to be split into economic classes. Because of this, then, the socio-political conflicts in the United States have been mainly of two types: (1) between the commercial and industrial capitalists on the one side, and the farmers on the other; and (2) between capital and labor.

In the following section of this chapter we shall discuss these conflicts under the points of view which have been developed in the preceding chapter. We shall in particular deal with the problem of class interest and consciousness as a factor in these conflicts and with the relation of farmers' movements and the labor movement to political parties.[2] Although the conflicts between agricultural and commercial interests were the first to rise to any significant extent in this country, we shall reverse the historical order and begin with a consideration of the American labor movement, because the conflicts in which it was involved are more easily understood.

THE LABOR MOVEMENT

In order to understand the peculiarities of labor's struggle in the United States and the relations between the labor movement and the major political parties, it is important to keep in mind that one can rarely expect to find the same pattern in all countries, not even in all societies belonging to the same civilization.

The Question of Class Consciousness

Whether American workers are less class-conscious than European workers, whether they are, instead, more job-conscious as some authorities think, is of course impossible to determine with exactness. If this be true, there is still a

[2] For a brief and able discussion see Cecil C. North, "Class Structure, Class Consciousness, and Party Alignment," *American Sociological Review*, Vol. 2 (June, 1937), pp. 365-371.

possibility that a greater class consciousness may develop among American workers, but it is not at all certain. Finally, the question of whether class consciousness is desirable or not cannot be answered objectively; we are not concerned with it.

One thing is certain: the American working class has played a different rôle politically than the European working class. The outstanding fact is the absence of a nationwide, class-conscious, consolidated labor movement. While the labor unions in the United States now (1951) count over sixteen million members, they are, as everybody knows, far from being united in one large body or federation. The consumers' coöperatives do not have anything like the significance of the coöperatives in Great Britain, or pre-Nazi Germany, or Sweden, or Belgium. And finally, there is no nationwide labor party.

Against these facts it means very little that parts of the wage-earning class have at times acted on behalf of their class interests with the same or even more energy than European workers. In general, American workers have been much less inclined than European labor to regard themselves as a distinct class and to base social action on this sentiment. Several factors have contributed to this situation. In the first place, the prospects have been relatively favorable for a wage earner to rise to a higher socio-economic position, such as land-owning farmer, independent businessman, manufacturer, or to rise within the hierarchy of personnel in industrial corporations. For a long time, their economic positions were considered temporary, by many wage earners, or they at least had the justified hope that their children would rise to higher socio-economic positions.

The very fact that even today, when the chances of rising are so much poorer for workingmen's children, the American worker considers it as desirable and almost natural that his children should get into the higher social strata; the very fact that he is proud if they do, indicates that his class consciousness is not as strongly developed as that of European workers. On the other hand, it is probably also significant that manual work as such, even if one engages in it out of financial necessity, is not considered as socially degrading, at least not if done temporarily and in one's younger years.[3]

The relatively high "vertical" social mobility, in which the wage earners participated, has thus been a major factor in delaying the growth of class consciousness among the American working class.

Another factor was the ethnic differentiation within the wage-earning class, and the inter-relation of this differentiation with vertical social mobility, each wave of immigrants entering the hierarchy of labor at the bottom and gradually rising to better-paid jobs.

But most important probably was the fact that the wages of skilled workers in many occupations were so much higher than in Europe and compared very favorably with earnings in many white-collar occupations, even in some of the professions. While this condition was basically a result of scarcity of skilled labor in a rapidly expanding economy, it was, of course, also an achievement of craft unionism and appeared so particularly in the eyes of the workers. No wonder then that they guarded their protected jobs anxiously against possible competition, even to the point of excluding from union membership large masses of workers, especially those who had recently arrived from economically backward areas in the United States or abroad, thereby relegating them to the low-wage jobs and low-wage-level industries.

This relatively high-income level of the skilled workers was of great importance, since all goods of standardized

[3] By way of contrast, when college students in Germany in the 1920's went to work in factories and mines in order to finance their studying, it was necessary to them to proclaim patriotic or educational motivations, in other words, to resort to rationalizations in order to maintain their self-respect and social status.

mass consumption, including the simpler types of houses, were sufficiently low-priced so that the better-paid wage earners did not live at a visibly lower level than the broad middle class of white-collar workers and small independent businessmen. In fact, the better-paid wage earners, as far as the level of living was concerned, did consider themselves as part of the middle class and were so regarded by others.[4] This is still the case in less industrialized regions, like the South, and in small towns.[5] In this respect American society differs sharply from European society, where, until the upheaval caused by the Second World War, the various social classes were rather clearly distinguishable even in dress, manners, and other observable traits. A lack of visibility of class membership will tend to reduce the awareness of it and consequently help to prevent or retard the development of class consciousness.

Finally, the church bonds and credos which cut across class lines and oppose class antagonism, proposing a solidaristic instead of an individualistic social order, are a much stronger influence among members of the working class than in European countries, with the possible exception of Great Britain. There is almost no anticlericalism among American workers; the churches have, since the end of the nineteenth century, concerned themselves with social problems and, although locally they have often been subservient to the employers' interests and demands, the top leaders and the proclaimed social policy programs of the churches have not been unfriendly to the labor movement and have, in many cases, embraced Christian Socialist ideals.[6]

[4] Richard Centers, *The Psychology of Social Classes* (Princeton, Princeton University Press, 1949).

[5] For a discussion of the development of class consciousness and sense of solidarity among Southern industrial workers, see Harriet L. Herring, "The Industrial Worker," in W. T. Couch, ed., *Culture in the South* (Chapel Hill, University of North Carolina Press, 1934).

[6] See Liston Pope, ed., *Labor's Relation to Church and Community* (Insti-

These factors have prevented the socialist, communist, and anarchist movements and parties, of which there have been quite a large number in the course of a little more than a century, from attracting masses of working-class voters and thereby from becoming major factors in American political life. Their existence has scarcely been felt as competition for the major parties, except in a few big cities. Here the presence of large masses of already class-conscious immigrants from industrial areas of Europe contributed to an intensification of class antagonism.

But the immigrants were to a very large extent originally small farmers, farmers' children, and agricultural laborers who had no previous contact with the European labor movement. Those among the immigrants who came from land-owning farmer families must have shared the social and political views of this class which were, in the nineteenth century, still largely conditioned by pre-capitalistic status-group consciousness. Consequently, these immigrants, even if they became miners or wage earners in mass-production industries, could not suddenly develop a working-class or proletarian class consciousness. Incidentally, the same observations hold true for the large masses of native-born people of rural origin who streamed into the new mass-production industries. The white migrants from the hills of Arkansas, Kentucky, and Tennessee who formed a substantial part of the labor force in the auto industry "brought with them their prejudices, their religious and racial bigotry"—but no experience in industrial relations. Under the influence of employer-supported sectarian preachers,[7] they were hard to win for organized labor and certainly did not realize their new class position until they had gone through some drastic experiences in actual class struggle.

---

tute for Religious and Social Studies, Jewish Theological Seminary of America; New York, Harper and Brothers, 1947).

[7] Kermit Eby, "Labor's Challenge to the Church," *Labor's Relation to Church and Community*, p. 96.

Character of the Movement

In view of these factors it is rather surprising to see the numerous manifestations of class sentiment and organized action for the attainment of equality, recognition, and improved economic conditions among American workers during the past hundred and fifty years. The Knights of Labor and, more recently, the Industrial Workers of the World (I. W. W.) were the best known and the most wide-spread of these movements.[8] Just because of the absence of the mitigating influence of social bonds, values, and norms surviving from the old status group society, the actual clashes between capital and labor have been much fiercer and more violent in this country than in most European countries. Especially is this true in those mass-production industries where the objective class conflict between employers and workers was sharpened by ethnic differentiation as in the mining, steel, automobile, textile, and logging industries. Incidentally, it is significant that in the garment industry, where no such ethnic differentiation existed, though the conflicts between employers and employees were bitter enough, a peaceful *modus vivendi* was established at a relatively early time.

In view of these outbursts of industrial conflicts, and of the appearance of many—though scattered and often sporadic—socialistic, communistic, and syndicalistic movements, it appears doubtful whether there was really any social basis for a nationwide class-conscious political labor movement in this country. This has been maintained by W. Sombart as well as by John R. Commons and his school.[9] The undeniable fact

[8] See H. W. Laidler, *Social-Economic Movements* (New York, Thomas Y. Crowell Company, 1944); Philip S. Foner, *History of the Labor Movement in the United States from Colonial Times to the Founding of the American Federation of Labor* (International Publishing Co., Inc., New York, 1947). Foner emphasizes the class consciousness of American workers.

[9] S. Perlman, *A Theory of the Labor Movement* (New York, The Macmillan Company, 1928).

is that toward the end of the nineteenth century, precisely those labor groups which in Europe had been the pioneers of a class-conscious political and economic labor movement, the skilled trades, resigned themselves to that type of business unionism and non-partisan policy which found its most representative expression in Samuel Gompers and the A. F. of L. Essentially, these American unions were, and often still are, cartels of wage earners, formed for the purpose of dividing the labor market into spheres of interest, each of which would be under the monopolistic control of a craft or amalgamated union, consisting mainly of skilled workers. Like other cartels, the unions went lobbying, and like all other economic groups, they put pressure on both political parties. It was part of their policy to approve or disapprove political platforms by endorsing candidates and congressmen friendly toward labor and denouncing others.

The implications of this policy can be understood only when we consider the nature of the two major parties. These, as is well known, originally reflected certain antagonisms and conflicts within the classes of property owners—that is, between agricultural interests on one side and commercial, financial, and manufacturing interests on the other. But they did so in a pattern which is quite peculiar to the United States. While in European countries it was possible to identify each of the major parties—the conservatives, the liberals, the progressives, and so on—with certain socio-economic classes which were dominant in their organization and policies, this could not have been done for the American parties —except within certain regions or sections of the country. (Compare Chapter 12.)

Thus we obtain a pattern, roughly speaking, as follows: The Republican Party, while representing mainly the financial, commercial, and manufacturing interests, or big business, has its progressive wing of Midwestern farmers; the Democratic Party, while in Northern and Eastern states a progressive party of the poorer urban classes, has its conservative wing of Southern businessmen and planters. The lack of uniting political ideas and principles compels both parties to rely, for a binding force, primarily on patronage and on loyalty to leaders. (See Chapter 14.) This reliance and certain factors inherent in the American system of government have produced the machines of professional politicians who serve their constituencies in very much the same way lawyers serve their clients: by obtaining the passage of legislation and appropriations suiting the interests of their constituents, or rather those of the most influential groups among them.

Non-partisan Policy

What then does the non-partisan policy of the labor unions mean? Instead of entering the political battle under their own chosen leaders, American workers have been seeking the services of politicians who have no close connection with organized labor, but who set their hopes on the labor vote. But these politicians are part of the machines of parties which are dominated by the very adversaries of labor and whose policies are, in the last instance, directed by rural and urban entrepreneurs.[10] The fact that, until quite recently, American workers by and large have been content with this kind of political action indicates, at least symptomatically, that their class consciousness cannot be very strongly developed. Opposition against this non-partisan course of the A. F. of L. unions has come early from the more class-conscious groups which were affiliated with the socialist movement.[11]

[10] See Harold J. Laski, *The American Democracy* (New York, The Viking Press, 1948), Chap. VI.

[11] Max S. Hayes, testifying before the U.S. Commission on Industrial Relations in 1910, stated the case succinctly in these words:
"... it is an absurdity to make demands upon the industrial field from the employing class and then turn around and elect attorneys to Congress and to the State legislatures who are dominated ... by large corporations and, naturally, side with the employers when it comes to a crisis, and make it

The communists have, of course, resumed the attack. We shall see what the consequences have been. When the refusal of the A. F. of L. to allow organization of unskilled and semi-skilled workers in mass-production industries led to the establishment of the C.I.O., many observers interpreted this schism as a sign of awakening class consciousness and expected the development of a new labor-class ideology in the industrial unions.[12] Have these expectations become true?

In a sense it is obvious that industrial unionism with its abolition of craft barriers and its policy of non-discrimination on account of race or color is *de facto* more of a class movement than the older craft unionism. It is also true that the political action of the C.I.O. unions, dating from labor's Non-partisan League of 1936 and now centered in the Political Action Committee (P.A.C.) has initiated a new phase in the political activities of American labor unions. This political action has induced the A. F. of L. and the railway brotherhoods to set up their own political action organizations (the A. F. of L. sponsors Labor's League for Political Education), but it is questionable whether these new adventures signify a greater degree of class consciousness. The more comprehensive political platform or legislative program of the C.I.O.-P.A.C. would seem to indicate that there is an increase in class consciousness; on the other hand, the continued adherence to the principle of non-partisan policy, the emphasis on the solidarity of interests of workers and farmers, and the appeals made to other non-labor voters,

difficult to secure the enactment of legislation which we have been demanding. . . . Hence in every contest where the lines are sharply drawn, the capitalist representatives usually are opposed to the enactment of remedial legislation for labor."

Quoted from *The Double Edge of Labor's Sword.* Discussion and testimony on Socialism and trade-unionism before the U.S. Commission on Industrial Relations, by Morris Hillquit, Samuel Gompers, and Max Hayes (Chicago, Socialist Party, National Office, 1914), p. 160.

[12] Max Handman, "Conflicting Ideologies in the American Labor Movement," *American Journal of Sociology,* Vol. 43 (Jan., 1938), esp. p. 534.

including small businessmen might indicate that class consciousness is still weak. The fact that communists have been able to gain control in some labor unions does not necessarily indicate greater class consciousness among the rank and file; the gaining of control was in many cases a fruit of more intensive activity and tactical superiority on the part of the communists. (More details in Chapter 17.)

It seems safe to say that the labor movement in the United States, while becoming more active politically, is not in its own consciousness a class movement, inspired by an ideology which ascribes to the working class a particular mission of salvation.

FARMERS' MOVEMENTS: AMERICAN AND EUROPEAN FARMERS

We shall now turn to a consideration of the nature of the second great conflict which has been so predominant in American party strife. Here we find that the antagonism between the "landed" and the "moneyed, commercial, and manufacturing" interests (as Madison would say) has been not so much a conflict between major social classes advocating different social-economic systems, as a conflict between various subclasses of capitalistic entrepreneurs. The meaning of this statement can be made clear by a comparison with similar conflicts in Europe. There, the differences in sociopolitical attitudes between farmers and the urban business classes have been sharpened by the adherence of large agricultural groups to pre-capitalistic conceptions of economy and society. Not only have family farmers, until quite recently, been opposed to the increasing commercialization and other effects of capitalism on agriculture, but there has also been considerable anti-capitalistic sentiment among the large landowners. Although many of the rural nobility were leaders in the development of improved methods of agriculture, animal husbandry, rural industry, and large-scale production of wool, grain, sugar beets, potatoes, and other crops for the market, the more status-conscious among them always felt pangs of conscience and a good deal of concern and regret about these developments.

Although it is true that in England, Scotland, and eastern Germany many yeoman farmers have been driven from the land since the sixteenth century by landlords desiring to enlarge their own estates for large-scale production of staple crops, it is also true that there has been considerable opposition to such practices among the nobility, many of whom detested the acquisition of wealth through commercialized farming and felt responsible for the welfare of their peasants. Wealth was to these people a means, a condition which enabled them to serve their country in the army, in the administration, or as parliamentarians and statesmen. The European farmers, even the most prosperous and most commercialized among them, have never ceased to look upon their farms as something more than a mere business investment or enterprise. The farm is to them the basis of the existence of their family, a foundation to last through many generations. It is from these attitudes that genuine conservatism has drawn its main strength, in England and Germany as well as in France. (Compare Chapter 2.)

Surface struggles involved tariffs, taxation, and other matters of immediate concern to the agricultural interests. Beneath these there has been the conflict between incompatible conceptions of life and society—between pre-capitalistic ideas of human relations and landed property and those which are characteristic of a commercial society. The rural aristocrat who was accustomed to care for his peasants in sickness and old age was disgusted by the urban manufacturer's impersonal and indifferent attitude toward the workers whom he employed. We recall that many measures of protective labor legislation were initiated or supported by the rural conservatives in England and in Germany. The increasing dependence of large-scale agriculture on the world market, the progress of mechanization, and the substitution of seasonal for temporary workers had made the realization of conservative ideals in European society increasingly difficult. Eventually these very ideals became quite unrealistic and out of line with actual possibilities of social organization.[13]

This antagonism did not exist in the United States. The American farmer as a rule does not share the European farmer's anti-capitalistic traditions and attitudes. Fundamentally, American farmers have always been agricultural entrepreneurs, exploiters of the range, the forest, and the cropland, with the main objective of acquiring wealth in a rapidly expanding home and overseas market for staple crops. Of course, there are exceptions, but we are here concerned with the prevailing and characteristic types of American farmers.[14] Even the planters in the South, despite their more or less aristocratic style of life [15] and their paternalistic rule over slaves and sharecroppers, were from the start essentially agricultural entrepreneurs. A plantation is primarily a capitalistic enterprise.

Thus there was in the United States no class which could constitute the basis of a genuinely conservative party. (Compare Chapter 3.) Both parties—the Federalists as well as the Republicans and their successors to the present day—were groupings of urban and rural entrepreneurs, who were holding essentially identical conceptions of life and society. But

---

[13] Ferdinand Tönnies, *Die Entwicklung der sozialen Frage bis zum Weltkrieg,* 3rd ed. (Leipzig, 1919), pp. 135 f., on transformation of the conservative party into an agrarian and industrialist bloc.

[14] See Carle C. Zimmerman, "The Effects of Social Change on Rural Personality," *Rural Sociology,* Vol. 14 (Dec., 1949), pp. 345-352. Zimmerman's quaint terminology should not prevent the reader from realizing that he really regards the typical American farmer as an entrepreneur.

[15] For an excellent discussion of Southern aristocracy, see W. J. Cash, *The Mind of the South* (New York, Alfred A. Knopf, Inc., 1941).

the concrete and immediate economic interests of farmers and planters were often opposed to those of the financiers, the merchants, and the manufacturers.

The Issues

Precisely because of the capitalistic nature of American agriculture, farmers were dependent much more, and much earlier, than European farmers, on credit and on the market at home and overseas. As a debtor class they have fought for low interest rates and pursued inflationary schemes of monetary policy. As shippers of grain, cattle, and other staple products, they have opposed the monopolistic control of freight rates by the railroad corporations, and as exporters and also as consumers, they have opposed industrial protective tariffs. As men desirous of free land for themselves and their sons, they have advocated legislation to prevent speculative acquisition of farm land by railroad corporations; in their endeavor as producers to increase their profits and to reduce their expenses for seeds, fertilizer, and other material through the organization of coöperative societies, they have encountered bitter animosity of the dealers, and had to fight for favorable legislation.

Organized Movements

Numerous farmers' organizations like the Grange, the Farm Bureau, the militant Farmers' Alliances, and the Tenant Farmers' Union have been formed to advance and protect the farmers' interests.[16] But all these conflicts have been essentially conflicts within the middle class, of which the farmer considers himself a part. Consequently, the farmers could stay in the two major parties and form a bloc in Congress which cuts across party lines. At times, however, the

[16] For a brief survey of organized farmers' movements, see Carl C. Taylor and others, *Rural Life in the United States* (New York, Alfred A. Knopf, Inc., 1949), Chap. 29, by Carl Taylor.

antagonism became so sharp that it threatened to burst the traditional two-party system. The regional concentration of farming interests and the possibility of controlling at least the government in their own states led to the formation of political movements of farmers and the establishment of farmer and farmer-labor parties. The farmers' movements in the United States have thus not been uprisings of peasants against landlords but movements of protest against exploitation and monopolistic practices of creditors, freight carriers, and distributors of farm products. It is characteristic that the most violent of these protest movements have occurred among farmers depending on one cash crop—tobacco, cotton, or wheat—and among such highly commercialized groups as the dairy farmers.[17]

Populism, the most militant and enduring of these movements, though largely a movement of the poorer farmers in the Midwest and in the cotton and tobacco belt of the South, was not directed against the wealthy farmers but against the industrial and commercial interests by whom the farmers felt exploited. The leaders in the Southern Farmers' Alliance were often planters, and so were many of the leaders in the People's Party. While there were socialistic tendencies in the populist movement, the platforms of the People's Party and of the alliances did not proclaim a new societal ideal; they consisted of demands for certain reforms and policies which, if carried out, would not fundamentally change the economic system. Had it been different, the major political parties would not have been able to take the wind out of the sails of these movements by adopting a good many of their demands.

Sectional or Class Cleavages

It has been stated by Holcombe, Rice, and others that these third-party movements were sectional, not class move-

[17] *Ibid.*

ments. This may be true if one considers all farmers as one homogeneous class with identical economic interests. That, however, is quite unrealistic. The entire farming population of this country consists of a variety of economic and social classes and subclasses. First of all, there is, at least in regions of large-scale, labor-intensive farming, as in the South and on the Pacific Coast, the class difference between land-owning farmers and landless agricultural workers. Leaving this aside, we find among farm operators a variety of subclasses with divergent and often antagonistic interests: planters, ranchers, and small farmers; owners and tenants; grain farmers and cattle grazers, and so forth. The concrete economic interests of these various groups are determined by the size of their holdings, the tenure condition, the marketing conditions for their main products, their dependence on credit, and similar factors. It must be remembered, of course, that tenants or renters do not in all parts of the country form a separate social class, insofar as renting is very often a step towards ownership. On the other hand, sharecroppers in the South are, as pointed out before, often only nominally tenants and should rather be considered as agricultural laborers.

It is true that because of the great uniformity of types of agriculture over very large areas—the various belts—sectional or regional groupings of farmers of one economic class are very distinct and quite characteristic of American rural society. But these sectional differentiations are in reality based on the prevalence of subclasses of farmers, as, for example, the typically Southern contrast between coastal plain planters and upland hill farmers. As in every country of the world, there is in the United States a basic class differential between farmers on rich soil and farmers on poor soil, between farmers in prosperous areas and farmers in agricultural trouble areas (exposed to drought, or flood, or subject to excessive price-changes of one-crop products), and between farmers who employ hired workers and those who rely on their own family.

If one looks closely enough, one will find, for example, in those Midwestern states which have been the cradle and stronghold of rebellious or radical farmers' movements, certain rather well-defined areas from which these movements have arisen and where they have found their main support. This has been shown by Stuart Rice and others. The farmers in these areas form a distinct subclass with concrete interests that differ quite significantly from the interests of the majority of Midwestern farmers. They are marginal farmers whose type of farming involves factors of great insecurity. (See Chapter 12.) The corresponding areas in the South are the hill areas of the cotton and the tobacco belts. Here the impact of crop failure or of a sudden slump in prices of the one cash crop is felt with incomparably greater severity than in the plantation areas of the lowlands. Here, too, the indebtedness of the farmer puts him in a situation much more precarious than that of the planter. It was in these areas that the Populist movement arose—here and in the corresponding areas of the Midwest. More recent "radical" farmers' movements had their strongholds in the same areas.

But these farmer movements cannot properly be understood if one sees them as sectional phenomena rather than as movements of subclasses. Furthermore, what we have called subclasses in economic respects tend to be real social classes with regard to general social intercourse and to intermarriage in particular. Imagine a Southern planter's daughter marrying a hill-billy! Or an Iowa farmer's daughter marrying a farmer from the dust bowl of Oklahoma or South Dakota! Standards of living are too different, consciousness of one's position in rural society too definite.

The New Deal certainly helped to bring these class differentiations among farmers into the limelight. The presidential elections up to the last pre-war election of 1940 showed a rather clear split of the farmer's vote for and against Roosevelt, a split which was well correlated with the indicated class lines. (See Chapter 12 for detailed discussion.)

Relation to Labor Movement

In one respect we find practically all farm owners politically in the same boat. In relation to organized labor they all tend to stand on the employers' side. There are, however, some differentiations in this respect between the larger farmer who is an employer of hired labor and the small farmer who is employer and worker in one person. The latter is perhaps inclined to be more progressive in his political attitudes, or more resentful of the monopolistic practices of big business. But is he more pro-labor? Very rarely.

The farmer is interested in low prices of industrial products, especially of farm machinery, and is therefore inclined to look at union activities merely as a cost- and price-increasing factor. Besides, he is often himself an employer. His reaction to organized labor takes the form of resentment against what appears to him exorbitant wages, which city workers get for a shorter day and seemingly lighter work. No wonder then that farmer-labor parties have always been shortlived. They were alliances based on the common opposition against the railroads and other monopolistic interests, lacking a foundation of common values and principles.[18] Being mere alliances, they could not develop a comprehensive political program.

[18] For an excellent discussion of the political rôle of farmers in the United States (and abroad), see C. Arnold Anderson, "Agrarianism in Politics," in J. S. Roucek, ed., *Twentieth Century Political Thought* (New York, Philosophical Lib., Inc., 1947).

CONCLUSION

Up to the present, the two-party system in the United States has been maintained not on a class basis, but through the strength of tradition and the tendency of organized parties to self-perpetuation. (Compare Chapter 14.) However, within each of the two major parties there have been quite serious conflicts between the subclasses which are their components. Furthermore, one should not close one's eyes to the fact that many conflicts between social classes, especially between labor and capital, have taken place outside the political arena. The employers as well as the workers have been fighting their battles to a large extent by direct action. Lockouts and strikes, the employers' frequent recourse to violent methods of strikebreaking, violence by organized labor against "scabs," the sitdown strike, and many other aspects of labor conflicts in the United States are perhaps consequences of this situation. Much of this violence has been due to the carrying over of rural folkways into industrial communities; the mountaineer who is wont to bear arms and use them in self-defense will insist on bringing his shotgun when he goes on a picket line. Other countries, of course, have also had their periods of violence in labor-capital conflicts,[19] but nowhere has direct action, as a mere factual practice without any ideological foundation, been resorted to so widely and so persistently as in the United States.

In countries like England, Sweden, or pre-Hitler Germany, where political labor parties are old, strong, and powerful, direct action is rare and violence at a minimum. (More in Chapter 16.)

[19] England in the 1820's and 1830's in connection with machine wrecking (Luddites) and with the Chartist movement.

IV

ECOLOGY, AND METHODS
OF QUANTITATIVE ANALYSIS

10

Methods and Techniques

AN INQUIRY INTO THE relations between social groups, in particular social classes, social movements and political parties in a particular country or area which aims at quantitative results could begin with a study of attitudes and opinions of individuals in regard to significant political issues. One effective method of doing this is the so-called public opinion poll.

Polls and Interviews

Insofar as their findings can be classified by occupation and by socio-economic status of the persons questioned, the polls provide data which lend themselves more or less to an analysis of the social and political attitudes and opinions predominant in various social classes. Technically, the poll may be considered as a short-cut for mass interviews. By asking a few significant questions from a large sample of the population the poll-takers expect to detect the main tendencies of opinion on a certain issue or a complex of issues.

Thorough interviews by sociologically trained investigators would, of course, be a better method of finding out what people think about social and political issues. But this technique, if it is to be used on a large scale, is too slow and expensive. A well-designed poll must, of course, be based on hypotheses which have been developed by experimental interviews.

195

To attempt a comprehensive digest of the poll findings pertaining to the political opinions and attitudes of social economic classes would go beyond the scope of this book.[1] It would require a separate study. But in order to show what kind of insight can be gained from the polls, and at the same time in order to submit some quantitative evidence in support of our general statements concerning the correlations between economic class position and political opinions and attitudes, we shall present a few examples. The first is taken from a poll of the American Institute of Public Opinion (Gallup) in 1943. The question was: "Do you think the ____ _____ [various social classes were inserted here] will be better off if the Republicans or the Democrats win the presidential election next year?" The results are presented in the following table:

	If the Dem. | Rep. Win		Makes No Difference	No Opinion	Total
	%	%	%	%	%
Do you think the *farmers* will be better off if the Republicans or the Democrats win the presidential election next year?	36	24	17	23	.100
Do you think the *businessmen* will be better off?	23	41	14	22	100
Do you think skilled and (or) unskilled *workers* will be better off?	40	19	19	22	100
Do you think *white-collar* workers will be better off?	27	27	21	25	100

Source: American Institute of Public Opinion (Gallup), June 3, 1943.

[1] Results of public opinion polls are published in *Public Opinion Quarterly*.

These questions intend to ascertain what individuals *think* of the willingness and ability of each party to care for the interests of the major social classes. They do *not* intend to provide any evidence of the political preferences of people in these classes themselves. The results show with amazing clarity the tendency of the interviewed persons to associate the Republican Party with business interests and the Democratic Party with labor interests. It is also significant that with regard to the interests of white-collar workers, the public—that is, the interviewed sample—had no clear conception of the parties' standing. This may be due to the lack of a clear conception of the nature of white-collar workers' interests. The opinions concerning farmers were not much more definite. If the answers were classified by social-economic status of the interviewed persons, one would most likely get a clearer picture of what each social stratum thought about the relation of its own interests to the policy of the two parties. On the other hand, the data also seem to show quite clearly how far each party is from being considered a one-class party.

A study of pre-election voting intentions by John Harding of the Office of Public Opinion Research, Princeton University, shows the following percentage of Republicans among occupational groups: [2] Of 100 farmers interviewed as to how they intended to vote, 56 per cent said Republican in 1938, but 61 per cent indicated a preference for the Republican Party in 1942. The corresponding figures for other groups were as follows: professional persons, 59 per cent in 1938, 60 per cent in 1942; businessmen, 67 per cent in 1938, 64 per cent in 1942; skilled workers, 50 per cent in 1938 and 47 per cent in 1942; unskilled workers, 43 and 48 per cent; and so forth.[3] There is, in principle, a strong positive correlation

[2] "The 1942 Congressional Elections," *The American Political Science Review*, Vol. XXXVIII, No. 1 (Feb., 1944), pp. 41-58.
[3] *Ibid.* Table 12.

between occupational status [4] and Republicanism in 1938, which also persists in 1942, but with a slight shift toward the Democratic Party among businessmen in larger cities. Therefore, the author has arrived at the conclusion that "apart from sentimental ties, the main determinant of Congressional voting was the voter's conception of his own economic interest." [5]

The public opinion poll has the advantage of permitting the breakdown of data according to a great variety of characteristics of the interrogated persons: sex, age, occupation, income, residence, present party preference, party membership, previous party preference, and voting in past elections. If properly planned, the poll is a very flexible method of gauging opinion on political issues. However, various objections and criticisms have been raised concerning polls, which we shall review briefly. First, there is no control over the truthfulness and accuracy of the answers; under certain conditions, where people are afraid of discrimination or retaliation, many of the answers are likely not to be truthful. [6] Also, in many cases the questions are framed so broadly that a wide margin is left for interpretation of its meaning by the interrogated persons; in that case, the answers will not be strictly comparable. The results of polls may of course also be distorted by the interviewed person's direct reaction to the interviewer—he may, out of fear or resentment, not give a true answer, or the interviewer may lead him on to give an answer harmonizing with the interviewer's own opinion. Or the person interviewed may have a preconceived idea of the kind of answer which the interviewer expects. Southern

[4] This means that the percentage of Republicans in each occupation tends to increase as one proceeds from lower to higher occupation groups. This part of the study was based upon Gallup Poll data (*ibid.*, p. 51).

[5] *Ibid.*, p. 58.

[6] For example, see George Gallup and Saul Forbes Rae, *The Pulse of Democracy, The Public Opinion Poll and How It Works* (New York, Simon & Schuster, Inc., 1940), p. 158: "In New Orleans one in every five persons interviewed [in 1939] indicated that he was 'afraid to talk'."

Negroes, for example, are very likely to give answers which they think will please a white interviewer.[7]

Most serious is the fact that the samples of the American Institute of Public Opinion (Gallup) and of the National Opinion Research Center have not always been accurately representative of the occupational structure of the population. They contain too many proprietors, professional, semi-professional, and clerical workers, too many service workers (who are easily met, for example, at filling stations), and not enough factory workers and farmers. This deficiency was one of the reasons for the failure of the Gallup Poll to predict the Democratic victory in the 1948 elections.[8]

[7] Stuart A. Rice, "Contagious Bias in the Interview," *American Journal of Sociology*, Vol. 35 (Nov., 1929).

[8] See Stuart A. Rice, "Polling Methods" *Washington Post* (Nov. 12, 1948):

". . . those who sample *people* have been mainly divided into exponents of probability sample and 'quota' sampling, respectively. The first depends upon the principle of random selection to obtain a sample that is representative of the whole. The degree of reliability is ascertainable.

"Quota sampling depends on "stratification." It seeks to obtain in the sample persons among whom there is the same distribution of certain previously counted characteristics as in the whole group or 'universe.' These characteristics are presumed to be related *to some other* characteristic the distribution of which, formerly unknown, is ascertained in the sample survey. The distribution found in the sample is then imputed to the universe. The reliability is indeterminate.

"In a public opinion poll on election issues, for example, a quota sample may have the same proportions as the general electorate of men and women, of different age groups and of different economic classes, since these factors are presumed to be related to voting preferences. The total number of persons to be interviewed is 'broken down' into subtotals, each containing the number of persons having a particular combination of the known characteristics. These subtotals are the *quotas* and the interrogator sets out to find people that possess the predetermined characteristics—first found, first interviewed. . . .

"But suppose that some of the most important characteristics associated with the characteristics under study (political opinion) have not been identified. The committee of technical experts advising the Anderson Committee stated: '. . . even though the enumerator does obtain the proper quota of persons of a given age or income level, he may unwittingly obtain persons who are not representative with respect to education, church affiliation, employment, attitude toward the war, or other characteristics . . .' that may be associated with political opinions.

Furthermore, the Social-Economic Status (SES) classification of the interrogated persons is determined either by
them, at best according to their own estimation of themselves, or by the interviewer; in the first case there is likely
to be some raising of position; in the latter case, the interviewer may be misled by the appearance of the interviewee.
In any case, there is a wide margin of error.

From the sociological point of view, perhaps the most
serious objection to polls as a technique of studying public
opinion has been raised by Clyde Hart, who himself has been
the director of a polling agency. In agreement with Herbert
Blumer,[9] with whom he has been closely associated, Hart
points out that by interviewing a large "sample" of the adult
population in private conversation one cannot find out what
these people would say in the company of their colleagues,
friends, neighbors, or wives. One does not get, therefore, a
true picture of those opinions which are really effective
within a social class. Furthermore, by interviewing samples
taken at random, or samples of individuals representative of
the sex, age, and socio-economic composition of the population one does not ascertain what opinions are being held,

"If all the quotas are filled with people interviewed on the street, trends
of opinion on the candidates may be missed that are associated with the
place of work, the place of residence, or even the place where those in the
sample are interviewed. The sample then is not really representative but only
appears to be. The sample design may reflect erroneous judgments as to the
factors really associated with the characteristic in question; or it may be
dependent upon data chosen because they are available and not because
they are most relevant to the purpose.

"Probability sampling obtains randomness and a measure of reliability
by resting upon sample areas or locations. People are interviewed by virtue
of their residence—as in every nth house in every nth block—and the interviewer must be indefatigable in his efforts to interview *all* of these people
and no others.

"Good samples for public opinion polls, as for any other purpose, can be
drawn. While they may be more costly than bad samples, a sound criterion
for such work is quality of the result rather than cost."

[9] Herbert Blumer, "Public Opinion and Public Opinion Polling," *American
Sociological Review*, Vol. 13, No. 5 (Dec., 1948).

and propagated, by the more influential persons in each category.[10]

The phenomenon which statesmen and historians have called *public opinion* is not the mere sum of individual opinions; it cannot be ascertained by adding up what people are willing to tell a stranger on the doorstep or at the street corner. It would be methodologically useful to distinguish conceptually between (1) *a* public opinion, that is, an opinion on important issues which is regarded as valid in a significant social collective—for example, among businessmen—and which tends to guide and orient relevant social actions of members of this collective, and (2) *the* public opinion of society, that is, the predominant and effectively valid opinion on matters of public concern which serves to orient social

[10] Hadley Cantril, *Gauging Public Opinion* (Princeton, Princeton University Press, 1944) gives an intensive critique of polls and polling techniques based upon experimental polling. Six sources of error are discussed. (1) Difficulties are encountered in conveying the correct meaning of a question to a large number of respondents. (2) The wording of a question, even its placement on the ballot, tends to influence the answers. (3) The technique of interviewing—that is, the use of secret or non-secret ballots—influences the results. (4) The ratings of respondents by interviewers—that is, the rating of social-economic status—are not very reliable. (5) The interviewer's own bias and his rapport with the respondent tends to influence the answers. (6) Finally, in sampling, utmost care should be taken that the sample be really representative of all those subdivisions of the public which may be relevant to the issue studied; the various sampling techniques are not equally good for all purposes.

Cantril's book should be consulted not only by pollsters but by everybody engaging in opinion and attitude studies. However, in this discussion we are not concerned with polls as devices for predicting the result of elections, but merely as sources of information on attitudes and opinions. This is a different problem. For prediction, a much greater accuracy is required. The result of an election may depend on a few percentages more or less, while in establishing a correlation between class position and party preference a wider margin of error is permissible. Furthermore, we cannot, in this treatise, discuss the more extreme claims made by some of the pollsters who want their polls to be regarded as sampling referenda, as the modern town meeting of a large nation and eventually as a substitute for the referendum. For a comprehensive critique of polls see Lindsay Rogers, *The Pollsters; Public Opinion, Politics, and Democratic Leadership* (New York, Alfred A. Knopf, Inc., 1949).

action of the government.[11] The opinion of a social movement, which is *a* public opinion, is more adequately presented by resolutions of conventions, proclamations of recognized leaders, and similar expressions than by the sum of opinions of private members.

These deficiencies of the polling technique may eventually be overcome by the development of techniques of group interviews and by interviewing persons known as leaders within their social circles and groups, that is, trade-union functionaries, prominent club women, and so forth. None of these improved techniques would, however, be as quick and easy as the ordinary polling technique. Nevertheless, it is quite likely that in the future, more use will be made of fairly intensive interviews of relatively few but influential individuals.

A variation of the polling method which permits the study of various phases in the formation of political opinion is the repeated interviewing of a panel, that is, of a representative sample of the voters, the personnel of which remains unchanged over a considerable period of time. This technique permits analysis of the factors which produce changes in attitudes or opinions, but it is so costly that it cannot be used on a large scale. However, it lends itself to the intensive study of opinion-forming in selected, representative communities. It has been developed by Lazarsfeld and his associates [12] in a

---

· [11] On the concept of public opinion see Ferdinand Tönnies, *Kritik der Offentlichen Meinung* (Berlin, Jul. Springer, 1922) and Paul A. Palmer, "Ferdinand Tönnies' Theory of Public Opinion," *Public Opinion Quarterly*, Vol. 2 (1938), p. 584. See also R. Heberle, "The Sociological System of Ferdinand Tönnies" in H. E. Barnes, *An Introduction to the History of Sociology* (Chicago, University of Chicago Press, 1948), p. 240.

[12] Paul F. Lazarsfeld, *The People's Choice,* 2nd ed. (New York, Columbia University Press, 1948). The technique contains a pitfall: the people who are on the panel may be influenced in their thinking by the very fact that they are subjected to repeated interviews. This difficulty is common to all techniques of more or less continuous observation in the social sciences. It has its parallel in nuclear physics. Lazarsfeld and his associates therefore used control groups of changing composition in order to ascertain whether the opinions of the panel were significantly influenced.

study of pre-election opinion and voting in the presidential elections of 1940 in a county in the state of New York. The problem was to find out how large a proportion of voters come to a decision during the campaign, how many change their party preference in the course of the campaign, and what means of influencing voters are most effective (meetings, radio, press, and so on). As far as the association between socio-economic status and party preference is concerned, Lazarsfeld and his associates found that the inclination to vote for the Republican candidate became more frequent as one ascended from the lower to the higher socio-economic strata, while the inclination to vote for the Democratic candidate increased in frequency as one descended the socio-economic scale. In general, the study confirms the hypothesis that social-economic class position is a foremost determinant of party preference, even in an area of little class consciousness. Most of the more politically conscious voters had made up their minds early in the campaign. The proportion of voters who actually changed from one party to the other during the campaign was very small.

Registers of Voters

Another way of ascertaining party preference is presented by the registration of voters for party primaries. Registration records permit a classification of voters by occupations and therefore by socio-economic classes. This procedure has been used by Anderson and Davidson in a study of two elections in Santa Clara County, California, a traditionally Republican county.[13] The average percentages registering in the Republican primary in the state elections of 1932, and in the national elections of 1934 were computed by status groups, by income classes, by occupations, and by real estate property ownership and non-ownership. On the whole the results

[13] Dewey Anderson and Percy E. Davidson, *Ballots and the Democratic Class Struggle* (Stanford, Stanford University Press, 1943).

show that the higher social strata had a stronger preference for the Republican Party than the lower.

While 69 per cent of registrants who were classified as manufacturers declared themselves as Republicans, only 48 per cent of the mechanics registered as Republicans; book-keepers and foremen showed a more intermediate position, with 65 per cent in both groups. Ownership of real estate in all occupational groups was also definitely correlated with Republicanism, except for those owners found among un-skilled laborers.[14] "The high Republican group was chiefly made up of professional and proprietory and a considerable number of clerical occupations; the low Republican group consisted chiefly of manual labor occupations (from each of the major categories)." [15]

A comparison of registrations in the two elections indicates that manual workers in this Republican stronghold were swinging toward the Democratic Party; "Not so the white-collar classes, who still clung to the Republican Party as their means of political expression." The same tendency to break away from the Republican Party was observable among ten-ant farmers and farm laborers; this is explained by the grow-ing cleavage between them and the farm owners.[16] It should be recalled that the study was made in an area of highly commercialized farming where owners, tenants, and farm laborers form quite separate socio-economic classes.

The validity of this technique may be questioned since it does not take into consideration the possibility of bolting from one's party. This might be a serious criticism if the technique were used to predict the result of an election. But merely as a device of determining party preferences in vari-ous social collectives at a certain date, it seems acceptable. Although bolters or voters who change over from one party

[14] *Ibid.*, pp. 150, 162.
[15] *Ibid.*, p. 162.
[16] *Ibid.*, pp. 197 ff.

to the other during a campaign, are a large enough group to affect the victory in a close election, they are too few to affect the correlation between social classes and political parties with which this technique is concerned.[17]

Perhaps more serious is the objection that occupational information derived from voters' registration is likely to give a distorted picture of the socio-economic stratification among the electorate, since registrants are inclined to do some "upgrading." In any case, these data are not strictly comparable with United States Census of Population data.

Election Analysis

An election or a referendum may be considered as the most comprehensive form of polling. However, an election usually involves a great variety of issues, especially in the United States, where elections usually are not held over a central issue, as they are sometimes in England. Only if the candidates stand very definitely for certain policies can one assume a fairly great homogeneity of political thought among their supporters—except for those supporters who always vote for the party because of habit, or because of connections with the machine. The political issues are usually more sharply formulated in a referendum. The voting on measures which involve issues of rather vital class interests reveals better than ordinary election voting the existing class alignments and attitudes. Elections, on the other hand, are of greater political importance, and the comparison of voting in several elections makes it possible to study trends and changes in political attitudes.

The secrecy of the ballot, however, prevents classification and tabulation of votes by occupation or other characteristics of the voters, except by residence and in exceptional cases by sex. Therefore it is impossible to ascertain directly how the various social classes vote. This can be done only indirectly,

[17] Compare Lazarsfeld's findings; see page 203.

by comparison of voting in areas of different socio-economic structure. This method has been widely applied in various countries.[18]

The first step in the analysis of election statistics is the choice of territorial units. Here one encounters a dilemma. Small areas are likely to contain a voting population of greater socio-economic homogeneity than large areas (for example, ward versus county); therefore, the smaller the areas for which election results can be obtained, the better. On the other hand, the number of units may become too large for manipulation with available personnel. Also, data on the social and economic characteristics of the population which could be correlated with the voting returns may not be available for the same small areas. In most cases, the investigator will have to make some kind of compromise between ideal and practicable ways of proceeding.

Election returns for the units may then be tabulated. If a frequency distribution table is constructed, one can draw map diagrams showing the percentages of the total vote obtained by each party in the various territorial units. Similar maps, graphs, and tables may be prepared for sociologically significant characteristics of the population and serve for preliminary visual comparisons.

A more complex but more precise technique of graphic presentation of voting results is the map graph with circular diagrams inserted in each territorial unit. Each circle gives with sufficient exactness the percentages of votes cast for each of several parties simultaneously instead of merely indicating the class into which the area falls. Through the varying size of the circle the total number of votes cast in each area can also be represented. This technique thus gives in one graph what would require several maps if cross-hatch-

18 See W. F. Ogburn and Nell Snow Talbot, "A Measurement of Factors in the Presidential Election of 1928," *Journal of Social Forces*, Vol. 8 (Dec., 1929). Other studies quoted are in Chap. 12.

ing of areas were used.[19] In order to find out whether any correlation exists between the voting results and certain social levels, the areas may be grouped (for example, plantation areas, family farm areas) and group-averages of voting strength may be compared with averages for social characteristics.

Another useful technique in analysis is the scatter diagram. Finally, coefficients of correlation may be computed to test the correlation between the voting strength of one or more parties with one or more social characteristics or factors. In most cases the rank correlation coefficient is the most adequate measure.[20]

It is essential that such correlations be computed for all parties, since in a multiple-party system, the proportion of the total vote obtained by each party in each unit is to some extent dependent upon the proportion obtained by other parties; for example, in German elections before the Nazi régime, a county showing a very high percentage of Social Democratic votes was not likely to have a very high Communist vote, as these two parties were in competition for the working-class vote. Only an area with an extremely large proportion of the working class among the voters could return very high percentages of the total vote for each of these two parties.

If one wants to study the importance or weight of a certain factor for the success or failure of a given party—for example, proportion of wage earners in the electorate—it is important to keep all other factors constant.[21] One must therefore have a very comprehensive knowledge of all the voters' characteristics which may eventually turn out to be significant factors influencing party preferences in certain areas.[22]

[19] For an example of this technique see p. 254.
[20] For explanation of statistical techniques, see Margaret Jarman Hagood, *Statistics for Sociologists* (New York, Reynal & Hitchcock, 1941).
[21] This can be done by the technique of partial correlations.
[22] However, caution is advised in using "partial correlations" in a mechan-

In using election returns for measuring political volition, one has to take into account quite a number of technical complications. First, one has to make sure that the returns are not falsified by stuffing the ballot boxes or by similar means of fraud. Second, abstentions from voting should be considered: they may be due to intimidation, or they may be merely an expression of indifference; but they may also, under certain conditions, be a way of expressing opposition to the candidate of the party in power—or to candidates of all major parties. It is also possible that certain classes of voters—like domestic servants or farmers in remote areas— encounter difficulties in finding the time for going to the polls. In some situations, therefore, the total number of persons eligible to vote, or the total number of registered voters may give a better base for the computation of percentages voting for each party than the total number of votes cast. In some cases, invalid votes may have to be taken into consideration.[23] Third, one has to keep in mind that in most

ical, uncritical way. See Arnold M. Rose, "A Weakness of Partial Correlation in Sociological Studies," *American Sociological Review*, Vol. 14 (Aug., 1949).

[23] For a comprehensive survey of information on participation in elections, see Herbert Tingsten, *Political Behavior, Studies in Election Statistics* (London, P. S. King & Son Ltd., 1937, Stockholm Economic Studies No. 7). In connection with our discussion, Tingsten's findings on inter-occupational variations in election participation are most interesting. Even where balloting is secret, those persons who have cast a vote are marked off in the register of voters and can therefore be classified by occupation. Occupations can be combined into social-economic classes, and the percentages of participating voters in each category can be computed. Tingsten finds that (1) among working-class electors participation tends to increase with the proportion of working-class people in the electorate or population of an area (pp. 126, 134) and (2) the proportion of socialist votes tends to rise with the frequency of voting among working-class people (pp. 127, 134, 179). He finds that in Sweden, the socialist vote remained below the proportion of working-class electors where the latter was low, while the socialist votes exceeded the proportion of working-class electors where the latter was large.

More recently, Sten Sparre Nilson has discussed the significance of quantitative studies of political behavior for the elaboration of historical laws. His book, *Historie et sciences politiques, essai sur la méthode quantitative* (Bergen, John Griegs, 1950), contains summaries and critical

cases, except where a very large number of parties compete with each other under a proportional representation system, the voters have only two or three choices, so that for a very large proportion of voters the casting of a vote for a certain party (or candidate) is not an expression of their true political convictions but the choice of the smallest evil. This explains why sometimes a new party can gain a sudden and sweeping victory; it attracts the votes that had previously been cast reluctantly for one of the older parties. In any election where there are more than two opponents, their strength is the result of a variety of circumstances concerning the mutual relationship of the candidates or parties.[24]

These considerations suggest that election analysis with the purpose of investigating factors of political behavior requires more than the study of single factors. It is desirable to take into consideration the interrelations between various parties in each significant area and also to study complexes or constellations of factors in those areas.

Studies of voting behavior which meet these requirements

---

evaluations of many recent studies and a comprehensive bibliography of Scandinavian, German, French, English, and American literature on the subject.

[24] Suppose we are dealing with a situation where three parties—Conservatives, Liberals, and Socialists—are presenting candidates. In the first ballot, the votes in district A are cast in the following proportions: Conservatives, 35 per cent; Liberals, 25 per cent; Socialists, 40 per cent; while in district B the proportions are: Conservatives, 35 per cent; Liberals, 40 per cent; Socialists, 25 per cent. Suppose the Liberals and Socialists have entered into a general pre-election alliance. The second ballot shows a Socialist majority of 65 per cent in district A, and a Liberal majority of 65 per cent in district B.

Now let us assume there is no pre-election agreement between any of the three parties. In the second ballot the Conservatives win with small majorities (55 per cent) in both districts. In district A, the Liberals, afraid of a Socialist victory, have switched about 20 per cent of the vote to the Conservatives; in district B, the Socialists, afraid of a Liberal victory (which is quite conceivable if the Liberal candidate happens to be anti-labor while the Conservative is not) have switched a sufficient part of their vote to the Conservatives. In this case, 55 per cent Conservative votes in A are not the same thing as 55 per cent Conservative votes in B.

are known in this country as studies in the social *ecology* of political parties and movements.

ECOLOGY

General Principles

The sociologist, in using statistical analyses of factors determining voting behavior, merely reverses the process of thinking which every politician uses in calculating his chances of winning an election. The political candidate knows approximately which social groups are his best potential supporters, and knows roughly the relative strength of these groups in each precinct, ward, or other area of his election district; knowing this, the politician will attempt to predict in which of these areas he is likely to have a safe majority and which areas will be doubtful. On the other hand, the social scientist knows the returns in an election precinct by precinct, ward by ward, and so forth. By taking the percentage of the total vote cast in each area for each candidate and comparing it with the relative size of certain significant groups in each area (for example, proportion of farmers or wage earners) the sociologist can *infer* which groups gave the main support for the candidate or party.

More difficulties arise if one attempts to explain *why* particular categories of voters supported one party or the other. For instance, one may find a high correlation between the proportion of Poles and the Democratic vote in certain areas; but it would be hasty to attribute the Democratic successes to the nationality of the voters, if it so happens that the Poles in these areas are predominantly industrial workers and the Democratic candidate has won a large proportion of the labor vote. In such cases one would have to hold one or more factors constant in order to determine the weight or significance of each factor. In our example, the Democratic candidate, being a Catholic, may have had a particular appeal to the Polish voters, not only as a pro-labor candidate but also because the Polish Catholic clergy endorsed him. To recognize all possible factors, one must have a thorough knowledge of the entire structure of society in the areas concerned, and also be familiar with the economy and culture of the areas. The same applies, of course, in any comparative study of political phenomena other than election results.

The planning as well as the interpretation of statistical analyses presupposes, therefore, (1) a comprehensive knowledge of all the possible factors, and (2) a general theory of political behavior which enables us to make a methodical selection of factors. Actual research in this field is a give-and-take between theory and empirical knowledge.

Furthermore, one has to keep in mind that political parties have changing relations to one another. Sometimes they are competitors for the votes of the same people, sometimes potential allies, sometimes antagonists supported by entirely different groups among the voters. In this sense, each country has its particular party system, and each region or area has its own variation of the national system, depending on the social structure and cultural characteristics of the regions and areas.

In other words, the comparative geographical approach in the study of political behavior involves the study of complexes of social phenomena *in their geographical distribution and in their interrelation.* This kind of approach to the study of social phenomena is called *social ecology.* The meaning of this term is related to the concept of *human geography* but is more comprehensive. It refers not simply to the geographic distribution of socially relevant phenomena, but also to their causal or functional interrelations. Just as the plant ecologist studies not merely the distribution of a single species but the entire flora of an area and the ways in which various plants depend on or interfere with each other, so the social ecologist concerns himself with the entire range of social phenomena in a given area and with their interdependence and conflicts.

Of basic importance in ecological studies of political behavior is the fact that one's voting is to some extent influenced by one's neighbors. However, in a highly stratified society, other influences arising from occupational and class groupings, tend to be more important than those of geographical proximity. Nevertheless, to the extent that people of like and similar occupations and class position tend to be concentrated in the same voting areas one may expect to find patterns of voting behavior which are more or less constant and more or less definite.

From theoretical deductions and empirical observations, we can develop a few general principles about the ecology of social movements and political parties, at least tentatively, as guiding rules in the study of election returns.

1. The correlation between social classes, social movements, and political parties must lead to geographical differences in the relative numerical strength of political parties and social movements if the class structure varies between areas.

2. The constellations of political parties and social movements vary between areas, because the class structure varies, and because parties and movements react upon one another. For example, in certain rural areas of Germany during the 1920's there existed a strong positive correlation between the Conservative and the combined Socialist and Communist votes, indicating a sharp political cleavage between landlords and farm workers.

3. Geographical differences in the strength of social and political movements and parties, especially between larger geographic regions, may be partly the result of differences in the political history of the regions; certain experiences in the past may affect the present attitudes, opinions, and party

preferences prevalent in a certain region (for example, as in the North and South in the United States, the old and the new provinces of Prussia, and the various regions of France).

4. Differences in the ethnic composition of the population of various areas may result in differences in attitudes and opinions, intensity of participation in social movements, and in party strength. An illustration of this is the influence of immigrants from European countries where labor was socially and politically oppressed; these immigrants are partly responsible for the strength of the socialist and related movements in New York and other big American cities in the nineteenth and early twentieth centuries.

Two problems arise with regard to the ethnic composition of a nation: first, a particular ethnic minority group may have traditional specific political preferences and antipathies. These will influence the expressions of political opinion of the entire area in accordance with the size of the ethnic group in question. Second, the presence of a particular ethnic minority may influence the attitudes of the politically dominant groups. For example, anti-Semitism developed in certain areas of European countries where Jews used to control farm credit and trade in agricultural products; anti-Oriental sentiment developed in the Pacific Coast states of the United States. The former situation favored the growth of Nazism in such areas of Germany as Hesse and Franconia (Franken); the latter contributes to the strength of Republicanism on the West Coast.

Hypotheses

The following hypothetical assumptions may guide the ecological analysis:

The geographic characteristics of *a region*—topography, soil quality, resources, climate, physical accessibility, and nearness to markets by various routes—determine the development of the economy of that region—the kind and relative importance of agriculture, of manufacturing industries, commerce, transportation, and so forth. The economy determines the economic class structure—the planters and share croppers; family farmers, renters and hired help; factory owners and workers. The economic class structure determines the nature of local social and political issues as well as the local reactions to national issues. Hence the rise, development, and persistence of constellations of specific social movements and political parties in the region.

The validity of these assumptions has to be proved in each case, and one must consider additional factors such as the political traditions and the religious affiliations of the population.

The same schema, with some modifications, can be applied to the study of ecological differences of political attitudes and voting behavior *in large urban communities.* Here the topography determines which locations in the city may be considered most desirable for certain purposes—commercial, industrial, residential, with subclassifications in each of these categories; the result is a pattern of land uses and land prices and rents. This again determines the social stratification of the population in each area. Class position in its turn determines the susceptibility of the people for specific social movements and their party preferences. This schema is of course an oversimplification.

As previously stated, additional factors, such as the ethnic composition of the population and certain relevant cultural traits may have to be taken into consideration in order to understand the entire complex of socio-political groupings in any given urban area.

In evaluating the geographical characteristics of a region, one should always keep in mind that the present geographical conditions are, as a rule, the result of man's changes of the original environment; in ecology we are concerned with the *Kulturlandschaft.* Every *Kulturlandschaft* is the result of man's response to the challenge of a natural environment.[25]

The determination of social action by the geographical environment which we referred to earlier is therefore not a simple, unilateral process. It is rather part of a process of interaction, of man's struggle with nature and his more or less ingenious utilization of his natural environment. In the process of this creation of the *Kulturlandschaft* certain habits, attitudes, and social institutions are formed which may influence the political behavior of the present inhabitants just as much as their immediate economic interests influence them. We mention as an example the ancient institutions of self-government which developed among the dike-building peoples of the North Sea marshes in Europe.[26]

A natural landscape poorly suited to human habitation may be completely changed through human effort if there is a sufficiently strong incentive, such as population pressure or the lure of exploitable natural resources. Technological progress, such as the invention of artificial fertilizer, may enable men to develop hitherto poor land into farms of high productivity, while neglect of soil conservation may have the opposite effect. The result may be two farming populations with quite different political attitudes.

The way in which men utilize a particular natural environment depends very largely on their system of values. Thus we observe that the same type of land under the hand of one kind of people is turned into highly productive, stable farming areas, whereas other groups after a few years of bumper crops, exhaust the land and let it return to a condition of semi-wilderness. The importance of evaluations for the dif-

[25] A. Toynbee, *A Study of History*, 2nd ed., Vol. I (London, Oxford University Press, 1934).

[26] The tasks of flood control and land reclamation compelled the dwellers in those coastal marshes to form close coöperative groupings beyond the village level. At an early time the entire tribal areas of the various Frisian and Dithmarsian peoples reached an intensity of integration which was attained elsewhere in medieval Europe only through submission to a prince.

ferentiation of land uses is especially evident in cities. The fact that a certain location—a lake shore or a hillside—is considered a desirable location for residential dwellings by specific groups of the population and therefore attracts, let us say, the people with highest social prestige, is a result of human evaluation, which may in some cases be quite irrational and which certainly cannot be explained in terms of simple environmental determinism.[27]

However, since the natural environment tends to set certain limitations to economic activity under given technological conditions, it is permissible to use our scheme of determinant factors as a starting point, or as a guiding principle, always keeping aware of the possible significance of additional factors.

The importance of cultural traits, for example, is well illustrated by the geographic distribution of "dry" and "wet" majorities in the United States in state and federal elections and referendums.[28] Those ethnic groups whose members drink in order to enjoy company, and prefer light drinks which they take sitting down, for example, the Germans and Italians, voted "wet," while the "dry" majorities occurred in areas where those groups prevailed who prefer quickly intoxicating beverages, taking them standing up.

The influence of past political events on voting behavior may be illustrated by the observation that radical or oppositional movements may attract certain groups not by their program but merely because the voters want to express their opposition to the existing régime or to the ruling groups. In such cases, regional radicalism may not mean agreement with the ideas of the radical movement but merely a protest against the powers in control. Thus, the rather strong vote cast for the Social Democratic Party in certain parts of Ger-

[27] See Walter Firey, *Land Use in Central Boston* (Cambridge, Harvard University Press, 1947).
[28] See W. F. Ogburn and Nell Snow Talbot, *op. cit.*, pp. 175-183.

many after 1871 was, to many voters, an expression of protest against the hegemony of Prussia in the new Reich, and not a confession of socialist ideals.

The growth and diffusion of a social movement or of a political party in a given area depends upon the strength, solidarity, and social importance of other social groups: the family and kinship group, the neighborhood, the village community, the church, vocational or occupational associations, special-purpose organizations as well as clubs, social circles and other informal groups without a special purpose. These groups serve as conductors or channels which facilitate the diffusion of political opinions and attitudes. Where kinship groups, neighborhood relationships, and local community solidarity are well developed, a new social or political movement will rapidly gain mass support once the leading citizens of the area have decided in its favor.

We shall now discuss some representative studies in political ecology, in order to show the kind of problems to be studied and the techniques and methods that have been used.

11

Representative Ecological Studies — Europe

A REGION IN FRANCE

The first important study of political ecology, was the work of André Siegfried, a French political scientist who is also quite well known in this country. Unfortunately the book, *Tableau politique de la France de l'Ouest sous la Troisième République*, was published at the time of the outbreak of the First World War and therefore did not receive as much attention as it deserved.

The French political scene was particularly conducive to regional studies. On the one hand, there were not at that time in France well-organized political parties, as there were in England and Germany, but only loose groups in the French Parliament, which represented tendencies among the masses of voters rather than definite party programs. The only exception were the Socialists, whose party had been recently reorganized after the pattern of the German Social Democratic Party. On the other hand, those tendencies or political attitudes among the voters varied significantly from one section of the country to the other, and also between social classes. The sectional variations were again largely conditioned by traditions which stemmed from the time of the French Revolution. The various sections of France had fared differently during those decisive years; not all of the old regional units had participated with equal intensity in

218

the revolutionary movements and not all had been in sympathy with the new régime. These variations in attitude towards the events of the revolution are still an influential factor in forming the regional political atmosphere or the tendencies.[1]

To speak of sectional or regional tendencies is not quite correct. There were in France, as in other countries, areas in which one party had almost a monopoly, at least in rural election districts; in the majority of regions, however, and in the larger cities, two, three, or more parties or political groups competed with each other. The result was that the social stratification of an area would be reflected in the relative strength of various political tendencies. It is with these constellations that we have to deal if we want to understand the political geography of France, past or present.

These regional constellations of political tendencies show a remarkable constancy which stands in apparent contradiction to the changing party preferences expressed in elections. Siegfried speaks of regional political "climates" which correspond closely to the ancient regions or *pays* of France. They form, so to speak, the real political geography underneath the artificial divisions of *departments* and other administrative units.[2]

Observations of this kind induced Siegfried to undertake an intensive study of the constellation or ensemble of the political tendencies in one large region of the country, which he calls the West. It includes Bretagne, most of the Vendée, Normandy, and parts of Maine, Anjou, and adjoining provinces. The first part of the work contains detailed descriptions

[1] Compare Charles Seignobos, *Études de politique et d'histoire* (Paris, 1934), the chapter on "La répartition géographique des partis politiques en France." Also Pierre de Pressac, *Les Forces Historiques de la France* (Paris, Libraire Hachette, 1928)—a kind of Baedecker on political tendencies in the French provinces, unfortunately without maps and charts and bare of any sociological method.

[2] André Siegfried, *Tableau politique de la France de l'Ouest sous la Troisième République* (Paris, Armand Colin, 1913).

of each subdivision of the entire region: the significant geographic features, the systems of land-holding, the distribution of the population, the types of farming and other occupations, the resulting social stratification, the location of power with certain classes, and the prevailing political attitudes and tendencies of these classes. The second part treats in a systematic order various factors which, from the preceding discussion, appear to be instrumental in forming the political climate; then follows a discussion of the political attitudes of each of the major social classes, their subdivisions, and their changes. Finally, the author discusses the characteristics of the major blocs of political parties and their geographic strongholds.

It is this procedure of careful analysis which refrains from hasty mono-causal explanations and considers all possible factors in their actual ensemble that justifies calling Siegfried's book an ecological study. The author himself calls it a study in human geography. Indeed, one of its best qualities is the author's feeling for the political relevancy of geological and topographic conditions.

The core of the West is the Vendée, or *bocage,* a region of granite which maintains a sparse and scattered population, has almost no villages and only a few cities (whereas adjoining chalk regions are characterized by village settlements). It is a region of large land-holdings, but agriculture—mainly livestock-breeding and grazing—is carried on by share-tenants and renters on small allotments living on isolated farmsteads. This is the region where in 1793 the peasants and noblemen under the leadership of the priests rose against the new régime. At the time of Siegfried's study, the relations between landlord and tenant were still patriarchal. The noblemen resided in the country, took active part in community life, held most of the offices and, aided by the priests, maintained almost unchallenged authority over the country people and the small towns. Consequently the political climate of the *bocage* was anti-republican, clerical, and generally speaking rightist (which means royalist in the interior, conservative in the fringe areas). Low enrollment in the secular public schools (while church schools flourished) and the social pressure exerted upon government officials who did not abide by the wishes of local landlords and priests indicated that the influence of the government was minimal.

Adjoining this region were areas of smaller holdings owned by grain-producing farmers who predominatly had anti-clerical, progressive, republican, or Bonapartist leanings.

In the cities of the region, Siegfried found, as one might expect, a sharp cleavage between the bourgeoisie and the proletariat. The latter voted predominantly socialist, while the former, in its various subdivisions presented diverse tendencies. On the whole, and this corresponds to a general rule as far as Europe goes, the entire bourgeoisie was at that time involved in an evolution from the extreme left (1789) to the extreme right.

In particular the petite bourgeoisie, including the low-salaried employees in big industry, were filled with fear of the socialistic proletariat and with resentment against the conservative and reactionary upper classes. It was this element which showed a strong inclination towards Boulangism, Bonapartism, and related plebiscitarian parties, or, as we would say today, authoritarian groups. Disappointed with parliamentary democracy, the petite bourgeoisie favored a strong national non-party government under a chief who would be solely responsible and not subject to the whims of parliaments.

It is of course impossible to give an adequate idea of this monumental work in a brief summary. If Siegfried's thesis of the constancy of political tendencies is true, one should be able to use his findings as a basis for the understanding of the political scene in France since the Second World War.

If, for example, the de Gaulle movement should become a major political force, some of its strongholds will be in the cities and peripheral rural areas of the west. It is also interesting to note how much the political climate of the French west must have had in common with such regions as East Prussia and the Mississippi delta. The similarities concern not merely the internal structure of the three regions, but also their relation to the national government. Just as the Third Republic had little influence in the Vendée, so was the Weimar Republic almost powerless in East Prussia, and the New Deal strongly opposed by the dominant classes in the lower Mississippi Valley.[3]

A REGION IN GERMANY

Taking Siegfried's book as a model, this writer in the years of 1932 to 1934 made a study of political movements and parties in the region of Schleswig-Holstein in Germany from 1918 to 1932.[4]

[3] Since Siegfried's book was published, numerous regional studies have been made in France, especially since 1945. For a list of references see Nilson, *op. cit.*, Appendix C.

For Great Britain see Edward Krehbiel, "Geographic Influences in British Elections," *The Geographical Review*, Vol. II (New York, December, 1916), p. 419. This study covers the period from 1885 to 1910. Although the political situation in Great Britain has changed considerably since the study was made, it is still very interesting. It shows a tendency of relatively poor agricultural regions to vote for the Liberal Party. In the fertile regions, however, where the aristocracy predominated and was able to control the vote of tenants and lower-class voters, the Conservatives had their strongholds. There is a great deal of interesting detail in this short paper. In general, Krehbiel's findings agree with our own and with the findings of the studies reviewed in the text.

[4] Rudolf Heberle, *From Democracy to Nazism; A Regional Case Study on Political Parties in Germany* (Baton Rouge, Louisiana State University Press, 1945). This book is a condensed translation from the unpublished German study entitled *Die Politische Willensbildung auf dem Lande in Schleswig-Holstein, 1871-1932*, augmented by an introductory chapter on the rise of Nazism in general. See also "The Political Movements among the Rural People in Schleswig-Holstein, 1918-1932," *Journal of Politics*, Vol. 5 (1943), and "The Ecology of Political Parties...", *American Sociological Review*, Vol. 9 (August, 1944).

This region was chosen for several reasons. First, since 1930 it had become one of the strongholds of the Hitler movement. In the elections of July, 1932, the election district of Schleswig-Holstein was the only one where the N.S.D.A.P. obtained a majority of the valid votes cast (51 per cent), although in the years before and after the First World War this region had been a stronghold of the Liberal and Social-Democratic parties. Second, the division into three distinct geologic, topographic, economic, and social subregions made Schleswig-Holstein an excellent field for a comparative study of political tendencies among rural people. Furthermore, because of this differentiation, the structure of rural society in Schleswig-Holstein was representative of the much larger region of the north German plains: it had large estates, owned by nobility engaged in grain production in its eastern Hill Zone; it had wealthy commercial farmer-entrepreneurs in the *Marsch* (Marsh) subregion on the west coast,[5] and relatively poor family farmers on the sandy, central *Geest*. These traits and the corresponding social structure types recur in the larger part of northern Germany. The marshes extend along the North Sea Coast, the *Geest* into the *Lueneburger Heide*, the Baltic Hills run eastward through Mecklenburg and Pomerania.[6]

Finally, the general picture of changes in voting behavior from 1919 to 1932 in Schleswig-Holstein corresponded very closely to that in the Reich, except that the decline of the moderate parties was more pronounced, owing to the weakness of the Catholic Center Party in this predominantly Protestant region (see table on page 224).

[5] The marshes are not wild and waste land. They are either river-bottom lands, as along the Elbe and the Eider, or land reclaimed through the centuries along the seacoast. They are protected against flood by levees and are drained by an ingenious system of ditches and locks. The soil is heavy and of high fertility. Some areas have been under cultivation for centuries, others have been reclaimed more recently. A marsh farmer is as a rule a wealthy farmer of high social status.

[6] Rudolf Heberle, *From Democracy to Nazism*, Fig. 1, p. 35.

PERCENTAGES OF TOTAL VALID VOTES OBTAINED BY PARTIES IN SCHLESWIG-HOLSTEIN IN URBAN AND IN RURAL COMMU-
NITIES, 1919 TO JULY, 1932 (REICHSTAG ELECTIONS) *

	FASCIST		CONSERVATIVE	LIBERAL				MARXIST		
	NSDAP	Landvolk	DNVP	DVP	Landes Partei	DDP	Zentrum and other	SPD	USPD	KPD
All Communities										
1919			7.7	7.8	7.2	27.2	1.0	45.7	3.4	
1920/21			20.5	18.4	3.8	9.4	1.5	37.3	3.0	6.1
1924 I	7.4a		31.0	12.1	0.7	8.1	5.6	24.9	c	10.2
1924 II	2.7b		33.0	14.6		8.7	4.0	30.3	c	6.7
1928	4.0		23.0	13.7		5.7	10.1	35.3		7.9
1930	27.0	0.3	6.1	7.3		4.7	10.7	29.8		10.6
1932	51.0	3.8	6.5	1.4		1.4	2.8	26.2		10.7
Urban Communities										
1919			5.4	8.6	0.4	28.3	1.4	50.9	5.0	
1920/21			16.2	19.6	1.2	10.5	1.9	39.8	3.2	7.6
1924 I	7.8		25.6	12.0		8.6	6.2	26.9	0.9	12.0
1924 II	2.9		27.8	14.5		9.2	3.9	32.8	0.4	8.5
1928	3.5		19.1	13.6		6.2	9.3	38.5		9.8
1930	23.2		5.3	8.4		5.7	8.7	33.1		13.1
1932	44.8	0.6	5.2	c		c	7.0	29.9		13.1
Rural Communities										
1919			10.7	6.7	16.4	25.8	0.3	39.0	1.1	
1920/21			28.6	16.1	8.6	7.3	0.6	33.0	2.6	3.2
1924 I	6.4		42.1	12.2		7.1	3.1	21.1	1.3	6.7
1924 II	2.3		43.4	14.9		7.8	2.4	25.4	0.5	3.3
1928	5.4		37.3	13.9		4.4	11.6	27.6		3.8
1930	35.1		7.9	4.8		2.5	11.1	28.8		5.1
1932	63.8	10.7	9.2	c		c	2.6	18.6		5.8

a Deutsch-völkische Freiheitspartei.
b National Sozialistische Freiheitspartei.
c Combined with Zentrum.
* Adapted from Rudolf Heberle, *From Democracy to Nazism*, Tables 3 and 4, pp. 94, 95.

We start by testing the hypothetical assumption that parties may change while basic political attitudes tend to remain constant as long as the economic interests and other structural factors in a society remain unchanged. The study begins with a survey of Reichstag election returns from 1871 to the First World War and from 1918 to 1932.

From the end of the nineteenth century (elections of 1893, 1898) to the elections of 1921 the Socialist (Marxist) parties regularly obtained between 39 and 49 per cent of the total valid vote. Among the *bürgerliche* or middle-class (non-Marxist) parties there was a persistent shift toward left-wing liberalism which lasted until the first elections after the war, then gave way to a shift towards the conservative parties and finally to the ascent of the National Socialist Party (N.S.D.A.P.). The Marxist parties regained their relative strength in 1928 and 1930, and did not lose much in the election of July, 1932. They commanded a rather stable group of voters, but within this group there was a shift from the Social Democratic to the Communist Party, the latter obtaining over 10 per cent in the two last elections. (Compare the table on opposite page.)

The study then concentrates on voting behavior in rural areas. It begins with a comparison of the geography, economy, socio-cultural structure and traditions in each of the subregions and reaches some tentative conclusions concerning the relation between these factors and the constellations of political tendencies in the subregions.

These conclusions are then tested with statistical methods. Thereafter, the various factors which may have contributed to the change in voting behavior are discussed systematically. Finally, the development from a predominantly liberal-progressive political climate to one predominated by Nazism is traced historically. Special consideration is given the various social and political movements among the rural people which served as path-makers and fore-runners to the Hitler movement and as channels through which the N.S.D.A.P. gained control of large blocks of voters.

The technique of statistical analysis consisted in the usual comparison of percentages and ratios and in the use of simple rank correlation coefficients. $\left(s = 1 - \dfrac{6\Sigma D^2}{N(N^2 - 1)} \right)$ For certain phases of the inquiry, election returns for *Gemeinden* (communities) were used, instead of returns for *Kreise* (counties), because the latter cut across the boundaries of subregions.

When the percentages of votes cast for the N.S.D.A.P. in July, 1932, in the rural communities were plotted on a topographical map, it soon became evident that the real strongholds of the Hitler movement were on the *Geest*, the central subregion. Here were concentrated the village communities where more than 80 per cent, sometimes close to 100 per cent, of the vote was cast for the N.S.D.A.P. Towards east and west the Nazi vote, although generally heavy in that election, thinned out, and the Conservative and Marxist parties showed comparatively high percentages.

This led to the discarding of one initial hypothesis: that the Nazi movement was, among the farmers, essentially a debtors' movement, comparable perhaps to the Greenback movement and similar phenomena in America. For the most heavily indebted farms were not those of cattle-breeders and dairy farmers on the *Geest* who neither needed nor could obtain much credit, but those of the well-to-do cattle-grazing and wheat farmers in the Marsh. It was true that in villages all over the region, heavily indebted farmers and businessmen were conspicuous among the early supporters of the Hitler movement, but the factor of farm indebtedness could not have been the sole or even a major factor.

In 1919 to 1921 the *Geest* had been an area in which the liberal or democratic parties had won the greatest support among the rural people. It was here where the *Schleswig-*

Holsteinische Landespartei which advocated regional autonomy found its main support.[7] How was this shift from one extreme to the other to be explained? Time series of election returns from 1919 to 1932 for the major parties and party groups in each of the three subregions showed clearly a greater instability of voting on the *Geest* than in the Marsh and Hill zones. The *Geest* showed 65 per cent liberals in 1919; 50 per cent conservatives in 1924, and almost 80 per cent Nazis in 1932.

The other two zones did not show such extreme variations;[8] the socialists retained greater voting strength throughout the period and the conservative vote was also more stable. Thus the margin within which the voting strength of the N.S.D.A.P. could vary was smaller than on the *Geest*.

These observations led to the conclusion that there must be differences in the structure of rural society in the three zones. These differences, in combination with certain economic factors that accounted for the greater or lesser severity of the crises in agriculture in the three zones, might be regarded as determinants of the changes in political attitudes. Foremost among the economic factors causing instability of voting behavior in general and toward Nazism in particular was the dependence of certain types of farming on one or

[7] Parties which opposed the trend towards centralization appeared in various provinces of Prussia, which had been annexed in 1866; they are not to be confused with separatist movements in the Rhineland. The ideology of the *Landespartei* contained many elements which later on became part of the National Socialist ideology. See R. Heberle, *From Democracy to Nazism*, pp. 43 ff.

[8] The following table gives the subregional differences in the percentages of the total vote in the three most important elections, showing that party or group of parties which was leading in each of these elections:

	Liberals: 1919	Conservatives: 1924	N.S.D.A.P.: 1932
Marsh Section	46.5%	41.4%	61.6%
Geest	64.9%	49.9%	78.7%
Hill Section	42.3%	40.9%	57.1%

Source: R. Heberle, *From Democracy to Nazism*, p. 99, Table 5.

a few marketable products which were subject to extreme price changes. The *Geest* farmers depended largely on the two extremely sensitive markets for young beef cattle and for hogs. Having but meager financial reserves, they were, as a rule, in a worse plight than their wealthier neighbors in the Marsh Zone or the more diversified farmers in the Hill Zone.

The *Geest* was a zone of medium and small family farms, operated almost entirely without hired help. Contrary to the two other zones, the *Geest* had no broad class of a landless proletariat. Consequently, the villages were distinguished from the rural communities in the other two zones by a much higher degree of social solidarity, which was reflected in more unanimous voting.

In the Hill Zone, the social distances between landlords and tenants, and large and small farmers, were very pronounced; antagonism of class interests showed itself in the relative strength of conservatives and Socialists (Communists). The same was true of the Marsh, although no large estates existed in this region; but the Marsh people were differentiated into two very distinct classes: farmers and laborers, who tended to live in separate parts of the communities.

These findings led to the conclusion that in each of the three zones the main support of the Nazis came from the small, independent family farmers rather than from the owners of estates and large farmers. This hypothesis was tested and confirmed by a series of correlations between voting strength of the major parties and the proportions of gainful workers on farms of various sizes. Since tenant farms and cottagers' allotments on estates were counted as farms, the largest and smallest farm classes had to be combined in order to get an index for large estates.

Of course, a positive statistical correlation, for example between the proportion of people employed on small farms and

SCHLESWIG-HOLSTEIN—RANK CORRELATIONS BETWEEN PARTIES AND CLASSES
OF FARMERS, BY KREISE [*]

Positive			Negative		
Socialists [a] and estates .	1921	+.95	Conservatives and large farms	1921	—.04
Socialists and estates .	1930	+.92	Conservatives and small farms	1921	—.19
Democrats and small farms	1919	+.89	Conservatives and large farms	1919	—.34
Socialists and estates .	1919	+.88	Conservatives and large farms	1932	—.40
Nazi and small farms .	1932	+.85	Socialists and large farms	1932	—.40
Socialists and estates .	1932	+.83	Socialists and large farms	1919	—.43
Conservatives and estates	1932	+.83	Socialists and large farms	1930	—.43
Democrats and small farms	1921	+.80	Nazi and estates	1930	—.43
Nazi, Landvolk and small farms	1930	+.79	Socialists and large farms	1921	—.45
Conservatives and estates	1919	+.76	Conservatives and large farms	1930	—.49
Conservatives and estates	1930	+.61	Conservatives and small farms	1930	—.60
Landvolk and small farms	1930	+.59	Landvolk and estates .	1930	—.64
Democrats and large farms	1919	+.52	Conservatives and small farms	1919	—.70
Nazi and large farms .	1932	+.49	Democrats and estates.	1921	—.77
Nazi, Landvolk and large farms	1930	+.45	Conservatives and small farms	1932	—.80
Nazi and small farms .	1930	+.43	Socialists and small farms	1932	—.80
Democrats, Landespartei and large farms .	1921	+.34	Nazi, Landvolk and estates	1930	—.82
Landvolk and large farms	1930	+.26	Nazi and estates	1932	—.89
Nazi and large farms .	1930	+.26	Socialists and small farms	1930	—.92
Conservatives and estates	1921	+.02	Democrats and estates.	1919	—.94
			Socialists and small farms	1919	—.97
			Socialists and small farms	1921	—.98

[a] i.e., SPD, USPD, KPD together.

[*] Source: R. Heberle, *From Democracy to Nazism*, p. 114, Table 8.

the percentage of votes obtained by the N.S.D.A.P. in 1932, does not mean that every small farmer voted Nazi, but it indicates that this class had a tendency to vote that way. A comparison with the corresponding correlation for large land owners will show that these were less inclined to vote Nazi and more to vote Conservative (*Deutschnational*). The preceding table gives correlations between percentages of votes obtained by the major parties and indices of farm sizes by counties; it covers all elections from 1919 to July, 1932.

The farmers alone could not have furnished such large numbers of Nazi voters. Additional support of the Hitler movement came from businessmen in towns and villages and from persons in other non-agricultural occupations. Among them the small entrepreneurs (and perhaps their employees) who shared the economic insecurity of the small farmer, were especially inclined to vote Nazi, as was shown by a series of correlations between party votes and various indices of economic class structure of the rural population (see table on page 231).

In these computations, the ratio of the number of employees to the number of employers in an industrial division is taken as an index of the size of establishments in this division. Thus a high ratio in industry and handicraft in a county indicates the prevalence of large plants, whereas a low ratio would indicate small plants. These ratios were found to correlate positively with the voting strength of the Marxist parties, negatively with that of liberal parties in 1921 and the Nazi Party in 1930 and 1932. Thus these correlations indicate that the N.S.D.A.P. was stronger in areas where small crafts and small-scale manufacturing prevailed, and weaker in areas of predominating large-scale manufacturing.

An additional factor which favored the success of the Hitler movement among the small farmers and small businessmen was the lack of experience in political activity among these classes. The industrial workers had long been trained

SCHLESWIG-HOLSTEIN—CORRELATIONS BETWEEN PERCENTAGES OF VOTES OBTAINED BY PARTIES IN 18 MINOR CIVIL DIVISIONS (CITIES OF 10,000 OR MORE POPULATION EXCLUDED) WITH PERCENTAGES OF POPULATION IN SPECIFIED SOCIO-ECONOMIC CLASSES (BERUFSZUGEHOERIGE) BY MAJOR INDUSTRIAL DIVISIONS

Party	Year	Agriculture, Forestry, Fishery				Industry and Handicraft			Industry, Commerce and Transportation			All Industrial Divisions including Public Services, Domestic Service, etc.		
		Proprietors (a)	a+m	Wage earners (c)	$\frac{b+c}{a}$	a	c	$\frac{b+c}{a}$	a	c	$\frac{b+c}{a}$	a	c	$\frac{b+c}{a}$
Socialists SPD, USPD, KPD	1921	−.84	−.88	+.86	+.85	−.68	+.65	+.68	−.70	+.62	+.64	−.93	+.95	+.93
	1932	−.79	−.78	+.77	+.77	−.84	+.82	+.84	−.81	+.69	+.80	−.94	+.88	+.94
Liberals DVP, DDP, Landespartei, Center	1921	+.81	+.85	−.77	−.85	+.50	−.48	−.50	+.54	−.53	−.49	+.84	−.86	−.96
Conservatives DNVP	1921	−.20	±0.0	+.22	+.20	+.23	−.24	−.23	+.15	−.31	−.17	+.08	+.07	+.10
	1924 II	+.40	+.45	−.41	−.39	+.68	−.66	−.68	+.57	−.71	−.59	+.52	−.47	−.52
	1932	−.26	−.28	+.31	+.28	+.09	−.08	−.09	+.09	−.15	−.06	+.02	+.12	+.12
Landvolk	1930	+.67	+.69	−.64	−.68	+.58	−.30	−.53	+.49	−.39	−.26	+.74	−.77	−.74
NSDAP	1930	+.37	+.43	−.43	−.40	+.32	−.39	−.31	+.24	−.40	−.67	+.36	−.38	−.64
	1932	+.76	+.79	−.78	−.76	+.71	−.69	−.70	+.63	−.53	−.64	+.83	−.79	−.69

Explanation of occupational classifications:

a = proprietors
m = family members employed on farm
c = wage earners

b = salaried employees

$\frac{b+c}{a}$ = ratio of all employees to proprietors

Source: R. Heberle, *From Democracy to Nazism*, p. 118, Table 9.

231

by trade unions and by the very well organized Social Democratic Party, but the rural and urban middle classes had been accustomed to the political leadership of land owners, big businessmen, and the professional classes affiliated with these. Now, for the first time, the small farmer, the minor agricultural expert, and the small businessman rose, through activity in the organizations of the Nazi movement, into the political élite.

Another factor which contributed to the success of the Nazi Party in Schleswig-Holstein was the lack of profound religiosity among the rural people. Wherever pockets of intensive religious life existed, in particular in pietistic circles, the Nazis met considerable resistance (for example, in Angeln).

Finally, an ecological factor should be mentioned. The villages on the *Geest* are rather small and it was shown by statistical analysis that, with the exception of estates, the smaller the community the larger the percentages of votes for the N.S.D.A.P. tended to be. However, this situation is not very difficult to explain, since a strong party can exercise more influence and pressure in a small community than in a large one.

In summary, the following conclusions were drawn concerning the dependence of party strength upon social structure:

1. Where social stratification was not pronounced, where the village community was well integrated, the Marxists tended to be weak, the conservatives only temporarily strong, the liberal parties strong and relatively constant during the earlier years, the N.S.D.A.P. and its forerunners very strong towards the end of the period.

2. In areas of sharp differences of wealth and class, the Marxists were strong, the conservatives also strong and comparatively constant, the liberals weak, the Nazis late in coming to predominance. Family farm areas with little strati-

fication offered the best chances for the Nazis, the poorest for the Marxists.

3. Other things being equal, the chances for the extreme parties were better the more specialized and therefore more sensitive to business cycles the farms were. The tempo of change from Liberalism to Nazism was slower in areas of diversified farming and well-to-do farmers than in specialized areas of less wealthy farmers.

4. In areas where the rural upper strata, farmers or landlords, had been politically active for a long time, new parties could less easily gain a foot-hold than in areas where no broad politically trained stratum existed. Where class consciousness among rural laborers was still in its infancy, political radicalism was more likely to develop than in areas where labor had been organized politically and in unions for considerable time.

ON THE ECOLOGY OF NAZISM

The main findings of Heberle's study have been confirmed by Loomis and Beegle in a study of Reichstag election returns of 1932 in Hanover and Bavaria.[9] Hanover, like Schleswig-Holstein has been Prussian only since 1866; sentiments of loyalty to the old dynasty and demands for autonomy were still strong in this province. In Bavaria, anti-Prussian attitudes were as common as anti-Yankee sentiment in our own South.

In the *Heide-Kreise* of Hanover, or the Lüneburger *Heide*, which can be regarded as a southward expansion of the *Geest*, the patterns of voting behavior were strikingly similar to those in the corresponding zone of Schleswig-Holstein; the Nazis obtained 56 per cent of the rural vote in this area.

[9] Charles P. Loomis and Allan Beegle, "The Spread of German Nazism in Rural Areas," *American Sociological Review*, Vol. 11, No. 6 (December, 1946).

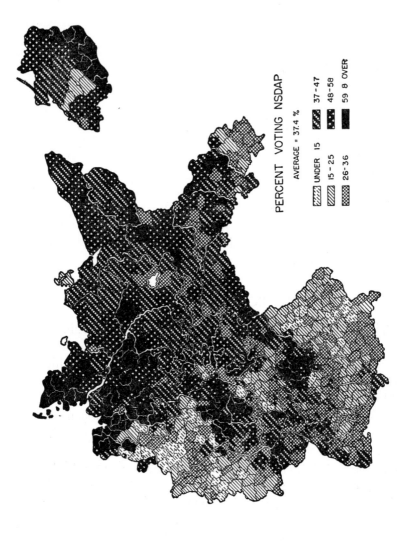

PERCENT VOTING NSDAP

AVERAGE = 37.4 %

UNDER 15 37-47

15 - 25   48-58

26 - 36   59 8 OVER

MAP 1. Percentages of total votes obtained by N.S.D.A.P. in the elections, July, 1932, by counties. (From Loomis and Beegle, "The Spread of German Nazism in Rural Areas," *American Sociological Review*, Vol. 11, No. 6 [Dec., 1946].)

In Bavaria, it was in the predominantly Protestant region of Franconia (*Franken*) and not in the Catholic provinces that the Nazis obtained the highest proportions of the vote. The country around Nürnberg was the stronghold of the Hitler movement in 1932. Correlations between party strength and socio-economic characteristics of the rural population, which Loomis and Beegle computed, correspond closely to the pattern for Schleswig-Holstein, except that in Catholic Bavaria, the coefficients tend to be smaller, especially for the N.S.D.A.P., because of the influence of the Catholic Center Party, which in Bavaria stands for conservatism and had retained a stronger hold on agricultural workers than the conservatives in Northern Germany. The Marxists and the Catholics constituted the two large blocks of voters who proved to be immune to Nazism. The ideologies of these groups were directly opposed to essential elements of Nazi ideology, and both groups had acquired political discipline and experience in well-established political machines.

Loomis and Beegle have also prepared a map (opposite page), of the entire Reich, showing the percentages of the total vote obtained in rural areas by the N.S.D.A.P. in the elections of July, 1932, by counties, cities of 10,000 or more inhabitants being omitted. This map lends some support to Goetz Briefs' thesis that Nazism had the greatest following in those regions which were outside the ancient *limes*—the Roman border fortification—that is, outside the sphere of early and continuous influence of the Roman Church.[10] While this thesis still needs to be tested, it is obvious that, apart from Hesse and Franconia, the major Nazi domains were east of the Weser and east of the *limes*. Especially interesting is the situation in East Prussia, which was generally regarded as one of the strongest Nazi areas.[11]

[10] G. A. Briefs "Limes Germanicus—Bridge and Frontier," *The Review of Politics*, Vol. I (1939), pp. 261, 444.

[11] James K. Pollock, "An Area Study of the German Electorate, 1930-33," *American Political Science Review*, Vol. 38 (Feb., 1944). Pollock uses only

Actually the Nazis obtained majorities only in the poor, sandy, small-farm subregion of Masuren, along the Polish border, while the Catholic Ermland showed less than 25 per cent Nazi votes. The rest of the Province, the typical *Junker* areas, showed approximately the same percentages of Nazi votes as Mecklenburg and Pomerania[12]—areas which have a similar social structure.

IMPORTANCE OF FOREIGN REGIONAL STUDIES

This example shows once more the necessity of studying small, relatively homogeneous areas whenever one is concerned with a causal explanation of political behavior. The use of too large areas tends to conceal those differentials which give one the clue to an inquiry into possible factors.

The reader may wonder why we devote so much space to foreign studies. There are two reasons for this. First, through the study of political ecology in foreign areas one can learn a great deal about one's own country. The political climate of the Southern states of the United States will, for instance, appear less unique and perhaps less strange to Northern students when they realize that this region has many political traits in common with European regions of similar social

---

the large election districts, which are much too heterogeneous to reveal any factors of political behavior; furthermore, he includes the elections of March, 1933, which were not longer free elections, as well as the elections of November, 1933, which were characterized by a great deal of pressure on would-be left-wing voters; finally he used averages of votes obtained in four elections, instead of analyzing the changes and tendencies. If one wants to show the degree of constancy of voting, it is better not to use arithmetic means of several elections, but to compute coefficients of correlation between proportions of the total vote obtained by a party in each area (state, county, and so forth) in several elections.

[12] There is, as far as one can judge from Loomis and Beegle's chart, no indication that the Nazis were particularly strong in typical *Junker* areas. One would have to see corresponding charts for the Conservative and the Marxist parties before one could say whether this was due to the conservatism of the *Junkers* or to the fact that the agricultural workers voted Socialist and Communist.

structure. Second, the increased importance of foreign relations of the United States makes it desirable that we know
more about foreign areas in which American interests exist,
and what is equally important, that we learn how to acquire
significant knowledge about such areas. During the Italian
elections of 1948 there appeared in a college campus paper
an editorial predicting a large communist vote in southern
Italy, since that is the poorest region of the country. This
was, of course, wrong. The writer had not considered that
the controlling power in southern Italy is the church, which
puts a curb on communism; he should have known that the
industrial north has always been the stronghold of socialistic,
anarcho-syndicalistic, and communistic movements.[13] It is
true that the Popular Front (Communists and left-wing socialists) made significant *relative* gains "in the south where
Marxism had hardly penetrated in 1946, and where the communist party had concentrated its main efforts to win over to
its side the landless proletariat"; however, the main strength
of the communist movement remained in the Po Valley and
in the Tuscan provinces, not in the south.[14]

[13] Marion Einaudi, "The Italian Elections of 1948," *The Review of
Politics,* Vol. 10 (July, 1948).
[14] Einaudi, *ibid.*

12

Political Ecology in the United States

~~~~~~

SECTIONALISM IN THE UNITED STATES

STUDIES ON THE American political scene which may be considered ecological are numerous, but scattered largely in periodicals. Relatively few books which cover the entire country or larger regions of it have been written. And yet, the political scene in the United States, with its conspicuous regional variations in party preferences, offers a real challenge to the political ecologist.

The field has been opened by A. N. Holcombe with a rather detailed analysis of the major economic interests which dominate the electorate in the various politically relevant regions.[1]

Holcombe starts from the observation that a political party, in order to gain power, must carry a majority of the states and also of the congressional districts. To achieve this it is not enough for a party to secure a majority of all votes cast; it is necessary that the party win the support of those local and regional interests which together can constitute majorities in a majority of states and congressional districts. If the party wants to maintain its power, it has to gain the support of a lasting combination of such dominating local and regional interests. Most important are the economic interests,[2] and most important among these are the agricultural,

[1] Arthur N. Holcombe, *The Political Parties of Today* (New York, Harper and Brothers, 1924).
[2] *Ibid.*, pp. 39-41.

238

manufacturing, and mining interests because of their ability to control majorities of voters in certain areas.[3] Holcombe discusses in detail the political attitudes of various groups of agricultural entrepreneurs (for example, with regard to the tariff question), their regional distribution, and the relationship between agricultural regions and congressional districts. The approximate number of congressional districts comprised by each economic region gives a measure of the political power of the dominating economic interest or interests of that region. Holcombe shows, for example, that in about 1920 the cotton belt comprised one-sixth of all congressional districts (73 out of 433) and one-fourth of the rural congressional districts (59 out of 238). The cotton growers, together with the cotton merchants and the cotton textile manufacturers in the South therefore formed one of the most outstanding sectionally concentrated combinations of economic-interest groups in the country.[4]

In a similar manner, Holcombe discusses the urban interests, in particular those of the major classes of manufacturers. In this connection he takes cognizance of the division and eventual antagonism of interests between employers and employees.[5]

Holcombe next turns to a delineation of political sections, and on the basis of election returns by states, he divides the country roughly into twelve political sections.[6] The problem then is to clarify the relationship between economic regions and political sections, and "between the economic interests which dominate particular regions and the political interests which dominate particular sections."[7] To this end Holcombe analyzes the congressional elections of 1922. By cross-classifying congressional districts according to party strength, rural

[3] Ibid., p. 55.
[4] Ibid., pp. 69-72.
[5] Ibid., p. 75.
[6] Ibid., p. 105.
[7] Ibid., p. 109.

and urban characteristics, and agricultural regions, he demonstrates on which combinations of sectionally concentrated economic interests the strength of each of the two major parties was founded.[8] Particular attention is given to the doubtful sections, that is, those states and districts where the leading economic interests are not traditionally aligned with one or the other major party. A majority of the doubtful congressional districts were in the winter-wheat region and in the corn belt, that is, in the Midwest.[9]

The remainder of the book is devoted to a historical explanation of the party alignment and its sectional pattern. Although Holcombe recognizes, at least for the urban areas, the significance of social classes, he attributes greater importance to the sectional cleavages. However, in a more recent book, he points out that class differences are gaining in importance over sectional alignments.[10]

In the present discussion we are mainly interested in the methodological contribution of Holcombe's book to the ecology of political parties. From this point of view, it constitutes the first, and as far as we know, only attempt at a political ecology of the entire United States. It is very much one-sided in emphasis on economic interests, neglecting religious and ethnic groupings, but in its time it was a pioneer study.

REGIONAL STUDIES

The Midwest

Since Holcombe's study, numerous more limited works on sectionalism in American party politics and elections have been published. Barnhart studied the effect of insufficient rainfall on Populism in the great plains; he found that the People's Independent Party (Populists) gained its strongest

[8] *Ibid.*, p. 123.
[9] *Ibid.*, p. 125.
[10] A. N. Holcombe, *The New Party Politics* (New York, W. W. Norton & Company, 1933).

support in the elections of 1890 and 1892 in the central parts of Nebraska, where farmers had gone beyond the zone of sufficient rainfall and pushed farther west into a semi-arid country better suited to extensive grazing than to grain production. However, he finds that unrest and a determination to resort to political action had been noticeable *before* the drought summer of 1890. The drought merely contributed to the rising Populist sentiment by making the farmers see more clearly how precarious their situation was.[11] One of the main issues raised by the Populist Party concerned railroad rates, and it is conceivable that in a year of crop failure the western settlers became more conscious of the importance of shipping costs.

The same general problem of the influence of environment on social behavior is the central issue in an earlier study by Lundberg.[12] He wanted to see which conditions in the physical and social environment tend to create radicalism and conservatism (using the terms in the popular sense). He arranged the counties in two states, North Dakota and Minnesota, on the basis of their support of or opposition to the Nonpartisan League in the North Dakota elections of 1916, 1918, 1920, 1922 (and 1924 in Minnesota), taking the ratio of votes for the League to votes against the League in each county and computing averages for four elections. Lundberg then selected from each state's list the five highest and the five lowest counties. Socio-economic and demographic characteristics of the population of these counties were gained mainly from the United States Census, averages were computed for the four groups of counties and for the combinations of radical and conservative counties. Lundberg states that better results would have been obtained if areas

---

[11] John D. Barnhart, "Rainfall and the Populist Party in Nebraska," *American Political Science Review*, Vol. 19 (1925).

[12] George A. Lundberg, "The Demographic and Economic Basis of Political Radicalism and Conservatism," *American Journal of Sociology*, Vol. 32 (1926-1927).

smaller than counties could have been used.[13] But even so, his findings indicate quite characteristic differences between the social environment in the two groups of counties.

"The distinctly radical counties are on the whole relatively new and undeveloped";[14] they had a sparser population but a higher rate of population increase, larger proportions of foreign-born, and slightly larger proportions of persons of foreign or mixed parentage. The central issue in the League's program was state ownership of public utilities, and Lundberg believes that the high proportion of Scandinavian and Slavic immigrants in the radical counties, who were accustomed to the idea of public ownership of utilities, may have been an important factor in gaining support for the League. On the other hand, he finds that the small-town people were usually more conservative than the rural farmers, and points out that the radical counties had less of their population in cities and villages. Economically, the people in radical counties were less fortunate than those in conservative counties; the value of land, farms, crops, and several other indexes of wealth were much lower than in the conservative counties. Lundberg comes to the conclusion that

... greater economic insecurity is generally apparent in the radical counties and this economic insecurity and the radicalism with which it is associated must be accounted for in terms of the degree or stage of development of the community, rather than in terms of any static differences in the people or the areas affected.[15]

The first part of this statement is interesting in view of our own findings for Schleswig-Holstein, where radicalism (in Lundberg's sense) was very definitely associated with economic insecurity. The last part, however, cannot be generally true, although it may fit the American Midwest during the period of Populism and Progressivism. In Schleswig-Holstein, however, we found no indication of greater radicalism in re-

[13] *Ibid.*, p. 727, footnote.
[14] *Ibid.*, p. 728.
[15] *Ibid.*, p. 730.

cently developed rural areas (for example, along the North Sea Coast), than in older communities. Economic insecurity, then, seems to be the more important factor of radicalism, rather than recentness of settlement. Economic insecurity in the area which Lundberg studied was primarily a consequence of one-sided farming. Here, as in the cotton belt of the South and in certain regions of France and Germany, the farmers' annual earnings depend largely on the market price of one kind of farm product—wheat, or cotton, or wine, or cattle. These specialized commercial farming areas are the typical breeding grounds of militant agrarian movements; diversified farming areas tend to be adverse to any kind of radicalism. Lundberg could have gone a bit further in his analysis had he inquired more thoroughly into the reasons and sentiments which induced rural voters in both states to vote for or against the Nonpartisan League.

Very interesting ecological observations on the same region are contained in Chapter X of Stuart Rice's *Quantitative Methods in Politics* (1928). Here Rice studies the spatial distribution of political attitudes. His particular problem is to explain geographical differences in the strength of the conservative and the radical (or progressive) vote in the Midwestern states of Iowa, Minnesota, North Dakota, South Dakota, and Nebraska. For each of the states he used certain significant elections or referenda in which a definitely radical or progressive party or faction contended with the conservative, or regular, major party or parties. Briefly, he finds that in the Missouri River Valley, the corn-growing and prosperous farming counties in the states of Iowa, Nebraska, and South Dakota constitute an area of conservatism. In North Dakota, however, the relatively conservative eastern counties along the Red River face the relative radical counties of western Minnesota. Another area of radicalism is found in central Nebraska.

From these observations Rice draws the following conclusions: first, that the spatial differences in the political attitudes as expressed in voting were due to geographical or sectional cleavages and not to occupational or [*sic*] class distinctions; [16] second, he offers the hypothesis that the concepts of culture area and culture diffusion, developed by American anthropologists out of their studies of the culture traits of primitive peoples, might be applied to the origin and spread of political attitudes. In the light of this hypothesis, the Missouri River Valley might be regarded "as a culture center of conservatism, or conversely an outer fringe of some culture area of radicalism." [17]

We cannot follow here Rice's painstaking and technically ingenious attempts to test this "culture area" hypothesis by investigating barriers to the diffusion of political attitudes and the rôle of transportation and communication lines in that diffusion. He himself has to admit that while the hypothesis is consistent with his data, "it has not yet been established empirically." [18] It does seem that studying the diffusion of political attitudes before obtaining a definite idea of the location and characteristics of the surmised central culture area means putting the cart before the horse. Furthermore, even if a "culture area of political discontent" could have been delineated—and we have no doubt that this could be done—it would not explain anything.

On the other hand, if we reconsider Rice's first findings for each of the states, a much simpler, almost common sense explanation is suggested. This however involves discarding Rice's first conclusion.

Rice's own findings involved four states. In Minnesota, he found a distinct concentration of the radical and conservative vote in certain areas along geographical lines "with their cor-

[16] Stuart A. Rice, *Quantitative Methods in Politics* (New York, Alfred A. Knopf, Inc., 1928), pp. 126, 129, 131-133.
[17] *Ibid.*, p. 136.
[18] *Ibid.*, p. 155.

related areas of crop specialization"; [19] there was strong support for the progressive candidate in the gubernatorial election of 1920 and the United States Senatorial election of 1922 in northwestern wheat counties, very light support in southern corn counties.[20] Now, everybody knows that farms in the corn belt tend to be more diversified than wheat farms in the region concerned, that the farmers who specialize in wheat are therefore subject to greater economic insecurity than the corn belt farmers. This factor alone would be sufficient to explain the voting differences.

In South Dakota, the picture was the same: the eastern, wheat-growing section cast the heaviest vote for the progressive candidate for governor in 1920, while the corn section—which is concentrated in the southeastern counties along the Missouri River—gave the candidate only a very light vote.[21] In Iowa a study of voting in a senatorial primary between Brookhart (radical) and Cummins (conservative) in 1920 showed that the conservative candidate's support came from counties in the Missouri River Valley and in the central area of the state; these were also the counties "in which the average value of all farm property was the highest." [22] Again, these were the areas where "the maximum production of corn occurs" and where "the maximum expenditures are made for feed and for farm labor." [23] With the reference to expenditure for farm labor, the influence of economic class differences is implicitly indicated, although Rice denies it explicitly on the preceding pages. To the factor of insecurity which induces the wheat farmers to vote radical more often than the corn farmers is now added the factor of differentiation between wealthy and less wealthy farmers (in terms of farm property value) and the corresponding differentiation between farm-

[19] *Ibid.*, p. 126.
[20] *Ibid.*, p. 126.
[21] *Ibid.*, p. 129.
[22] *Ibid.*, p. 132.
[23] *Ibid.*, pp. 132-133.

ers who hire labor and those who rely on their own and unpaid family labor. Anybody familiar with criteria of social stratification in rural society will see that here a differentiation between two social classes of farmers is involved.[24]

In Nebraska, the conservative counties along the Missouri River form a region of corn production, high farm values, and high expenditures for farm labor, forming the same type of farming area as on the opposite bank of the river in Iowa and South Dakota. And still Rice maintains that the lines of political cleavage in Nebraska were sectional rather than occupational. Rice does not discuss the social and economic characteristics of the radical area of the center of the state. Finally, we are told that in North Dakota the eastern counties (those facing the radical counties of Minnesota) were more conservative, the western counties more radical. This distinction, Rice says, "corresponds also to areas of comparative rural prosperity within the state."[25]

The location of the more conservative counties within the state along the Red River, opposite the most radical counties in Minnesota is the disturbing point. Two suggestions might be made. First, as Rice says, North Dakota as a whole might be more radical than Minnesota; second, a significant difference in types of farming may exist between the counties on the right and left banks of the Red River. The second possibility is not mentioned by Rice, and the first suggestion is not investigated. We recall that the Red River Valley area was a wheat farming area. We also know from the studies of Lundberg and Barnhart that in the Dakotas and Nebraska, the radical areas are those of greatest economic insecurity due to the risks of drought. They form the western fringe of

[24] The farmer who can afford to hire labor is inevitably placed in a higher social class than the farmer who can not. Economically, the latter is still largely a farm laborer, while the former is mainly a manager and employer. Mechanization may have levelled these differences, but at the time of Rice's study, they were still significant.
[25] Rice, p. 126.

the wheat belt. The Red River counties in North Dakota are located in the heart of the wheat belt; there wheat farming is relatively secure and political attitudes are less radical than in the western part of the state, but more radical than in eastern or southern Minnesota.

It appears, then, that the political radicalism of the 1920's in these states among the rural people was indeed concentrated in certain sections; furthermore, it also appears that the predominant occupation of farming was in these areas of a different, less secure and less prosperous type than in the conservative sections. Instead of resorting to borrowing from the tool shed of the anthropologists a concept derived from their studies of primitive peoples, we may simply recognize that differences in political attitudes are associated with differences in types of farming. Whether we want to call these occupational differences or not makes no difference. We should, however, realize that even in this presumably classless American society, farmers engaged in different types of farming constitute definite social groups with different and often antagonistic economic interests, and corresponding differences in political attitudes. These differences in types of farming do in some cases constitute real social class differentiations, as for example between Southern planters and family farmers, or between wheat farmers and cattle ranchers in the Great Plains area. Had it occurred to Rice to pay some attention to the differentiations between classes of farmers, he might have found a more fruitful hypothesis than that of the culture area.

The concept of a culture area characterized by the prevailing kind of political attitude is, of course, useful if adroitly applied. It has, in fact, much in common with André Siegfried's idea of a region or subregion characterized by a particular political climate. In Siegfried's terms the Midwest, especially the highly commercialized wheat-farming areas, constitutes a region where a temper of rebellion and a political climate of radicalism existed.[26] Siegfried would of course immediately proceed to analyze the class and subclass structure of rural society in this region. It would then become apparent that the so-called sectional cleavages within this region and between the region and the surrounding country were actually conditioned by differences in types of farming and by the resulting differences in class structure, very much in the same way as the political climate of the northwest of France is differentiated from that of neighboring regions. Instead of trying to establish lines of diffusion of political attitudes along railroads and highways one would study the distribution of soil types and rainfall zones, and their influence upon types of farming and corresponding political behavior.

Without belittling Rice's contributions to the application of quantitative methods in political science, we may, at this point, make a general critical comment. It seems that too much eagerness to ascertain quantitative regularities concerning voting behavior can prevent pursuit of the most promising course of inquiry, and can lead from a careful ecological study of concrete constellations of political behavior to a highly abstract, purely statistical treatment which misses the most significant aspects of social reality.

SELECTED STATES

A definite approach to a political ecology of the United States is contained in Gosnell's *Grass Roots Politics,* a study of voting in selected states, each of which represents a particular type of situation. The states are Pennsylvania, Wisconsin, Iowa, California, Illinois, and Louisiana.[27]

Writing soon after the third Roosevelt election, Gosnell is

[26] See the discussion of the Progressive movement in Siegfried's *America Comes of Age* (New York, Harcourt, Brace & Company, 1927).

[27] Harold F. Gosnell, *Grass Roots Politics, National Voting Behavior of Typical States* (Washington, D.C., American Council on Public Affairs, 1942).

primarily concerned with explaining the shifts in party preference which occurred since 1924, when the Democratic vote in the nation was at its lowest point. He takes into account such variables as party tradition, party discipline, economic conditions, the influence of the foreign-born and Catholic elements, and urbanization (or ruralization). The significance of the variables is tested by the use of correlations and by factorial analysis. While Gosnell makes ample use of statistical methods, he does not do so in a mechanical way, but relies first of all on detailed and concrete knowledge of economic, social, and political conditions in the states. What makes his analyses especially valuable from an ecological point of view is the consideration given to regional differentiations within each state.

A good example of Gosnell's method is found in his chapter on Wisconsin. In this state the Republican Party had been split for many years into two factions, the regular or stalwart Republicans, and the Progressives under the leadership of Robert LaFollette and his sons. The city of Milwaukee had been a center of the Socialist movement, even sending a Socialist to Congress. In 1932 Roosevelt carried the state with 67 per cent of the vote; the Democratic Party became the majority party in the lower house of the state legislature, and the Democrats won the senatorial and gubernatorial elections. The Roosevelt vote came mainly from the larger industrial cities and from the poorer, economically more vulnerable, rural areas in the central sands and the northern cutover regions. The elections of 1938 brought a comeback for the Republicans and those of 1940 resulted in the election of a Democrat (Roosevelt) for President, a Progressive for United States Senator, and a Republican for Governor. In other words, the voters showed a great deal of independence, although party discipline and party tradition were quite strong in some areas.

Wisconsin's agriculture recovered rather soon from the de-

pression, and the prosperous dairy farmers refused to participate in the AAA program; they were therefore not tied to
the Roosevelt administration by benefits, and they rather resented Mr. Hull's foreign-trade policy which exposed them to
competition from Canada. On the other hand, the traditionally progressive cut-over and poor central sands farming
areas remained quite faithful Roosevelt supporters.

The other area of strong support for Roosevelt was in the
urban and industrial counties along the shores of Lake Michigan and Lake Winnebago; the Socialist vote in Milwaukee
was obviously swung toward Roosevelt and supported him
throughout the New Deal era and beyond. The regular Republicans and anti-New Deal forces were thus to be found
among the more well-to-do farmers and in the small towns
and small cities. The Catholics, unless wealthy, tended to
vote Democratic, whereas the poorer (and foreign-born)
Protestants tended to vote Progressive—speaking in terms of
areas where those elements predominated.

The South

From the Midwest we may now turn to the Deep South.
The political ecology of the South is obscured today by the
predominance of the Democratic Party. The real cleavages
are between factions of this party and appear in the primaries rather than in presidential or congressional elections. But
before the establishment of what is virtually a one-party rule,
the sub-regional differences expressed themselves quite
clearly in the antagonism between political parties. For instance, the sectional conflict between Whigs and Democrats
that tore Alabama apart during the first four decades of the
nineteenth century was in reality a conflict between the
slave-holding planter class, which dominated the southern
part, and the smaller farmers—who as a rule did not own
slaves—in the northern part. The main issue was not slavery
but the tariff. Sectionalization came about through the sub-

mission of the Democrats in the south of the state to the Whigs, and through the gradual merger of the Whigs in the northern part with the Democrats of that section.[28] This pattern occurred all over the South and is still existent in many Southern states; but today the two parties have become factions in the Democratic Party.

If one regards all farmers as one class, the sectional cleavage is the only observable phenomenon. It is, however, undeniable that planters, small farmers, hill-billies, and even the farmers of the more fertile river bottoms and coastal plains form separate social classes between which there is little intercourse, almost no intermarriage, and little community of economic interests. If one looks at sectionalism from this point of view, it becomes evident that it is the result of the predominance in one section of one class of agricultural people and of another class in another section.

These underlying class antagonisms are, however, in the Solid South often obscured by the preëminence of personalities over issues. Even in gubernatorial campaigns it would be dangerous for the candidates to emphasize issues as much as one could do in a two-party state, because it might impair party solidarity, which is needed in congressional and presidential campaigns.

Louisiana

The correlation method does not lend itself very well to the analysis of factors influencing voting in states where one party dominates and where the political struggles are fought out between factions of the same party. Gosnell's chapter on "Huey Long's Louisiana" shows these limitations of the correlation method quite clearly. In this state, and particularly during Huey Long's political career, the influence of personal loyalty to leading politicians makes itself strongly felt on all

[28] T. H. Jack, *Sectionalism and Party Politics in Alabama, 1819-1842* (Menasha, Wisconsin, G. Banta Pub. Co., 1919).

levels—national, state, and local—and there are the disturbing
factors of cultural (and religious) sectional division between
French southern Louisiana and Anglo-Saxon, Scotch-Irish
northern Louisiana.

Gosnell thinks that no association can be established between the Long vote and "any social and economic groupings
in the state"—at least not through the use of census data. This
statement seems questionable. If one could use election returns in areas smaller than parishes and correlate them with
indices of socio-economic structure, one would probably, at
least in the earlier Long elections, find a fairly significant
association of the small-farmer class (white) with the Long
faction and of the planter class with the opposition. In the
cities, the division would be between the wealthier business
and professional classes on one side, and industrial workers
and small business people on the other side, except where
anti-Long employers were able to influence the voting of the
employees—as, for example, in Baton Rouge. The map of the
gubernatorial elections of 1924 which Gosnell reproduces
shows quite clearly that the Long vote was concentrated in
the poor hill parishes of northern Louisiana, clustering
around Long's home parish (Winn Parish); other strongholds
were in the poor cut-over areas along the Texas and Mississippi borders. The support was—in 1924—weak in French
Louisiana,[29] and also in the delta parishes of northern Louisiana. To the anti-Long area also belonged the two sparsely
populated Feliciana parishes where the impoverished but
proudly aristocratic planters still control public opinion.

[29] The reader who is not familiar with Louisiana should realize that the
French in this state comprise at least four different social classes: the
wealthy creoles of New Orleans and their often impoverished descendants;
the relatively wealthy planters; and the small farmers, fishermen, and
trappers, largely of Canadian origin (*Acadiens* or "Cajuns"). The more
recent urban off-shoots of the last two classes merge partly with the
petty bourgeoisie and partly with the urban working class. In other words,
in Louisiana French culture and Catholicism are not at all synonymous
with poverty or backwardness except in the case of the relatively few
inhabitants of remote villages and swamp settlements.

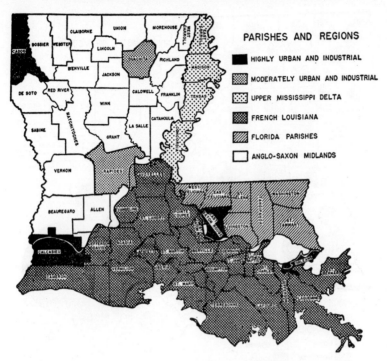

MAP 2. Politically significant regions of Louisiana.

A study by Heberle and Bertrand of the gubernatorial primaries in 1948 shows that the same groups of voters which
helped Huey Long into the saddle were also the main supporters of his brother Earl, when after a period of pro-busi-
ness reform government (1940-1948) the Long faction came
back into power. Again, the picture would be much clearer
had election returns by wards or precincts been used. Yet
even the parish returns show pretty clearly that the main
Long support came from northern Louisiana, and by and
large from the hill areas rather than from the river parishes.[30]
    The Feliciana parishes and East Baton Rouge Parish—

[30] Rudolf Heberle and Alvin L. Bertrand, "Factors Motivating Voting
Behavior in a One-Party State," Social Forces, Vol. 27, No. 4 (May, 1949).

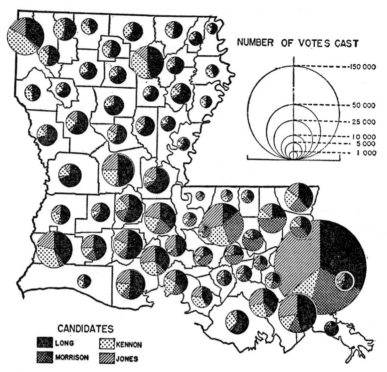

NUMBER OF VOTES CAST

MAP 3. Number and percentages of votes cast for candidates in first gubernatorial primary in Louisiana January 20, 1948, by parishes. (This map and Map 4 are reproduced from R. Heberle and A. Bertrand, "Factors Motivating Voting Behavior in a One-Party State," *Social Forces,* Vol. 27, No. 4, May, 1949.)

home of Standard Oil and seat of the Jones-Davis government in power—were again anti-Long. On the other hand, voters in St. Bernard and Plaquemines parishes supported him almost unanimously, as in 1940, indicating a highly disciplined party machine in those two parishes.[31]

The first primaries also show what a strong influence the personal connections of the candidates must have been, since

[31] Compare V. O. Key, *Southern Politics* (New York, Alfred A. Knopf, Inc., 1949), p. 178.

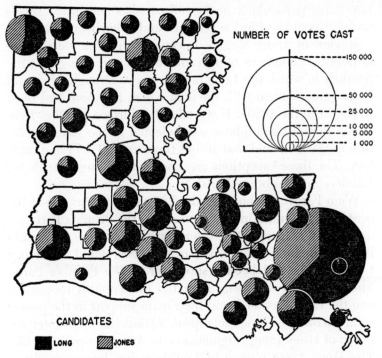

NUMBER OF VOTES CAST

---------- 150 000

— 50 000

— 25 000

— 10 000
— 5 000

— 1 000

CANDIDATES

LONG   JONES

MAP 4. Number and percentages of votes cast in second gubernatorial primary in Louisiana, February 24, 1948, by parishes.

each of the four candidates had the strongest support in his home area, except that Sam Jones did not carry his home parish of Calcasieu. (Map 3.)

The second primaries are, of course, much less revealing than the first primaries, because a very large proportion of the one-third of the voters who had voted for the minority candidates in the first primaries must have regarded the run-off as a choice between two evils. And yet, if one indicates on Map 4 the parishes where Long received more than the average of 66 per cent of the vote in the second primary, it becomes evident that his main strength still lay in northern

Louisiana, particularly in the hill parishes and in the small-farm areas of the Florida parishes and French Louisiana.

In view of André Siegfried's contention of the persistence of political climate or temperament, it is interesting that the territory in which the Long faction has its stronghold should be largely identical with the area where Populism had been strongest in the 1890's. If we take the thirteen parishes from which Populist candidates were elected to the state legislature in 1896, we find that all but three are in Earl Long territory. The three exceptions are East Baton Rouge Parish, St. Landry, and Claiborne Parish.[32]

Winn Parish, the home of the Long family, was one of the centers of Populism in Louisiana. Here the People's Party acquired a newspaper, the *Winn Parish Democrat,* and published it as the *Comrade.* It has also been stated that Huey Long's father had been a supporter of the People's Party. More generally speaking, both the old Populist movement and the Long faction found their main support in the poorer rural parishes.[33] These facts speak against the usual interpretation of Huey Long's significance in American political life. The Huey Long régime in Louisiana has been considered mainly as a manifestation of American fascism, or as an indication of potential fascism. In reality, if one looks at the originally supporting forces and even at the accomplishments of Huey and the policies of his brother Earl, this interpretation does not seem to be quite fitting; it would be much more

[32] Compare Melvin J. White, "Populism in Louisiana During the Nineties," *Mississippi Valley Historical Review,* Vol. V, No. 1 (June, 1928), pp. 12 ff.

Carleton Beals, *The Story of Huey P. Long* (Philadelphia, J. B. Lippincott Company, 1935), mentions the fact that Huey's father was "something of a Socialist," and that his son grew up in this atmosphere (pp. 29-30). Huey Long in his autobiography records as one of his first experiences the forced sale of a neighbor's farm, which made a terrible impression on him. Railway and lumber companies were at that time making inroads into the previously agricultural Winn Parish.

[33] "Populism never gained much of a foothold in the cotton parishes of the delta or in the sugar parishes, and its support was never strong in the cities," White, *op. cit.,* p. 15.

appropriate to regard the Long faction as a continuation of Populism.

The sentiments of those who believed in Huey Long's share-the-wealth program were probably very similar to the sentiments of those who about forty years earlier voted for William Jennings Bryan and his "free silver" slogan. Neither Huey nor Earl Long ever exploited the race question. Finally, it speaks against any fascist element in the Long faction that organized labor, in 1948, gave Earl Long its support.[34]

This interpretation of the Long faction was confirmed by V. O. Key, *Southern Politics,* which was published a few months after the article by Heberle and Bertrand.[35]

A Hypothesis Concerning the Solid South

Key's book contains the most comprehensive and thorough study in political ecology yet made in the United States. The monographic chapters on party politics and voting behavior in various Southern states give, for the first time, a detailed analysis of the regional and subregional differences in political behavior as well as the class and other group factors involved.[36]

In a synthesis of these monographic studies Key arrives at the hypothesis that the Southern Democratic Party is held together, no longer by common economic interests, but solely by the Negro issue. To test this hypothesis, Key analyzes

[34] A more thorough analysis of voting behavior in Louisiana is presented in Perry Howard, "Political Ecology of Louisiana, 1860 to 1948," unpublished M.A. thesis in sociology, Louisiana State University, 1951. Howard's study confirms the statements made above. He computes a rank-correlation coefficient of +.621 between the Huey Long vote in 1928 and the Populist vote in 1896, by parishes.

[35] An earlier interpretation of the Huey Long movement as a revival of Populism is found in D. F. Saposs, "The Rôle of the Middle Classes in Social Development; Fascism, Populism, Communism, Socialism," *Economic Essays in Honor of Wesley C. Mitchell* (New York, Columbia University Press, 1935), p. 404.

[36] There is no sense in trying to abstract these chapters; they should be read in connection with this treatise.

the voting in two presidential elections when large masses of traditionally Democratic voters bolted: the elections of 1928 and of 1948. Key shows that in the Smith-Hoover contest of 1928 the Republican Party gained the strongest support in states and counties with small proportions of Negroes, while in areas with large proportions of colored population the Democrats were still able to gain majorities. This general tendency was modified by two factors: strong traditionalistic party loyalty which kept certain counties with low proportions of Negroes in the Democratic camp, and urbanization, which tended to strengthen the Republican vote. Generally, the highland areas of the South have few Negroes and a strongly Protestant population which, theoretically at least, favors prohibition; hence the tendency in these areas, in 1928, to vote for the Republican candidate Herbert Hoover rather than for the Catholic, "wet" Democratic candidate, Al Smith. On the other hand, the lowland areas—coastal plains and river bottoms—tend to have many Negroes, and the planter class there is probably less excitable over religious issues and not so "dry" as the hill people; for them, the Negro issue has prime importance. Therefore one finds, in 1928, greater loyalty to the Democratic Party in these areas.[37]

In the 1948 presidential elections the same areas with high proportions of Negroes gave the strongest support to the Dixiecrats. This time the industrial interests joined the revolt, especially since the tide-lands problem became an issue in the campaign. Therefore planters as well as industrialists (represented by such organizations as The Associated Industries of Florida or the Arkansas Free Enterprise Association) supported the Thurmond-Wright ticket of states righters.[38]

[37] V. O. Key, *op. cit.*, pp. 325-328.
[38] *Ibid.*, pp. 329-341.

URBAN ECOLOGY AND VOTING BEHAVIOR

The existence of geographical patterns of voting behavior in American cities and their close relationship to the distribution of major social classes has been noticed by numerous scholars. Schattschneider, who subscribes to the sectionalistic interpretation of party cleavages, observes that within cities, when small areas are compared, the class cleavages become quite visible. He remarks, somewhat naïvely, that "on a microscopic scale, class and sectional alignments seem to be identical." [39] The explanation for this miraculous transformation from section to class lies, as we see it, in the fact that small areas (precincts, even wards) within very large cities tend to be inhabited mainly by people of one class. Therefore the inhabitants tend to be more homogeneous in terms of class position than are the voters in the larger units of county or state. This is perhaps more true of American than of European cities. In continental Europe, owing to the greater frequency of many-family dwellings (tenements and apartment houses) one finds a greater variety of rental levels within the same city block and consequently a greater range of income levels and a greater mixture of social classes—at least in the older parts of the cities. On the other hand, there is a closer association between social classes and political parties in most European countries. The result is that voting differentials correspond rather closely to the class differentials between urban areas. [40]

The idea of social ecology was first developed by sociologists at the University of Chicago and applied to the study of urban society. Influenced by these studies, Harold F. Gos-

[39] E. E. Schattschneider, *Party Government* (New York, Farrar & Rinehart, Inc., 1942), p. 116.

[40] A series of maps showing the distribution of votes for the major parties in the city of Hamburg, Germany, in the Reichstag election of 1930 has been published by Andreas Walther in *Aus Hamburgs Verwaltung und Wirtschaft*, Vol. 8, No. 6. (1931).

nell used an ecological approach in parts of his *Machine Politics—Chicago Model*. In the chapters "The Voters' Response" and "The Relation of the Press to Voting," he analyzes a large number of variables which were of some significance in contributing to the Democratic victories in the presidential elections of 1932 and 1936 and in the congressional election of 1934. These studies, in which ample use was made of simple and partial correlations, are based upon intimate knowledge of the various social areas in the metropolis of Chicago, and comprise inquiries into the interrelations of factors. Information concerning the political ecology is available for several other cities besides Chicago. A recent paper on the ecology of voting in Bloomington, Illinois,[41] shows by a series of map diagrams how the Democratic Party spread its precinct majorities from west to east between 1928 and 1936 and then receded. In 1928 the Democratic candidate for president carried only three precincts—largely Irish and Catholic—in the northwestern part of this traditionally Republican city. In 1932 and 1936, Democratic majorities were obtained in 22 and 23 precincts, covering the entire area west of Main Street and a contiguous area east of this axis. This left a fairly solid but shrunken Republican area in the eastern and southeastern parts of the city, where most of the professional and business-class voters live. In 1940 and 1944, the Democrats held almost all the precincts on the west side, but lost every precinct on the east side.[42] The authors point out that this political division of the city corresponds in a general way to the customarily recognized social class or status differentials between east side and west side, but they do not, however, offer any quantitative proof for this contention.

[41] John A. Kinneman and Shirley E. Shipley, "The Ecology of Pluralities in Presidential Elections," *American Sociological Review*, Vol. 10, No. 3 (June, 1945).

[42] The size of the majorities is not indicated on the maps, but some percentages are given.

A more thorough study of a similar kind is contained in Calvin Schmid's "Social Trends in Seattle." [43] In the 1920's the Republican Party carried the city of Seattle in virtually all national elections. In 1928 Hoover obtained almost two-thirds of the votes cast (65.1 per cent). But in 1932 a complete reversal occurred: Hoover received only 36 per cent of the votes cast, and the Democratic candidate in the gubernatorial elections received 55.8 per cent. Even in 1940 Roosevelt carried the city with 58.3 per cent against Willkie, who received 40.4 per cent.

Within the city there was a wide variation in the proportion of the Roosevelt votes from one precinct to another.[44] Roosevelt's greatest support came, as one would expect, from the poorer areas of the city. The correlation between the percentage of votes cast for Roosevelt in 1936 in each precinct and the mean rental of housing units by precincts was $r = -.722$. Other correlations tend to confirm the relation between the Democratic vote and income level. The lower the economic level, the higher the proportion of Democratic votes. The new ecological pattern of voting behavior proved to be very constant: the correlation between the Roosevelt vote of 1940 and of 1936 by precincts was extremely high: $r = +.938$, and correlations between percentages of votes received by all Democratic candidates in presidential, gubernatorial, and congressional elections were also high. Even in municipal elections the geographic pattern of voting corresponded very closely to the voting in national elections, as is shown by several correlations; this applies to candidates of both major parties.

Furthermore, the constancy and consistency of the ecological pattern is apparent from a study of voting on initiatives, referenda, tax levies, and similar measures involving issues of

[43] Calvin F. Schmid, "Social Trends in Seattle," *University of Washington Publications in the Social Sciences*, Vol. 14 (Seattle, University of Washington Press, Oct., 1944), Chap. XI: Political Trends and Characteristics.

[44] *Ibid.*, p. 257.

vital interest to different economic groups and social classes. For example, the vote against a strike-control initiative in 1938 (which was defeated by a 52.4 per cent majority) showed a correlation with mean rentals of −.808 and with the Roosevelt vote in 1936 of +.938. Schmid presents the voting data in a series of well-designed maps, and some of the correlations are demonstrated by scatter diagrams.

The value of this study would have been greatly enhanced had its author seen fit to correlate voting behavior and social-economic status. His book contains several maps showing the distribution of persons in major occupation groups by census traits (especially charts 65, 66, 67, 68, 69, 70), which permit at least a rough visual comparison in voting behavior between the geographic distribution of wage and salary workers on the one side and employers, managerial, and professional workers on the other.

A finer statistical analysis, applying correlation methods, would require the combining of precincts and census tracts into approximately comparable areas. It would also require the re-calculation of data on voting and on social-economic status for these areas—a highly expensive and time-consuming procedure. One would, however, like to see a more detailed ecological analysis on the basis of the data in their present shape. For instance, it is quite interesting that the predominantly professional voters around the University of Washington gave little support to Roosevelt in the elections of 1936 and gave him even less in those of 1940; his strength lay quite obviously in the precincts with high proportions of wage earners.

Conclusions: Possibility of a Comparative Ecology

A comparative, international ecology of political behavior would be very interesting. It might disclose certain general regularities of voting behavior. It might show broad rules concerning the influence on political behavior of such variables as the system of land holdings, socio-economic stratification, and migratory mobility of population.[45]

Such an undertaking would of course encounter the following difficulties: (1) The election systems vary from country to country, so that election returns are not strictly comparable. (2) The party systems are not alike in number, organization, or their relation to social classes. (3) The same party name (Socialist, Liberal, Conservative) may mean quite different things in different countries.

For all these reasons, the data with which one would work would not be strictly comparable. To put it more concretely: one Socialist vote in, let us say, Sweden, does not mean exactly the same thing as one Socialist vote in the United States or in Chile. Neither are the *intentions* of the voters the same, nor is the *function* of a Socialist vote in each of these countries the same. And yet, our previous discussion has shown us a fair number of parallels of voting behavior and constellations of political attitudes in different countries, and this as a by-product of rather scattered and casual observations. A more methodical procedure might produce even more and better results. Starting with the rural people, we can quite safely say that on the best soils we will find rather stable and mostly quite conservative political attitudes. Wealth, of course, does not produce conservatism, but the best soils tend to be in the possession of the ruling classes in rural society, and these classes tend to be the defenders of the status quo. Of course, if our observations happen to be made after a social and political revolution, we are likely to find counter-revolutionary attitudes and movements associated with the best soil regions. On the other hand, people on poor soils tend to be susceptible to new political movements and parties and sometimes they are quite inclined to demand a fundamental change in the political system. In other words,

[45] Sten S. Nilson, advances some suggestions for general principles of political ecology in his *Histoire et sciences politiques* (Bergen, 1950).

radicalism in rural society tends to be associated with the poorer soils, again not because poverty breeds discontent, but because the poorer soils tend to be in the possession of the lower, less influential, and less respected classes in rural society, who quite naturally tend to bear resentment against the "big shots," "fat heads," and so forth.

A variable of major importance seems to be the dependence of farmers on markets. It seems that highly commercialized and at the same time specialized farming which results in a high degree of economic insecurity tends to result in a basic tendency towards radicalism. Apparently, commercialized, specialized farming results in instability of political attitudes which makes the rural voters susceptible to any new political party that promises to reduce oscillations in farm prices, to lower the interest rate on farm credit, to reduce the margin between farm and consumer prices or that proposes similar measures. Industrialized rural areas tend to have a political complexion of their own. If the industrial labor force is native, of farm or peasant origin, they are likely to go through a cycle from habitual conservatism through a radical land-reform progressivism to socialism or communism, as industrialization progresses. If the labor force consists of immigrants from other industrial areas, they will most likely import those attitudes and party preferences that were predominant in the areas of their origin. If they come from other agricultural areas, especially from economically backward regions, the spread of socialism may be retarded, or there may spring up among such workers an attitude of radicalism, given to violence, which may open the field for communist infiltration.

Variables of major importance are: (1) the size of plants and enterprises and the resulting quality of labor-management relations, (2) the presence or absence of the owner, (3) the existence of ethnic or religious differences between employers and employees, and (4) the existence of racial differences.

A major question of political ecology which still needs much empirical investigation is whether regional political climates are really as persistent as some scholars, like André Siegfried, maintain. The persistence may be great if the social structure of a region remains unchanged; in that case, parties may come and go as their platforms become worn out or their leaders gain and lose popularity, but the basic attitudes concerning the functions of government, the institution of private property, the relation between Church and State, and so on, may remain the same. On the other hand, if the social structure changes (for example, through concentration of landholdings, through mechanization in agriculture, or through the growth of big industrial enterprises and large manufacturing plants), the political attitudes are also likely to change. In this case there may be a rapid change from one party to the other, even a succession of new political movements and parties.

It is possible, though, for party machines to be so firmly disciplined and cemented by the patronage which they control, that they can weather the storm. In such situations the parties must meet new demands of the voters through changes in their platforms and policies, and offer nominations to new leaders who otherwise might start a secession.

V

STRUCTURE
AND ORGANIZATION
OF SOCIAL MOVEMENTS
AND POLITICAL PARTIES

13

General Principles

THE CONCEPTS OF ORGANIZATION AND STRUCTURE

SOCIAL MOVEMENTS according to our definition are not organized groups (see Introduction). According to Tönnies they are "social collectives"—that is, large groups consisting of enough individuals to be able to endure a change in membership without undergoing a change in quality; united and held together by a sense of belonging together and a consciousness of sharing the same opinions, values, and goals, not necessarily with a formal organization. However, the rule is that organized groups are comprised within a social movement.

Some degree of organization is indispensable for any kind of concerted social action in which large numbers of persons participate; the larger the group, the more elaborate the organization needed. We say a group is organized if certain of its members are authorized to give orders to members of the group and to represent the group in relations with outsiders and other organized groups. Organization consists in attributing to certain members definite powers and duties relevant to the functioning of the group; these certain members are thereby authorized to demand and prohibit particular actions from other members, and expect obedience to their requests.

The empowered persons act, within the sphere of their authority, not as private individuals, but as agents of the group, they do so also in relation to outsiders. Their actions are regarded as actions of the entire group. Since, in the ideal case, all of the functions delegated in this way are essential and interdependent, the officers of an organized group can be compared to the organs of a living body, hence the term *organization.*

Organization may or may not be of an elaborate and formal nature, depending on the characteristics of the group. For this reason one can discern many different degrees of organization. For example, a group of young people who meet regularly to discuss matters of common intellectual or vocational interest may be considered as an unorganized social circle; as soon, however, as they appoint a committee of three who are authorized to prepare the programs and to call meetings, we have the beginnings of organization. A group of college students going out on a picnic does not necessarily have an organization; if, however, the group consists of ten persons or more, it will probably be practical to agree on what each member is to contribute in the way of transportation, food, drinks, and entertainment; in that case there is some degree of temporary organization.

Any more elaborate form of organization contains two additional structural elements: first, the officers of the group are aided by clerical and technical staffs in carrying out their duties, and in larger groups some of the staff members will have authority over subdivisions of the group or certain fields of group activity. Second, there will be an established set of rules regulating the actions of all members of the group. These rules determine the ways in which decisions of the group shall be made and the procedures by which they are to be carried out. Such rules for an organized group are, in general, what constitutions and laws are for the state, and they are usually called *constitution* and *by-laws.*

In order to define the sphere of power of an organized

group it is essential to know exactly who belongs to the group and who is an outsider. If the group is not closed, but open, as political parties usually are, it is also necessary to determine by general rules who may become a member of the group and who would not be eligible even if he wanted to join.

Furthermore, in order to achieve consistency and continuity of action, all but the most simple organized groups need records of their actions and of the actions of their officers. The importance of such recording increases with the size of the group, the variety of its activities, and the complexity of its organization. This is of importance because possession of the membership lists and other records of the group's activities is one of the conditions of control over the group. If a conflict within the organization leads to a split, that faction which remains in control of the organization's offices and files will be at an advantage.

Since any large organized group needs office space, meeting halls, and other material equipment, as well as funds out of which expenses and salaries of officers and clerical personnel can be paid, it will have to design a method of financing its activities. This can be done in various ways: through membership fees; assessments; collections; donations from wealthy members or sympathizers; contributions from affiliated organization; revenue from newspapers, periodicals, or publishing firms,[1] or income from other profit-making enterprises owned or controlled by the organization. The method of financing a political party or social movement depends of course to a large extent on the financial resources of the individual members of a movement or party, that is, largely on the class position of the membership. Parties and other organizations representing the well-to-do and rich can be financed by voluntary contributions, whereas those representing people with moderate means or representing poorer people will

[1] For example, the N.S.D.A.P. had considerable revenue from its press.

have to rely upon dues and assessments. The larger the number of contributors to the organization, the smaller the chances that a few wealthy individuals or groups will gain control over the policies.

The ways in which financial means are allocated and redistributed within an organization have great significance for the location of control within the movement. It makes a great difference whether, for example, all dues collected by the labor-union locals are transmitted to the "international" which redistributes them, or whether a larger or smaller proportion is retained by the locals for free disposition. The latter way seems to prevail among American labor unions, whereas the former arrangement is characteristic of present-day union organization in Western Germany. In external and internal relations, he who holds the purse string is likely to be in a position of influence and eventual control over a group.

Even a group which is not organized will have a social structure, that is, a spontaneous division of functions, which originates by more or less tacit agreement among members. Because the nature of the group's activities demands it, and because individual members are inclined to and gifted for different rôles, a social structure arises easily. In any group, whether organized or not, we can observe that certain individuals are more influential than others in some respects of group activity. We also find that certain members usually tend to initiate action, whereas others merely follow. In this sense we can speak, for example, of structure in a play group of children or in a boys' gang, although neither group may require a formal organization.

"Social structure" thus means an attribution of rôles and positions within the group to its various members—a mere factual arrangement which may not be formally recognized, nor regulated by statutes, constitution, or other formal rules of conduct. This, however, is only the primary aspect of structure.

In a large and complex social collective there will usually be found several subgroups, some organized, some not. This is another aspect of structure and a very important one in regard to social movements. In the labor movement, for example, we find labor unions, consumers' coöperatives, workers' educational associations, clubs of various kinds, and political labor parties. The interrelation between these groups is sometimes not organized, that is, not regulated by definite rules, and yet it is very important for the understanding of the whole. In addition to such organized groups we find in every larger social movement unorganized debating and reading circles, friendship groups, cliques, wings and factions, followings of certain leaders, and so forth, all of which make up the structure of the movement. Incidentally, these informal, unofficial groupings within a larger social movement may be of as great importance for an understanding of its functioning as the official or formal organization.

The terms *structure* and *organization* thus do not designate two contrasting aspects of a group. Every group has some kind of structure, but not every group is organized; one might be tempted to say that structure is potential organization, but this would not be an adequate definition, since many structural groupings and relationships are by their very essence not capable of formal organization. A friendship circle, for example, would change its sociological character if organization was attempted; and furthermore, there are in any organized group structural interrelations and groupings which escape formal organization and which exist, so to speak, in the interstices of the organization. It would be more adequate to say that organization is a particular kind of structure.

The main structural problems in social movements are: the relation between leaders and followers, the type of leadership, the hierarchy of leaders and functionaries, the organization of the staffs, the existence of and interrelation between subdivisions of the movement, the characteristics of formally organized groups within the movement, and the relation of the movement to other collectives and to political parties in particular.

POLITICAL PARTIES

The Concept

The term *party* has many meanings and connotations, as any good dictionary will show. The usage of the term has changed greatly since the Middle Ages. Derived from the French word *partie,* the term has its origin in the Latin *partire:* to divide, to separate. It has therefore the meaning of a detachment from a larger group, for example, in military language, a troop detailed for foraging or reconnaissance. At an early time, it acquired the connotation of an antagonism to another division of similar kind. The term *party* thus is given the meaning of a collectivity of persons holding similar views in matters religious, philosophical, scientific, or political in contrast to and in conflict with groups of people who hold opposite views. Thus, the philosopher Kant refers to "Leibnitz' party." We find the two great factions in medieval Italy and Germany, the *Guelfs* and *Ghibelines,* referred to as *partien* in contemporary poetry; but only in the nineteenth century did the political connotation become the most frequent one. However, *party* always has the connotation of conflict, more specifically, of an antagonism and struggle by a social order within a larger social order. This last point is important because it implies that in spite of the antagonism, the parties must have some things in common—that all genuine parties recognize certain values and certain rules, just as both teams in a ball game must be agreed as to the rules and objectives of the game.

Parties in this sense occur in all kinds of groups, particularly in corporate bodies or organized groups, such as churches, learned societies and academies, labor unions, and town meetings. By *political parties* we mean those that form antagonistic divisions within the "bodies politic" of ancient and medieval city-states, medieval kingdom-states, and modern states. The typical political party in the modern state is an association of citizens recruited by free solicitation with the purpose of securing power for the leaders. A party awards to its active participants chances of attaining objective ends or of gaining personal, ideal, or material benefits.[2]

Organization

Since parties are action groups, they are bound to be organized, if only temporarily for a campaign, or if merely in the legislature as a parliamentary party or group. The need for a minimum degree of organization arises from the functions of a political party: the preparation of resolutions and bills, the nomination of candidates, the conduct of election campaigns.

In harmony with a general sociological principle, mass parties are likely to be more elaborately organized than small parties. The evolution of party organization is therefore largely a consequence of the extension of the franchise to ever-larger masses of voters. However, other factors are also to be considered: the state constitution and election system under which a party operates, the concept which its members have of the function of their party, and the social position of the rank and file of its membership. Consequently, political parties vary greatly in degree and kind of organization, not only from one country to the other, but also within the same country. The general trend has been towards more and more elaborate organization. The extreme in this respect is represented by the Communist and Fascist parties (see Chapter 15).

[2] Max Weber, *Theory of Social and Economic Organization,* trans. by A. H. Henderson and T. Parsons (New York, Oxford University Press, 1947), pp. 407 f.

Membership

A peculiar problem is presented by membership. Strictly speaking, a political party consists of its organized members. But in many cases, there are no membership dues, no membership cards, or any hard and fast rules about party membership. In such cases, it is virtually impossible to determine the exact expanse of the organized party. Most parties are open groups, that is, they admit any bona fide supporter who is willing to join. Some require the payment of membership dues, others ask only for voluntary contributions.

In democratic countries the parties with the most rigid membership rules are the Socialist, Communist, Labor, and Catholic parties. Adherence to the party principles, payment of party dues, and membership in the appropriate auxiliary organizations of the party are the usual requirements demanded of those who wish to remain on the party rolls. The Socialist and Communist parties are the most successful in making effective the requirement of the regular payment of contributions. . . .

Non-socialist and non-confessional parties in democratic countries are usually very loosely organized with few or no formal rules regulating membership . . . [in England] only rarely are dues required of those who belong to the local party clubs or associations.[3]

Parties in democratic states are as a rule desirous of getting as large a membership as possible. The most notable exception from this rule are the Communist parties which have been organized after the model of the Russian Bolshevist party. Lenin's conception of the Communist Party as a closely-knit, highly disciplined organization of professional revolutionaries has led to the establishment of rigorous conditions for party membership, to the policy of keeping the party relatively small, and to periodical purges—that is, expulsion of unreliable or undisciplined members. The basic idea is to keep the party fit for the preparation of a revolution, and in those countries where the Communists are in

[3] H. F. Gosnell, "Political Parties—Organization," *Encyclopaedia of the Social Sciences* (New York, The Macmillan Company, 1942), p. 193.

power, to preserve it as an instrument for the execution of the Communist program and policies.

The organization of the Italian Fascist Party was largely copied from the Bolshevik model, and the organization of the N.S.D.A.P. from both.[4] Membership in the N.S.D.A.P. was open only to persons of "Aryan race" and involved quite heavy demands on the individual member's time and finances, which had a restricting effect. After the seizure of power in 1933 the party was from time to time closed until the new members had been adjusted. It was intended that eventually access to party membership would be possible only through the youth organization.[5]

Both the Communist and Fascist parties are organizations of activists; members who confine their party service to the paying of dues and to voting in elections are not tolerated in this new type of party. The statutes of the N.S.D.A.P. (Art. 4, Sec. 3c) provided for expulsion of members because of "disinterestedness."[6] The same applies to communist parties. The constitution of the Communist Party of America (1919) states that only persons who "agree to engage actively in the work of the party shall be eligible to membership. It is the aim of [this] organization to have in its ranks only those who participate actively in its work." (Art. 3, Sec. 1.)

After a militant party has become a major political power,

[4] More accurately speaking, the Fascist and Nazi parties borrowed from their arch-enemies, the Communists, many organizational and tactical devices. Both the Communists and their antagonists were influenced by Georges Sorel and French revolutionary syndicalism.

[5] The principles of selective membership on which the party was organized are presented in Adolf Hitler's *Mein Kampf*, ed. 1933, Chap. 11, pp. 649-657. Here Hitler makes a very definite distinction between members of the organized party and sympathizers (*Anhaenger*); of the latter kind he wants as many as possible, but as party members he welcomes only those who are willing and capable of participating in political action, to carry on the fight for power. What he wants is a party consisting of political activists. That is essentially the same idea as Lenin's conception of the Communist Party as the spearhead of the proletarian communist movement.

[6] Karl Stumpf, *Die Struktur der Modernen Partei und ihre Stellung im Staate, Dissertation* Jena, 1934, p. 30.

it becomes increasingly difficult to preserve the activistic character of its membership. In this connection the following note on developments in Soviet-controlled Czechoslovakia is of interest:

> The Communist Party, which is the driving force, is concerned meanwhile with problems created by a bandwagon psychology. Rudolf Slansky, referring to membership in the Communist Party (which recently passed the two million mark), warned that "opportunists pursuing their personal careers or people without character must not be accepted. If any dishonest elements succeed in infiltrating into the party, they will soon be discovered and removed." On the other hand, "Those who wish to join the Communist Party must do so because of their own conviction, and membership must never be imposed on anybody," he said, directing his remarks to party officials who in certain offices had handed out membership forms to be filled in by the next day." [7]

One of the few devices left to the opposition under a totalitarian régime is to infiltrate into the ruling party.

Relations between Social Movements and Political Parties

In view of these variations in membership requirements, it is not easy to define the relation between political parties and the broader social movements. Generally we can say that many individuals belong to political movements—for example, socialism—who are not members of an organized political party. In this respect the relation between a party and a movement resembles the relation between a church and a religious denomination: not all who share the faith are members of a church group.

There are often, in one and the same broad social movement, several political parties. For example, within the communist movement of today there exist the Stalinist (orthodox) parties in the various countries, the Trotzkyist parties, and

[7] David Scott, "Czech Rubber Stamp," *New Republic*, Vol. 118 (June 7, 1948).

the recent Titoist [8] parties in Yugoslavia and the Western Zones of Germany. On the other hand, a party may comprise or absorb several social movements, partly or entirely, by adopting their programs and enlisting their membership.

In any social movement, as in a political party, one can distinguish various degrees of intensity of participation among the members. The most active members usually belong to one or more organized groups and devote a great deal of time to work in these groups; others participate intermittently in elections or in public meetings and mass demonstrations; others are merely sympathizers without participating much in group action; some may do nothing but contribute more or less regularly to campaign funds; finally, there is always a fringe of opportunists who do not actually sympathize with the party or movement but think it safer to buy protection. (Compare Chapter 5.) However, as in political parties, the general tendency in any social movement is toward complete and intensive organization of its adherents. The structure of a social movement can thus be said to consist of one or more formally organized cores or nuclei surrounded by a mass of less formally and less intensively attached supporters. In many cases, but by no means in all, one of the organized cores is a political party—as in the case of the communist and fascist movements. [9]

Notwithstanding the manifold and often complex nature of the empirical relations between political parties and social movements, four basic types can be discerned.

1. A party may be part of a broader social movement, as is the British Labor Party, which forms one of the three branches of a labor movement.

2. The party may be independent of any particular social

[8] Titoism is the orthodox Communists' opprobrious term for the tendency towards national independence among Communists outside Russia.

[9] The National Socialists made a distinction between the N.S.D.A.P., which was a registered, incorporated association, and the movement, which consisted of all followers of Adolf Hitler, regardless of party membership.

movement and embody in its membership all or part of several social movements; this has been the tendency in the major American parties.

3. The same social movement may be represented in several political parties: for example, the socialist movement in various socialistic parties, the labor movement in socialistic, communistic, and other parties.

4. Finally a social movement may reject on principle the affiliation with any political party, as for example did the anarcho-syndicalistic movement or the I.W.W.[10]

Elements of Party Organization

In studying the structure and functions of a movement or party it is of great importance to determine whether the officers and workers as a rule receive payment for their services, or whether they work merely for the honor of the offices and positions entrusted to them. The difference lies not merely in the effects upon the finances of the group but even more in the kind of personnel which is selected under the two arrangements.

Types of Party Workers

a. Honorary workers can be recruited only from occupations which leave a man (or woman) ample leisure time, or at least allow a certain flexibility in the daily work schedule. Honorary workers are therefore usually people whose occupation affords them opportunity to take time off to work for the party or movement. Such persons might be large landowners, *rentiers,* or wholesale merchants. Often they are persons who have the use of an office: perhaps lawyers, businessmen, or physicians. Innkeepers, saloonkeepers, storekeepers,

---

[10] This case is not to be confused with the non-partisan policy of American labor unions; the anarcho-syndicalists do not put any trust at all in parliamentary action (see Chap. 16), while the labor unions attempt to gain influence in all major parties.

physicians, lawyers, newspaper editors, and (in some countries) school teachers are very valuable because their voca-
tions bring them in contact with many members or prospective
supporters of the movement or party. The vocational recruit-
ment of honorary party workers depends of course on the
nature of the party. Conservative parties in Europe used to
rely upon landowners, pastors, lawyers, and other professional people; the liberal parties had to rely more on the
petite bourgeoisie; the Catholic parties can always rely on
the clerics.

b. In all organizations, some of the routine work is likely
to be done by *paid office workers,* who are usually employed
only in administrative work, not in policy-making positions.
Naturally, members of the party or movement and their relatives are preferred for such jobs. In this way, fairly large
numbers of individuals and families acquire an economic interest in the organization. The English parties—the Liberal
Party first, later the Conservatives—started to employ paid
secretaries about the middle of the nineteenth century for
routine administration and for the execution of technical administrative work relating to elections. These secretaries are
not politicians and are not supposed to influence the policies
of their party. Many social movements which are centered
around an organized core employ paid executives who are
under the authority of honorary policy-making officers.

c. Some parties and movements, because of the social position of their members, cannot secure enough honorary workers. These groups usually combine paid administrative positions with policy-making offices by assigning *paid jobs to
officers who lack other means of support.* This has been the
situation in the labor movement in all countries, in the political labor parties as well as in the trade union and coöperative
movements. In the local units of the German Social Democratic Party, the *bonze* or "porkchopper" was usually the paid
secretary or some other kind of administrative officer who at

the same time would participate in policy making. Sometimes these paid functionaries were also members of the municipal or provincial assembly or of the state or national legislature. Such officers drew per-diem compensation, which reduced the strain on the financial resources of the party. In some cases, a party elected deserving workers to legislative assemblies in order to secure financial support for them. This practice was greatly facilitated under the Weimar Constitution by the system of proportional representation with long ballots for very large election districts.

Bureaucratization

In general, these tendencies in organization lead to *bureaucratization;* by this term we mean the creation of large bodies of hierarchically arranged professional party workers who are assigned to well-defined tasks of administration and who are selected and promoted on the basis of efficiency in routine work rather than because of their political attitudes and judgment in political matters. This tendency towards bureaucratization is a very widespread trait of modern society which is found not only in government, but also in industry, since bureaucratic administration is the most efficient form of keeping a large social organization functioning. Adolf Hitler realized this; in 1919 when he assumed the position of propaganda chief in the original seven-man *Deutsche Arbeiterpartei* (out of which he created the N.S.D.A.P.), he saw that only a permanent office organization, headed by a paid employee, could guarantee the smooth functioning of routine business. He also established the principles of business efficiency in the administration of party-owned enterprises —even to the point of hiring non-Nazis, who of course, if they stayed with the organization, were sooner or later converted.[11]

The general disadvantages of bureaucracy are well known.

[11] Adolf Hitler, *Mein Kampf* (München, 1933), pp. 662-666.

In the case of political parties and related organizations one drawback is that the growth of a large administrative staff of people who acquire an economic interest in the organization may generate an attitude of opportunism and tend to reduce the militancy of the group.[12] This is especially likely if members of the administrative staff also hold political offices. The German Social Democratic Party seems to have suffered severely from this structural trait. In the N.S.D.A.P. it was counterbalanced by the concentration of power with the supreme leader.

The major American parties are not as highly organized as some of the European parties, and their bureaucratization is not very highly developed. It is the volunteer workers and honorary staff members who do a great deal of the routine work, and it is the *boss* who is the backbone of the organization or machine. The boss is not an employee of the party but rather a kind of political entrepreneur or *condottiere* in politics whose function consists in securing a following and in mobilizing this following at election time in order to "deliver the vote." The boss, in the stricter, technical sense of the term, does not hold public office and therefore cannot be held responsible for the policies of the party. This distinguishes him from the party leader, who is also often referred to as the boss.

The politically irresponsible boss is a fruit of the separation of powers in the American system of government. He is the man who, behind the scenes, serves as a coördinator of party actions. Sait says: "The English counterpart of our boss is the Prime Minister who rules the country without being known to the law. He is the party boss. . . ." Here the point of analogy is the lack of a constitutional provision for the function of the boss. Later on Sait points to the significant difference between the prime minister and the boss: "But the

[12] See Robert Michels, *Political Parties*, tr. by Eden and Ceder Paul (Glencoe, Ill., The Free Press, 1915, 1949); p. 498, German edition).

Prime Minister soon after Walpole became responsible, while the American boss is irresponsible." [13]

Oligarchic Tendencies

Most of the older political parties and social movements in Western society have a democratic form of organization. The local membership meeting and the assemblies of delegates to various levels of party conventions constitute the supreme organs; party officials are usually elected by these bodies and are subject to control from the rank and file. However, in political parties and in other organized cores of social movements, there is always a tendency towards concentration of power in the hands of a small group of leaders—a tendency towards *oligarchy*.[14]

Officers and functionaries tend to retain their offices for long periods of time by re-election, or, this failing, they tend to rotate offices among themselves. Movements and parties with democratic ideologies and democratic constitutions are no exception to this rule. On the contrary, the dependence of the labor parties and mass movements among the lower-income groups on paid functionaries tends to strengthen this tendency. Experience in routine administrative work as well as in the know-how of policy making tends to raise the office-holders far above the rank and file. The prestige of established political leaders makes it difficult and often unwise to replace them.

We will understand this curious paradox in the structure of democratically constituted organizations even better if we consider that the rank and file are usually content with a low degree of participation in group action. They are willing to pay dues and to attend meetings, though not too frequently; they are quite eager to participate in general policy making

---

[13] Edward M. Sait, *American Parties and Elections* (New York, Appleton-Century-Crofts, Inc., 1927), pp. 345, 346.
[14] R. Michels, *op. cit.*

through resolutions, and on the whole, to participate intermittently in the activities of the group. But as a rule the rank and file are not ready to work constantly and continuously for the organization or to assume personal responsibility for the group's actions.

This kind of work requires a great deal of persistence and devotion to details which often seem trifling even to the most enthusiastic supporters. Besides, it requires the ability to guide and lead other people. Also, it involves the ability to negotiate with outsiders, be they opponents or potential allies, and this ability has to be acquired by experience. The lower the educational level of the rank and file and the smaller the proportion of available individuals, the more indispensable will be the established élite of more or less permanent office holders. Parties consisting of members of the nobility or other notables, that is aristocratic parties, usually have a relatively large supply of available honorary workers and therefore are much less subject to this tendency towards oligarchy than are democratic parties and mass movements. However, the control over membership lists, funds, newspapers, and other instruments needed in running a party or movement is in any case bound to give the established officeholders many advantages over any competitor from the rank and file.

There are of course variations in the degree of concentration of power in the hands of the leading oligarchy. But the problem of the existence of oligarchy and the relation of the leaders to the masses, is universal in all action groups. It exists in practically every kind of voluntary association. Much has been said about dictators and tsars in the American labor union movement, but autocratic abuses of power on the part of elected officials are also to be found in other organizations. In the case of labor unions, it is true that some union leaders have entrenched themselves so firmly in their control of the union hierarchy that it is virtually impossible to dislodge them. Close inspection of some of the more notorious instances shows, however, that these men enjoy an enormous popularity and loyalty with the rank and file. A successful labor leader who has built up a powerful union in a previously unorganized industry and has achieved significant improvements in the conditions of life and work of the wage earners in that industry is sure to be worshipped like a hero, regardless of how autocratic he may become in his later years.

There is another factor contributing to stability of officialdom in labor unions and labor parties. Each individual who has climbed from a job in a factory or mine to a leading position in the movement, be it merely that of an educational director in the local of a large union, represents, so to speak, an investment on the part of the members. Their dues and fees have maintained the leader and paid for his education—why should they want to waste all this effort if the leader in question does his job to their satisfaction?

Michels' discovery of the tendency towards oligarchy in democratically constituted groups was of course grist to the mills of the opponents of democracy. However, it seems that these opponents have little reason to gloat, particularly in view of the debacle of the two most decidedly anti-democratic régimes (Nazis and Fascists), which, incidentally, were indirectly influenced by Michels' findings. The implications of the principle of oligarchic tendencies in democratic groups will become clearer when we consider the various types of authority and leadership that occur in social movements.

Types of Authority and Leadership

The term *leader* as used in popular language may designate all kinds of persons who exercise influence, power, or authority over others. A minister of the church may be called a leader in the community merely because his office automatically places him in the group of prominent citizens who are asked to serve on all sorts of committees; or he may be called a leader because he is one who initiates social action in the community, through proposing new ideas. It would perhaps be better to reserve the term *leader* for those individuals who, whether they hold an office or not, take the lead in group action, and to call the others *officials* or *functionaries*. The latter are obeyed and respected because of the dignity and powers of their office, the former because of their personal ability to impose their will on others. One should realize, however, that no permanent position of dominance is possible without a certain amount of consent on the part of the dominated individuals. This applies to boys' gangs as well as to labor unions, political parties, and the state. Even a régime which seems to rest upon force alone presupposes not only the existence of an administrative staff supporting the rulers, but also a minimum of support from the masses, even though the latter submit passively out of fear.

It is advisable to distinguish between mere power and authority. We speak of the latter when the power of an individual over the members of a group is not merely factual but is considered by all or most members as valid and legitimate. The various bases for belief in the legitimacy of an authority furnish an important criterion for the differentiation between basic types of authority.[15]

In social movements and also in political parties one can distinguish two main *types of authority:* institutional and charismatic. The institutional or legal or rational type of authority is founded on the belief in the legality or constitutionality of certain statutes and in the right of those elevated to positions of power under such statutes to issue orders and commands. Obedience is due and given to the legally established, impersonal order. However, obedience is due to persons exercising the authority of office only by virtue of the formal legality of their commands and only within the scope

[15] Max Weber, *op. cit.*

of authority of the office.[16] The prototype of this kind of authority wielder in social movements is the elected officer (chairman, president, vice-president, and so forth) on all levels of the organization. These officers may be brilliant men or quite mediocre individuals, and yet the degree of authority which they exercise legitimately is determined by statutes defining the functions of their offices.

The very opposite is the leader in the strict sense, or the charismatic type of authority. *Charisma* means, in theological language, a particular gift of grace—prophets and founders of new religions are endowed with charisma. In political or sociological terminology, *charisma* means the real or imagined extraordinary qualities of any group leader, therefore charismatic authority means a type of authority which is based "upon the devotion of the group members to the specific and exceptional heroism, sanctity or otherwise exemplary character of an individual person, and on the belief in the validity (sanctity) of the normative order revealed or ordained by him." [17] The typical charismatic leader is regarded as the creator of the movement and of its ideas, and he himself believes or pretends that this is so; therefore he claims absolute authority over his followers and demands unqualified loyalty; "he who is not for me is against me." Mussolini and Hitler had many characteristics of the genuine charismatic leader. Hitler believed that he had been chosen by the grace of God to lead "his" people out of disgrace and despair to new power and fame, and Hitler certainly was considered by his really devoted followers as a kind of demi-god and savior of the German people.

A grain of charisma enters into all political leadership, even into the legal authority of elected functionaries in democratically organized groups. Rarely can a person win an election

[16] *Ibid.*, pp. 328 ff.
[17] *Ibid.*, p. 328. See also S. Neumann, *Permanent Revolution* (New York, Harper and Brothers, 1942), Chaps. II, III.

unless he is capable of building up a personal following, and in order to do that he will have to evoke a certain amount of personal loyalty, of enthusiasm for his personality, of confidence in his ability, and so on. (Exception: the election of a compromise candidate—a "dark horse"—of whom his supporters expect mainly patronage and not leadership.)

These two types of leadership condition two entirely different *types of administrative staffs:*

1. In the first case, the administrative functionaries derive their authority from the same basic statute or constitution as the leaders. The division of labor is likely to be bureaucratic, each functionary having a logically constituted sphere of duties and rights. Selection is supposedly made rationally on the basis of objective qualifications.

2. In the second case, all authority is derived from the leader. He bestows duties and offices on those with whom he has worked closely: the old guard, the first followers, the original disciples, those whom he can trust because their loyalty has been tested. Assignment of tasks does not follow logical, systematic lines but appears to be quite arbitrary. However, there is method in the madness of office distribution insofar as the most important offices are given to the most trusted of the inner circle, and so distributed among them as to achieve a balance of power by which the leader is protected against any *coup* from his lieutenants. The same principles apply also on the lower levels: each of the subleaders will have his trusted followers and will distribute offices among them, primarily on the basis of nearness to the subleader.

In most parties and in most organized cores of social movements, the two principles of staff structure are mixed. The higher positions will often be given to trusted members of the old guard, men who have acquired a great deal of prestige among the rank and file, whereas the lower positions are filled with experts in various fields. Even the Nazi Party could not do without the services of expert clerical workers, accountants, and so on.[18] In labor unions it is quite common to fill policy-making positions by election through the rank and file or its delegates, whereas administrative positions are filled by appointment. As the unions grow and gain in power, more and more administrative and research jobs are filled with experts, either self-taught men or college graduates who have received the particular kind of training needed for the position.

It should be clear now that the form of organization of a political party depends on a variety of internal and external factors. The party's conception of its function, the social position of its supporters, the size of the electorate, and the political system or régime under which the parties operate are the most important factors. The last point needs some elaboration. If parties are recognized as essential to the political system, they will be organized differently than if they are outlawed or suppressed and therefore compelled to work in secrecy. The fact that in England parties have been considered as inevitable and not evil for more than two hundred years has affected their form of organization. In the same way the oppression of the socialist movement in Tsarist Russia has left a deep imprint upon the communist parties everywhere.

INTER-RELATIONS BETWEEN POLITICAL PARTIES AND OTHER GROUPS COMPOSING SOCIAL MOVEMENTS

Special-Purpose Groups

Political parties often seek to win votes and to bind their supporters more closely to the party by organizing *special-purpose groups* for various categories of party followers and for various kinds of activities. Thus we find women's groups

[18] Hans Gerth, "The Nazi Party; Its Leadership and Composition," *American Journal of Sociology*, Vol. 45 (Jan., 1940).

and clubs attached to political parties. We find also the very important youth organizations: Young Democrats, Young Republicans, Young Socialists (in Germany), the *Komsomol* in the Soviet Union, the Hitler Youth, the Free German Youth in the Eastern zones of Germany, and so forth. Even children have been organized in party-affiliated organizations such as the *Rote Falken* (Red Falcons) of the old German S.P.D. and the *Jungvolk* of the N.S.D.A.P.[19] Among the special-purpose organizations we find athletic clubs and associations, singing societies, and beneficial societies. The Social Democratic Party in pre-Hitler Germany was said to comprise the workers' entire life, from the cradle (organization for the care of mothers and children) to the grave (proletarian associations for cremation).

Types of Inter-relations

Organizations of this kind are not always created by the political party; sometimes they are older than the party—like the British trade unions which form the backbone of the British Labour Party. In major social movements one finds a great variety of interrelationships between the various subgroups, and sometimes the interrelationships between political parties and other components of a movement are very complicated. With a great deal of simplification, one can distinguish the following types of interrelationship:

1. The party creates or sponsors associations of particular categories of voters or prospective voters. This was often the case in Germany where the Social Democratic Party, the liberal parties and the Catholic (Center) Party began, about the middle of the nineteenth century, to sponsor and

---

[19] H. F. Gosnell, *Why Europe Votes* (Chicago, University of Chicago Press, 1930), p. 190. In general, the European parties have made greater efforts than the American parties to organize the young people. The British Conservative Party after the defeat of 1906 organized the Junior Imperial League; after 1918 young women were admitted, "and the functions of the organization became more of a social nature." (*Ibid.*, p. 30.)

even to create a great variety of specialized groups and in particular their own trade unions.

2. The party is created by or with substantial aid from already existing functional organizations. For example, the British Labour Party came into being as an alliance between various socialist groups and the trade unions; the Peoples' Party (Populist Party) in the United States of the 1890's was largely a creation of the two major Farmers' Alliances.[20]

3. Special-interest organizations may use an existing political party as a vehicle through which to gain influence with, or control over the government. In this case there may be either a close affiliation with one political party—as in the case of the Conservative Party or the Agrarian League (*Bund der Landwirte*) in Germany before 1918; or the special-interest association may pursue a non-partisan policy of bringing pressure upon several parties—as in the case of manufacturers' associations, farmers' organizations, and labor unions in the United States. This pressure group relationship presupposes a particular type of political party and a situation in which the party is not part of one particular social movement.

4. A party may infiltrate or penetrate an existing organization in which it finds its prospective supporters already sifted and organized. By converting the key persons in the organization or by placing its own members in key positions, a party may gain control of the other group. By acquiring new supporters in this wholesale fashion, the party may gain power much faster than by canvassing voters individually. This technique was used very successfully by the Nazi Party between 1926 and 1933, and it is the essence of the communists' tactic of boring from within. If this technique is used not merely to gain control but as a method of recruiting, it may result in making the membership more hetero-

[20] Solon J. Buck, *The Agrarian Crusade* (New Haven, Yale University Press, 1920).

geneous. A socialist party recruited from trade unions is likely to absorb a large proportion of non-socialist unionists, since the members of special interest organizations who are drawn en bloc into the current of a social movement are not all likely to be equally convinced of the righteousness of the cause and many may be motivated by opportunistic considerations. Or, the party may come under the dominating influence of efficiently organized particular interests which may lead to splits or secessions.

In the case where a social movement divides itself by creating certain special interest groups, it is likely to gain thereby in strength, just because the fate of so many varied groups is tied up with the success or failure of the movement. However, the movement may thereby lose in militancy, because any risky action it takes will put all the affiliated institutions at stake. This was one factor in the tragedy of European labor.

In the case of existing associations aligning themselves with a party, the latter may come under the domination of special-interest groups. Since much of the campaign funds comes directly or indirectly from such organizations or their members, these organizations can often present certain requests to the political party leaders concerning the choice of candidates and the formulation of platforms and policies. This was quite noticeable in Germany even before the First World War, especially in the Conservative Party, which, because of its affiliation with the farmers' league (*Bund der Landwirte*) became more and more the party of the east German landlords and their retainers. After the First World War, under the system of proportional representation, the influence of special economic-interest organizations on political parties became even stronger. Many candidates, lower down on the tickets, were nothing but representatives of such organizations.

Through these affiliations, the class foundation of political parties becomes clearly visible, whereas in the earlier nineteenth century before the advent of mass parties, the same class affiliations were effected through less obvious informal connections, mostly of a more personal nature and on the local levels.

Pressure Groups

The type of relationship between special interest groups and political parties which was mentioned above under (3) (p. 292) refers to what is usually called the influence of pressure groups upon political parties. The kinds of pressure groups vary. There are reform movements with broad and idealistic programs; there are highly self-centered economic-interest groups who engage in lobbying for a particular prospective tariff or a similar type of legislation; and there are various kinds of groups in between. The common characteristic of all genuine pressure groups is that they do not seek to win elections or to assume the responsibilities of government; their purpose is to obtain legislation for a minority rather than a majority of voters (although exceptions to this statement can be found). Their tactics vary: they range from persuasive argument to more or less outright bribery. As a rule they approach legislators in all the major parties, pursuing a so-called non-partisan policy, although their chances of winning influence may be better with one party than with others. However, the distinction between pressure groups and social movements is fluid, since many pressure groups also engage in propaganda directed at the broad masses of voters in order to gain the support of public opinion.[21] Many social and political reforms were the result of such pressure tactics employed by organized groups out-

[21] For a detailed classification of pressure groups in the United States see A. Cousens, *Politics and Political Organizations in USA* (New York, The Macmillan Company, 1942), pp. 26 ff. On the rôle and technique of pressure groups see V. O. Key, *Politics, Parties, and Pressure Groups* 2nd ed. (New York, Thomas Y. Crowell Company, 1947), Chap. 7.

side the legislatures. The great reforms of 1832 and subsequent years in England were largely brought about in this way. The Anti-Corn Law League was a pressure group in the wider sense. Groups like this are indispensable and were particularly important as long as no party organizations existed except in Parliament.[22]

In the United States, pressure groups are a characteristic element of the political system. Since there are no special elections and since legislators are elected for terms of two years or more, between elections politicians are compelled to gauge the sentiments and opinions of voters by any means available. This furnishes an opportunity for minority groups to create the impression that they represent a powerful block of voters. In the absence of a definite mandate from the voters and of guidance and discipline from the party leaders, American legislators are perhaps more inclined to listen to pressure-group lobbyists than legislators in Europe.

> Congressmen succumb to pressure by organized minorities not because the pressure groups are strong, but because Congressmen see no reason for fighting [them] at all: the party neither disciplines them nor supports them.[23]

We pointed out in Chapter 8 that the various groups of businessmen tend to be associated with different political parties because they have different and often antagonistic interests concerning such matters of economic policy as foreign trade or domestic railway freight rates. But, as employers of labor, their interests tend to be alike. Employers' associations, in distinction from manufacturers' and other businessmen's associations, therefore tend to pursue a nonpartisan policy with regard to all parties (except of course

22 M. I. Ostrogorski, *La Démocratie et l'organisation des partis politiques* (Paris, Chalman-Levy, 1903), pp. 43 ff., 135 ff.

23 Elmer E. Schattschneider, *Party Government* (New York, Farrar & Rinehart, Inc., 1942), pp. 193-196. See also his article, "Pressure Groups versus Political Parties," *The Annals of the American Academy of Political and Social Science* (Sept., 1948).

the labor parties). Under the American two-party system this has been practically a necessity, but the same policy has been pursued in European countries, even in Germany before the Hitler régime.[24]

Labor Unions

Labor unions are, as mentioned before, more or less closely affiliated with political parties in all countries where socialist, communist, or labor parties exist. In this kind of situation, the unions, the party and the consumers' coöperatives form the three major divisions of the labor movement; this is the case, for example, in Great Britain and Sweden. The situation in Germany, before Hitler, was more complicated. The largest group of unions, the Free Trade Unions, were closely affiliated with the Social Democratic Party. Their officers usually belonged to both organizations, and the majority of the rank and file voted the Social Democratic ticket and many held S.P.D. membership cards. After 1918, however, the Independent Social Democrats and later the Communists gained members among the Free Trade Unions.

Furthermore, there existed since the latter part of the nineteenth century a federation of Liberal trade unions whose main strength lay with white-collar workers, and finally there were the Christian trade unions which, although

[24] The first association of industrial employers in Germany to advocate independent political action was the *Verband Sächsischer Industrieller,* founded in 1902 and directed for a long time by Gustav Stresemann, later foreign minister. This organization at one time controlled almost one-third of the members of the second chamber in the legislature of the highly industrialized state of Saxony. The national employers' association (*Verein Deutscher Arbeitgeber-Verbaende*) acted as a non-partisan organization of all industrial and commercial employers irrespective of their party affiliations, and supported reliable friends of employers in elections in complete neutrality. It was pointed out by the association that the like interests of employers in issues of labor policy and labor legislation were more important than their divergent interests in such matters as foreign trade agreements. The latter, it was argued by one of the association's spokesmen, are raised only every ten or twelve years, while labor relations problems are the employer's daily concern and are almost constantly at issue in the legislatures.

interdenominational, were closely affiliated with the Center Party. The largest block of their Protestant membership was contained in the *Deutschnationaler Handlungsgehilfenverband*, a powerful organization of commercial employees, which had strong nationalistic rather than Catholic leanings.

Where such an affiliation to a party exists, the unions are faced with the problem of including among their membership political dissenters who are nevertheless loyal unionists. Where the Communist Party has gained mass support among the workers of a country, a much more serious problem arises for the unions, which is not so easy to solve. Generally speaking, the solution has been, in western Europe and Scandinavia, to keep union membership and party membership separate, leaving it to the individual union member whether he wants to join the party with which the union is affiliated or not. The union's functionaries, on the other hand, are party members, and party functionaries who are eligible do hold union cards. There are joint boards and committees on all levels and there are usually other organizational bonds, such as joint operation of newspapers and union-party office buildings and assembly halls.[25]

The European pattern of union-party affiliation was abandoned in the American Federation of Labor at the insistence of its founder and long-time leader, Samuel Gompers.[26] Although himself a socialist, Gompers saw that to pledge American unionists to a political doctrine which presupposed a class-conscious proletariat would severely limit the recruiting possibilities of the unions. He realized that unions, in order to become effective in collective bargaining, had to organize all workers in a given trade, irrespective of their political opinions. Consequently, political issues and political cleavages such as those between the various socialistic and

[25] For Sweden, see R. Heberle, *Zur Ideengeschichte der Arbeiterbewegung in Schweden* (Jena, 1925).
[26] See Chap. 9.

communistic groups, had to be banished from the internal activities of the unions. On the other hand, since unions would inevitably be concerned with matters of legislation, they had to win influence in state legislatures and in Congress. In view of the insignificance of the socialist parties in the United States, this could be done only by working through the major parties. Thus, a technique of political action was developed which consisted, briefly, in (1) supporting candidates who had shown that they were friends of organized labor, and (2) refusing endorsement of candidates with anti-labor records. In addition, the representatives of the A. F. of L. would attend the national conventions of both parties and attempt to attain pro-labor commitments in the platforms.

Some unions were socialistic in their ideology, like the Amalgamated Clothing Workers, and individual labor union members and functionaries were quite often active in one or the other party, especially on the local and state levels. Many of the state secretaries of labor, and some of the U. S. Secretaries of Labor, were union leaders. But on the whole, and in principle, there prevailed in the A. F. of L. an attitude of distrust of government; that is to say, the leading men had more confidence in collective bargaining and self-help (for example, old-age pensions from union funds) than in state aid and labor legislation. The result was that political action within the framework of non-partisan policy tended to be limited to matters of immediate concern to unions. A major deviation from this policy occurred in 1924 when the A. F. of L. supported Robert M. LaFollette's candidacy for president. The result was a defeat so devastating that A. F. of L. leaders returned to strict non-partisan policy in subsequent years.

A new phase in organized labor's relation to the political parties began when in 1943 the C.I.O. formed a Political

Action Committee; the A. F. of L., aroused by the Taft-Hartley Act, followed in 1947 with the establishment of Labor's League for Political Education. Now each of the top organizations, including the Railway Brotherhoods, has its particular agency for political action.

The new feature in the policy of the C.I.O.P.A.C. is the great intensity of campaigning and the broad range of issues included in its legislative program or platform. There is no longer any hesitancy in taking a stand on matters of foreign policy and other issues which the older school of American labor leaders would have regarded as outside the sphere of sound non-political unionism. The C.I.O. considers political action through legislation as more expedient than trade-union self-help or Gompers' tactics of direct pressure upon, and negotiation with employers. The strategy of the C.I.O. to get labor union functionaries elected to various party committees and conventions, from the precinct up to the national conventions is also new, as is the policy of encouraging members to run for elective public offices. In summary, the C.I.O.P.A.C. has departed decidedly from the Gompers tradition in the A. F. of L.

The A. F. of L.'s League for Political Education is patterned after the P.A.C. and differs from it only in minor points. Like the P.A.C., it is a permanent organization which functions not only at election time but continuously. This is a significant innovation. The first purpose of the L.L.P.E., like that of the P.A.C., is to "get out a large vote in every election." [27] Realizing that this requires intensive "campaigning of local union officers and rank and file members at the grass roots in each district and precinct," the L.L.P.E. duplicates the machinery of the P.A.C.: leagues or committees are set up on local, state, and congressional district levels. The local leagues have to remain "completely independent and

[27] Minutes of the National Committee of L.L.P.E. (Oct. 5, 1949), p. 7.

non-partisan." [28] In other words, if in a district where organized labor has traditionally supported the candidates of one party the opposing party presents a more acceptable candidate, labor will be asked to vote for the latter, irrespective of existing ties between local unions and the machine of the first party. But endorsement of candidates will come, if possible, in open primaries or in any case before the nomination. No longer will organized labor be content with voting for the "lesser evil": "We want candidates who will win and who will vote for liberal legislation and repeal the Taft-Hartley Act on Capitol Hill." This means that the local leagues have "to make sure that able and liberal candidates are brought forth in either or both parties." [29] The L.L.P.E. stresses also the community of interest between farmers and labor, emphasizing the experience in the political arena "that the enemies of labor are also the enemies of the farmer." Political coöperation with farm groups, therefore, "is not only possible but it is the key to victory on election day." [30]

Differences in structure and tactics between P.A.C. and L.L.P.E. arise from differences in the structure of the two parent organizations. The structure of the A. F. of L. is more that of a confederation of autonomous internationals, and the Federation has less control over member organizations than the C.I.O. has. Because of the craft union heritage, the number of member unions in the A. F. of L. is larger than in the C.I.O. and the membership is not, as in the C.I.O., concentrated in a few mammoth unions. There are a few very large unions, but they cannot dominate A. F. of L. policy as the Auto Workers and Steel Workers can in the C.I.O. Consequently, the A. F. of L. and Labor's League for Political Education avoid taking a stand on issues on which not all member unions are agreed—for example, the basing-

[28] *Ibid.*, p. 8.
[29] *Ibid.*, p. 10.
[30] *Ibid.*, p. 6.

point system on which the Cement Workers defend the cement industry interest.

A further deviation from the Gompers tradition shows up in the more systematic and intensive efforts for spreading information on political issues among the union members and other groups. In particular, there is more systematic evaluation of legislators' voting on issues with which labor is concerned, and the spreading of this information among constituents is improved.

In summary one may say that the new techniques result in the creation of a continuous political-action movement within the unions. Officially the P.A.C. and L.L.P.E. are entirely separate organizations, but actually a great deal of coöperation exists on all levels, particularly in local communities. Even at top levels there is consultation between the two agencies and with the political committees of other labor groups.[31]

When one considers the implications of this mobilization of the rank and file of union members for political action, one begins to wonder whether this may not be the beginning of a labor party in the United States. So far, all spokesmen of organized labor definitely reject the idea of a labor party. They point out that no party which appeals to one particular

---

[31] In view of the fact that it was largely the Taft-Hartley Act which gave the stimulus to the new type of political action, the following news item concerning organized labor's political action in Senator Taft's state is interesting:

"Columbus, Ohio.—Philip Hannah, secretary-treasurer of the Ohio Federation of Labor, is co-chairman of the newly formed United Labor League of Ohio spearheading the drive to defeat proposed changes in the state's voting laws in November.

The league represents, 1,200,000 trade unionists in Ohio belonging to the Ohio State Federation of Labor, Ohio CIO Council, United Mine Workers, International Association of Machinists, Communications Workers of America, Brotherhood of Locomotive Firemen and Enginemen, Brotherhood of Railroad Trainmen, Brotherhood of Locomotive Engineers, Order of Railway Conductors, Brotherhood of Railway Clerks and Maintenance of Way Employes." From *A. F. of L. Weekly News Service Supplement* (Oct. 28, 1949).

economic-interest group can hope to win a presidential
election, since the candidate would not only need a majority
of the popular vote, but a majority in the electoral college
as well. Under the present system, states with large proportions of wage workers tend to be under-represented in the
electoral college. The C.I.O.P.A.C. therefore "advocates election of the President of the United States by direct vote of
the people." [32]

In spite of the rejection of the labor party idea, there are
many indications that the American working class, under the
leadership of labor unions, is becoming increasingly aware of
political interests, both in the short- and long-run perspective.
The influence of organized labor in the major parties is considerable, especially in the Democratic Party, and the labor
vote is a factor which all political candidates and office
holders have to take into consideration.

The non-partisan policy, originally conceived as a safeguard of unity within the ranks of organized labor, has not
prevented very bitter and disrupting schisms within some
unions, especially among those which belong to the C.I.O.
The bitterness of the animosity between the pro- and anti-
communist factions within the C.I.O. unions is primarily due
to the right wingers' resentment of the way in which the communists use their influence in the unions for political ends
which are set by the Communist Party of America (or by
the Politburo) and which are not often objectives which a
majority of union members would approve. The presence of
Democratic Socialists in labor unions, on the other hand, has
never caused serious trouble, since the Socialist Party has
not attempted to gain control of labor unions.

[32] Dillard Stokes, "Direct Election of the President," *Presidential Elections:
The Twenty-Third Annual Debate Handbook* (1949), p. 155.

14

Historical Trends and National Variations in Party Organization

COMMON BEGINNINGS

GENERALLY SPEAKING, modern political parties originated as factions or caucuses in the elected legislatures and as committees and clubs among the voters. In order to understand the social processes involved, one has to remember that in all countries concerned there had been in existence parliaments composed of status groups or estates. The English House of Lords is a direct descendant of these. In the assemblies, the nobility and higher clergy sat in person, in contrast to the third estate, the burghers, who were represented by the delegates of cities. The peasants were represented in Scandinavian parliaments but not in England, France, or the German principalities.

When these parliaments of estates were replaced by elected legislatures representing the people on the basis of a more or less universal and equal franchise, the individual legislator was free of all formal group affiliation. Theoretically, he represented the people at large, not any social or territorial group of them. Anybody who has had some experience in the operation of assemblies which pass resolutions and legislate will know that it is impossible to conduct business unless at least some of the members have come to an understanding beforehand about the election of officers, and about general policy concerning the issues which are to come

303

before the whole body. And everybody who has sat in such assemblies knows that a small, well-knit group, which has a definite policy and operates and votes accordingly, will be in a position to dominate the meetings. This is the quintessence of a legislative caucus.[1]

Theoretically, the legislative caucus is one source from which parties develop, for no sooner has a caucus started to operate, than there will arise at least one opposition caucus. Actually, the caucuses developed usually from religious and class groupings outside the legislature. In all constitutional assemblies and legislatures of the eighteenth and nineteenth centuries, the estate groupings were thus replaced by free, voluntary factions or caucuses. These had little formal organization, but were flexible, loose circles, gathering around the more outstanding men in the assembly and often named after their leaders, or after their meeting-places in coffee houses or taverns. The nature and the number of these divisions depended upon the issues.[2]

When factions developed in the legislature, similar groupings appeared among the voters; but in Great Britain and in the American colonies, political clubs existed even before and independently of parliamentary factions.[3] In colonial

[1] Elmer E. Schattschneider, *Party Government* (New York, Farrar & Rinehart, Inc., 1942), pp. 40-44, give an excellent analysis of a caucus.

[2] The two-party system, the origin of which has been the object of much speculation, seems to be the most logical system sociologically. Since in any political body—city or state—a ruling oligarchy is bound to develop, an opposition is likely to arise of those who do not belong to the ruling élite; as long as the mere antagonism against the "ins" is strong enough to hold the "outs" together, a two-party system will arise. It may be concealed in the form of cliques among the status groups (the nobility, and so on) or it may be public and nationwide where representative government exists. If, however, strong and irreconcilable clashes between economic class interests arise within one of the two parties, it may split—and a three-party system is born.

[3] The earliest British club was that of the Presbyterian opposition to William III of Orange, which dominated the Scottish parliament and had close affiliations with the Jacobites in England. It is significant for the structure of seventeenth-century Scottish society that this club was really a federation of clans. This illustrates, incidentally, the importance of kinship

America, the movement for independence, organized in the Committees of Correspondence, became the first political party which completely dominated the Continental Congress, constituting "a dictatorship of the insurgents." [4]

In France, as in England, the custom of coffee-drinking which spread over Europe during the eighteenth century, seems to have had a stimulating effect on party formation. Coffee-houses became the gathering points of political clubs.[5] Another basis of political organization in France was the Masonic Lodge. Many of the lodges sent their officers as delegates to the provincial assemblies in 1787, and in 1789 the lodges all over France transformed themselves from secret societies into public political clubs.[6] The example of the British and French political clubs was later imitated in the United States.[7]

In Germany, where the modern type of legislature came into being after the revolution of 1848, the structure of parties followed the French pattern of loosely knit parliamentary groups which were paralleled by political clubs and associations among the voters. (The parties were those in the National Constitutional Assembly at Frankfort-on-the-Main in 1848 and in the diets of the various states.) The turn towards elaborate organization of voters and strict discipline within the parliamentary groups came much later.[8]

---

and religion in the early phases of party formation in Great Britain. Wilhelm Wachsmuth, *Geschichte der politischen Parteiungen*, Vol. III (published 1853-1856), p. 43.

[4] E. E. Robinson, *The Evolution of American Political Parties* (New York, Harcourt, Brace & Company, Inc., 1924), pp. 33-36.

[5] M. I. Ostrogorski, *La Démocratie et l'organisation des partis politiques*, Vol. I (Paris, Chalman-Levy, 1903), p. 143. See also H. Cunow, *Politische Kaffeehaeuser* (Berlin, Dietz, 1925).

[6] Claudio Janet, "Les Francs-Maçons pendant la révolution," *Revue de la révolution*, Vol. I, No. 4 (Paris, 1883), pp. 278-280.

[7] Charles A. Beard, *The Rise of American Civilization*, Vol. I (New York, The Macmillan Company, 1927), p. 384.

[8] The historian of the German *Zentrumspartei*, Karl Bachem, relates that the consolidation of the members of his party in the Prussian Diet of 1852

It seems that during this period everywhere in Europe and even in America the progressive parties made more use of formal clubs and associations than the conservative parties. The latter, representing the ruling forces, could easily rely on informal relations among the leading land owners and prominent businessmen in each election district and also on the aid of the bureaucracy, whereas the middle-class parties whose supporters were less interrelated through primary groups needed more formal organization. However, most of the early political clubs and associations of constituents were rather informal groups, without membership dues, and without formal requirements and procedures of admission.

THE DEVELOPMENT IN ENGLAND

A radically new phase of party organization was initiated in England with the reorganization of the Liberal Party after the pattern of the so-called Birmingham Caucus in the late 1870's. There had come into existence registration societies which attempted to mobilize the masses of voters whose size had been increased as a result of the Reform Acts of

---

into a *Fraktion* (caucus) through a formal order of procedure and the elaboration of a program was something new in the party life of that time. Until then the parliamentary groups had been mostly loose followings of outstanding personalities; he claims that the Catholic *Fraktion* had been the first "to show the way towards a sound caucus formation."—Karl Bachem, *Vorgeschichte, Geschichte und Politik der Deutschen Zentrumspartei*, Vol. II (Köln, 1927), p. 109.

The same author, speaking of conditions about ten years later, mentions the "lack of a developed system of political clubs (*Vereine*)" as a disadvantage for the Center Party.—*Ibid.*, p. 209.

After the founding of the new German Empire in 1871, the Center Party was reorganized for representation in the National Parliament (*Reichstag*) of the Catholic interests; this time the organization grew from the "grassroots," through conferences, peasant societies, and the *Katholiken-Vereine*. —*Ibid.*, Vol. II, pp. 21, 49.

Bachem gives a great deal of valuable, sociologically interesting information about organization and structure of the party in the *Reichstag* and among the constituents.—*Ibid.*, Vol. III, pp. 127 ff.

1832 and 1867.[9] The Liberal Association which Joseph Chamberlain founded in his home city of Birmingham in 1868 was a new type of organization and was therefore regarded with apprehension by the older school of politicians— Liberals and Conservatives alike. It signified the end of the notables' parties and the beginning of highly centralized mass parties with rather strict discipline and large staffs of professional functionaries.[10] It was an innovation of general sociological significance.

Birmingham Caucus

The essential objectives of the Birmingham Caucus were to activate as many liberal voters as possible and to concentrate their votes in a way which would secure majorities for the Liberals in as many districts as possible. This was important because the voting system gave advantages to the Conservatives. Contrary to the oligarchic American caucuses of the time, the Liberal Association was a step toward the democratization of the British Liberal Party; it was launched by the radical opposition within the party against the resistance of the Whigs.[11] On the other hand, the new system served also to coördinate the Liberal vote in local elections. The "Six Hundred" of the Liberal Association, determined

[9] Ostrogorski, *op. cit.*, Vol. I., p. 143.

[10] W. A. Rudlin, "Political Parties in England," *Encyclopaedia of the Social Sciences* (New York, The Macmillan Company, 1942). "Extra-parliamentary organization on the modern scale began virtually with Chamberlain's highly disciplined Liberal Association in the late 1870's. The success of the Birmingham association led to the general adoption of similar measures by both parties.... The part played by the central offices has become increasingly more important...."

[11] J. L. Garvin, *The Life of Joseph Chamberlain,* Vol. I (London, Macmillan & Co., Ltd., 1932), p. 253 and *passim.* Garvin claims, in criticizing Ostrogorski's interpretation, that "the caucus system as organized by him [Chamberlain] in this country [England] owed nothing whatever to American example." He points out that Birmingham had been a strong center of unions, clubs, and various schemes for national political action since before the Reform Bill of 1832. This tradition was revived after passing of the Reform Bill of 1867.

to direct the liberal vote most rationally, resorted, therefore, to "vote-as-you-are-told" tactics.[12]

The Birmingham Liberal Association was based on formal membership (although no dues were required in its beginning) and on a system of membership representation on various levels. The rank and file elected ward or district committees and these sent elected delegates to a central council (the so-called Six Hundred in Birmingham) which became the policy-making body for the city.[13] Later on, when Liberal Associations had been established in other districts and had formed a National Federation, national Liberal conventions were held. The Birmingham organization grew out of a local tradition of civic action on a democratic basis and was intended to mobilize and activate the masses not merely at the polls but to let them participate in nominations and in formulation of policies. The Birmingham organization met much criticism from the older generation of politicians because, in Chamberlain's words, it "puts aside and utterly confounds all that club management and Pall Mall selection which has been going on for so long." [14]

The new organization also introduced stricter discipline into the Liberal Party. As one critic said, "the Liberal voters are no longer free lances but armies of disciplined men." [15]

[12] *Ibid.*, p. 255.

[13] "The Liberal Association which organises this vast majority [in Birmingham] is actually the whole Liberal constituency, every Liberal having right of membership on expressing his readiness to accept decision of majority after fair discussion. No subscription is required, and it happens that three-quarters of the great committee of the 600 are workingmen." From a letter by Chamberlain to Morley, Nov. 25, 1876, *ibid.*, p. 258.

[14] "The opponents of the Caucus are not to be convinced—they hate it for its virtues—because it puts aside and utterly confounds all that club management and Pall Mall selection which has been going on for so long and which has made of the Liberal Party the molluscous, boneless, nerveless thing it is. The Caucus is force, enthusiasm, zeal, activity, movement, popular will and the rule of the majority—the Seven Deadly Sins in fact." From a letter by Chamberlain to Morley, Sept. 29, 1878, *ibid.*, p. 263.

[15] W. Fraser Rae, "Political Clubs and Party Organization," *Nineteenth Century* (May, 1878), p. 921.

The same critic observed that the Birmingham organization seemed to have been fashioned after the American system and would lead "to the creation of a new avocation, that of the politician" which "honest men despise and condemn." He felt that the new form of organization would require more time than good professional men or businessmen could afford to give; the only people who would give their time would be those who were unable to get patients or clients, or artisans and mechanics after their daily work was done. In other words, Rae deplores the passing of the gentleman-politician and fears the rise of people who instead of living for politics would have to live off politics. "When politics become perfectly organized, politicians are thoroughly demoralized." [16]

Another objection was that the central Liberal Association allowed itself the right to recommend candidates, even nonresident persons, the objection being that this would put the party "into a strait-jacket." Another critic feared that the new organization would weaken the contacts between voters and their representatives.

> They would practically be unknown to each other, and would never really come in contact. It is the Caucus, and not the mass of nominal electors [whom they controlled] that the M.P. would regard as his real constituents. . . . He would in fact become their [the Caucus'] delegate.[17]

The new system proved to be so efficient that it was adopted by every party in Great Britain and Ireland.[18] In the course of time, however, the oligarchic tendency, so characteristic of all mass organizations, prevailed, and the system "was more and more used by all of them [all parties] to deter

[16] *Ibid.*, p. 924.

[17] "The Government and the Opposition," *The Edinburgh Review* (Jan., 1879), pp. 132 ff.

[18] "The Caucus, gathering in new workers and improving all former arrangements, polled Liberal voters to the last available man, and undoubtedly turned the scale in many constituencies where Liberals won by a narrow margin." Garvin, *op. cit.*, p. 281.

or crush personal independence." [19] Even Chamberlain experienced conflict with his own creation and was forced to secede, whereupon he formed the Radical Union. [20]

One important factor in this schism among the Liberals was that the professional organizer for the Liberal Association, M. Schnadhorst, took a stand against Chamberlain. Generally, the paid organizers or agents who form the backbone of party organization, were restricted to supervising the registration of voters, organization of meetings, raising of campaign funds, and so on. "There is no class comparable to them in the U.S.A. or on the Continent of Europe." They are professional electoral experts, not politicians; they are not in competition for mandates or offices and they do not participate in policy-making—at least not in the Conservative and Liberal Parties. The Labor Party often entrusts to the secretary of the local trade union council the functions of a party agent, and such a man is definitely in politics. [21]

Centralization

The extension of the franchise to virtually all adult citizens, which occurred in two major acts of 1911 and 1919, increased the need for formal organization and led to a growth of party bureaucracy. At the same time the size and importance of the Central Office increased and became "the focal point of party control. . . . This is especially true of the Conservative and Liberal Parties, where all electioneering work is done by the Central Office and its subordinates in the constituencies," [22] rather than by the local associations. In the Labour Party, "where the annual Conference really amounts to something," the Central Office is controlled by the National Executive,

[19] *Ibid.*, p. 264.
[20] *Ibid.*, pp. 217-219.
[21] H. F. Gosnell, *Why Europe Votes* (Chicago, University of Chicago Press, 1930), pp. 27 f.
[22] James K. Pollock, Jr., "British Party Organization," *Political Science Quarterly*, Vol. 45, No. 2 (June, 1930), pp. 161 ff.

which is elected by the party conference. Control of candidacy rests with the Central Office, or in the Labour Party with the National Executive; all candidates must be sanctioned by these central agencies and all candidates are expected to accept the policy of the leader of the party. "The M.P., when elected, is expected to support in Parliament the policies of the party as laid down by the leaders." [23] Party discipline in the Commons, which had been strong since the 1870's, was greatly strengthened by the mid-twenties.

Bureaucratization

Along with centralization went bureaucratization. The Central Offices employ

large staffs of trained workers covering the country in systematic fashion, performing the multitudinous tasks which a good party organization must perform. There are also provincial branches, of the Conservative Central Office, for example.... Hundreds of full-time paid workers, usually the most experienced ones ... are selected to do this work, and they do it under Central Office guidance.[24]

The result has been a lessening of the influence of local constituencies in control even of their own affairs, but especially in matters of nomination of candidates and selection of agents. In all three major parties, responsibility for party organization and discipline outside Parliament and inside Parliament rests with different officers, but in all of them the central party organizations have become more powerful. This is, according to Pollock, a consequence of the increase in the power of the Cabinet. The scope of party activity has greatly increased through the formation of youth organizations which began in 1908, and through the increased use of press and publicity, all of which require a large number of trained and paid party workers.[25] Obviously, urbanization, the enlargement of the constituencies, and the firm estab-

23 *Ibid.*, p. 165.
24 *Ibid.*, p. 166.
25 *Ibid.*, pp. 179 f.

lishment of party government have been the major factors contributing to the centralization of control and the bureaucratization of the party offices. The Labour Party, which was originally a federation of trade unions and various socialistic groups, is still largely controlled by the trade unions. But the introduction of individual membership has made it easier for persons not belonging to the working class to become members and to exert influence in the central offices of the party.

DEVELOPMENT OF AMERICAN PARTY STRUCTURE

The structure of the major American parties was in the beginning very similar to that of the European parties, but later they developed quite different patterns. In the growth of American party organization one can, with Charles Beard, distinguish four phases: (1) the period of informal caucuses in colonial times; (2) the period of legislative caucuses and committees of correspondence after the revolution; (3) the period of state conventions after 1824 and of national conventions after 1832; (4) the period of legal regulation of parties and of direct primaries.[26]

Four Periods

In the colonial period, and even during the first decades of independence, voters belonged largely to the property-owning and educated classes and were few in number, so that little formal organization was needed. The political leadership by men prominent through wealth and education was accepted as a matter of course in the communities.[27] The political ruling class took it for granted that only men of eminence were qualified to occupy leading positions in the

[26] Charles A. Beard, *American Government and Politics* (New York, The Macmillan Company, 1944), p. 157.

[27] Edward M. Sait, *American Parties and Elections,* (New York, Appleton-Century-Crofts, Inc., 1927), pp. 238, 241.

parties, and they resented any action which involved the political activation of the masses. The Federalists in particular, as the party of wealthy merchants and planters, relied on informal connections much longer than the Republicans who, much to the distress of their adversaries, began to organize the masses for county and state nominations.

Furthermore, there were significant regional differences. The development of party machinery in the South was delayed, as Ostrogorski has pointed out,[28] because the small upper class of planters, merchants, and professional men could easily control the elections. However, in the more stratified North, where the lower middle classes entered politics, and also in the more equalitarian West, where ties of family and class were weak, more formal organization was needed and actually did develop at an early date.

Before the building of railroads it was quite difficult in this vast country to assemble delegates from local voting areas and party clubs for any large state or for the nation as a whole; therefore control of the parties stayed for a long time in the hands of members of Congress and state legislatures. When population density increased and travel conditions improved, an intermediate control-institution was developed: the state convention, in which the constituents as well as the parliamentary factions were represented. Since all party work was done either by honorary workers—that is, people of some leisure—or by professional politicians, the party structure was definitely oligarchic. No change in this situation occurred when national conventions of elected delegates were introduced between 1832 and 1852.

The voters' attempts to establish control through legal regulation of party organization and direct primaries, which began about 1890, had an unfortunate result: "the parties lost the right to determine their own membership and [could] at any time be invaded, looted, despoiled of their

[28] Ostrogorski, *op. cit.*, Vol. II, pp. 111-112.

leaders, and driven into an utterly new course." [29] None of the major parties controls membership by formal admission and payment of dues. On the other hand, in most states, a public declaration of party affiliation or preference is sufficient to establish a voter's right to participate in the direct primary. This registration is a unilateral act and does not establish a mutual relationship of rights and duties between the voter and his party. The party cannot reject a bona fide registrant, nor can it expel a voter who in the election votes for the candidate of another party. This is the strange result of well-intended attempts to curb, by legislation, the inherent tendency towards oligarchy or boss rule. The boss—typically a politician who does not hold public office and therefore is remote from popular control—is necessary to coördinate party activities, especially nominations, under a constitutional system which prevents the formation of a strong national party leadership and which, at the local level, tends to decentralize power rather than to centralize it.

Characteristics of the American Parties

One of the fundamental differences between the British and the American political systems is that the British parties must at all times be ready for an election, whereas in the United States elections come at definite intervals; American parties therefore do not need a large permanent administrative staff.[30] This is true at least on the national level. On the state and municipal levels, elections occur more frequently and the large number of elective offices to be filled requires a great deal of preparatory work. But on those levels, effective party work can be done to a large extent by volunteer workers under the direction of professional politicians. The result is that while the state and municipal party

[29] Sait, op. cit., p. 106; also Theodore W. Cousens, Politics and Political Organizations in America, (New York, The Macmillan Company, 1942), pp. 350, 358.

[30] H. F. Gosnell, op. cit., p. 35.

organizations are very closely knit machines—though not much bureaucratized—the national party organizations are comparatively loose federations.

Patronage

The bond of patronage, which is lacking in no party organization, has gained much greater significance in the major American parties than in the ideologically differentiated parties of Europe. This is due to the absence of definite and distinguishing ideologies, as well as to the weakness of statutory disciplinary power of party leaders, including the President (or presidential candidate).

Patronage is perhaps the strongest bond which holds municipal and state machines together; it is also one of the strongest bonds in the national party organizations, especially in the Democratic Party, where the President's power of patronage constitutes the most effective device of disciplining the Southern branch of the party.

Let us assume that a political party can be held together by four factors: ideas, institutional or legal authority, charismatic leadership, and expectation of material advantages in case of victory (that is, patronage in return for services rendered to the victorious party). It is clear that a party which has no control over its membership and no ideology will have to rely on the third and fourth factors, and this is obviously the case of the two major American parties. Similar tendencies were observable in the German Center Party (the Roman Catholic Zentrumspatrei). As a religious party it comprised voters of all classes, and its immediate political aim was to secure the position of the Roman Catholic Church in the new empire. This achieved, the party developed largely into a patronage party, because patronage was essential in overcoming cleavages between Catholic manufacturers, Catholic trade unionists, and Catholic farmers. The German National Liberal Party (*Nationalliberale*

Partei), in the period of its decay between 1900 and 1914, when its original aim—the establishment of a unified *Reich*—had been accomplished, began deliberately to substitute public office patronage for the defunct ideological bond.[31] Patronage means giving not only offices but government contracts and other tangible rewards for services rendered to a winning party.

The fact that American political tradition adheres to the principle of nominating only persons who are residents of their election district—in contrast to the British practice—tends to strengthen the patronage power of local and state leaders and bosses. Hence, the tendency to divide each national party into numerous semi-independent state and local organizations. The two major national parties may therefore be considered to be loose alliances of state machines "to win the stakes of power embodied in the presidency."[32] Today they are structurally very different from the British political parties, which have gone through a development towards ever greater centralization of control in their parliamentary leaders.

The essential importance of patronage, incidentally, is also one of the most effective obstacles for third-party movements. Nobody who is in politics, in the sense that he expects a tangible pay-off for his campaign services, is likely to render such services to a party whose chances of winning are extremely slight.

We have seen before that the class basis of the two major American parties varies between regions and communities (Chapter 9); we have now shown and explained the significance of personal loyalty to patronage-wielding bosses and leaders. Consequently, it should be clear that the often lamented traits of the major American political parties (lack

---

[31] Theodor Eschenburg, *Das Kaiserreich am Scheideweg* (Berlin, 1929).
[32] A. W. MacMahon, "Parties, political; United States," *Encyclopedia of the Social Sciences*, Vol. II, p. 596.

of definite ideas, boss rule, and the spoils system) are closely interrelated with (1) the absence of effective control over party membership, (2) with the relatively fluid class structure of American society, and (3) with certain constitutional limitations, especially in presidential elections. The minor parties, which cannot expect to gain control of the federal or even a state government, have no patronage to offer and therefore rely upon principles and doctrines as uniting bonds. Consequently, they exert a rather strict control over membership. To become a member of the Socialist Party, for example, one has to endorse in writing the constitution and platform of that party, to renounce all relations with other parties, and to pay annual dues.[33]

It is the peculiar structure of the major American parties which enables them to act as political brokers for various special-interest groups and enables them to absorb major and minor social movements by incorporating their immediate goals into party platforms. The alternatives would be either a close affiliation of each political party with certain special-interest groups, as in the German multiple party system before the Nazi régime (a system which is now emerging once more) or a system of loosely organized political groups representing different political tendencies more or less in agreement in regard to particular interests, as in France.

THE GERMAN PARTY SYSTEM

The German party system was characterized from the beginning by a close correlation between parties and social classes, and, as a consequence, by an increasingly rigid affiliation of parties with economic interest organizations. This was hardly concealed by the strongly emphasized party ideolo-

[33] Harold R. Bruce, *American Parties and Politics* (New York, Henry Holt & Company, Inc., 1927), p. 244. About the Communist Party, see below, Chap. 15.

gies and programs. Party organizations became elaborate, comprising many auxiliary organizations, and party bureaucracy became more and more developed, especially under the Weimar Constitution. At the end of the Republic, all parties had established formal party membership based upon the payment of dues, and party discipline was strictly enforced.

Each of the German parties had an official program which took a stand on all important political issues and was from time to time revised. The discussion about program revisions was a major event at the annual or biennial party congresses, particularly at those of the Social Democratic Party. These programs were not mere platforms consisting of immediate demands and promises calculated to catch votes; they were based upon the political philosophies of the parties.

Tendencies in the Pre-Hitler Period

The typical traits of German political parties in pre-Nazi days [34] can best be demonstrated by two opposites: the Social Democratic Party (S.P.D.) and the Conservative Party (later German National Party or *Deutschnationale Partei*). The Social Democratic Party, being rather strictly Marxist, was, roughly speaking, a working class party closely affiliated by dual and triple membership with the trade unions (*Freie Gewerkschaften*) and consumers' coöperatives, which were developing simultaneously with the party and were sponsored by it. The party was one branch of the socialistic labor movement. Consequently,[35] it had to rely from the beginning on membership dues for financing, and on paid, full-time secretaries and clerical staffs for administrative work. Its large group (*Fraktion*) in the *Reichstag* as well as the groups in state legislatures were subordinate to the party congresses and to the party's elected central com-

[34] A good analysis of the organization of German parties is given in Karl Stumpf. *Die Struktur der modernen Partei und ihre Stellung im Staate,* Dissertation, Jena, 1934.

[35] That is, in the absence of wealthy contributors.

mittee (*Partei Vorstand*); further, each legislative member was obliged to abide by the majority decisions of the *Fraktion* (group in the legislature). This was a general characteristic of the structure of the parties of the left.[36]

Thus the individual parliamentary representative of the party was subject to: first, the authority of the officers of his *Fraktion;* second, to the authority of the central committee (*Vorstand*) of his party, and in the last instance, to the authority of the party congress. Since most of the Social Democratic legislators were dependent for a living on some kind of office or job in the party organization or in other branches of the Social Democratic movement, party discipline could be enforced quite strictly. As long as the election districts were small enough to be thoroughly worked by a candidate, as was the case before 1918, a member of the *Reichstag* who had held his seat for a couple of legislative periods could preserve a good deal of independence even if he did not belong to the leading circle in the party. After 1919, however, under the new system of proportional representation, election districts became much too large to be intensively canvassed by a candidate. Therefore the power of the central committee of the party increased and members of the *Reichstag* and of state legislatures became less independent. This tendency was reinforced by the technique of voting for a list of candidates on the party ticket rather than for individual candidates; the number of votes cast for the party determined the chances of candidates down the list. This was, with modifications, the general trend in all German parties. In addition, the special-interest groups were gaining in direct influence, since the new election system with its long lists of candidates gave them an even better opportunity to get their leading officers elected. In 1930, before the first great success of the N.S.D.A.P., the personnel of the *Reichstag* comprised (1) a large proportion of trade-union

[36] R. Heinen, "Fraktionen," *Staatslexikon* (1927).

secretaries—both Socialist and Catholic, (2) a large proportion of *syndici* of employers' and manufacturers' associations
as well as (3) representatives of various farmers' organizations.[37]

The Conservative Party was in philosophy, class basis, and
structure the exact opposite of the S.P.D., and yet it developed a very similar structure. The constitutive ideas and
the origin and initial structure of the Prussian Conservative
Party have been treated in Chapter I. It has been pointed
out that, at an early stage, very close affiliations developed
between this party and various farmers' associations and that
towards the end of the second empire the Agrarian League
(*Bund der Landwirte*) had gained control of the party. During this period of seventy years (1848-1918), the party was
not in need of bureaucratic, that is, professional administrative, staffs. Its leading members were men of wealth and
sufficient leisure; they could rely upon bonds of kinship
and neighborhood, their authority as land owners, and their
connections with the state bureaucracy (civil service)
through kinship, friendship, and power, to reach the rank
and file of voters.[38]

After 1918, when the franchise had been extended to
women, when the discriminatory class system of voting had
been abolished in Prussia and when the party spread all over
Germany and gained the support of urban big-business
circles and middle-class nationalists, it became necessary to
change the form of organization. Formal membership was
introduced, with dues moderate enough to permit impecuni-
ous clerks, professional people, and even students to join.
Paid full-time party secretaries were employed (many an

[37] The beginning of this trend was noticed and discerned by Emil Lederer
before the First World War. See Emil Lederer, "Das Ökonomische Element
und die Politische Idee im Modernen Partei-Wesen," *Zeitschrift für Politik*,
Vol. 5 (1912), pp. 535 ff.
[38] Erich Jordan, *Die Entstehung der Konservativen Partei und die
preussichen Agrarverhältnisse von 1848* (Muenchen, Leipzig, 1914).

ex-army officer found a new career in this way) and students
and other youth groups as well as women's groups were organized. By 1928, that is to say, within eighty years after
its foundation, the Conservative Party had developed from
a regional party of the rural gentry to a nationwide party supported by property owners, entrepreneurs, and salaried employees. From a small organization relying mainly on primary
group relations, it had developed into a mass organization
run by more or less professional politicians and paid administrative staffs. This entire structure burst asunder during
the next five years, partly because its leader, Hugenberg,
did not understand the art of reconciling divergent economic
interests within his party and partly because many of the
younger members were attracted by the more militant Nazi
movement.

The Party Press

The picture of German party structure would be incom-
plete if the relation between political parties and the press
were overlooked. Each major party owned and controlled
at least one big daily newspaper with nationwide circulation
and many regional and local papers. The Conservative Party
was the first to acquire a newspaper, but the Social Democratic Party probably had the most complete network of
party newspapers.

Pressure Groups

Pressure groups also existed in Germany, but they were
probably less numerous than in the United States for the
simple reason that the parties themselves were so closely
allied with special economic interests. Broader issues, however, were sometimes taken up by large pressure groups
and propaganda organizations, like the Colonial Society
(*Kolonial-Verein*), the Navy Association (*Flotten-Verein*),
and the Land Reform League (*Bund der Bodenreformer*)—

organizations which in true pressure-group fashion created a public opinion and attempted to win influence with various more or less congenial parties in the national parliament.

Resurrection of Party System Since the Second World War

Since the fall of the Hitler régime in 1945, political parties in Germany have been resurrected under the Allied Military Government. The most striking feature is the revival of the multiple-party system. By 1949 more than thirty party names could be listed.[39] This large number is explained partly by the fact that military governments prohibited the formation of nationwide organizations and permitted parties only on a state or zone basis, and partly by the election system which retains most of the provisions of proportional representation of the pre-Hitler system, though with modifications in the British Zone. Proportional representation does not necessarily produce a multiple-party system, but it makes it easier for any group to develop its own party organization. In the last analysis, the German multiple-party system is a product of the complex class structure of German society and of the large variety of issues over which political dissension could develop. Underneath this multiplicity of parties can be discerned the same basic tendencies and attitudes which determined the German party system in pre-Nazi days.

In contrast to the period of the Weimar Republic, party membership in the Western zones is small in proportion to the general following of the parties—probably only about 2 per cent. Indifference seems to be great among the young people in spite of party efforts to re-establish youth organizations.[40] The publication of party newspapers was prohibited

[39] Klaus Mehnert and Heinrich Schulte, *Deutschland-Jahrbuch 1949* (Essen), pp. 60 ff.

[40] *Ibid.*, p. 68. In the Soviet Zone, where the Socialists and Communists are merged into the Communist-controlled Socialist Union Party (S.E.D.) and the other parties have been compelled to join the S.E.D. in a bloc which comes very near a single party system, participation in political

in the American Zone, but all parties publish some kind of periodical. The forms of party organization are regulated by military government and state law. Each party is democratically organized from precinct or local community level to state level, and working agreements exist between the various state party organizations.

Generally speaking, the German parties were and still are characterized (1) by the emphasis placed on political *Weltanschauungen* on the one hand and the close affiliation with economic-interest organizations on the other hand, (2) by the resulting strong correlation between social classes and party preferences (see Chapters 8 and 11) and, structurally (3) by elaborate formal organizations and relative weakness of the party leaders' position. One might say that, while the individual representative was subject to strict party discipline, the parties, except for the N.S.D.A.P., were led by committees rather than by personalities.

THE FRENCH SYSTEM AND ITS CHANGES

Late Development of Formal Organization

The structural development of political parties in France during the second republic was very different. Like the economic structure whose development had been arrested after an early start towards modern industrial capitalism, the French party system, with a few exceptions, represented the earlier phase of party development: loosely knit parliamentary groups which permitted the individual *député* or *sénateur* a high degree of independence from the party machine. One exception was the Socialist Party (*Parti Socia-*

---

activities is greater; the trade unions are integrated with the bloc on all levels, and since the Communists control the unions, a great deal of pressure to attend meetings can be exerted upon individuals. Employees in the socialized plants, civil servants, and other government workers are required to attend party meetings, political indoctrination courses, and so forth.

liste) which in 1904 was reorganized after the pattern of the
German Social Democratic Party in compliance with instructions from the Second International of Amsterdam.[41]
The other exception was the Communist Party, which in
1920, under the influence of the Third International (Moscow), had separated itself from the Socialist Party and
adopted "a régime of foreign origin," which will be discussed
later.

Seignobos, to whom we owe one of the best descriptions
of party structure in France, compares the organization of
the German Social Democratic party and the *Parti Socialiste*
to that of the Catholic church

... with its councils (*conciles*), its clergy, its dogmas and excom-
munications. ... This kind of organization places these two parties in
contradiction with the French tradition, according to which the representative is responsible only to his electors. The interference of a
party machine with the decisions of certain groups of *députés* has
caused a revolution in the political life of France.[42]

Apart from these two exceptions there were no parties in
the American, English, or German sense. There were factions
in the legislature, but as far as the voters were concerned,
there were only the tendencies or movements characterized
by the intentions of the candidates. The faction was a definite
formation: it had a chairman, a meeting place, an agenda,
and sometimes even a program. Its name was known, and
so was the number of members, for since 1910 the Committees of the *Chambre des Députés* were elected on the principle of proportional representation; and since 1914 the
groups were seated in the chamber according to their general
political shadings. The tendency on the other hand is only a
loose community of opinions and sentiments.[43] We might
say they are political movements rather than real parties.

[41] Charles S. Seignobos *Études de politique et d'histoire* (1934), p. 357.
[42] *Ibid.*, pp. 357-58.
[43] *Ibid.* See also André Siegfried, *Tableau des partis politiques en
France* (Paris, B. Grasset, 1930).

The older parties in France, as Seignobos describes their structure,

> ... have never had a central committee, nor a national convention, nor an officially recognized chief or party directorate, nor a program, nor discipline, nor a press, nor a treasury—in short, no organization of the voters or of the *députés*.
>
> In an election, each candidate presented himself with his personal profession of faith; he paid his own election expenses; eventually he might have the support of a temporary local committee and of a local paper published by him or printed at his expense. Frequently the candidate had himself nominated by an assembly of local delegates. But he chose at his will his political label; he could at his will call himself a liberal, democrat, republican, radical or socialist without being obliged, on account of the label, to follow a determined political line.
>
> In the Chamber, the *député* joins a group which pleases him or remains outside any group if he prefers, or he can pass from one group to another when he wants.[44]

There was no compulsion to participate in group conferences or to adhere to the group's resolutions. Even if he had participated in a caucus decision, he retained the freedom to abstain from voting in the house or to vote against his group's majority. In both houses of the legislature these groups represented unstable formations which split or merged with others, or changed their names, sometimes even during one and the same legislative session. "This is possible only because the members of a group are not tied to it by restrictions of discipline or by a personal bond to a chief who is recognized by all, or by any pledge made to the voters." Seignobos and André Siegfried agree that the tendencies were deeply rooted and durable, the factions, temporary affairs. The voters had little concern with the latter, but they would scrutinize the *tendence* of the candidate.[45]

We have encountered some of these *tendences* in the preceding chapters where we discussed their geographical dis-

---

[44] Seignobos, *op. cit.*, p. 355.
[45] Seignobos, *op. cit.*, p. 359. Compare also Jules Véran, *Comme on devient: Député, Sénateur, Ministre* (Paris, 1924).

tribution and their relationship to the social classes. It has been observed [46] that this very freedom of the candidate serves to maintain the notion that the *député* or *sénateur* is the representative of all citizens and thereby to preserve the "sentiment of democratic unity." And as a matter of fact, the *député* would feel and act as the trustee of the entire population of his district, even to the point of supporting petitions of political adversaries before the minister.[47] In other words, the multiplicity of parties and their frequently changing alignments should not be interpreted—as is often done by foreign observers—as a sign of discord.

However, the days of such loose and flexible structures were counted when the Socialists introduced the new party type. Then the Radical Socialists (who were really less radical than the usual Socialists) felt compelled to follow their example, with the result that the party was split over the issue of party discipline.[48] Some of the other parties also introduced formal membership lists and membership cards.[49]

However, membership *per se* did not mean much. In order to be really in politics one had to belong, not to a formal club, but to the local cercle of the party, that is, a group of *camarades* who met regularly in a café.[50] From this cercle was usually recruited the local party committee, which in turn sent delegates to the various cantonal, departmental, and national congresses of the party. It is significant that nominations were, among the parties of the right, often made by "a few gentlemen meeting in a drawing room," whereas

[46] R. P. Rohden, *Demokratie und Parteien* (Wien, Seidel and Son, 1932) p. 145.
[47] *Ibid.*, p. 140.
[48] *Ibid.*, p. 127. A number of politicians seceded from the two socialist parties and formed the *Indépendents de la Gauche* (The Independents of the Left), who refused to be told how to vote.
[49] For example, the *Alliance démocratique* and the *Fédération républicaine;* Véran, *op. cit.*, p. 28. See also Emile Veysset, *De la nécessité des partis organisés en régime parlémentaire* (Paris, 1933).
[50] Véran, *op. cit.*, p. 29.

candidates of the left parties had to have the official endorsement of the departmental party convention. Campaign expenses were moderate; the candidates themselves usually paid for drinks or gave a few dinners, except for the Socialists, who were the guests of their electors.[51] Generally speaking, until the Second World War, the French parties, at least those which were supported by the bourgeoisie, the petite bourgeoisie, and the farmers, had not changed much in structure since the beginning of the nineteenth century. This was possible largely because of the smallness of election districts, which permitted thorough canvassing and personal acquaintance of a candidate with his constituents. This was probably also possible because of the rule that in run-off elections only a simple majority or plurality was required.

Post-war Developments

Since the end of the Second World War, the tendency towards formal and disciplined party organization has gained momentum by three important developments: the growth of the communist movement and the participation of the Communist Party in post-war coalition governments; the organization of a Catholic, essentially Christian socialist party—the *Mouvement républicain populaire* (M.R.P.)—whose organization is deliberately shaped after the Communist Party pattern;[52] and the emergence of a militant nationalistic movement under a quasi-charismatic leader, Charles de Gaulle. The M.R.P., which was recruited from an older Catholic party, from Catholic youth organizations, from the resistance movement, and from disintegrating liberal groups, is small in organized membership and so heterogeneous in its following that really strict party discipline has never been enforced.

[51] *Ibid.*, p. 44.
[52] Gordon Wright, *The Re-Shaping of French Democracy* (New York, Reynal & Hitchcock, 1948), p. 76.

Structure and organization of communist movements and parties will be discussed in the next chapter. A word should be said here about the de Gaulle movement.

It is not at all unusual that a victorious general becomes a political leader, nor is it unusual that a defeated nation turns to a popular general for political leadership, or that a military leader attempts to gain political leadership in a defeated nation; Boulanger in France after 1871 and Ludendorff in Germany are two well-known cases. Hindenburg's presidency was of another type: he did not seek leadership but was drafted by the conservatives, so he can scarcely be regarded as a political leader—he was a symbol. However the case of de Gaulle does not fit into these categories.

During the war, that is, after France had been vanquished and had made peace with the victor, this general in exile, who had not held a high command in the field and was unknown outside military circles, became, by agreement with the British prime minister, "supreme commander of a French force of volunteers." He proceeded to form a kind of government in exile (the *Comité National* of September, 1940), declared the legitimate government of France as non-existent, and demanded that the Allies recognize him and his *comité* as a political power representing France. Although these political ambitions were curbed, he became a demi-god for the French resistance and, after the liberation, he became president of the French state, supported by a coalition of the Communist, Socialist, and Catholic parties. Without a definite political program, but favoring a form of government in which power is concentrated in the hands of the president, he resigned when the political currents seemed to go against him. Actually rejected by an electorate suspicious of politically ambitious generals, he then assumed the rôle of the "Savior in withdrawal," [53] the charismatic leader who is wait-

[53] The term is borrowed from Arnold J. Toynbee, *A Study of History* (Oxford, Oxford University Press, 1947).

ing for his hour. In the meantime, fascistic and anti-republican elements among his followers formed the de Gaullist Union, without gaining the sanction of their hero. After his estrangement from the left-wing parties, de Gaulle assumed the leadership of this movement—renamed *Rassemblement du Peuple Français* (*R.P.F.*)—ousting its founder, René Capitant, from the leading position and installing his own henchman Soustelle.[54] Within a few months, the new movement was able to claim nearly a million followers, and in municipal elections it won almost 40 per cent of the vote. Like the Republican régime of Weimar origin in Germany about 1930, the Fourth Republic was now threatened by the Communists on the one side and the de Gaullists on the other. The Communists' strength lay not only in their very capable leadership but also in their control of the trade unions. The strength of the R. P. F. lay in the still enormous prestige of its leader and in the resentments, disillusionments, and fears of the bourgeoisie and petite bourgeoisie. In the fall of 1947 the chances of survival for Western democracy in France looked rather bleak.[55] Today—in the spring of 1951—it seems that the republican tradition has reasserted itself and that democratic constitutional government is saved once more.

The Communist Party, because of its increasingly obvious dependence upon Moscow, has lost much of its former support among the intellectuals and among the middle classes, while it is still a force in big cities and the centers of mass-production industries.[56] De Gaulle has lost a great deal of

[54] Gordon Wright, *op. cit.*, p. 252.

[55] *Ibid.*, pp. 256-57.

[56] On Communist influence in trade unions, see Joseph Mintzes, "Labor Movement Developments in France, 1944-49," *Monthly Labor Review*, Vol. 69, No. 1 (July, 1949). The officially neutral, but actually socialistic *Confédération Générale du Travail* (CGT) fell under Communist domination after reuniting with Communist unions at the end of the Second World War. Politically motivated strikes in 1947 under Communist direction led to secession of non-communist minority in December, 1947 and formation of CGT-FO (Workers' Force). Communist-dominated CGT has its main strength among semi-skilled and unskilled workers in heavy industries, construction,

middle-class support, because of his more and more apparent megalomania and because of the barely concealed fascism of his entourage.

Summing up, we may say that the French political scene today is characterized by a surprising persistence of traditional political attitudes or tendencies; by the survival of a multiple-party system which gives to French governments the appearance of instability but would permit a strong leader to rally the republican and democratic forces in a coalition of the center; and by the continuation of pre-war tendencies toward more elaborate and centralistic organization in the political parties.

---

railroads, and the textile industry. CGT-FO support comes mainly from skilled and white-collar workers.

15

The Totalitarian Movements and the New Political "Orders"

THE NEW PARTY TYPE

THE CONCEPT OF PARTY in the modern sense implies the willingness to recognize an opposition. A genuine party, as we have pointed out before, is considered as part of a larger whole; parties intend to gain influence in, but not to become identical with, the larger corporate group. The willingness to compromise logically follows from this proposition. It is characteristic of a democratic government that the party in power realizes the necessity of reaching compromises with the opposition. We shall discuss the functions of parties in detail in the last part. Here it is sufficient to point out that government by parties rests on these presumptions and that it works only where a community of basic political values exists among all groups participating in political action.[1] Democratic processes cease to function when powerful groups in a society abandon the idea of compromise and seek absolute domination.

The present crisis of Western democracy, which began approximately with the First World War, has brought about the rise of movements and parties of a new type which cannot be regarded as genuine parties at all since they deny

[1] See Chap. 20 for more detailed discussion. A recent treatise on the subject is Sebastian de Grazia, *The Political Community, a Study of Anomie* (Chicago, University of Chicago Press, 1948).

opposing groups the right of existence and have, where they came to power, established one-party régimes of a radically new character.

As soon as the Fascist régime was established in Italy in 1922, observers were impressed with the great structural similarities between it and the Bolshevist régime in Russia, as well as with its similarities to the structure and procedures of the fascistic and communistic movements in other countries. The structural similarities between the two great ideological antagonists were so fascinating that the differences in structure, which follow from the antagonism in ultimate goals, have been almost overlooked.

Before we go into these matters, we may attempt to give an idea of the significance of these two movements. A study of the single-party systems made about 1935 [2] listed the following totalitarian régimes and parties: the Communist Party in Russia, in power since 1917; the People's Republican Party in Turkey, in power since 1919; the Fascist Party in Italy, in power since 1922 and legally recognized as single party since 1928; the N.S.D.A.P. in Germany, in power since 1933; the National Union in Portugal (1933); and the Spanish Falange—at that time still fighting for control. Apart from the communist parties which existed in practically every state, dominion, and colony, the study listed nineteen totalitarian, fascistic movements in Denmark, Norway, England, Belgium, Holland, Switzerland, Austria, Hungary, Rumania, and Bulgaria. One might have added the Kuomintang in China, and one could now add the Peron régime in Argentina, the de Gaulle movement in France (discussed in the last chapter) and the communist régimes in the satellite countries of eastern Europe—including that of the heretic Tito—and the recently established communist régime in China. Of the five major powers, only three have retained democratic multiple-party systems.

[2] Mihail Manoilesco, *Le Parti unique* (Paris, 1936).

Although proposing different political philosophies, all of these movements and parties are alike in their discontent to rule on the basis of the majority principle and claiming or striving for absolute and exclusive power. The régimes which they have established attempt to regulate all spheres of social life, every kind of social activity and to control every kind of group and institution, not leaving neutral any spheres —private or political. Hence the designation as *totalitarian* movements and parties.

We have seen that in all modern parties there exists a trend toward more definite organizational integration of supporters, a tendency towards oligarchic leadership and a trend toward strict party discipline. The parties of the new type have all these characteristics in a higher potential, so to speak. Instead of being open to as large a membership as possible, they choose their members according to highly selective standards, the guiding principle being that of the creation of an élite of political activists (see Chapters 4 and 5). Members are methodically indoctrinated with the movement's constitutive ideas not by free discussion, but by drill, and the right of dissension is denied. No opposing faction is tolerated within the party, no criticism of valid decisions taken by party leaders is permitted. Party discipline is much more strictly enforced, and expulsion from the party involves much more serious consequences than in old-style parties, especially when the totalitarian party is in power. On the other hand, voluntary resignation from the party in power is virtually impossible, and resignation from a party struggling for power is not without serious risks. The oligarchic character of party leadership is not only frankly recognized, but theories of party function are developed which justify the establishment of a hierarchy of functionaries in which authority is delegated from the top downwards, though in the conception of the nature of authority, differences exist between the communist and fascistic parties. The new pattern was set by the Russian Bolshevists and later imitated by anti-communist movements. We shall therefore begin with an analysis of the structure and organization of communist parties.

THE COMMUNIST MOVEMENT

In order to avoid misinterpretations of the relationship between goal and structure in the communist movement, it is important to remember that the communist parties which are recognized and authorized by the Third International—now the Cominform—do not constitute the entire communistic movement; there are, in almost every country, the Trotskyites and other minority groups. In these groups, certain of the principles of organization of the regular communist parties are rejected: the Trotskyites, as a rule, insist on more freedom of discussion.[3] It is quite safe to say that a communistic society does not necessarily have any intrinsic relationship to the authoritarian structure of the communist parties which belong to the Third International; nor does Marxism necessarily lead to the formation of authoritarian parties. This new party type was largely the creation of Lenin, and a product of the political situation in Russia as he saw it.[4]

[3] James P. Cannon, *The History of American Trotskyism* (New York, Pioneer Publications, Inc., 1944).

[4] Of the early communist movement in the United States, James P. Cannon says that, since a very large part of the proletariat were foreign born, the Communist Party was dominated by leaders whose "minds were not really in the U.S.A. but in Russia," who were "absolutely unfamiliar with the American economic and political scene" and "did not understand the psychology of the American Workers." It was in the rival organization, the Communist Labor Party, that the native Americans and americanized foreign born dominated (pp. 5 ff.). From this latter group, which later merged with the Communist Party but retained its identity as the Cannon faction, the American Trotskyist movement, which was initiated by Cannon in 1928, was to draw its main strength. *Ibid.*, pp. 35, 50.

Tendencies in Western European Marxism

In order to gain the proper perspective of the Bolshevist principles of organization, we will have to survey briefly the earlier forms of organization in the communist and socialist movement. In the first decades of the nineteenth century, Communists and Socialists (the names were used almost synonymously) in all countries were compelled to work more or less in secrecy. Few in number, they formed study circles and other small groups. Their structural models were the secret societies of the Free Masons and in Germany the patriotic leagues like the *Hainbund*, the Turners' League, and certain semi-secret student fraternities. The secret communistic societies in France were characteristic of this phase of the movement; among them was a group of German socialist craftsmen living in exile in Paris—the Federation of the Just (*Bund der Gerechten*). After the failure of Blanqui's insurrection in 1839, this society moved to London. Together with other groups of German revolutionary workers in exile in London, Brussels, and Paris, this group founded the Communist League (*Bund der Kommunisten*) in 1847.[5]

When Karl Marx and Friedrich Engels joined the Communist League in 1847, they found a predominantly favorable attitude toward Blanquist conspiracy and a tendency among the leaders to ascribe unlimited authority to the Central Committee of the League. This was a natural outgrowth of the idea that a communist social order could be established simply by a *coup d'état*. Blanqui and his followers believed that a conspiracy among a small élite of workers would be a sufficient preparation for revolution, while Marx and Engels were convinced that a successful revolution could be staged only by an organized mass movement of class-conscious proletarians and only when the society in which

[5] G. M. Stekloff, *History of the First International* (New York, International Publishers Co., Inc., 1928), p. 16.

the movement operated had become ripe for a revolution.[6]

Although Marx's and Engels' writings are by no means free of controversial statements on this point, their conception of the communist movement was certainly opposed to the conspiratory tradition. The controversy between them and the revolutionary anarchist Bakunin led to the early end of the First International (1864-1872). By 1900 an evolutionary and essentially democratic conception of the proletarian movement had become predominant in the socialist parties in western and central Europe.

This was not merely a fruit of Marxism but even more a consequence of the rising power of the trade unions. The latter, essentially democratic in structure and led by men who were primarily concerned with immediate, tangible results in the advance of labor, were equally averse to revolutionary adventures and to personal leadership of radical intellectuals. Many of the intellectuals had realized in the meantime that Marx had over-estimated the tempo of disintegration of the capitalistic society. Revisionism (see Chapter 4) and confidence in gradual ascent to power through democratic processes characterized the Social Democratic parties in Germany and other Western countries.

Lenin's Party Model

In Russia, the situation was different. There, the Social Democratic party consisted mainly of students and intellectuals, most of whom did not seriously want to go beyond a bourgeois liberal democracy. The masses of workers, although already engaged in direct conflicts with the employers, were not yet thinking in terms of a revolution leading to a socialist order.

In this situation Lenin proposed the creation of a new type of party. This would be a cadre of hand-picked professional revolutionaries, trained in Marxist theory and willing to de-

[6] Compare Otto Bauer, *Die illegale Partei* (Paris, 1939), pp. 20-33.

vote their entire lives exclusively to political action.[7] Neither
the masses of politically untrained wage earners nor the
democratic intellectuals should be admitted to the party. This

[7] Lenin's conception of the structure of the Communist Party can be traced
as far back as the year 1900. In that year he wrote in an essay, "The Urgent
Tasks of Our Movement," as follows:

"We must train people who shall devote to the revolution [sic] not only
their spare evenings, but the whole of their lives; we must build up an
organization so large as to be able to introduce division of labor in the
various forms of our work." (*Collected Works*, Vol. IV, Book I, p. 56.) In
other words, Lenin was not satisfied with a socialist party in the ordinary
sense; he wanted an organization of professional political activists (revolutionaries, not merely holders of socialistic ideas); and he wanted specialists
in the various tactical methods of preparing and executing a revolution. Two
years later he formulated his ideas as follows:

"The fact is, of course, that our movement cannot be caught precisely
because it has hundreds and hundreds of thousands of roots deep down
among the masses, but that is not the point we are discussing. As far as
'roots in the depths' are concerned, we cannot be 'caught' even now in spite
of all our primitiveness; but, we all complain of the ease with which the
organizations can be caught, with the result that it is impossible to maintain
continuity in the movement. If you agree to discuss the question of catching
the *organizations*, and stick to that question, then I assert that it is far more
difficult to catch ten wise men than it is to catch a hundred fools. And this
premise I shall defend no matter how much you instigate the crowd against
me for my 'anti-democratic' views, etc. As I have already said, by 'wise men,'
in connection with organization, I mean *professional revolutionists*, irrespective of whether they are students or workingmen. I assert: (1) that no movement can be durable without a stable organization of leaders to maintain
continuity; (2) that the more widely the masses are drawn into the struggle
and form the basis of the movement, the more necessary it is to have such
an organization and the more stable must it be (for it is much easier then for
demagogues to side-track the more backward sections of the masses); (3)
that the organization must consist chiefly of persons engaged in revolution
as a profession; (4) that in a country with a despotic government, the more
we *restrict* the membership of this organization to persons who are engaged
in revolution as a profession and who have been professionally trained in the
art of combatting the political police, the more difficult will it be to catch the
organization; and (5) the *wider* will be the circle of men and women of the
working class or of other classes of society able to join the movement and
perform active work in it.

".... we can never give a mass organization that degree of secrecy which
is essential for the persistent and continuous struggle against the government. But to concentrate all secret functions in the hands of as small a
number of professional revolutionists as possible, does not mean that the
latter will 'do the thinking for all' and that the crowd will not take an active
part in the movement."—Lenin, "What Is to Be Done?" *Collected Works*,
Vol. IV, Book II (New York, International Publishing Co., Inc., 1929) pp.
198-199.

was the issue over which the Russian Social Democratic party split into *Mensheviki* and *Bolsheviki* since 1903. The Menshevist party developed after the pattern of western social democracy; the Bolshevist party became an organization of professional revolutionaries, highly skilled in the techniques of illegality and trained in Marxist theory. A Central Committee which resided abroad in exile exercised unlimited control and authority over the members, who had to accept what assignments were given to them. The party was deliberately kept small, but it carried its propaganda into the masses through workers' study circles, trade unions, clubs, and benevolent societies. In these organizations, the Bolshevists operated as disciplined factions (*Fraktionen*) under the commands of the Central Committee. "Thus the Central Committee led the Party; the Party, the trade unions, . . . and these the working class." [8]

The organization which Lenin created was thus an outgrowth of two peculiar political and social conditions under which the socialists had to operate in Russia. First, it grew out of a political régime which forced the party to resort to tactics of illegality and compelled most of its leaders to live in exile; second, it grew out of a state of socio-economic development which produced a great deal of social unrest but prevented the masses of workers from acquiring the intellectual and political maturity which would have been the prerequisite of a socialist mass movement and of a democratic form of party organization.

Since Lenin calculated that the proletarian revolution in Russia would be accompanied by a revolt of the peasants, the leaders of the revolution would have to direct practically illiterate masses.[9] The leaders would have to be men and women well educated in Marxism—intellectuals, but at the

[8] Otto Bauer, *op. cit.*, p. 48.
[9] Sir John Maynard, *Russia in Flux* (New York, The Macmillan Company, 1942), p. 367, suggests that in his ideas regarding the peasants, Lenin was under the influence of Russian Populism. See Chap. 4.

same time activists willing to serve like soldiers in the vanguard of the revolution. Lenin knew very well that few intellectuals are fit for this kind of political action; thus his insistence upon a highly selective and strictly disciplined party.

In 1909 when he conducted a school of communism in Paris, Lenin told students who had come from another communist school (Lunacharsky's, on Capri, Italy), "You won't find intellectual liberty and right of private judgment here." [10]

The new party type was deliberately conspiratorial. Again and again Lenin called it this to denote the difference between the Bolshevist party concept and that of the Menshevists and the revisionistic Social Democrats in Germany. [11] One might say the new type amounted to a regression, a relapse into Blanquist and Bakuninist principles. This was not so strange in a society which, as we have explained before (Chapter 4), never knew the Western meaning of freedom of conscience, of opinion, or of legitimate opposition. But the fact that the Bolshevist idea of party prevailed and persisted in the first large socialistic society to be established is a fact of tremendous historical significance. For, after the successful revolution and the establishment of a socialist régime in Russia, the new party type became the pattern which was imposed on communist parties everywhere, regardless of the political traditions of the country.

[10] Quoted by Sir John Maynard, *ibid.*, p. 137.

[11] "Only an incorrigible utopian would want a *wide* organization of workers with elections, reports, universal suffrage, etc., under autocracy. The moral to be drawn from this is a simple one. If we begin with the solid foundation of a strong organization of revolutionists, we can guarantee the stability of the movement as a whole, and carry out the aims of both Social-Democracy and of trade unionism. If, however, we begin with a wide workers' organization, supposed to be most 'accessible' to the masses, when as a matter of fact it will be most accessible to the gendarmes, and will make the revolutionists most accessible to the police, we shall neither achieve the aims of Social-Democracy nor of trade unionism; we shall not escape from our primitiveness, and because we constantly remain scattered and dispersed, we shall make only the trade unions of the Zubatov and Ozerov type most accessible to the masses."—Lenin, *op. cit.*, p. 194.

Organization of the Communist Party
in the United States

By way of illustration, we may consider the organization of the Communist Party of America.[12] On the local or shop level, members are organized in clubs; on the state level, members are organized in state organizations or in districts comprising two or more states. The highest authority of the party is, according to the constitution, the National Convention, which meets at least every two years, and is composed of delegates elected by the state and district conventions. Actually, the National Committee, which is elected by the Convention, and which "has the right to make decisions with full authority on any problem or development facing the party between conventions" has more power. It elects the National Board, which carries out the decisions of the Committee. The Committee meets at least three times a year, whereas the Board is continuously in function. The latter is therefore bound to be the real seat of control. It corresponds to the Politburo of the Russian Communist Party.

The first constitution of the Communist Party of America defines as eligible to membership "every person who accepts the principles and tactics of the Communist Party and of the Communist International" except such persons who have "an entire livelihood from rent, interest, or profit." Certain classes of government employees in politically important positions are also disqualified.

Applications for membership must be endorsed by two members of the party, and all applicants are placed on probation for a period of two months. Of greatest significance is the rule that only persons who "agree to engage actively in the work of the Party shall be eligible to membership. It is the aim of [this] organization to have in its ranks only

[12] A description of the organization of the Communist Party of France is to be found in A. Rossi, *A Communist Party in Action*, W. Kendall, ed. (New Haven, Yale University Press, 1949).

those who participate actively in its work." [13] The last point is most important, because it constitutes a fundamental difference in the structure of the Communist Party as compared with the traditional party, which was well satisfied if members paid dues and voted for the party's candidates.

Methods of Recruiting

One cannot become a member of a communist party except by joining and working actively in a local group. This is in accord with a principle pronounced by Lenin in 1903 against Menshevist proposals. Lenin thought that individual membership would swamp the party with irresponsible intellectuals, impair its class character, and encourage opportunism. The full significance of the membership rules of the communist parties will appear when they are considered in connection with the methods of recruiting new members. It is the duty of communist party members to be constantly on the look-out for prospective recruits, but on the other hand, precautions have to be taken, in most countries, against the infiltration of police agents and other undesirable individuals into the party organization. Therefore the psychological fitness of a prospective new member has to be investigated as well as his social qualifications. He must be an activistic type and he must not be encumbered by social connections which would become a source of danger to the party. Therefore biographical data on each prospective member have to be submitted to the personnel officers of the party, and psychological reports on him (or her) are requested.[14]

The first approach to a prospective recruit can of course be made in many different ways, depending upon the partic-

[13] Constitution of the Communist Party of America of 1919, Chap. III, Sec. 1.

[14] Rossi, *op. cit.*, relates that when the Communist Party of France went underground in 1941 (after the German attack on the U.S.S.R.), it requested an elaborate biographical report from each member, based upon a detailed questionnaire that left no side of the member's private life untouched. Rossi reproduces the questionnaire on pp. 167-169.

ular situation and also on the strategic position of the party;
it can be open in a country where the party is already a large
and powerful organization; it has to be more or less clandestine in a country where the party operates in semi-legality,
and it has to be made with extreme caution in a situation of
illegality (when the party is an underground organization).
Special emphasis is placed on the recruiting in industrial
plants, where the communist cells serve as recruiting agencies.[15]

A particular problem is the admission of intellectuals.
From the very beginning a tendency in the Communist Party
has been to keep the proportion of intellectuals small in order
to preserve the proletarian character as well as the militant
spirit of the party.[16] The Communists have developed an
elaborate technique of recruiting new members through
groups outside the party: trade unions, reading circles, discussion groups.[17] Obviously, this technique has the advantage that the approach can be made inadvertently and that
the prospect can be observed as he behaves within a group.
If the recruit is an intellectual, the approach is likely to be
one of rational, critical discussion of social conditions and political issues of the day. During the period of illegality of the
party in Germany under the Hitler régime, contacts of this
kind were often made in anti-Nazi discussion circles camou-
flaged as mere friendly social gatherings or as musical evenings in private homes. A communist would participate in a
circle of this kind where his party membership was unknown
and where his political views were never scrutinized in detail; he would then approach those members of the circle
who seemed to be most determined in their opposition to the

[15] G. Antonow, *Die Erfahrung der KPdSU(B) bei der Regulierung des
Wachstums und der sozialen Zusammensetzung der Partei* (Moskau, 1933),
pp. 64 ff.
[16] *Ibid.*, pp. 9, 19. Lenin's distrust in the revolutionary elan of intellectuals
was not unopposed.
[17] *Ibid.*, pp. 19, 20.

Nazi régime and most likely to accept the communist interpretation of the political situation. These prospects were then
exposed to more definitely Marxist-Leninist views. If the candidate responded favorably, he might be asked to join the
party. If he hesitated, it might be made clear to him that as
a man of communist conviction, he should show less concern
about his family and other private affairs and devote himself
entirely to the great cause.

The value of a recruit depends of course not only on his
personal qualities but also on his social position; an important
official in an important ministry may be worth considerable
effort in this conversion process. Converts in such positions
of public service are, however, sometimes not given a membership card; their name is merely carried on a secret roster,
which is kept by the party. This is done especially in situations where the member would lose his position if the fact
of his party membership became known.

In a situation of legality, recruiting can be done on a large
scale through party-sponsored youth organizations—a device
which is in our day used by all kinds of parties.

The principle of active participation which converts the
party into a militant organization of professional revolutionaries may also be applied in testing the reliability and loyalty
of new members and at the same time as a means of binding
them to the party. Although the assignments are usually in
the field of propaganda (distribution of handbills, participation in demonstrations, conducting discussion groups outside
the party),[18] they may be of a more serious nature. In the
Canadian spy case, for instance, according to the Royal Commission's report,

... within a very short time what had been merely a political discussion group, made up of Canadian scientists as members of a Canadian
political party, was transformed on instructions from Moscow into an
active espionage organization working against Canada on behalf of a

[18] *Ibid.*, p. 74.

foreign power. [The report adds;] it is particularly startling that none of the initiative for this transformation was supplied by the three scientists themselves.[19]

The Canadian case is especially interesting because it demonstrates, through the testimony of participants, how persons who would never have stooped to do espionage work for money were so conditioned psychologically to loyalty to the Communist cause, that when they were told the Canadian Communist Party needed certain confidential or secret information, they furnished the information, apparently without ever considering the possibility that it might be wanted for espionage purposes.

Indoctrination

The indoctrination which forms part of the conversion process is continued after formal admittance into the party. Each party member is obliged to devote one hour a day to the reading of Marxist-Leninist literature, which now includes of course the writings of Stalin.[20] But the most effective indoctrination is achieved in small study groups which are organized on each party echelon under a leader, and which serve as seminars for the training of additional instructors.[21]

We have used the term *indoctrination* on purpose, because these study courses within the party treat Lenin's and Stalin's

[19] "The Report of the Royal Commission to investigate the facts relating to and the circumstances surrounding the communication, by public officials and other persons in positions of trust, of secret and confidential information to agents of a foreign power" (Ottawa, Controller of Stationary, June 27, 1946), p. 48.

[20] Rossi, *op. cit.*, pp. 207 f. Rossi contends that every Communist must read the *History of the Communist Party of the Soviet Union (Bolsheviks)*, prepared under the personal direction of Stalin, "and learn it by heart." Rossi's contention that "having once learned it by heart, no Communist is required to study anything else" seems a biased exaggeration. Among the books to which a particularly ambitious comrade may be referred, is the *Communist Manifesto*. By neglecting to mention this, Rossi gives the impression that Marxism is abandoned for Stalinism.

[21] *Ibid.*, p. 209.

writings as revelations of absolute and final truth. Since the groups are small and have no connection with one another, except through vertical channels, any deviation from the orthodox doctrine can easily be detected and prevented from spreading.

In this respect the communist (Bolshevik) movement has again much in common with the fascist movements. However, it must be said that within the N.S.D.A.P. a great deal of ideological controversy existed, probably mainly because of the vagueness of the National Socialist ideology. On the other hand, the official indoctrination bestowed upon party members and members of affiliated organizations through official instructors was often of an intellectual quality far below even the poorest communist levels.

Discipline

In order to maintain a high degree of militancy, discipline, and ideological uniformity, the new parties resort from time to time to mass expulsions or purges. The more spectacular purges in the Soviet Union and satellite countries have attracted much attention because of the bloodshed connected with them; they were directed mainly against old revolutionaries (some of them former Menshevists) who were accused of having committed heresies or of having conspired against the party leaders. However, there have also been numerous mass expulsions among the rank and file of insufficiently active members and of opportunists who had joined the party during one of the membership drives after the party's seizure of power.[22]

Of course, outside the orbit of Soviet Russia's sphere of influence, purges are a much less serious matter; however, for

[22] Antonow, op. cit. Walter Duranty, Stalin and Co.—The Politburo (New York. William Sloane Associates, Inc., 1949, p. 85), states that during the great purge in 1936-1938, about two-thirds of the leading Communists in the Soviet Union were removed from public life by expulsion or execution; the two-thirds ratio was applied on all levels, down to the locals.

a professional politician to be cut off from his party office, from party funds and, in case of expulsion, from association with his political friends, is a hard fate. No wonder then that even outside of Soviet Russia party discipline is quite strictly maintained.

The Communist Party of America entrusts the maintenance of party discipline to the National Review Commission (Art. VIII of Constitution of 1945) which "shall consist of tested members with exemplary records" and at least five years of active membership in the party.[23] The N.S.D.A.P. had a corresponding commission which exercised jurisdiction within the party.

The essential sociological peculiarity of the communist parties becomes even more manifest in times of repression when a party is forced to work illegally. It then assumes an entirely different scheme of organization: small units of not more than three members at the lowest echelon, no horizontal communication whatsoever, and communications upwards and downwards only through the appointed leaders of each unit.[24] The advantages of this kind of organization are increased security and the training of a very large proportion of the members in functions of leadership.[25]

Comparison With Fascistic Movements

In the history of warfare it has often happened that one power borrowed strategic and tactical innovations as well as new weapons from the enemy and adapted them to its specific purposes. Fascism, National Socialism, and the other fascistic movements, being essentially anti-communist move-

[23] On January 18, 1950, *The New York Times* reported on the expulsion of John Lautner. "Mr. Lautner was head of the New York State Review Commission of the party.... This committee investigates and tries members accused of treason to the party, heresy, and disobedience." One charge against Mr. Lautner was that he had failed to detect and expel a certain F.B.I. undercover agent.

[24] For a detailed description, see A. Rossi, *op. cit.*, Chaps. 19, 20.

[25] *Ibid.*, p. 165.

ments, have borrowed organizational as well as strategic and tactical ideas from the Bolshevists, to such an extent that structurally they look very similar to one another. People who have lived first under the Nazi régime and later under the Soviet régime claim they are not fundamentally different in operation. Whether the similarities are entirely a result of direct imitation is hard to say. However, it is possible to trace common sources in French revolutionary syndicalism and in pre-Marxist Russian revolutionary social movements. It is also likely that both Bolshevists and Nazis have borrowed from Russian anti-revolutionary movements like the Black Hundred.

Here we have to confine ourselves to a morphological comparison, that is, an analysis of the similarities in structure and organization. The Fascist and National Socialist parties' relationship to the fascist and Nazi movements was similar to the relationship of the Communist Party to the communist movement. The N.S.D.A.P. was conceived as the trusted élite of the movement, composed of fanatic, militant, active believers. Concentration of power with the party leader, delegation of authority from the top down were even more clearly designed than in the Communist Party. Discipline was enforced by a special committee that acted as a party court of arbitration and discipline. Active participation in various party activities was expected of all members, and there developed, as we have mentioned before, a hierarchy of full-time, professional party workers. Qualifications for membership were not very selective—apart from the disqualification of non-Aryans. The recruiting methods of the N.S.D.A.P. were similar though much less subtle than those of the Communists, and the alternating periods of drives, closure, and purges were to be found here, too, as were training institutions of various kinds. (See Chapter 19.)

A difference between the parties is found in their social bases: the fascist movements are not class movements but rather movements of *dé-classés*, of people who have fallen out of their social class or are marginal to it. Such movements are supported by insecure elements in the petite bourgeoisie and by certain large entrepreneurs (Chapter 8; therefore they cannot develop a clear-cut doctrine but merely an ideology (see Chapter 2). Consequently, they have to rely, to a degree quite unknown in the communist movements, upon the solidifying and integrating power of a leader.

Leadership

In the position of the leader there exists a fundamental difference between the two types of movements, which is usually overlooked and sometimes intentionally not pointed out: Mussolini and Hitler were regarded as charismatic leaders—inspired men who considered themselves endowed with extraordinary gifts of statesmanship, who claimed to be the sole creators of the movements which carried them to power, and the supreme source of all important decisions. The will of the leader is law in a fascist movement. The authority of the leader has irrational foundations. Such ideas are quite foreign to Marxist theory. Theoretically, the chairman of the National Committee of a communist party is the elected representative of the rank and file. He certainly does not claim to be the founder of the movement—this rôle is ascribed to Karl Marx—nor does he claim to possess any extraordinary, unique gifts of intuition. The fact that Lenin has become the first and only saint of orthodox Marxian Communism (Trotsky being the first devil) and that Stalin receives the kind of adulation which is awarded a charismatic leader, should not make us blind to the more significant fact that Lenin never claimed to be more than the leading functionary of the party, and that the party never proclaimed anything resembling the leadership principle. Stalin himself, while he tolerates the popular cult of his person, is not known to have given encouragement to it. On the contrary, we know the blunt rejection in his letter to Comrade (Professor) Razin (Feb. 23, 1946): "The dithyrambs in Razin's letter in honor of Stalin grate on the ears and simply make one uncomfortable to read them," [26] a sentence which Hitler would never have written.

It is also significant that the decisions of the Politburo are— at least *de jure*—presented as collective decisions; and if we may trust authorities like Duranty [27] it seems that Stalin actually consults a great deal with its members.[28] With regard to subleaders in the Russian Communist Party, there is not even a trace of charisma.

As for communist parties in countries outside the Soviet Union, there is no question at all that the authority of their commanding officers is legal or institutional, and in no way charismatic. These leaders are elected, can be recalled, and have in fact been quite frequently ousted from office on orders from Moscow, without any serious disruptions within their party organizations. Their position is very similar to that of officers in any army, who are and must be replaceable at any moment in order to secure smooth and effective functioning of the group.[29] The one outstanding exception seems

[26] Quoted verbatim from *Political Affairs*, 1946, p. 417. See also Walter Duranty, *op. cit.*, p. 64: "Stalin does not think of himself as dictator-autocrat, but as the guardian of the 'party line.'" Duranty, who has thorough first-hand knowledge of Soviet Russia, points out the democratic elements in the Soviet régime. (pp. 27 ff.).

[27] *Ibid.*, p. 90.

[28] To over-rate the charismatic element in Stalin's position may lead to serious miscalculations concerning the durability of the Soviet régime. Whether Stalin has been motivated, in his struggle with the left and right oppositions within the Party, by a yearning for personal power as some former Communists maintain (for example Rossi, p. 239), has no bearing upon this problem; Stalin may be the Russian Napoleon, but he is no Mussolini or Hitler.

[29] This view is confirmed by Martin Ebon, *World Communism Today* (New York, McGraw-Hill Book Company, Inc., 1948), p. 175: "The Communist movement outside the Soviet Union has shown itself relatively independent of personalities. In France, the frequent replacement of top leaders is hardly remembered at all. Still, Thorez, who became his party's secretary-general in 1932, today symbolizes French communism more than any other man. His personality is decisive in determining popular opinion of Communist qualifications and patriotism."

to be Marshall Tito, whose personal prestige in combination
with great cunning and determination have enabled him to
hold his own against the Cominform.

RELIGIOUS MODELS FOR POLITICAL ORDERS

It should now be clear that the new parties are structurally
quite different from the old. There remains the task of grasp-
ing the nature of these new structures more precisely. Just as
the new political idea systems have been called political religions,[30] so the new parties have been compared to certain
types of religious brotherhoods or orders.

One of the best authorities on Russia, Sir John Maynard,
has characterized Lenin's conception of the Communist Party
as that of

a disciplined order of devoted adherents, more nearly resembling the
Society of Jesus than any of the lax aggregations of political sympathizers to which we are accustomed to apply the name of political
party.... We can trace the germs of it to Bakunin, Nechayev and
Tkachev.[31]

Rossi, in comparing the structure of the Communist Party
with that of the other political parties in his country, points
out that these make only political demands in the strict sense
on their members; party influence

does not extend beyond the threshold of their private lives.... It is
quite otherwise with the Communist Party.... The Party asserts
control over every department of their [the militants'] lives, and recognizes no dividing line between the political and the personal....
The Party is a movement [sic] to which he [the militant] belongs, a
community in which he lives, a way of life in which he participates....
His personal interests and his personal feelings count for nothing in
so far as they conflict with his duties that attach to his party membership. The Party is, on this showing, less a party in the ordinary ac-
ceptation of the term than an ecclesia [church].[32]

[30] Eric Voegelin, *Die Politischen Religionen* (Stockholm, Berman-Fischer,
1939).

[31] Sir John Maynard, *op. cit.*, pp. 128, 293 ff.

[32] Rossi, *op. cit.*, p. 102.

Among the National Socialists, the medieval orders of religious knights—the Templars and especially the order of Teutonic Knights (*Deutschritter-Orden*)—were favorite models for the structure of the party.[33] It is worth noting that the training schools for future party leaders were given the name of *Ordensburgen* or castles of the order (compare Chapter 19).

What made the medieval militant orders appealing to the Nazis was the high evaluation of physical prowess, courage, and the virtue of unconditional obedience. There was still another idea involved, namely the theory that the state had its origin in the *Männerbund,* or fraternal group of youthful warriors who rally around a heroic leader. In the Teutonic order the Nazis saw a modified *Männerbund,* and the fact that the state of Prussia issued from the state of the order seemed to confirm their theory.

Actually, if one wants to draw such analogies at all, the National Socialist movement showed just as striking structural analogies to the Jesuit order as did the Communist Party. We find in all three groups the principle of strict selectivity in the recruiting of new members, very similar techniques of infiltration, very similar methodical techniques of indoctrination and testing of loyalty, the same renunciation of intellectual freedom, the same unconditional submission to the authority of superiors, the same devotion of one's entire personality to the group, without reservation of a private sphere; we find the same military or quasi-military hierarchy, and very similarly organized institutions of training (Jesuit colleges, party schools, *Ordensburgen*). We find even the same differentiations between various stages of development of converts and the concomitant differentiation between organized members and the fringe of non-initiated workers; and finally a system of penalties and enforcement agencies for the

---

[33] A. Rosenberg, *Der Mythos des 20. Jahrhunderts,* (München, Hoheneichen-Verlag, 1942).

preservation of discipline which makes each of these groups a state within the state or a church within the church.

We find, furthermore, the same combination of centralized authority with flexibility of strategy and tactics—that is to say, the subordination of means to ends. Just as the defense of the church is the supreme end of the Society of Jesus, so has the defense of the Soviet Union become the supreme end of the orthodox Communist movement, even to the point where Communist parties in foreign countries are expendable. It was the flexibility of the Jesuits' lines of action together with the principle of perfect obedience to a superior who was—according to the contention of the order's adversaries—not bound by any general rules, that aroused most of the antagonism which the Jesuits encountered within the church and without. They were indeed regarded as a foreign, if not heretical element within the Church.

Similarities in organization are of course no proof of actual imitation. However, it is certain that the National Socialists imitated the Fascists and that both also borrowed a good deal from their arch-enemies, the Communists. It is also reasonable to assume that the Italian Fascists and some National Socialist leaders like Josef Goebbels were familiar with and influenced by the organization of the Society of Jesus.

Perhaps the similarity to the Jesuit order [34] should not be over-stressed; strict discipline, and even blind obedience is a

[34] The comparison between certain types of political parties and the Jesuit order is not a new idea. In a German liberal encyclopedia of politics of the second half of the last century, we find the following statement:

"It is also an important question whether parties should be free to adopt a permanent strong organization which would establish the party as a formal hierarchical power, and which functions perhaps under secret officers (Vorständen), which substitutes its own bureaus and binds its members by oath to absolute obedience and persecutes those who leave the party or refuse to join. This kind of party organization constitutes a state within the state, establishes a dual government (Nebenregierung) and authority and is just as intolerable (unzulässig) as the Jesuits."—Politisches Handbuch, Staatslexikon für das Deutsche Volk (Leipzig, Brockhaus, 1869-1871), p. 301.

common norm in many religious orders. The position of the chief officer varies.[35]

In any case, the structural similarities between the new totalitarian parties and the religious orders are strong enough to warrant the designation of the former as *political orders*.

The political order reaches perfection when it seizes the powers of government, abolishes all other parties, and establishes itself as *parti unique*; it then sheds all semblance of party and becomes an organ of the state, a ruling élite. Fascist theory considers the one-party rule as final. In Communist theory, the dictatorship of the proletariat is intended as a transitory phase in the creation of a classless society where the proletarian state will wither away.

The abolition of political parties does not remove the reasons for party formation. Parties may be prohibited, but controversies over issues, as well as factions and cliques are bound to develop even in a one-party régime. Since the political order claims to be in the possesion of the political truth, all such factions appear as heretical sects and are dealt with very much in the same way as religious heretics have been dealt with by the churches: through demotion, banishment to a remote part of the country, expulsion from the party (which means political death), exile, and physical liquidation. Again, the Fascists and Nazis have borrowed from the

[35] For a sociological analysis of the structure of the Society of Jesus and other religious orders, see E. K. Francis, "Toward a Typology of Religious Orders," *American Journal of Sociology*, Vol. LV, No. 5 (March, 1950). Francis states that among the oldest of the monastic orders, the Benedictines, the abbot was "the absolute paternal master of a given family of religiosi and their 'living rule' in all temporal as well as spiritual matters. The Dominican prior, on the other hand, is rather a minister of the community with strictly limited rights and functions."

Compare also Gustav Gundlach, S. J., *Zur Soziologie der Katholischen Ideen-Welt und des Jesuiten Ordens* (Freiburg, 1927). Gundlach states that the authority of the general in the Society of Jesus is more limited than that of the Benedictine abbot, since he is dependent upon the general congregation. However, since the general is elected for life, the constitutional limitations of his power do not have much practical force.

Bolshevists methods of controlling and repressing heresy. The fundamental difference between these methods and those employed in the democratic states is that the political orders are not content with punishing the political offender, but have developed techniques of breaking his morale and bringing him to confession of his "sins."

Louis Fischer, in his *Men and Politics* (pp. 527 f.), when discussing the penitent behavior of the old guard of the Bolshevik Party during the trials of 1936–1938, points out that most of the accused had been for many years subjected to methodical breaking of their self-respect. Fischer gives good reasons why it is unlikely that these men were physically tortured before or during the trial, but for years they had been suffering demotions, had been humiliated and shunned, in short, exposed to a treatment which undermined their morale. In the end, they were in a state of mind that made them ready to "confess." The threat of execution without trial in case they refused, and the slight hope, on the other hand, of being spared if they played the rôle of repenting political criminals as the prosecution wanted them to, made them pliable and submissive.

The Nazis resorted to cruder methods, including extremely beastly physical torture, always making it a point to humiliate their victims by exposing them in ridiculous or even repulsive physical condition—even in death. Such treatment of political opponents is psychologically possible only when the ruling élite has ceased, in its own consciousness, to be one party among others, and poses instead as the incarnation of the community.

At this stage, the party has ceased to be a mere political order—it has become the political church.[36]

---

[36] "The Russian religious conception of the presence of truth in the congregation, and there alone, passed to the Communists."—Sir John Maynard, *op. cit.*, p. 441. The same author, *ibid.*, p. 20, calls the Communist Party in U.S.S.R. a new form of an ancient institution—the priesthood.

CONCLUSION

Political parties have thus developed from cliques of clans-
men or neighbors and from factions within status groups
(estates) to bureaucratically administered mass parties; the
transformation of the latter into political orders and their rise
to exclusive power closes the circle. The parties of the old
style, the genuine parties, were often hardly distinguishable
from the broader social movements, but the new-style political orders, aiming at the establishment of a totalitarian
régime, actually renounce the very idea of social movement.
In the society which they want to create there would be
no room or reason for movements, since the political order
would monopolize all initiative toward social change.

VI

TACTICS AND STRATEGY

16

General Principles

~~~~~~

THE CONCEPTS OF TACTIC AND STRATEGY

THE TERMS *tactic* and *strategy* are frequently used to denote the ways and means by which a movement or party seeks to attain its goals. Strictly speaking, both terms should be used only in reference to the principles or doctrines concerning methods or techniques of action and not to designate the ways of action as such. *Tactic,* according to the great military scientist Karl von Clausewitz, is the theory of the use of forces in battle; *strategy,* the theory of the use of battles for the conduct of war. Clausewitz used the term *theory* in the sense of *general principles,* and one should therefore apply the terms *tactic* and *strategy* to political action only where a movement or party has developed a set of principles concerning ways and means. Actually, however, the terms are often applied with reference to observable patterns of action.[1]

---

[1] For example, Feliks Gross, *European Ideologies* (New York, Philosophical Lib. Inc., 1948), pp. 5-15, discusses the concepts of strategy and tactics in their relation to each other and to the concepts ideology and program; in analogy to von Clausewitz's famous definition, Gross states, ".... political tactics denote the use of political forces in a current, actual, historical, concrete situation for coöperation with, or struggle against, other political forces; political strategy is the use of tactical moves to approach the great ideological objectives, determined by the whole ideology. Political strategy and tactics correspond to 'policy making' and practical politics. Programs and tactics change more frequently than ideology and great political strategy...."

Stalin has given a definition which is obviously derived from Clausewitz's:

Tactics are the determination of the line of conduct of the proletariat for the comparatively short period of the ebb or flow of the movement, of the rise or decline of the revolution, the struggle to carry out this line by replacing old forms of struggle and of organization by new ones, old slogans by new ones, by combining these forms, etc. While the aim of strategy is to win the war, let us say against tsarism or against the bourgeoisie, to carry the struggle against tsarism or against the bourgeoisie to its end, tactics concern themselves with less important aims, as they strive, not to win the war as a whole, but rather to win a particular engagement, or a particular battle; to carry through successfully a particular campaign or action corresponding to the concrete circumstances of the rise or decline of the revolution. Tactics are a part of strategy, subordinate and subservient to it.[2]

This definition refers by implication to ideas, to theory or principles rather than to actual behavior. Since in the field of politics no forces are used and no battles fought, it is clear that the terms *tactic* and *strategy* can be used only in a metaphoric sense. One might say that the Marxist-Leninist theories of class struggle and worldwide revolution belong in the sphere of strategy, while the principles of making a *coup d'état* belong in the sphere of tactics.

However, there is a deeper justification for the use of these terms in denoting political action. Clausewitz himself has seen the inherent, sociological relationship between war and politics:

War belongs not in the field of arts and sciences but in that of social life. War is a conflict of great interests which must be resolved by bloodshed and only in this is it different from the others. Better than with any kind of art can it [war] be compared with commerce, which also is a conflict of human interests and activities, and much closer to it is politics, which again may be regarded as a kind of commerce on a larger scale.[3]

The three phenomena—war, commerce, and politics—have

[2] Joseph Stalin, "Foundations of Leninism," *Leninism*, Vol. I (New York, International Publishers Co., Inc., 1933), p. 75.

[3] Karl von Clausewitz, *Vom Kriege* (Berlin, F. Dümmler, 1832-34) (R. Heberle's translation).

in common the conflicts of interests and the rational methods of resolving these conflicts. This is the formal sociological aspect of their relationship; the material relationship between war and politics, and politics and commerce is too obvious to need further elaboration in this context.[4]

It is quite difficult in particular cases to draw a sharp line of distinction between tactics and strategy, just as it is difficult to distinguish in particular cases between strategic ideas and ideology, since the latter inevitably includes certain ideas on the ways and means by which the ultimate goal can be attained. Ideas on strategy are in some cases part of the set of ideas which distinguish a movement from others and may therefore be called *constitutive ideas* (see Chapter 2).

Furthermore, a very close interrelation exists between strategy and organization: certain forms of action require certain forms of organization; on the other hand, the choice of action patterns is limited by the form of organization.[5]

For example, a party which is loosely organized and not strictly disciplined can not prepare a *coup d'état;* a movement which anticipates attainment of its goals by social evolution needs no strict discipline, no high degree of centralization. Because of this interrelationship of strategy, tactics, and organization, it is inevitable that some repetitions will occur in the following discussion. Nevertheless, it is advisable to devote a special chapter to the treatment of strategy, and especially of tactic.

[4] One will recall Clausewitz's famous sentence, "War is a mere continuation of [the state's] policy by other means." Karl von Clausewitz, *On War,* Vol. I (London, N. Trübner & Co., 1873). p. 12.

[5] "It was not at all accidental that the points which resulted in the split of the Russian Social Democracy were on the one side the conception of the character of the coming revolution and of the tasks resulting therefrom (whether the Social Democrats should fight together with the progressive bourgeoisie or on the side of the peasants) and on the other side the question of organization. The dialectic interrelationship of the two questions has unfortunately not been understood in the movement outside Russia,"—Georg Lukacs, *Geschichte und Klassenbewusstsein* (Berlin, Der Malik-Verlag, 1923) pp. 298 f. (R. Heberle's translation).

SIGNIFICANCE FOR THE SOCIOLOGY OF
SOCIAL MOVEMENTS

The consideration of the tactics of a social movement or a political party is of practical importance, because it is in the sphere of tactical action that conflicts with the existing régime are most likely to arise. Furthermore, it is not too difficult to repress and prosecute actions which violate the normative order of a society; it is very difficult, however, to combat successfully the mere holding and expression of ideas opposed to the existing social order or to a particular political régime. It is therefore in the field of tactic rather than in the sphere of ideas that social movements are vulnerable. One would be inclined to assume that movements which are radically opposed to an existing socio-political order would tend to favor tactics which are incompatible with the legal order, whereas movements which are principally in agreement with the existing social order would be inclined to respect the law in tactical actions. This, however, is by no means generally true.

The Social Democrats, though striving for a radically different social order, do not advocate and favor tactics which would violate the law of the land. On the other hand, employers' associations, farmers' movements, labor unions of the business union type, and similar groups which do not intend to change the existing social system often resort to intimidation, violence, and other actions which may constitute violations of the law. In fact, the temptation may be greater for groups who feel that the courts will sympathize with their conduct than for those whose intentions are considered subversive by the ruling strata.

The Problem of Legality

It will thus be clear that the tactics of a social movement or of a political party are of essential importance when the question arises whether the movement should be tolerated or outlawed. Since the modern state has a monopoly on the legitimate use of force, the use of violence or force in a political party or social movement will constitute an illegal act. The persons who commit the act are subject to criminal prosecution. This seems a simple and clear-cut principle. However, it gives rise to a host of problems.

In modern Western democracies, where freedom of opinion is a constitutional civil right, the mere belief in and expression of ideas opposed to the existing social order can not be considered as a criminal offense. But what about the advocation, in the doctrine of a party or movement, of the illegal use of force? Should the possible incitement to violence contained in such doctrine be tolerated? And if acts of violence have been committed by members of a movement or party which advocates or condones such conduct, should only the persons who committed these acts be punished, or should repressive action be taken against the entire organization to which they belong? What kind of action could be taken against members without violating the freedom of association and without establishing the principle of guilt by association, which is foreign to the legal system in Western democracies? Finally, in case of a movement or party which, though observing strict legality in tactical action, aims at the ultimate abolition of democracy, what kind of action, if any, can a democratic government take for its self-protection without violating the very principles of democratic procedure?

This is not the place to attempt an answer to these questions. We raise them merely to demonstrate the practical significance of a study of tactics.[6]

[6] For a scholarly and competent discussion of the ways and means of controlling an anti-democratic movement, see Professor W. Y. Elliot's statement and testimony before the House Committee on un-American Activities, Subcommittee on Legislation, Hearings on Proposed Legislation to curb or control the Communist Party of the United States, Feb., 1948, esp. pp. 410 f.
While Elliot opposed the persecution of individuals merely because at one

These problems concern not only the state but other groups in society as well; they arise even in the relations between social movements. The immediate reason for the American labor unions' recent policy of excluding Communists from offices and expelling Communist-controlled unions from the big federations lies in their objection to Communist tactics rather than to the ultimate ideals of communism.

Tactical Controversies

This last observation touches upon another reason why the tactics and strategy of a movement are so important from a sociological point of view. We are referring to the fact that the same objectives can be pursued by quite different and often incompatible ways of social action. Some members of a social movement or party may have no confidence in the tactical and strategic principles to which the majority in the

---

time or other they held Communistic ideas ("you can't control thought"), he recommends repressive measures against those who are actively engaged in carrying out the policies of the Communist Party, as such work is done in the service of a "foreign *political* and *hostile* power" [Heberle's italics].

Professor Elliot's colleague, Zechariah Chafee, Jr., of Harvard University, criticized the proposed Mundt Bill most severely in his article, "Freedom and Fear," *American Association of University Professors Bulletin,* Vol. 35, No. 3 (Autumn, 1949). Taking the Communist danger in this country much less seriously than Professor Elliot, he emphasizes the possible abuse of repressive legislation. Since legislation of this kind would have to designate certain kinds of action as a criminal offense, it is quite likely that it would be applied sooner or later against individuals who do not at all belong to the orthodox communist movement, but who happen to commit actions defined as criminal in the law.

Professor Thomas Reed Powell of the Harvard Law School, in a letter to the House Committee on un-American Activities, says, "I cannot believe that the mere espousing of an apocalyptic gospel [an allusion to the Communists' belief in the coming world revolution] would be judicially held to be such an overt act as is requisite for a finding of the guilt of treason, or that it affords such a fairly conclusive presumption of active affiliation with a foreign power as to justify a compulsion to register as an agent of such power." He then draws the parallel between the Communists' allegiance to Moscow and the Catholics' subordination to the Vatican. He believes there must be many members of the Communist Party of the United States who are not in fact agents of a foreign power.

group adheres. Many of the historically important splits and schisms in social movements and political parties had their beginnings in controversies about questions of tactics or strategy. It has been suggested that such disagreement about ways and means among individuals who are in agreement as to ultimate ends has its source in differences of temperament (see Chapter 5). Tactical controversies may indeed be a consequence of a more or less optimistic or pessimistic appraisal of human nature and conduct; they may result too from differences in opinion concerning man's ability to follow consistently a preconceived plan of action. In particular, disagreements may arise out of different appraisal of the number and quality of factors which are either unpredictable or beyond control.[7]

These controversies may also arise from differences in judgment, experience, and social rôles. Generalizations in this field are risky, but it seems as if those who carry a great deal of responsibility as group leaders are inclined to be more cautious, more flexible in tactics, and more willing to compromise than those who are not responsible for the success of a large organization. By way of illustration: the intellectuals in the socialist movement usually seem to be more concerned about ultimate goals and principles and are therefore more intransigent in tactics and strategy than the trade union leaders, who are inclined to give priority to immediate improvements in the conditions of the workers. This difference in evaluation of immediate and distant goals often underlies the controversies between the right and left wings, between moderates and radicals, and between the intransigents and those who are willing to make compromises and enter into alliances with groups whose ultimate aims are not in agreement with their own. The bitterness of factional strife arises from moral implications. The radicals accuse the moderates

[7] Walter Sulzbach, *Die Grundlagen der politischen Parteibildung* (Tübingen, Mohr, 1921), pp. 136 f.

of treason and opportunism, while the moderates charge the radicals with lack of realism, accusing them of having no sense of responsibility. The radicals have greater chances of gaining control of a movement the more it is supported by emotional-affectual attitudes, rather than by value-rational motivations.

Even where agreement exists on the principles of strategy, controversies concerning the timing of certain actions may cause a severe schism. The conflict between Stalin and Trotsky developed largely, though by no means exclusively, out of such disagreement about proper timing. Both wanted the collectivization of agriculture, both wanted the world revolution, but Stalin advocated a slower tempo.[8]

REVOLUTION: THE CONCEPT

To define *revolution,* we must first make the important strategic distinction between evolution and revolution, or between reformers and revolutionaries. The terms are used in the popular sense. *Reform* means gradual, step-by-step action towards the intended objectives, resulting in slow changes in the socio-political structure of the society; *revolution* means sudden and therefore usually violent social action for the attainment of the movement's objectives. However, the terms, if used in this way, do not refer to the ultimate result or effects of social movements. A gradual but radical reform movement may bring about a fundamental and lasting

[8] An interesting analogy to the schism between Stalin and Trotsky is found in the French revolution of 1789, when a schism arose within the democratic party between Robespierre, who wanted an isolationist policy, and the majority, who advocated propagation and extension of the revolution beyond the borders of France. The latter tendency benefited by the formation of a coalition of European princes against France. The republican Democrats became the protagonists of the idea of a pan-European crusade against the enemies of the revolution—of "a league of nations against the princes".—A. Aulard, *Histoire politique de la révolution Française: origines et développement de la démocratie et de la république (1789-1804)* (Paris, Librairie A. Colin, 1901) p. 111.

change in the allocation of economic and political power and thereby change the entire social structure, whereas a sudden and violent political revolution may not produce very great and lasting changes in the social system.

The term *revolution* is therefore often used in a technical sense to denote a process of relatively quick, but not necessarily violent, social change through which the power relations of social classes are changed and a new social order is established. Examples are the French revolution of 1789, the Russian revolution of 1917-18, and the Chinese revolution of 1911. It is doubtful whether the German revolution of 1918, despite its violent character, can be regarded as a genuine revolution in the technical sense. It was neither planned nor wanted at that time by the socialists who came through it to power, nor did it change the social order in a fundamental way. One may call it a stalled revolution, one that bogged down, because the new rulers were afraid of the consequences of a really revolutionary strategy. Revolutions in the strict, technical sense are much less frequent than revolutions in the popular sense of a violent overthrow of government. Most of the revolutions, for example, in Latin America led merely to the replacement of one clique of a dominant minority by another clique of the same social group. In this popular sense of the word, a movement which opposes genuine revolution, a counter-revolutionary movement, may apply revolutionary tactics, as the example of fascistic movements shows.

It is the change in power relations and institutions, not merely the violence, which characterizes a revolution in the sociological sense. A change in power relations is usually expressed by a change in the written or unwritten constitution of the state and in the legal system in general. The new constitution, and the revolutionary legislation reflect the changes in the relations of power, status, and prestige between the various social strata.

Revolutions can occur in large societies as well as in small communities, but it is a characteristic of genuine revolutions that they tend to spread beyond the confines of local communities and even national societies until they have affected more or less intensively all parts of a civilization.[9]

Causation

Since each revolution springs from specific conditions and leads to peculiar, widely varying results, it is difficult to develop a general theory of revolution, although attempts have been made to generalize about types and phases as well as processes of revolutionary action.

One generalization can be made concerning the causation or origin of revolutions: a real revolution does not start unless certain conditions are given. First, there has to be a social class or several social classes dissatisfied with the existing distribution of political power; this usually happens because the classes feel the discrepancy between their actual importance in society and their legal and political position. Second, a revolution, although carried mainly by one social class, has to have potential support among broad masses of malcontents in other social classes. Third, the groups which control the government must have suffered a loss of confidence in the righteousness of their own position, in the justifiability of the existing social system, and in the possibility of resisting a popular uprising.

It is a mistake to assume that poverty and misery as such cause revolutions. The poorest, most underprivileged classes seldom start a revolution, although they may give it support. The actively revolutionary groups are usually those classes or subclasses that, just because they are no longer poor, feel unduly restrained in their economic activities or in their participation in political decisions. Seemingly excessive taxation

[9] T. Geiger, "Revolution," *Handwoerterbuch der Soziologie* (Stuttgart, 1931), pp. 511-518.

without visible returns for the main taxpaying classes can produce a revolutionary situation. An inadequate or miscarrying attempt at basic social reforms may have the same results (for example, Stolypin's land reform, which resulted in the proletarization of large parts of the Russian peasantry).

The ruling class is always in a dangerous position when there are in the society a large number of *dé-classés,* that is, impoverished families and individuals whose vocational careers are blocked or thwarted by circumstances beyond their control—ex-soldiers after a lost war or an intellectual proletariat, as in Tsarist Russia.[10]

Conditions of this kind, unless produced by war, can only come about as the result of slow changes in the economy and in the social structure of a society. A genuine revolution, therefore, is usually the final link in a long chain of events, or the final phase of an evolutionary process. If the changes in the distribution of power are made by gradual adaptation to the changing socio-economic conditions, a violent revolution may be avoided. The longer the institutional adjustments that are demanded by the changes in the actual economic and social relations between classes are deferred, the more violent is the revolution likely to be.[11]

Course and Outcome

Even when started in a mature situation in which all these conditions are present, a revolution can never be sure of success. Although the revolutionaries may reach the immediate goals, the ultimate effects of the revolution can never be fore-

[10] Crane Brinton, *The Anatomy of Revolution* (New York, W. W. Norton & Company, Inc., 1938), pp. 44 ff., points out that the economic distress of underprivileged groups is not in itself a cause of revolution; more important is the feeling of being restrained in economic activities and in chances of social advancement by political institutions. Also *ibid.,* pp. 52 f., pp. 63 f., pp. 75, on stoppage in the circulation of élites as a cause of revolution.

[11] Marx, "Revolution is the spurt-like completion of a frustrated evolution." (*Revolution ist die ruckartige Nachholung verhinderter Entwicklung.*)

seen, and they may in fact be quite unforeseen in character. The classical example is the French Revolution. It aimed originally at the redress of certain alleged injustices committed by the king and the abolition of certain feudal institutions which had become meaningless; it led, however, to radical changes in French and European society in general. On the other hand, the German revolution of 1918, aiming at the establishment of a socialistic society under a democratic constitutional government, failed in its economic aims and succeeded only temporarily in its political aims, due to a variety of new factors which could not possibly have been foreseen in the fall and winter of 1918.

This uncertainty, this unpredictability of the outcome of a revolution illustrates how social action can lead to unpremeditated, unforeseen, and often unwanted results which may impair, cancel out, or completely ruin the intended achievements. This phenomenon is well known to all students of history and in particular to those familiar with the history of social and political reform legislation. This unpredictability is due to the great number of variables which would have to be taken into account in accurately predicting the effects of social action—a feat which apparently surpasses the capacities of even the most astute minds.

A further observation shows that an initially successful revolution is likely to reach a point where its achievements are at least partially destroyed by the mounting resistance and eventually successful counter-action of those classes whose interests have been hurt. Any revolution is accompanied by a counter-revolutionary movement, in many cases by emigration of the counter-revolutionary elements, who then attempt to overthrow the new régime with foreign aid. It is the threat of counter-revolution that leads to terror.

The counter-revolution may be the result of a direct restoration movement—as in England after Cromwell—or it may be the result of a mounting disunity among the revolutionary groups—as in the French Revolution—when the politically dissatisfied bourgeoisie attempted to put a stop to the democratic and socialistic tendencies which came to the fore in the latter phases of the revolution. The outcome was the Caesaristic régime of Napoleon I, which, after its collapse, was followed by the restoration of the monarchy. Or the counter-revolution may be due to the failure of the driving groups in the revolution to secure sufficient support from other groups. This was the case in Germany after 1918; in order to suppress the radical wing of the revolution (the *Spartakus Bund* or Communist Party) the Social Democrats leaned upon the counter-revolutionary professional army and its voluntary auxiliary forces. They failed to win the support of the small farmers and the salaried employees. This initial tactical inconsistency led to further alliances with the wrong forces and alienated many potential supporters and sympathizers within and without the working class.

A successful revolution is rarely a single uprising. Usually the decisive action is preceded by a series of unsuccessful attempts (such as the revolutions of 1830 and 1848 in many European countries, or the Russian revolution of 1905); and in any case it is preceded by a long period of social unrest, with occasional flare-ups of violence here and there. The history of the American Revolution offers ample illustrations.

A successful revolution requires some kind of group organization. Unorganized masses, assembled crowds and mobs, can not start or carry out a revolution. Even if the revolution is not the work of a political party, there are usually a fairly large number of more or less secret, more or less intentionally revolutionary circles, clubs, or committees formed in advance of the outbreak of a revolution. Such groups furnish leadership, and also serve sometimes as executive agencies in the first phases of a revolution. If special new institutions or agencies are created during the revolution in order to carry the action, they are usually staffed with people who had previous connections through other kinds of groups such as political parties, labor unions, social clubs, occupational associations, students' fraternities, and so on. The same principle applies to counter-revolutionary movements.

The recognition of this principle is the reason why modern totalitarian régimes insist upon the control of any kind of association (the "coördination" or *Gleichschaltung* of the Nazis); even if the group in question is merely a shepherd-dog breeders' society, totalitarian régimes will attempt to prevent the formation of any informal private circles beyond their control.[12]

Effects Upon the Structure of Society

A genuine revolution leads not merely to a redistribution of power between social strata but it results in a change of the entire system of stratification.[13] The victorious class itself ceases to be what it was before the revolution. The French Revolution, by abolishing obsolete political institutions, revealed the fact that French society had changed from a status-group society into a modern class society. The proletariat which supported the revolution in Russia is no longer a proletariat today. The entire pre-revolutionary class structure of Russian society has been destroyed by the revolution, together with what survived of the old status-group society which had already crumbled in the preceding abortive revolution of 1905. The Bolshevist intelligentsia which led the

---

[12] Even inconspicuous, a-political friendship circles may become dangerous to an authoritarian régime; four of the leading men in the opposition against Hitler, all of whom were executed after the 20th of July, 1944, belonged to the *Mittwochsgesellschaft* (Wednesday circle)—a small, informal dinner club of civil servants and scholars in Berlin. See Hans Rothfels, *The German Opposition to Hitler* (Chicago, Henry Regnery Co., 1948), p. 72.

The *Kreisau* Circle, which is treated in detail by Rothfels (pp. 112-129), was a larger and politically oriented friendship circle.

[13] Geiger, *op. cit.,* "*In der Revolution verschiebt sich nicht [nur] das Machtverhältnis zwischen nach wie vor gegebenen Schichten, sondern das Schichtungsprinzip selbst ändert sich.*"

revolution was transformed into a ruling élite of commissars and government officials.

The counter-revolution, on the other hand, although carried by the individuals whose dominating position in society was abolished by the revolution, is not really carried by the same social class, because the social position of the counter-revolutionaries has changed during the revolution. From a firmly-entrenched élite of civil servants, large land owners, army officers, and others, they have become converted into political, and often social outcasts, economic pariahs leading a life of insecurity, depending even on jobs in the service of the new political powers—they have become *dé-classés*. Even their standards of value tend to change, which explains much of the moral deterioration and sadism that is displayed in such movements. Because they have to find support among other social strata, the counter-revolutionary program or ideology incorporates certain ideas borrowed from the revolution and rarely proposes an outright return to the pre-revolutionary state of affairs.[14]

Again the principle of unforeseen results may become effective, and what started as a counter-revolution may get out of control and result in a real revolution. It may be said that this was the case with Nazism in Germany. Even before the war it had brought layers of society into the élite which hitherto had played a very minor rôle, such as the petty bourgeois, the small farmer, and the common laborer of rural background. And it had wrought such complete havoc with traditional values and institutions (even those respected by the revolution of 1918) that it would have amounted to a real revolution except for one important fact: the preservation of ultimate control over the German economy by members or agents of the big-business class, who were incorporated into the hierarchy of the party and its affiliated organizations.

[14] A. Meusel, "Revolution and Counterrevolution," *Encyclopaedia of the Social Sciences*. (New York, The Macmillan Company, 1942).

Another of the paradoxes of revolution is that the movement which began in the name of liberty, which promised freedom not only for the revolutionary class, but for everybody, almost inevitably leads to a régime of terror, of dictatorship, or of tyranny, directed not only against the old ruling classes but also against those among the old revolutionaries who do not agree with the actual course of the new régime. The new ruling group then is in a precarious situation: the legal or traditionalistic authority of the old régime has been destroyed, general respect for law has been shaken, many social values are in transformation, and the authority of the new régime is not yet firmly established in the beliefs and attitudes of the people. Therefore it can maintain itself only by force; force, however, if not accepted as legitimate, generates opposition and resistance which can be broken only by more force and threats of force. This is, in short, the way in which terror develops. It will of course arouse the disgust, criticism, and active opposition of those among the revolutionaries who took the promise of liberty seriously and who do not believe that it may be impossible to grant freedom during a period of transition from one régime to the other. Those in power will regard these objectors as heretics and traitors and deal with them severely.

It is a peculiar trait of modern Communism that the phase of terror is, so to speak, officially incorporated in its strategic doctrine under the name *dictatorship of the proletariat*. The long duration of this phase was unforeseen by Lenin, and it seems doubtful that he visualized the possibility of terror exercised against old and venerable leaders of the revolutionary movement.

Destructive and Constructive Aspects

A revolution therefore has destructive and constructive aspects. The old institutions are destroyed, many of their supporters are killed in civil war, executed as political criminals, imprisoned, exiled, deprived of their property or debarred from public office, and even from certain occupations. With them and their social position perish many cultural values, and much tangible and intangible cultural heritage is destroyed in the process. On the other hand, the revolutionary groups create new institutions, allegedly better adapted to the welfare of the broad masses. The hitherto oppressed classes are emancipated, liberated from obsolete fetters of law and custom, and a new social philosophy, a new social attitude, and new cultural values are created.

The two aspects of revolution are so closely intertwined that it seems a vain and hopeless undertaking to attempt a distinction between an initial, destructive phase, and a later, constructive phase of a revolution.[15] The same action, such as the liquidation of the *kulaks* in Soviet Russia, has destructive and constructive aspects. The very destruction of the *kulak* class was an essential step in the building up of the collective economy of the village.

It is also alleged by some authors, like P. A. Sorokin, that the first, destructive phase is followed by a declining phase in which "the revolution destroys much of what it sought to accomplish in the first period, and rebuilds much of what it destroyed in its first phase," with the result that "generally only the moribund institutions, values, and trends eliminated in the first phase fail to re-establish themselves."[16]

Certainly the new régime is often forced to retrace its steps, to make temporary concessions to adverse forces and circumstances, and even to restore what it destroyed—but such adjustments do not change the long-run trend of the

[15] Vierkandt and Sorokin make this distinction; see A. Vierkandt, "Zur Theorie der Revolution," *Schmollers Jahrbuch*, Vol. 46 (1922), and P. A. Sorokin, *Society, Culture, and Personality* (New York, Harper and Brothers, 1947), Chap. 31. T. Geiger, *op. cit.*, emphasizes the interrelatedness of the two phases of a revolution.

[16] Sorokin, *op. cit.*, p. 487; see also *Sociology of Revolution* (Philadelphia, J. B. Lippincott Company, 1925).

revolution. Most likely the new ruling groups will reach a point where they will call a halt to any attempt to push the revolution any further—even if this attempt may be made from among the ranks of their own followers. However, the idea that every revolution runs through a cycle, returning after a relatively brief period of excesses to the level whence it originated, is hardly confirmed by historical observation. On the contrary, the speculation upon such return to normalcy has been a grave mistake in dealing with both the Soviet Union and the Nazis. The illusion is probably caused by the fact that certain basic attitudes and even institutional traits which are anchored very firmly in the culture of a people are likely to survive even the most radical revolution. Thus one may see in Napoleon I a social reincarnation of the *Roi de Soleil,* or in the collective farm in Soviet Russia a revival of the ancient *mir,* and in the Communist Party of the U.S.S.R. (Bolshevik) a secularized version of the Orthodox Church. However, these resuscitations rarely amount to a restitution of the past. The *kolkhoz* is a very different institution from the *mir.*[17]

The illusion of a cyclical course and return to the starting point, together with the more realistic principle of the unpredictability of the effects of a revolution, provides one of the most frequent and powerful arguments against deliberate revolutionary tactics. The price, so the evolutionists argue, is too high. It would be much safer and much less reckless to accomplish one's aims by gradual reform, making one safe step after the other, observing, while one goes, the effects of each measure and correcting one's mistakes before the process of change has got out of control. The revolutionist, on the other hand, scorns such caution. He agrees that the price is high, that many will perish—friends as well as enemies—and that great risks will have to be taken. But, he argues, it is

[17] Sir John Maynard, *Russia in Flux,* S. H. Guest, ed. (New York, The Macmillan Company, 1948), pp. 390 ff.

better for a few to perish than for many to continue living in squalor, oppression and injustice. Curiously enough, the revolutionist who professes to fight for the liberation of his fellow men from the evils of the existing social order is, as a rule, very little concerned about the life, liberty, and happiness of actual human beings; he tends to be so convinced of his own righteousness that he is quite willing to sacrifice millions of lives for the realization of a political idea, the value of which has not been, and cannot be, empirically demonstrated. In this respect he and the religious fanatic have much in common.

TACTICS

Turning now to a consideration of tactics, we realize that a comprehensive treatment is practically impossible, within the scope of this book. All the devices of propaganda, persuasion, and intimidation, of negotiation and deception—the whole arsenal of the experienced politician and statesman—would have to be considered. In particular the ancient and the modern techniques of arousing emotions in assembled masses, the use of symbols, slogans, and ceremonies might be included.

Much of what is technically known as *social control* has significance for the tactics of social groups. We can mention only a few devices which are of particular importance and sociological interest.

Political and Direct Action

One of the more important, though not widely known, tactical distinctions is that between *political* and *direct* action. This distinction stems from the labor movement, but it has wider applications. *Political action* aims at a change in institutions and policies by legislation and eventually by control of the government. In democratic countries it presupposes

378 TACTICS AND STRATEGY

attainment of influence in the legislature and eventually participation in or control of the executive branch of the government.

Direct action consists of various types of measures employed directly against such individuals and groups as oppose or resist the movement. Most important devices of direct action are: boycott, sabotage, strike, and various forms of violence by which opponents are intimidated or persons whom the movement claims as potential supporters are compelled to join.

Devices of this kind are quite old and have been used in many and very different social and political movements. Machine wrecking, one of the most direct actions in the labor movement, is also one of the oldest patterns of direct action. In England, it was used on a large scale during the insurrection of workers known as the Luddite movement in the first decade of the nineteenth century. The destruction of machines was by no means an innovation but rather an old weapon of English workers.[18]

The *boycott* [19] has been used by such widely different groups as malcontent, rebellious farmers, conservative landlords, Zionists, and organized labor in many countries. Although mainly known as a weapon of the underprivileged, the boycott has also been applied widely by ruling strata to suppress movements and parties of the opposition. The Conservatives in Prussia used the economic boycott against businessmen, artisans, innkeepers, and even physicians who dared to oppose Conservative rule. About 1910, when political antagonisms gained in bitterness, the boycott was used more frequently as a means of intimidating political opponents, especially the local leaders of the liberal parties, in-

[18] Hermann Schlueter, *Die Chartistenbewegung* (New York, Socialist Literature Co., 1916), pp. 1-26.

[19] Origin of the word: action taken by the Irish against a land agent, Captain Boykott, in 1880, by severance of all social intercourse with him (Webster).

cluding the National Liberals.[20] In France, the economic boycott has been quite frequently used by large land owners and
big industrialists in the western regions to keep the petite
bourgeoisie under control—the grocer in a small town may
vote for the candidate of the *marquis* or manufacturer in
order to avoid being boycotted.[21] To these cases may be
added the boycotting of the town of Neumuenster in Holstein
by National Socialist farmers in 1928 because of the anti-Nazi
attitude of the city police. In this case the rural Nazis refused
for several weeks to trade in the town.

   In the labor movement, two kinds of boycott are used:
(1) the direct boycott by which trade union members are advised not to enter into wage contracts with an employer who
is involved in a labor conflict with their union, and not to buy
goods which are produced by non-union labor under sub-
standard conditions; and (2) the secondary boycott which
means the refusal of trade unionists to transport or process
goods produced by an employer involved in a labor conflict.
As a tactical measure, the boycott is especially useful where
the right of workers to unionize has not yet been established
and where the practices of collective bargaining are not yet
developed.

[20] Walter Koch-Weser, *Volk und Staatsführung vor dem Weltkriege,*
(Stuttgart, 1935), pp. 12-13. A banker who had been a National Liberal
member of the *Reichstag* was forced to abstain from running again when
the Agrarian League boycotted his bank. A professor at the Agricultural
College in Stuttgart-Hohenheim was compelled to renounce a National
Liberal *Reichstag* candidacy when the Württemberg Conservatives threat-
ened not to send their sons to the college any longer.
   In the winter of 1911-1912 the city of Sagan was boycotted by the large
landowners of Silesia because the mayor had been a progressive candidate
for the Reichstag. Similar tactics were used against the city of Leer in
Friesland in 1907, against the town of Schlawe in 1910.
   [21] R. P. Rohden, "Demokratie und Partei in Frankreich" Rohden ed.,
Demokratie und Partei (Wien, L. W. Seidel & Sohn, 1932). Also A. Siegfried,
Tableau politique de la France de l'Ouest sous la Troisième République
(Paris, Armand Colin, p. 1913).

Sabotage

Sabotage, that is, the wilful damaging of machines or materials, has been used mainly by anarcho-syndicalist groups in the labor movement. Well-established trade unions refrain from it since it infringes on property rights and may endanger the lives of fellow workers. But the *slow-down,* which is functionally related to genuine sabotage, is a widespread tactical device among workers, whether organized or not.

The Strike

The *strike* is today the most important means of direct action in the labor movement. Since the modern wage contract does not bind the employee to an employer for periods longer than a day or a week, the individual worker is legally free to stop working if he is dissatisfied with the conditions of work or the treatment he receives. If several workers quit their jobs at the same time after consultation with each other, we have the simplest form of a strike. This kind of spontaneous strike may lead to organization of workers in a union.

The modern strike, however, is usually a tactical measure of a union in industrial conflict and presupposes organization of the workers; it is not an imitative mass action nor a spontaneous action of a loosely organized group, but a deliberate and planned action of a corporate social body. Moreover, the workers do not intend to give up their jobs, but, on the contrary, want to be reinstated at improved conditions. The right to strike is now generally recognized by law and public opinion.

Very intricate problems arise, however, regarding the conduct of a strike and the counter-measures which an employer may take. The right of a striking worker to reinstatement after settlement of the dispute and the right of the state to prevent or repress strikes in establishments whose undisturbed functioning is considered essential for the community constitute difficult legal and political problems. In our modern Western society, with its closely integrated economy, an interruption of the production of essential goods and services can, if it is sufficiently extensive, bring all functions of society to a standstill and thereby shake the very foundations of a government. This is the reasoning behind the idea of the general strike for political purposes. Its actual success depends upon the power of the government to maintain at least the most essential industries and services and upon the support from the public which the strikers receive. In 1902 a political general strike in Sweden for an extension of the franchise did not receive sufficient support and failed to achieve immediate results;[22] on the other hand, a general strike in Germany in 1920 after the so-called Kapp-Putsch had widespread and intensive support in public opinion and achieved the collapse of a counter-revolution by conservative groups through forcing the illegitimate government to abdicate.

The idea of the general strike as a means of direct action in opposition to political or parliamentary action has assumed considerable significance[23] in certain labor-movement groups mainly under the influence of French revolutionary syndicalism and of French theorists of the labor movement, especially Georges Sorel.[24] This French theory of direct action dates from the beginning of the twentieth century. It is a non-Marxian idea partly of anarchist origin. Its adherents among the French trade unionists feared that the rivalries between various socialist parties would weaken the solidarity of the working class, that the compromises which the political leaders of the socialist movement had to make tended to kill the militant *élan* of the labor movement, and that the poli-

[22] Rudolf Heberle, *Zur Geschichte der Arbeiterbewegung in Schweden* (Jena, 1925), pp. 40, 42, 49.
[23] As a tactical idea it was first proposed in 1869.
[24] See Louis L. Lorwin, "Direct Action," *Encyclopedia of the Social Sciences;* see also H. W. Laidler, "French Syndicalism," *Social-Economic Movements* (New York, Thomas Y. Crowell Company, 1946), Chap. 22.

ticians' concern with issues of the day and with immediate social reforms would divert the labor movement from its ultimate revolutionary aims. The trade unionists were also apprehensive of the monopolization of political leadership by intellectuals and of the corruption of labor leaders through participation in coalition governments.

Direct action—sabotage, strike—on the other hand, appealed to them not merely because of its immediate results, but because of its activating effect on the masses of workers. Casting a vote did not require great courage, but active participation in a series of strikes would strengthen the class consciousness, the will to power, and the morale of the workers. The strike, and in particular a general strike, would bring the masses of workers in direct conflict with the enemy, the employer, and also with the forces of the capitalist-dominated state. Other kinds of direct action such as mass demonstrations, especially against imperialism and militarism would also lead the rank and file of workers into direct conflicts with the police and would thus arouse their revolutionary spirit.

Revolutionary Syndicalism

Georges Sorel developed the philosophy of direct action, especially the idea of the general strike as the final clash between capital and labor after which the unions would seize the factories and constitute the new political and economic order. He presented this idea as a myth, designed to unite and arouse the masses of workers.[25]

[25] Georges Sorel, *Réflexions sur la violence*, 1907 (edition Rivière, Paris, 1930), pp. 32-33. "The men who participate in the great social movements represent to themselves their future action in the form of visions of battle [*images de batailles*], assuring themselves of the triumph of their cause. I proposed to give the name 'myths' to these constructions, the knowledge of which offers so much of importance to the historian: the General Strike of the syndicalists and the catastrophic revolution of Marx are 'myths,' and so is the Ecclesia Militans of the Catholics. A myth needs not to be analysed or criticized, it should be reckoned with as a fact."

In view of the tendency among recent writers to use the term *myth* indiscriminately, we recommend that scholars make themselves familiar

The importance of this theory of direct action lies in its adoption by revolutionary syndicalists in other countries, including the I.W.W. in the United States, and by its direct influence on Mussolini and the Italian Fascists as well as in

---

with Sorel's discussion of the function of the myth in the revolutionary struggle of the proletariat. In Sorel's theory, myth has a very definite and specific meaning. It should not be confused with a mere belief or with erroneous ideas; it is a particular kind of belief or idea, one whose function is to catch the imagination and to arouse the will to revolutionary action in the masses. It is therefore an indispensable element in a revolutionary movement. No revolution is without its myth, because without a vision of battle there can be no militancy. The myth of the general strike has the function of immunizing the militant proletarian movement against infection by bourgeois ideas and ethics (p. 52). It is especially directed against those socialist leaders and theoreticians who want to substitute the ballot for the gun (pp. 71 f.). The governments fear the workingmen's violence (p. 94), the militant workers are aware of this and therefore use direct action to intimidate the authorities. The socialist parliamentarians on the other hand do not want to let the masses get out of hand and are therefore opposed to proletarian violence. Sorel believed that the bourgeoisie and the proletariat both tended to become soft under the influence of social reform, democracy, and humanism, but that proletarian violence would help them to recover their old energy and *élan*. His rejection of compromise, of reform, of democracy, his (personally purely theoretical) admiration for action and for violence, connects Sorel directly with the Fascists—Mussolini was his follower—and indirectly with the Nazis. This connection is intelligible only if one considers that Sorel regarded violence not as a unilateral tactical device of labor, but saw in it a cure for the moral and cultural crisis of our society. "Everything can be saved if, through violence, the classes could be reconsolidated and the bourgoisie could regain something of its [former] energy." (p. 130).

"The proletarian violence . . . appears thus as something very beautiful and heroic; . . . it is perhaps not the most appropriate method for obtaining immediate material advantages, but it could save the world from barbarism . . . because only by violent class conflict can we hope to achieve a better social order, an order under which true civilization is possible."

It is this philosophical glorification of *la violence* which was adopted by the Fascists. One can clearly see the straight line from Sorel's conception of the direct, unmitigated, constant class struggle to the "heroic life" of the Fascists and Nazis. On the other side, modern communism contains quite distinctly elements of the same philosophy. The distrust in parliamentary methods in capitalistic countries, the principle of active militancy as a duty of every comrade, the idea of the dictatorship of the proletariat executed through action committees, the under-rating of intellectual freedom, and the emphasis on party discipline are essentially syndicalistic elements in communism.

the indirect influence on German Nazism.[26] Traces of these
tactical ideas can be found also in Bolshevism and in the
Communist movement in general. The phenomenon that a
new essentially anti-democratic philosophy of political radicalism developed out of tactical questions is of course extremely interesting from a sociological point of view.

Other Forms of Direct Action

Springing from a different situation and quite remote from
any philosophic rationalization are vigilantism and lynching,
two forms of direct action characteristic of colonial frontier
societies where the orderly but slow action of the courts of
justice is thought inadequate in coping with dangerous
offenders. Related to these tactics are other uses of violence
designed to intimidate and demoralize the opponent, all of
which may be designated as tactics of terror. In recent times,
terroristic tactics have been used by the Communists as well
as by the Fascists and Nazis.[27] Direct action, including terroristic devices, may be used also as a means of keeping discipline within the ranks of a movement. The boycott as well
as violence or the threat of quiet liquidation are favorite disciplinary methods of social movements, especially in situations where enforcement of discipline by other methods is
hampered by an adverse legal order, or where a movement is
compelled to go underground.

Direct action can finally also be employed as a device of
propaganda; witness the assassinations, expropriations, and
so on, committed by the Russian Nihilists and revolutionary
anarchists in Tsarist times,[28] or the bombing of revenue of-

[26] See Lorwin, *op. cit.;* Sigmund Neumann, *Permanent Revolution,* (New
York, Harper and Brothers, 1942), Laidler, *op. cit.*
[27] S. Neumann, *Permanent Revolution* (New York, Harper and Brothers,
1942), Chap. VI.
[28] The Nihilists and revolutionary anarchists in Tsarist Russia had developed an elaborate theory of terrorism; the fundamental idea was to
prove by punishable acts of violence that one was capable of sacrificing
one's life or liberty for the salvation of the masses of the people. In some

fices by members of a radical farmers' movement in Schleswig-Holstein, in 1928 and 1929.[29]

This propaganda of action can, however, also assume the form of passive resistance against the forces of the state. The suffragettes in England engaged in mass picketing of Parliament with the intention of provoking mass arrests and criminal indictments. Historically the most important case of passive direct action is the tactic of non-violent resistance and non-coöperation which was invented and successfully employed by Mahatma Gandhi in the Indian movement for independence. According to Gandhi's friend, the Rev. J. J. Doke, the idea was inspired by Hindu sources (the Gujarati poem and the Bhagavad Gita), by the Sermon on the Mount, and perhaps also by the writings of Leo Tolstoi. It consists essentially in meeting hatred with love, physical force with soul force.[30]

Direct Action versus Democratic Procedure

Direct action is essentially un-democratic because it denies the principles of rational debate and deliberation,[31] of majority rule, of compromise; it does not give the opponent a chance to present his view of the issue. The extreme forms of direct action presuppose absence of any sense of community with the adversary; he is regarded as an absolute enemy, a traitor, a heretic, eventually a sub-human being. Since genuine inter-party relations presuppose a sense of community

---

cases, like the bank robberies and payroll holdups committed by Bolshevists, the immediate surface motivation was, however, quite simply to obtain funds for the party and at the same time to weaken the ruling classes morally and economically.

[29] Hans Fallada, *Bauern, Bomben und Bonzen* (Berlin, 1933), a novel.

[30] See Albert R. Chandler, *The Clash of Political Ideals,* 2nd ed. (New York, Appleton-Century-Crofts, Inc., 1949), pp. 317, 318.

[31] See Chapter 18 and the very instructive essay by Walter Bagehot, "The Age of Discussion," in *Physics and Politics,* 5th ed. (London, 1879), which, although starting from a different issue, brings out very clearly the contrast between activism and democratic procedure.

between all parties in a society, one can say that the philosophy of direct action tends to destroy any genuine party system. No wonder that its most ardent advocates are to be found in essentially anti-democratic movements.

What combination of tactical means a movement adopts and employs will depend on a variety of factors. One of the most important factors is the nature of the society in which the movement operates. In a society where freedom of opinion does not exist, and in a state where voluntary associations for political purposes are forbidden or restricted, social and political movements are bound to become conspiratorial and to advocate direct action. During the earlier period of the British Labor movement the cases of direct action—machine wrecking, violence against private property of factory owners —and the later tactic of mass petitioning (Chartism), which had its parallel in the United States in "Coxey's army," were a result of repressive measures on the part of the government.

The structure and tactics of the Russian revolutionary social movements were a response to oppression and persecution. In order to understand present-day Communist tactics, it is important to take into account the Russian inheritance of the movement which grew up under conditions which made conspiratorial tactics practically indispensable.

In a democratic society there is a choice between playing the game according to rules of democratic procedure and disregarding these rules. In the first case, the movement will pursue practically a course of reform, through gradually influencing public opinion and through gaining majorities in legislative bodies. In the second case, the movement may make use of democratic procedures and institutions to spread its ideas, but it will eventually also resort to direct action, intimidation, and other non-democratic devices. A movement which begins as an evolutionary reform movement may at times be compelled to abandon democratic tactics and resort to direct action when a ruling minority refuses to abide by the rules of democratic procedure in settling disputes. This is likely to happen if the dominant class is confronted with a mass movement which is threatening vital interests of the ruling groups and appears to have a fair chance of gaining the support of a majority of voters.

On the other hand, certain groups, especially among those workers who cannot be easily organized for voting in elections, are inclined to advocate direct action. Examples are the I.W.W., whose main strength lay with migratory workers, miners, and sawmill workers in isolated, employer-dominated communities.[32]

[32] Brissenden, "The I.W.W.," *Encyclopedia of the Social Sciences;* Carleton Parker, *"The California Casual and his Revolt," Quarterly Journal of Economics,* Vol. 31 (1915); Hans Bötcher, *Zur Revolutionären Gewerkschaftsbewegung in Amerika, Deutschland und England,* (Jena, 1922).

17

Strategy and Tactics of Communism and Fascism

~~~~~~

PROBABLY AT NO TIME in history have there existed two major antagonistic movements whose strategy and tactics have been developed to such a point of refinement as those of modern communism and its fascistic adversaries. None of the other social movements of modern times was in need of an elaborate system of strategic and tactic *theory*. The Bolshevists needed it because they started in a situation of illegality, the Fascists because they represented a minority aiming at total power.

The Bolshevists, as the revolutionary opposition to the Tsarist régime, were compelled to adapt their tactics to a constant struggle with the police.[1] The Fascists were in a more favorable position because they could rely to a great extent on the ruling classes, but the National Socialists had to cover up many of their true aims for fear of losing support and arousing foreign intervention. This explains the conspiratorial character of the tactics in both movements.

THE STRUGGLE FOR POWER: COMMUNIST STRATEGY AND TACTICS

The principles of Communist strategy and tactics were formulated in the program of the Fifth Congress of the Com-

[1] See Lenin's exposition of socialist strategy and tactics in "What Is to Be Done?" *Collected Works*, Vol. IV, Bk. II (New York, International Publishers Co., Inc., 1929).

intern in 1924, which was revised in 1928.[2] There have, of course, been later refinements, but the principles have not been changed. Although the Communist Party in each country is a small élite of the "most class-conscious, most active and most courageous members" of the working class, its success will depend on its ability to maintain close contact with the masses of the workers and the people in general. Therefore the party must "extend its influence over the majority of the members of its own class" especially by gaining followers and supporters among the members of proletarian mass organizations like trade unions, factory councils, coöperative societies, workers' sport organizations, and so forth. It must also gain influence over the "lower strata of the intelligentsia," the petite bourgeoisie, the peasantry, the agricultural laborers, and the rural poor in general.

In colonial and semi-colonial countries the party will support the national liberation movements against the imperialist rulers, establishing political coöperation between the proletariat in the oppressing countries and the peasants and workers in the oppressed countries. The struggle in these countries is directed first, against foreign domination, in alliance with the native upper classes against the bourgeoisie of the oppressing country and second, against the native bourgeoisie, particularly against the exploiting landlords. The agrarian revolution will thus be coupled with the national liberation.

Variability of Tactic

The tactical pursuit of the major strategic aims will depend on the particular situation in each country at a given time. When a revolutionary situation is developing, the party must

[2] Quoted after *The Strategy and Tactics of World Communism,* Report of Subcommittee on National and International Movements, Committee on Foreign Affairs, 80th Congress, House Document 619 (Washington, D. C., U. S. Government Printing Office, 1948).

390 TACTICS AND STRATEGY

use minor, every-day working-class needs to raise *partial demands*—demands for immediate reforms—in order to lead the proletarian masses into the revolutionary struggle.

When the revolutionary tide is rising, that is, when the structure of society is so disorganized that a revolution becomes possible, the party must lead the direct attack upon the bourgeois state by raising more radical demands and by organizing mass action. The latter includes strikes, demonstrations, combinations of strikes and armed demonstrations, finally the general strike together with armed insurrection. These last actions have to be prepared by formation of armed workers' and soldiers' councils and by propaganda and cell formation within the armed forces of the bourgeois state. The party must be careful not to push too far ahead and not to lose, by unsuccessful actions, the confidence of the masses; on the other hand it must not let the opportunity for insurrection slip by and thus "allow the initiative to pass to the enemy...."

When the revolutionary tide is not rising, the party must try to broaden its influence through the raising of partial demands and through united front tactics, especially through active work in the trade unions and by utilizing the parliament as a platform for agitation and propaganda. Quite detailed instructions are given concerning the kind of demands that may be raised in this kind of situation in the sphere of industrial relations, politics, agrarian reform, and colonial policy. These tactical rules are, as one can easily see, concerned mainly with what may be called the appeal to the masses, with measures aiming not so much at the winning of new members—this is done by the more intensive methods which have been discussed in Chapter 15—as at the gaining of support among the voters. The Communists, like the Fascists, are extremely adept in the art of varying the line of appeal in correlation with the specific interests of various groups: workers, farmers, tenants, intellectuals, and ethnic minorities. The Communists do not restrict their appeal to promises; rather they have developed an elaborate technique of actively taking the part of underprivileged groups. Rossi describes how this technique was applied in France.[3]

RAISING DEMANDS

Urban Tenants

As an example of its application in the main stronghold of communism in the United States, we may survey the instructions of the Communist Party of America for work among the poorer urban tenants contained in the *Manual on Housing Work*, prepared by District Housing Commission, Communist Party, New York State, ca. 1936. It begins with the following sentences:

Housing work can play a major rôle in establishing the Party branches and units in the neighborhoods. Its political importance at the present moment cannot be overestimated.

Both major parties, it is claimed, are trying to get popular support by some kind of housing legislation scheme, while at the same time the real-estate lobbies try to destroy existing regulations for the protection of tenants.

There are in New York City about 2 million men, women, and children who are living in "old law tenements" (erected before 1901). . . . These 2 million men, women, and children . . . must be organized. . . . The party must play a major rôle in organizing and leading the growing tenant movement. . . . Housing is an issue around which local neighborhood united fronts can be built and should be one of the main planks of a people's party.

The party also proposes organization of small landlords who are merely "janitors" for banks, insurance companies, and other mortgage holders. The main factor in the program is the organized tenants' movement—that is, the local tenant unions (leagues, associations) comprised in the Citywide Tenants Council. It "is yet in its organizational stage."

The manual states that

[3] A. Rossi, *A Communist Party in Action*, W. Kendall, ed. (New Haven, Yale University Press, 1949), pp. 57 f.

...on the Lower East Side, the issue of housing was utilized successfully by the Party in developing a local neighborhood united front. Over 40 organizations of the Lower East Side with comrades working inside, rallied to sponsor a tenants' union. When the banks started an organized campaign of mass evictions, the tenants' union won a temporary victory and stopped mass evictions.

The Communist Party organizes cells in the tenants' unions, which must see to it that the tenants' unions do more than engage in legal battles in the courts. Propaganda and direct action must be instigated. "The housing issue is one of the main ways in which to get into the neighborhoods. Recruiting can grow tenfold after proper work."

Directives are given in the pamphlet for approaching tenants in the rôle of a representative of the Citywide Tenants' Council. Conversation may start with a reference to the existing violations of the Multiple Dwellings Law of 1929 in the building visited. Meetings are to be arranged in the home of one of the tenants. Here an apartment-tenants' committee will be elected; it will call for inspection by the city's tenement-house department, then present requests to the landlord, and so forth.

The American Negro as an "Oppressed Nation"

The appeal to ethnic minorities has played an important rôle in the history of the Communist movement in the United States,[4] as we have previously indicated (Chapter 8). In that connection, the peculiar approach of the Communist Party to the American Negro problem was mentioned; since

[4] "The Report of the Royal Commission to investigate the facts relating to and the circumstances surrounding the communication, by public officials and other persons in positions of trust, of secret and confidential information to agents of a foreign power" (Ottawa, Controller of Stationary, June 27, 1946), p. 53; this contains some interesting information on the Communist workings on this continent. Mr. Gouzenko charged that the Soviet officials imitated the Nazis in this respect (p. 52). "In the same way Soviet officials are working with the Canadians of Russian and Ukrainian origin. They try to develop those people as a Communist-minded population. . . ."

it offers an interesting example not only of propaganda tactics but also of party doctrinairism, it may be appropriate to present this matter in some detail.

The Negroes—according to communist doctrine—constitute the largest underprivileged minority in the United States, which, on account of its socio-economic position, can be considered a potential ally and a recruiting cadre for the Communist Party. The Communist Party therefore acts as a defender of Negro rights and a supporter of Negro aspirations to political, economic, and social equality. In particular, the party has gone on record for land reform in the South, for full participation of Negro workers in trade unions,[5] and finally for "self-determination for the Negro people, that is, their right to realize self-government in the Negro majority area in the South." No detailed program for the realization of the last objective is given, and the proposition has been a subject of controversy within the National Committee of the Communist Party of the United States.

From a Marxist-Leninist point of view, the position of the Negroes in the United States and their relation to the Communist Party presents a number of theoretical difficulties. The Communists cannot recognize the Negroes as a separate and homogeneous race. Nor can the Negroes be considered as a class, although the vast majority may qualify as proletarians (indeed there is scarcely a more proletarian working-class group than the mass of the Negro wage earners); but the existence of a Negro petite bourgeoisie, consisting of bankers, undertakers, lawyers, and small businessmen, cannot be overlooked. Nor can it be denied that a fairly large number of Negroes are farm-owners. In short, the Negroes form a class-society of their own and they cannot be won

[5] "Resolution of the Communist International on the Negro Question in the United States," *The Communist*, Vol. 9 (January, 1930); James S. Allen, *The Negro Question in the United States* (New York, International Publishers Co., Inc. 1936); W. Z. Foster *et. al.*, *The Communist Position on the Negro Question* (New York, New Century Pubs. Inc., 1947).

over by an appeal to working-class interests alone. The theory of Lloyd Warner and his school, which views the Negroes as a caste, cannot be accepted by the Communists, since it would involve acquiescence in the present state of race relations. What kind of group, then, are the American Negroes from a Communist point of view? For an authoritative answer we turn to the comments by William Z. Foster, then National Chairman of the Communist Party of the United States.

> During the course of this discussion, we have clearly established three or four fundamental propositions regarding the mooted question of self-determination in the Black Belt of the South. First, that the Negro people in the Black Belt are a nation, that they possess the essential qualities of nationhood, as elaborated in the works of that great expert on the national question, Stalin.[6]

Now Stalin, as we learn from another speaker at the plenary meeting of the National Committee, defines *nation* as follows: "a nation is a historically evolved, stable community of language, territory, economic life and psychological make-up manifested in community of culture."[7] The application of this definition to the Negroes in the South, or to be more precise, in the Black Belt of the South, has caused the drafters of the Resolution considerable headache. Are the Negroes a "stable community"? Do they have an economic life of their own? Why, if they are a nation, do they not themselves raise the demand for national self-determination? Mr. Foster gives the answer to the last question.

> Fundamentally, the reason is that they are essentially a young nation, a developing nation; [their national consciousness is not yet fully developed, but] they, too, have put out, what are basically national [sic] slogans, very largely in a racial sense. . . . Behind these prevalent concepts of race are actually developing national concepts.[8]

[6] "Resolution on the Question of Negro Rights and Self-Determination," adopted at the plenary meeting of the National Committee of the Communist Party of the United States, Dec. 3-5, 1946, p. 14.

[7] Max Weiss, Secretary, National Education Commission, Communist Party, United States of America, *ibid.*, p. 48.

[8] *Ibid.*, pp. 14-15.

In other words, according to Communist doctrine we are here confronted with a case of false or under-developed group consciousness, similar and analogous to the phenomenon of false class consciousness (see Chapter 8). This is not the only difficulty. Mr. Foster realizes of course that "the Negro people most distinctly feel themselves to be Americans in the fullest sense of the word, and they are fighting resolutely for full participation in all phases of American life on the basis of complete economic, political and social equality." Nevertheless, there is "a second main trend in the orientation of the Negro people," namely, the development of a definite national consciousness as Negroes. Mr. Foster takes it as a symptom that "the Negro people no longer speak of themselves as a race, but rather as a people. When the Negro people begin to designate themselves as a people rather than as a race, they are already taking a long stride in the direction of national consciousness." Although these two tendencies seem to oppose each other, Mr. Foster says they do not.

Comrade Ed Strong made a good contribution when he stressed the basic harmony between these two streams of courses [sic] of development. . . . One of the major difficulties we have had to contend with has been a tendency of our opponents to pose [sic] one of these currents to the other, thus making it appear that the demand for self-determination slogan[s] is in contradiction to the proposition that Negroes fight for the fullest rights as Americans. Comrade Strong knocked this nonsense on the head when he pointed out so forcefully that it is impossible for the Negro people to achieve their full economic, political, and social equality as Americans unless they organize as a nation, unless they forward the slogan of self-determination for the Black Belt of the South.[9]

From this discussion it might appear to a sociologist who is not familiar with Leninist-Stalinist thinking that the Southern Negroes might be considered as something like a national minority. This label, however, is reserved for the Negroes in the North. Outside the South, according to Mr.

[9] *Ibid.*, p. 16.

James E. Jackson, State Chairman of the Communist Party of Louisiana,

> ...we view the problem as that of national minorities, that is, the cornerstone of the concept is the individual. On the other hand, the concept of the Negro in his heartland territory in the Black Belt of the South as that of an oppressed nation has as its cornerstone the mass.[10]

Before forming an opinion on the validity of this doctrine, one does well to realize that Communist doctrines are not necessarily meant to be statements of fact, but weapons in the struggle for the liberation of the workers. Mr. Foster in commenting on the movement of the Negroes shows this very frankly.

> This fight...is a struggle for full nationhood, for their rightful position of full equality as a nation. In recognizing the struggle for equal rights in the South as a movement towards full nationhood, the Communist Party supplies new power to the Negro liberation movement and also advances the perspective of full freedom for the Negro people.[11]

However, there remains among the Communist leaders a feeling of uneasiness, for the Negroes and even the white comrades might misunderstand the entire idea of Negro nationhood, and instead of solidarity of all workers there might develop tension and even conflict. Therefore one of the last paragraphs of the resolution admonishes,

> Negro Communists should systematically combat separatist tendencies and distrust of white workers among the Negro people, while building working class unity and alliance with other nationality groups, also suffering from discrimination, such as the foreignborn, the Jewish people, and Catholics.[12]

Considered as "nationality groups," these are certainly strange bed-fellows.

In reading the numerous articles on the subject which appeared during the year of 1946 in *Political Affairs,* one can-

[10] *Ibid.,* p. 28.
[11] *Ibid.,* p. 11.
[12] *Ibid.,* p. 13.

not escape the impression that the National Committee worked hard to reconcile the practical problems of the American scene with Leninist-Stalinist doctrine about national movements in colonial or semi-colonial societies. The reason for this scholastic *tour de force* is that Lenin, "as far back as 1913, emphasized that the Negro people constituted an oppressed nation." [13] There exists in an unfinished essay a "direct reference to the Negro people as an oppressed nation. . . ." [14] Thus an occasional remark of Lenin's gives direction to Communist propaganda on this regional and national problem of which Lenin could not have had a very intimate and concrete knowledge,[15] and within the Communist movement, it puts into the position of heretics all those who approach the question in a more realistic way.

Infiltration

The technique of raising demands is implemented by the technique of *boring from within*. This involves active participation in policy making and administration of mass organizations of the working class in order to gain influence and eventually control over such organizations. This has been mentioned in Chapter 13. The main objectives of infiltration have been the trade unions. The French General Confederation of Trade Unions at one time was practically under Communist control. In the United States, Communist infiltration has been successful in certain industrial unions—until the

[13] Claudia Jones, "On the Right to Self-determination for the Negro in the Black Belt," *Political Affairs* (Jan., 1946), p. 70. Also Lenin, *Miscellany, Collected Works*, Vol. XXX.

[14] *Ibid.*

[15] One should of course realize that in 1913 the concentration of Negroes in the "Black Belt of the South" was much greater than today. Lenin's statement was made before the great migration of Negroes to the North, which began during the First World War, and before the migration of Negroes to cities in the South had led to a greater dispersion of the colored population within that region. In this connection, it is important to realize that the Negroes do not want segregation, which autonomy would inevitably involve.

sudden changes of the Communist Party's policy during the war began to alienate the rank and file from Communist influence and gave the moderate leaders a chance to oust the Communists from leading positions. Fascists and National Socialists have used the same technique. Although infiltration is by no means an invention of the new political orders, it has been developed by them to a fine art, and it agrees perfectly with their conspiratorial character.

Infiltration consists in forming highly active cells within labor unions and other organizations and eventually gaining the control of the organization by getting members of the order elected to important offices. It requires a great deal of hard, persistent work, skill in the handling of parliamentary procedure, intimate knowledge of the organization's constitution and by-laws, and all the tactics of gaining nominations and winning elections. Under unfavorable circumstances no more may be possible than the planting of a few members in the organization who in case of a *coup d'état* will assume leadership by usurpation of offices. The National Socialists made much use of this technique, a fact which explains to some extent the ease with which they accomplished the coördination (*Gleichschaltung*) of all kinds of organizations. The method is very efficient because the infiltrators will have of course acquired a good knowledge of the political attitudes and personality traits of the more active members and are thus in the position to use blackmail, intimidation, flattery, and persuasion most effectively on recalcitrant members.

Of even greater tactical importance is infiltration into government offices and agencies, including the police and armed forces. In this regard the fascistic parties have the advantage that their adherents tend to belong to the same social classes and sets from which the government personnel is recruited and it is therefore not so difficult for them to win servants of the state for their cause or to place party members in government positions. The National Socialists, for example, had by the winter of 1932-1933 succeeded in gaining considerable foothold among the Prussian police (*Schutzpolizei*) and among the armed forces.[16]

Duplication of Government Units

In addition, the Nazis had, like their Fascist model, developed a *technique of duplicating*, in the organization of their own movement, the major agencies of the state—the Foreign Office was duplicated by Ribbentrop's bureau, and so forth. This device permitted the training of personnel for specific tasks as well as for the control of state agencies after the seizure of power.[17]

The Communists have developed a similar device, the "people's committees,"—future *soviets*, which, according to communist tactics are to be formed in factories, offices and specific areas, that is, in neighborhoods and on a local community basis. These committees comprise not only Communists but "all men and women of good will," [18] and they can serve a variety of purposes. In France, for example, they were assigned the task of getting the economy going again after the armistice, while the German-Soviet friendship pact was still extant.[19] Or, where the situation demands it, they can be used to slow down production, to perpetrate acts of sabotage, to harass the employers by presenting workers' demands for higher wages, shorter hours, and recreational facilities, and they can be used to stage mass demonstrations

[16] It seems that in the police a large proportion of the higher officers were Nazis, whereas in the armed forces, it was mainly the non-commissioned officers and enlisted men who were won over. The explanation of this difference is that many of the police officers came from the same petty bourgeois and farm families from which the bulk of the non-coms in the army, navy, and air force came; in fact, many had been non-commissioned officers in the army before 1918.

[17] Very effective was the incorporation of S.A. (storm troop) units into the state police in the spring of 1933.

[18] Rossi, *op. cit.*, pp. 57, 111, 115.

[19] *Ibid.*, pp. 57-58.

and mass action. They are especially useful in a situation where the trade unions are not controlled by the Communists, since the people's committees function outside the unions.

Their ultimate rôle, however, is an important part in the revolution. They are the cadres from which the higher echelons of soviets are to be formed, and they can be armed and thus be used to form "red guards" or revolutionary militias.[20]

THE SEIZURE OF POWER:
CONDITIONS OF A "COUP D'ETAT"

The actual seizure of power has to come through a *coup d'état*. The model for the Communists remains the Russian Revolution,[21] but the tactical details are of course to be adapted to the particular situation.

In 1923 the Nazis apparently planned a march on Berlin after Mussolini's example; the failure of this premature coup led to a complete revision of tactics. Observing constitutional procedure, they entered into a coalition government with the Conservatives (D.N.V.P.). Under the pretext of a clear and present danger to the state (demonstrated by setting fire to the national parliament building and blaming the Communists for it), they eliminated the Communist Party from the legal political scene and induced the rump parliament to endow the government with emergency powers. Since the ministry of the interior and the prime ministry in Prussia

[20] When in the German revolution of 1918 the first revolutionary soldiers' councils appeared, the High Command of the army ordered the election of soldiers' councils in all units. The effect of this order was to convert the councils, by and large—especially in the combat forces and in occupied countries—from potential tools of revolution into stabilizing agencies. The author remembers how the men in his own unit elected to the council their commanding officer—a man whose counter-revolutionary leanings were well known and who played an active part in various counter-revolutionary undertakings, until he was killed during the Nazi *putsch* in Munich in 1923.

[21] Martin Ebon, *World Communism Today*, 3rd ed. (New York, McGraw-Hill Book Company, Inc., 1948), p. 33.

were in the hands of Goering, he had control of the police force, and the party now was free to persecute and oppress all opposition and finally to oust its Conservative allies from the cabinet.[22]

The Communists have applied similar methods in several of the satellite countries; the most instructive example is perhaps the coup in Czechoslovakia. Here the control of the ministry of the interior with its jurisdiction over the police, together with the direct action of people's committees (which had been formed in every factory, store, and government bureau) were the decisive tactical factors. The people's committees intimidated, arrested, and liquidated resisting supporters of the democratic government. They initiated the dictatorship of the proletariat—a régime "not bound by any laws." The Nazi equivalents to this phase of the Communist technique were the direct actions of the S.A. (Brownshirts), S.S., and Hitler Youth during the coup of March, 1933. The psychological effect of such direct action varies directly with its ability to appear as spontaneous action of the "enraged" people.

Both the Communists and the Fascists have learned that a modern government cannot be overthrown by force except under the following conditions: it must have been weakened by defeat in war,[23] by an interior political reversal, and by fear among the ruling classes of a popular rising. This was the case in Russia in 1917. The other possibility is that the ruling class has been sufficiently demoralized and weakened so as to permit participation of the revolutionary party in the government, thereby giving the revolutionaries access to the

[22] For a detailed account by a close observer, see A. Brecht, *Prelude to Silence, the End of the German Republic* (New York, Oxford University Press, 1944).

[23] War at first intensifies national solidarity and postpones outbreak of a revolution which may have been threatening; defeat in war increases the revolutionary tension and improves the chances for a successful insurrection, because it demoralizes the ruling classes. Emil Lederer, *Einige Gedanken zur Soziologie der Revolution* (Leipzig, 1918), pp. 35 f.

instruments of state power. A third alternative is civil war; it presupposes that an anti-governmental armed force has established control over part of the country, as in the case of Spain (through the invasion from Spanish Morocco) and the recent case of China. In an economically highly integrated country with a well-developed system of communication and transportation at the disposal of the government, this way is not likely to be successful.

The Communists in this situation have resorted to the second scheme: the "united front" government with Social Democrats and other progressive parties (in eastern Europe these are especially the small farmers' parties). In agrarian countries the peasants are encouraged to seize the land— unless as in the Eastern Zones of Germany a radical land reform is legally enacted—while the banks, railroads, and other systems of transportation and communication, as well as the basic industries, are socialized. If the coalition partners object to such revolutionary measures, they are charged with plotting against the people's government, their leaders are arrested, made to confess, and the rival party organizations are either destroyed or merged with the Communist Party.

The Nazis applied a similar technique against the Conservatives; they gradually forced the "steelhelmets" (*Stahlhelm*), the Conservative private army, to enter into a compact with the S.A., and finally absorbed them into the latter.

To confirm the new one-party régime, an "election" is arranged in which the voters are given the choice of voting for or against the single party slate. By announcing that nonvoting will be considered as an expression of opposition and by spreading rumors that the party has ways and means to check how one votes, the voters can usually be sufficiently intimidated to attain very high percentages in favor of the régime. Where these devices fail, it is possible to resort to the usual tricks of falsifying the returns, provided that the police and the courts are under control.

The Communists in countries outside the Soviet Union have, today, the great advantage that for the preparation and execution of a revolution they can rely upon leaders who have many years of experience in party work and in most cases have been trained in revolutionary tactics and communist strategy in the schools of the Bolshevik party. Some, like the late George Dimitrov, have held important offices in the Comintern. The National Socialists had to learn their techniques through trial and error while preparing for the seizure of power; it is, however, certain that they learned a great deal from the Italian Fascists and also from the Bolshevists.

THE STABILIZATION OF THE RÉGIME: MAKING FRIENDS AND CONTROLLING ENEMIES

Once a *coup d'etat* has been successfully performed, the political order will have to consolidate and stabilize its régime by constant vigilance against three possible dangers: attack from abroad, opposition in the country, and dissent within the political order itself. The three are often interrelated; we recall the support given by foreign powers to the armies of various counter-revolutionary leaders, like Kolchak and Wrangel, during the period of civil war after the Bolshevik revolution. No serious attempts at intervention were made against the régimes of Mussolini and Hitler; even during the war the Western powers did not give political support to the German opposition to Hitler.

Any revolutionary régime will therefore resort to forceful repression of its internal enemies (see p. 370). Force alone, however, cannot stabilize a régime; on the contrary, it has the effect of creating enemies and therefore tends to lead to self-perpetuation of repression. Therefore, the political order has to make friends by enacting measures which will reconcile powerful groups in the society and by offering

careers and influence to outsiders who are either gullible
enough or opportunistic and ambitious enough to make
peace with the new régime. Hence, the alternating of membership drives and purges, which has been discussed before
(Chapter 15); hence also, the establishment of channels
through which young citizens can, after proper training and
indoctrination, hope to rise to eminent positions in the hierarchy of the political order or in the state bureaucracy. By
expanding the armed forces and the bureaucracy, the totalitarian régimes are able to increase their support among the
younger generation considerably and in a short time. The
new chances of advancement are likely to reconcile even
many former opponents. However, since the armed forces
and certain branches of the civil service cannot easily be
brought under party control, they may become a refuge for
opponents of the new order. This was the case, to some
extent, under the Hitler régime.

The very fact that a new political authority is established
will reconcile to the new régime many people without particular political convictions, and the peculiar characteristics
of a political order will attract individuals who desire security and comradeship more than liberty.

At the same time, the political order will have to gain
control of all possible seed-beds of resistance and opposition.
Since it is possible to convert even the most innocuous group
into a cell of opposition, the new régime will purge its declared enemies from all organized groups, and, if possible,
have its own members placed in controlling positions.

The result is an increasingly tighter network of social controls which omits practically no sphere of life. In the case
of Nazism and Fascism this was to be expected, since it
agreed with the basic philosophy of these movements. But it
was not to be expected in the case of Communism. If the
dictatorship of the proletariat has developed into a totalitarian régime which shows no signs of withering away, this

is the consequence, according to Communist doctrine, of the continuous danger of attack from capitalistic powers.

THE ISSUE OF "EXCEPTIONALISM" (TITOISM)

From its very beginning the Marxists have visualized the socialist revolution as a worldwide struggle in which the "proletarians in all countries" would form a united force.

The Bolshevists projected their peculiarly Russian conception of organization, strategy, and tactics of the movement into the field of communistic world politics by forming the Third International after the pattern of their own party. Instead of a loose world federation of independent national parties, they created a highly centralized and disciplined International as soon as they had established themselves in power in their own country.

The program of the Comintern states the need for strict discipline in the following words:

International Communist discipline must find expression in the subordination of the partial and local interests of the movement to its general and lasting interests and in strict fulfilment, by all members, of the decisions passed by the leading bodies of the Communist International.

The phrase "partial and local interests" refers to the interests of the Communist movements in countries outside the Soviet Union, and the "general and lasting interests" have come to be identified with the interests of the U.S.S.R. as the socialistic fatherland of the proletariat. What these interests are, is determined from case to case by the Comintern or its successors—the Cominform in the West and the Liaisonburo in the Far East—or lastly by the *Politburo*.

Obedience to the directives of the Cominform is demanded from all Communist parties outside the U.S.S.R. even if the interests of these parties—and presumably the interests of the working class in these countries—seem to require a different policy. In France, for example, the policy which the French Communist Party was ordered to pursue during the era of the Nazi-Soviet friendship pact brought the movement into the very dangerous position of virtually aiding the fascistic aggressor and later of supporting the German war effort.[24] One wonders whether, even from the standpoint of the U.S.S.R., this was a wise policy. In any case, it damaged the prestige of the party in France very considerably. However, they were able to more than recover their losses, because the episode was soon forgotten when the German-Russian war began and the Communists became very active in the leadership of the resistance.

Greater and more lasting was the set-back in the United States. Here the Communists had won a great deal of influence and prestige in some of the labor unions in mass-production industries. The decline of the Communists' influence began when, during the German-Soviet friendship pact, they opposed the unions' efforts to contribute to the aid lent to France and England. When, after the German attack on the Soviet Union, the Communists suddenly shifted to a policy of unlimited support of the war effort, even to the point that they were willing to give up hard-won union achievements, the impression was created that the Communists regarded the American unions merely as figures in the foreign policy of the Soviet Union. The result was a rising tide of anti-Communist sentiment, which led to the exclusion of Communists from leading positions in most unions. Public opinion in general began to take it for granted that the Communist Party of America was itself nothing but a fifth column in the service of the U.S.S.R.

In a country where the Communist Party is small and uninfluential, the Comintern can enforce international discipline, since the party leaders, as professional revolutionists, are morally and financially dependent upon support from

[24] See the well-documented analysis in Rossi, *op. cit.*

the Russian party. If they are expelled, they have nowhere to go, unless they want to desert the cause for which they have been living and become agents of anti-communist groups. But in a country where the Communists are strong, and the party large, as in France after the war, or where the Communists have formed a government, as in Yugoslavia, it is much more difficult for the Cominform to impose its policies against the objections of the party leaders in the country. Not only are these leaders financially independent, but they know also that policies which would antagonize the masses of workers, peasants, and other supporters, might lead to a severe defeat to the party, or an overthrow of the Communist régime.

The issues involved in these controversies have been mainly of the kind which may be called strategic questions. However, in the case of Yugoslavia more seems to have been involved: an attempt by the Russians to create in that country, as in Poland and other eastern European countries, a party organization and a secret service controlled from Moscow. This move was opposed by the Yugoslavian Communist Party which had established its régime without aid from Moscow.

Naturally the top leaders in the various countries—all of whom are well trained in Marxist-Leninist theory and in Communist tactics and strategy—ought to know best whether the situation in their country is ripe for, let us say, collectivization of agriculture, or direct action (which has been a party issue recently in Japan and in about 1948 in many Southeast Asiatic countries). If Moscow, against the objections of native leaders, insists upon premature steps, the impression will grow that the various Communist Parties are in fact regarded, in Moscow, as expendable auxiliary forces in the Soviet Union's struggle for hegemony.

There was no exact analogy to the Comintern in the Fascist and National Socialist movements. However, the

Nazis attempted, more or less successfully, to organize not only the German citizens in foreign countries and the native German minorities abroad, but also to control native fascistic movements in various countries. We know now these organizations were to function as fifth columns and that the Nazi leaders considered even the German minorities as expendable.

The Communist case is more complicated. Here we have to rely, so to speak, on circumstantial evidence, while the real meaning of the policy of the Russian leaders of the movement is known to them alone. If they insist on absolute obedience to the decisions taken by the Cominform, and denounce those party leaders outside the Soviet Union who hold that exceptions should be made for their country, they actually claim superior wisdom. Those among their opponents who have openly broken with the Stalinist organization charge—like Rossi—that the Russian Communist Party has abandoned the ideals of the early Bolshevists and is now indeed using the communist parties in other countries simply as fifth columns in the interest of Russian imperialism.[25] Thus the apparently strategic controversy may very well involve a real schism over ideological issues. In this controversy the positions would be reversed: the heretics being the true defenders of the faith.[26]

[25] Rossi, *op. cit.*, pp. 85-89, 234-242.
[26] This position has been taken by the Communist Party of Yugoslavia in a May-Day proclamation according to a dispatch by M. S. Handler to *The New York Times* (May 1, 1950). The proclamation, as reported in *The New York Times*, said:
"The current inside the international workers and the democratic movement, which defends the just cause of our country and the struggle against the revision of Marxism and Leninism [by the Russians], is becoming more and more powerful. The number of those who are participating in this current is increasing from day to day, and we send them our fraternal greetings on the occasion of May 1.
"The numbers of workers and entire trade union organizations, men of letters and science, as well as other progressive people in the world who are following our struggle with sympathy see in it the spark that will set off new victories for the forces of socialism and that will aid the development of socialism on its proper road."

VII

~~~~~~

THE FUNCTIONS
OF POLITICAL PARTIES
AND SOCIAL MOVEMENTS

18

The Formation of Consensus

~~~~~~

PARTIES AND MOVEMENTS AS FUNCTIONAL ELEMENTS IN DEMOCRATIC SOCIETY

Discord and Concord

THROUGHOUT THE AGES, political parties have been regarded with disfavor by the man in the street, by statesmen, and by political philosophers. Parties seemed to disturb the peace and harmony in the community which is the very foundation of any social order. The bickerings and intrigues of party leaders and the criticism from the opposition are of course annoying to the responsible statesman with autocratic leanings.[1]

---

[1] Henry St. John Bolingbroke, *Dissertation upon Parties*, 7th ed. (London, 1749), pp. 5 ff, 137 ff., regards the old parties of Whigs and Tories as sound divisions on the basis of principles; but he condemns the attempts of the court to create, by corruption, a new division between a court party and a country party and to identify the former with the national interest.

Wachsmuth, whose previously mentioned work is probably the oldest comprehensive history of political parties, observes: "The genesis of party formation leads into many and various depths and gorges of the human soul [Gemuet] and most rarely to the seat of a will [which is] enlightened and determined by reason. The spirit of party has its origin and nurture in the impure and chaotic sphere of the passions...avarice and ambition, revenge, love, and hatred, voluptuousness, lust, lack of self-control, insolence, wickedness, and personal sympathy or antipathy make up the mental dispensary of party mechanism like so many levers and springs...." Wilhelm Wachsmuth, *Geschichte der politischen Parteiungen alter and neuer Zeit*, Vols. I (1853-1856), p. 27.

Madison, in the famous No. 10 of the *Federalist*, begins his discourse on the danger of factions with references to "the violence of faction." "By a faction, I understand a number of citizens,...who are united, adverse to

But even the political scientist who is convinced of the superiority of democracy may be seriously disturbed by the rise of parties. He will point out, as a first principle, that any society can exist only through permanent and sustained consensus of the wills of the members who compose it. This consensus must not be thought of as a rational agreement; its basis at least lies deeper than that. In fact, the rational compromises, the majority decisions, the abiding of the opposition by majority decisions, the voluntary compliance with numerous administrative orders which make up the daily reality of this consensus would not be possible without a deeper, more affectual and habitual understanding which we may call *concord*.[2]

The German word *Eintracht* signifies even better than concord the nature of this consensus: it means that the members of the group desire one and the same basic goal, that their striving is coördinated. What is it they are striving for? In the first place, it is the preservation of their group, the

the rights of other citizens, or to the permanent and aggregate interests of the community."

For a comprehensive treatment of the changing opinions about parties see Carl Gösta Widell, *Staten och partiväsendet* [The State and the Parties] (Lund, 1939), pp. 109 ff.

Widell shows that parties were at first considered incompatible with the national interest and their existence was regarded as a contradiction to genuine representation; they were regarded as outgrowths of selfish interests and of unrestrained passions. The defenders of absolute monarchy as well as the advocates of constitutional monarchy held that the monarch alone represented the people and the state as a whole, whereas parties pursued particular interests, motivated by the baser instincts of the citizens; they were therefore regarded as dangerous elements. Behind these arguments was the fear of the increasing power of the people. The liberals were opposed to parties because they seemed to weaken the people's power of resistance against the crown. Liberals were also opposed to parties because of their encroachment on the liberty and freedom of opinion of the individual citizen.

Widell maintains that a change towards a more positive evaluation of parties occurred in England during the early decades of the nineteenth century, while the negative evaluation lasted much longer in France and still longer in Germany (pp. 120 ff.).

[2] In this we follow Ferdinand Tönnies, *Gemeinschaft und Gesellschaft.*

continued existence of their community, the living together in harmony. From this proposition follows the will to abide by particular decisions of the group which may not find everybody's specific approval, the willingness to compromise and the respect for dissenting opinions.

Concord does not exclude the pursuit of individual and particular interests, but it makes agreements possible between persons or groups engaged in such pursuits.

It is concord which makes it possible, in a relatively small group of people with diverse individual opinions, to arrive, through debate, at an acceptable expression of what is called *the sense of the meeting*.[3] That a decision arrived at by majority vote can be accepted as valid and binding by the opposition is of course also due to the existence of concord.

Representation

In larger groups, it is of course more difficult to ascertain the sense of the meeting. The main device by which these difficulties can be overcome is representation. Representative assemblies are supposed to operate on the principle that every member act as if he represented, not any particular

[3] A. D. Lindsay, *The Essentials of Democracy* (Philadelphia, University of Pennsylvania Press, 1929), pp. 22-23. Democracy, according to Lindsay, involves two principles: first, that nobody be bound to obey a government "that he hath not a voice to put himself under," as it was formulated in the debates in Cromwell's army; second, that the true will of the people—which ought to be the will of God—can be found through the weighing of individual opinions in public discussion. (p. 24) The second principle presupposes the existence of a recognized opposition. Since in a large society not every citizen can participate directly in the final discussion, but only through elected representation, the debate in and between political parties and other voluntary associations becomes an essential part of the entire process: "In a healthy democracy the discussions of the representative assembly will as it were act as chairman for the multifarious informal discussion of the nation as a whole, and the measure of the successful working of democracy is the extent to which the voting of the ordinary man and woman has been informed by this widely diffused public discussion." (p. 42.)

group, but the community as a whole. This at least is the modern theory of popular representation.[4]

If this principle were applied in the actual conduct of citizens, each would give his vote to that candidate who, in the voter's opinion, is best qualified to represent, not him or any particular group of voters, but the constituency as a whole and the entire people. These men, being elected and assembled, would in their turn be guided in their deliberations and decisions—not by any particular interests of their electors, but by considerations of the common good, the national interest. Ideally, in conducting themselves according to these principles, the representatives should arrive at unanimous decisions; in reality, because of the frailty of men's wisdom, that rarely happens, especially in assemblies representing large and highly complex communities. As a short-cut, in order to secure the functioning of representative assemblies, the majority rule has been invented. The minority or opposition abides by the majority decision as if it represented the will of the whole assembly. The majority rule is acceptable since, as long as every member of the assembly is free to vote on any issue according to his own opinion and conviction, no fixed and permanent majorities will crystallize and in the long run the decisions of the assembly will represent the sense of the community. The rules of parliamentary procedure, by guaranteeing a maximum of freedom of discussion, intend to give the dissenting members an assurance that their opinions have been heard and weighed, and that there may be, at a later date, an opportunity to have the matter reconsidered. In summary, the majority rule in representative assemblies operates on the assumption of fair play and a free meeting of minds.

[4] J. J. Rousseau, *Le Contrat Social, Livre II*, Chap. III, and Widell, *op. cit.*, p. 116.

Conflicting Opinions on Parties and Movements

However, if factions and parties are formed, so the argument runs, the individual representative will be guided by considerations of party interest rather than by considerations of the common interest. At the polls, the voters, instead of electing the men best fitted to represent the entire constituency, would vote for men of their own party. If this happens, the formation of a consensus will be hampered; decisions made in the representative assembly will no longer be an expression of the sense of the represented community but rather of the will of particularistic interests.[5]

This, indeed, is a severe indictment of political parties. And yet it is hard to see how a representative assembly could function without parties. The sociological reasons for the genesis of parties have been discussed in Chapter 14.

A more realistic school of thought developed during the struggles for popular government in European countries where progressive (liberal and democratic) statesmen and theorists began to advance the view that organized political parties were an essential guarantee of civil and political liberty.[6] The function which these thinkers ascribed to parties was, so to speak, a negative one—that of preventing the government from oppressing the people. The idea fitted the pattern of constitutional government as well as that of parliamentary government and the American system of checks and balances, A state without parties could not be a free state.[7]

[5] John C. Calhoun, "A Disquisition on Government," *Works* (New York, D. Appleton and Company, 1864), Vol. I, especially pp. 39-41, where he speaks of the danger·that a government based on the principle of absolute majority would come under the control of a majority within the dominant party.

[6] See, for example, "Parteien," *Staatslexikon für das Deutsche Volk* (1869-71), Vol. II, pp. 299 ff.

[7] Widell, *op. cit.*, pp. 126 f. The new evaluation of parties had begun in England at the end of the eighteenth century with Burke, Fox, Hume, and Grenville.

However, with the growth of formal party organization and with the activation of larger masses of citizens through the extension of the right to vote to practically every adult, it became evident that parties had more constructive functions.

When people began to debate the political issues within their party groups, and when party leaders were compelled to lend an ear to the many voices that arose from pressure groups, from the press, and from other vehicles of public opinion, it became clear that parties had also some important function in establishing the sense of the community. This idea is very clearly expressed in the following statement of a prominent jurist:

> The will of the people which we have contrasted with the parties does not originate without the latter, in any case not without the action of antagonistic forces which oppose each other under certain conditions in form of parties. The content of the people's will ... comprises always a number of compromises between conflicting interests and convictions, compromises which presuppose an antagonism of the forces underlying these interests and convictions. The unity of the will on which the social order is based can therefore be always only a limited one. ... It is perfect only in a formalistic regard, insofar as it demands that compromises be respected.[8]

No longer were parties regarded as mere disturbing forces, as necessary evils; a new and positive evaluation arose out of a more realistic understanding of the integrating processes in a large democracy.

Parties are now regarded as indispensable structural elements in any large-scale democracy.[9]

[8] Adolf Merkel, *Fragmente zur Socialwissenschaft* (Strassburg, Karl J. Trübner, 1898), p. 92.

[9] E. E. Schattschneider, *Party Government* (New York, Farrar & Rinehart, Inc., 1942), pp. 31, 50 ff. Herman Finer, *The Theory and Practice of Modern Government* (New York, Dial Press Inc., 1934), pp. 241 ff., 284 f. The political parties, according to Finer, set out to accomplish what other agencies do not do: they gather and disperse political information and they gather the politically talented—that is, the élite. The collection and dispersion of information by the parties is better organized in England than in most other countries.

Simultaneous with this reconsideration of the rôle of parties in forming the common will has been the realization, especially by students of comparative government and by sociologists, of the importance of parties in the selection of leading statesmen. It was found that under certain conditions the quality of the political élite depends very largely on the relation of parties to goverment.[10]

The prevailing opinion on social movements resembles the early opinion on parties. At least those who do not belong to a social movement usually tend to regard it as a nuisance or as a real danger to social solidarity. In particular, conservative people, who are content with the status quo of their society, tend to take this position. To them the leaders of social movements appear as agitators, rabble-rousers, or maladjusted personalities. It is quite significant that in our day the imputation of egotistic motives is often replaced by the psychiatric label. (See Chapter 5.) In saying this, we are not referring to serious psychological studies, but we refer instead to the partisan abuse of psychopathological categories.

An objective and detached appraisal of the function of social movements in a society is clearly even more difficult than in the case of political parties. Movements are more diffuse; they have no obvious connection with government, and their aims are more variable than those of parties. One can, however, state as a first generalization that social movements serve as creators and carriers of public opinion; and insofar as government is guided by public opinion the social

---

Hans Kelsen, *Vom Wesen und Wert der Demokratie*, 2nd ed. (Tübingen, 1929) takes the position that democracy is essentially a method of formation of group will and selection of leaders, and incidentally the most rational method (pp. 100 ff.). He emphasizes that the people can exercise their right to participate in the formation of the common will only through parties (p. 19); he shows that the hostility of the old monarchy towards parties was nothing but an ill-concealed hostility against democracy.

[10] Schattschneider, *op. cit.*, pp. 109 ff., 152 ff.

movements contribute indirectly to the formation of the political group will.[11]

Second, insofar as leaders of social movements acquire political influence and power, the movements contribute, like parties, to the formation of the political élite. The leaders of national minority movements in Russia and Austria became statesmen in the new states of eastern Europe which were formed after the First World War. The labor movement today furnishes the leading statesmen in many countries and contributes to the lower levels of the political élite.

Leaving the discussion of this second function until later, we shall now analyze the first function.

THE FORMATION OF COMMON WILL AND PUBLIC OPINION

The Group Will

The very notion of a group will has fallen in discredit among contemporary social scientists, although in the language of politicians, journalists, and the man in the street its existence is still implied in such phrases as: "Russia demands," "Great Britain concedes," "Labor supports." The personification of social groups, which is implied in these phrases, is, of course, incompatible with realistic sociological analysis. But if we recall what has been said about organization (in Chapter 13), it is easy to see what such phrases really

[11] A. D. Lindsay, op. cit., p. 39: "Some of the most creative political proposals in modern democracy originate, not with government nor with the permanent Civil Service, but with public-minded voluntary groups who have a public concern for this or that problem and who have together thought out a remedy for it. We make a great mistake if in considering political democracy we think only of individuals on the one hand and of the political organizations on the other, and neglect the enormous importance in the production of a real public opinion of the innumerable voluntary associations of all kinds which exist in modern democratic society....

"Nothing so much makes possible a public opinion which is real because it is based on free and frank discussion as the existence of independent voluntary organizations with public purposes."

mean. They refer to an expression of will which is the result
of deliberations and consultations within an organized group
and which is pronounced by responsible and authorized
organs of this group.

In the modern democratic state this group will is represented by the official proclamations of the legislative and
executive organs within their spheres of competence and in
some states also by the supreme organs of the judiciary
power.

If we assume that before the group will of the state can
be adequately and validly expressed by the branches or
organs of the government, a supporting public opinion must
have been formed, we are justified in discerning two levels
on which the group will or common will is formed: the plane
of public opinion and the higher level of the legally binding
decisions of organs of the state.

Public Opinion

Public opinion may be defined, for our purposes, as the
prevailing publicly expressed opinion on a matter of public
concern which can claim effective validity in a society.[12]
Not every opinion which is voiced by individuals in public,
and not every opinion sustained by a public is public opinion
in the sense of our concept. If, for example, a high state
official expresses in a public speech an opinion on what his
government ought to do in its relations to a foreign power,
he does not necessarily express public opinion; the very purpose of his address may be to "send up a trial balloon" in
order to find out how public opinion reacts to his proposition.

Many publics hold opinions which are not at all in agreement with the prevailing opinion; for instance, although
there is in this country a large public which believes in pub-

---

[12] See F. Tönnies, *Kritik der Oeffentlichen Meinung* (Berlin, J. Springer,
1922).

lic ownership of utilities, one can hardly say that this represents *the* American public opinion on the matter. The so-called public-opinion polls do not actually deal with public opinion; they merely count opinions which individuals are willing to express in private conversation to an interviewer. It is often highly doubtful whether the same individuals would express the same opinion in public, and furthermore, whether, if they did, their opinion would have much significance. For, as everybody knows, the opinions of different people have different weight: some are listened to by nationwide publics as to an oracle; some influence at least their neighbors and fellow workers; others do not make any impression. But in a poll, the opinion of a group leader has the same weight as that of a socially isolated individual. For these reasons it has been suggested (Chapter 10) that group interviews be held instead of individual interviews, and that some consideration be given to the influence of the interviewed persons' opinions. Even if this procedure or any other technique were applied to ascertain the opinion of groups, the results would not give a reflection of public opinion but rather a concert of public opinions. This concert of the voices of many different publics is not what men have in mind in speaking of *the* public opinion of a country or society.

The real meaning of the term, or rather, of the concept, can best be ascertained from a historical review of its origin and usage.[13]

Public opinion is a notion, an idea which became significant in practical political thought and action about the end of

[13] This discourse on the concept of public opinion follows F. Tönnies, *ibid.* especially pp. 129 ff., 131 ff.

See also Paul A. Palmer, "Ferdinand Tönnies' Theory of Public Oponion," *Public Opinion Quarterly*, Vol. 2 (Oct. 1938), pp. 584-595; R. Heberle, "The Sociology of Ferdinand Tönnies," in H. E. Barnes, *Introduction to the History of Sociology* (Chicago, University of Chicago Press, 1948); and Herbert Blumer, "Public Opinion and Public Opinion Polling," *American Sociological Review*, Vol. 13, (Oct., 1948).

the eighteenth century. Increasing literacy, the progress in communication, the rising importance of the press, the public discussion of political matters, and other issues of importance to the society—these brought the ruling élite in all Western countries to the realization that no government could disregard the sentiments, wishes, beliefs, and ideas of the ruled. The notion arose that there existed beside and outside the opinion of the ruling group another and sometimes more powerful opinion. It became an axiom of the art of politics that without the support of public opinion no government could endure. However, the real nature of this new force was difficult to grasp. Certainly it was not considered identical with the private opinions of individual citizens on every kind of subject.

Public opinion was thought to consist of opinions which were voiced and debated openly, in clubs, coffee houses, meeting and assemblies, at the stock exchange, in newspapers, and in pamphlets. It comprised opinions related to matters of state and to public affairs in general, and it was thought to be informed, critical opinion based on knowledge of facts. Finally, if it was to be a force, it had to be the accepted opinion of large groups of people—of many publics,— and, in the ideal case, it should be *the* public opinion, the only opinion in a society that is recognized as true, correct, and valid.

There are, however, few matters of public concern on which *the* public opinion of a society is actually quite definite and unanimous. In other words, one can distinguish between degrees of weakness and strength of public opinion. A firm public opinion is to be found more likely on fundamental principles than on current issues. For example, public opinion in the United States today is firmly opposed to communism as a possible social system, and it is likely to remain firm on this viewpoint for a long time. On the other hand, public opinion with regard to relations between the United States and Soviet Russia has been subject to frequent and rather sudden and sweeping changes.

Public opinion in the ideal case is not merely a statement of beliefs but it is also a will; it demands respect and obedience, it comprises norms of social action. Those who offend public opinion are likely to be ostracized or otherwise penalized, through censorious response from their fellow citizens.

Public opinion, like the public opinions of groups, is formed by relatively few individuals who enjoy the reputation of being well informed and of being experts, or who merely have a personal gift of convincing others of the validity of their opinion. The broad masses of group members, like the broad masses of the general public, are inclined more or less to accept those opinions, depending on how much they believe in the authority of those who form them. The very fact that many people come to accept the same opinion tends to reinforce the strength of each individual's conviction. Tönnies has shown how closely related opinions and beliefs are.[14] In fact, an opinion, if it becomes the opinion of an action group, may assume the intensity of a religious belief. We have seen this happen in various social movements.

Contribution of Social Movements

The constitutive ideas of a social movement may be regarded as *a* public opinion. Therefore, in propagandizing and in striving for universal acceptance of these ideas, the people who form the movement contribute to the formation of public opinion. In this sense one may say that public opinion in Europe has become more favorable toward socialism since the Second World War, insofar as the ideas of public ownership of certain types of enterprises and of some kind of planned economy are now fairly generally accepted. The socialist movement has thus contributed significantly to the formation of public opinion.

[14] Tönnies, *Kritik der Öffentlichen Meinung*, pp. 19 ff., 58 f., 77, 89.

Contribution of Parties to the Formation of State Will

The formation of the state will in a modern democratic society is the result of discussion, deliberation, negotiation, and compromise between many kinds of groups holding opposing and dissenting opinions. Gradually, the prevailing opinions in these groups converge into broader fronts or camps and, in political parties, merge into an officially adopted policy on issues and candidates. The political parties, both within the parliaments and outside, have the function of reducing this clamor of voices into a small number of dominant volitions and finally into parliamentary majorities capable of supporting a government. The legislature or parliament is thus merely "the receptacle for the extra-parliamentary forces of the people which have been organized into political parties in order to gain influence and institutional form"; if there were no parliament, these forces would nevertheless exist, and parties would be formed in an irresponsible and lawless struggle.[15]

The parties are thus an indispensable link in the chain of groups which contribute to the consolidation of individual wills into partial group wills and of these into the state will or political common will. However, the exact rôle of the parties in this process varies from one country to the other; the consolidation can occur on different levels, depending on the system of elections and other conditions. Under the majority rule,[16] the voters in each district are compelled

[15] Erich Kaufmann, *Zur Problematik des Volks-Willens* (Berlin and Leipzig, 1931), p. 15.

[16] The method of making decisions in and for a social group by majority vote is a relatively recent social technique. In archaic societies, unanimity is required, and deliberations continue until there are no dissenting opinions left. This was the procedure in Russian village assemblies until far into the nineteenth century. The important point is that the dissenting minority would not have felt to be bound by a majority decision. It takes a rather abstract way of thinking to understand the fundamental premise of the majority principle: that each group member pledges himself in advance to abide by any decision which is supported by any kind of major-

to choose between two lines of action, or the parties, if there are more than two, are compelled to enter into election alliances; under the system of proportional representation the final choice lies with the elected representatives who will have to form coalitions among the parliamentary parties or factions.

National Variations

Sait points out that in France the compromises and arrangements, which in the United States would occur within each of the great parties before the election, are made after the election, among the party groups in the Chamber of Deputies.[17] Sait thinks that the greater instability of political alignments in France is a result of this condition. He does not mention, in this connection, the cross-party blocs and bipartisan groupings in the United States Congress. However, relatively, in comparison with France, it is true that compromises in the United States have to be made largely before the election.

Quite the contrary situation existed in Germany from 1918 to 1933. Here the system of proportional representation, in combination with large numbers of mandates or seats for each election district and the large size of election districts, made it quite unnecessary for the voters to compromise; or at any rate the compromises did not have to go very far. There was a party for each major trend of opinion, and on each party ticket there was usually at least one candidate who appealed to the particular interest group to which the

---

ity of votes and to accept it as if it were the unanimous will of the group. See L. Konopczynski, "Majority Rule," *Encyclopedia of Social Sciences* (New York, The Macmillan Company, 1942), Kurt Wolf trans. and ed., *The Sociology of Georg Simmel* (Glencoe, Ill., The Free Press, 1950), Chap. 3, 5 on the majority rule. Also Willmoore Kendall, *John Locke and the Doctrine of Majority-Rule* (Urbana, The University of Illinois Press, 1941).

[17] Penniman, *Sait's American Parties and Elections,* 4th ed. (New York: Appleton-Century-Crofts, Inc., 1948), p. 196.

voter belonged. On the other hand, since a single party could rarely obtain a majority in the legislature, compromises had to be made between the *Fraktionen* in the legislatures.[18] In order to form a working coalition government, a party had often to support another party which it had been fighting bitterly during the elections. Thus the Catholic Center Party would form coalitions with the Social Democratic Party, although both had denounced each other vehemently during the campaign, and with very good reasons. This aroused the ire of the voters, who saw their political ideals betrayed by trading among politicians; it contributed greatly to the discredit of the entire institution of parliamentary representation.

In the United States, the integrating function of the major political parties is easy to see, at least in broad outline. The party organizations on all levels are subject to influences from many and diverse groups, organized and unorganized. The opinions, wishes, idiosyncrasies, prejudices, and sentiments of ethnic and occupational groups, of religious denominations and social classes are to be given consideration; the demands of organized pressure groups have to be heard. Politicians scrutinize, weigh, and sift these particularistic opinions and volitions and bring them into play in their intra-party deliberations and negotiations. In party caucuses on various levels and in nominating conventions and primaries, these many volitions are gradually reduced to a few main propositions aceptable to a majority of party leaders. Then platforms are drawn, and in the campaign the voters are presented with a simplified presentation of what each party or candidate stands for. The final decision then seems to lie with the voters. But this is an over-simplified picture. Significant differences exist between different state organizations of the same party. Sometimes the same outside in-

---

[18] Kelsen, *op. cit.*, p. 62; about 1929 Professor Kelsen thought this arrangement preferable.

fluences and pressures are felt in both parties, and blocs
cut across party lines. These circumstances increase the importance of the individual politician in the process of integration. The less strict the party discipline, the greater the
individual representative's responsibility to strive for the
kind of compromises which will satisfy the electorate. The
final integration into a state will, of course, occurs in Congress. On this highest level, the process is complicated by
the existence of two houses and by the Presidential veto.

The integrating functions of American political parties
have been clearly seen by Lord Bryce in his famous description of the parties as brokers whose business it is to serve
various interests and to reconcile them. More recently,
Schattschneider has emphasized this function of the major
parties.[19] A great deal of the formation of public opinion and
of the integration of the opinions of particular publics into
the political will of the American people occurs not in the
House and Senate chambers, but in the Congressional committees on the basis of public hearings. It is in these hearings
that the representatives of social movements—along with
those of pressure groups and of private interests—have an
opportunity to present their views and to influence legislation and policy making in a very direct way.

The integrating function of the major parties is recognized
by those defenders of the present two-party system who
claim that it serves to keep radicals out of practical politics
and to mitigate the class conflicts.[20] Harold Laski, on the
other hand, being less concerned about integration than

[19] E. E. Schattschneider, *Party Government* (New York, Farrar & Rinehart, Inc., 1942), especially p. 31. "The mobilization of majorities in recognition of the great public interests, the integration of special interests with
public policy, and the over-all management and planning involved in dis-
criminating among special interests, cannot be done by organized special
interests on their own initiative. These are the functions of an entirely
different kind of organization, the political party."

[20] Sait, *op. cit.*, pp. 160 f.

about pursuance of an ideal, advanced the opinion that a re-alignment of parties on the basis of real issues would be desirable; he suggested in particular the formation of a Labor Party, since the present system tends, in his opinion, to obfuscate, to cloud the real political issues and to maintain the rule of economically powerful minorities.[21]

From the preceding discussion one may draw conclusions concerning the merits of different election systems: proportional representation, while granting fair chances to minority parties, tends to hamper the process of integration. The latter is best served by simple majority rule and a two-party system. Proportional representation encourages the formation of particularistic interest parties and of radical parties. The majority principle compels the major parties to give consideration to popular radical movements and yet compels the adherents of such movements to cast their votes in favor of moderate candidates.[22] However, the importance of such technical arrangements as election systems should not be over-estimated. The number of parties in a given society depends on the intensity of cleavages among social strata as well as on the regional distribution of powerful special interest groups. Ethnic minority parties, for example, can arise under majority rule if the minority has a chance to win elections in a sufficiently large number of election districts (the Irish Nationalists did this in the British House of Commons before the granting of independence, as well as the Danes and Poles in the German Reichstag before 1918). As the cleavages grow in intensity, the parties will develop traits of military discipline and orderlike structure.

[21] Harold J. Laski, *The American Democracy*, (New York, Viking Press, Inc., 1948) Chaps. III, VI.
[22] Ferdinand A. Hermens, *The Tyrant's War and the People's Peace* (Chicago, University of Chicago Press, 1944), pp. 86 ff. and *passim*. See also Hermens, "Democracy and Proportional Representation," *Public Policy Pamphlets*, 1940.

Political "Orders"

The rise of political orders is thus a symptom of the breakdown of the integration process. In studying the integrating functions of these new pseudo-parties, one has to distinguish between the period of the struggle for power and the period when the régime is established. During the first period, the political order still retains many traits of a genuine party, and although its leaders are as a rule not at all interested in reaching compromises with other parties, the very existence of a political order may induce the other parties to reach an understanding among themselves. Within the political order, there can, at this stage, still arise opposition; controversies are indeed often quite fierce and lead to secessions and expulsions of opposition groups.

During the struggle for power, the political order participates in parliamentary debate, however it does not do so in good faith. The order does not want to contribute to the effort of finding the sense of the meeting or to arrive at a workable compromise. The Nazis in the German *Reichstag* as well as in state and municipal representative assemblies used the debates merely for purposes of propaganda; the rostrum became for them a tribunal, a public platform from which they could attack the government and other parties under the protection of parliamentary immunity. After the seizure of power, when the political order has established its régime, the situation changes, and the order ceases to be a party or a movement.

The N.S.D.A.P. was opposed to all democratic procedures. Orders and directives were to be issued from above and relayed down to the lower echelons. In reality there developed a great deal of uninstitutionalized and therefore unregulated discussion, and there developed as well much clandestine intrigue and wire-pulling within the party. This placed the *Führer* in the position of a final authority, of an umpire, which increased his power. On the other hand, party functionaries from the bloc leaders upward were requested to report on opinion and morale within their jurisdictions. The opinion-forming process in a totalitarian state can best be compared with the method of reporting on conditions and morale of combat forces in an army. Each echelon relays the information received from subordinate units to the next higher echelon. The amount of censoring and editing of the original reports which takes place in this process depends of course on a variety of factors: the attitude of the higher echelon commanders, the moral courage of the commanders of the lower echelons, the allocation of responsibility, and so forth. It is quite safe to say that the political order in a totalitarian régime has the function not merely of forming the dominant opinion but also of keeping the ruling élite informed on the sentiments, attitudes, and morale of the people—both inside and outside the party hierarchy.

The Communists' conception of democratic centralism does not preclude debate. It differs from ordinary conceptions of democratic will formation in this point: it does not permit any further discussion of an issue which has been decided by an act of the highest policy-making echelon. Presumably the debate could be re-opened by directives from highest party offices.[23]

In the U.S.S.R. the institutions in which issues can be debated are the soviets and the party. However, it is hard to know to what extent discussion is really possible. The Webbs [24] have given a very favorable picture, which is most likely exaggerated. Other competent observers maintain that there was in the beginning, and most likely still is, a great deal of opportunity for group deliberation and discussion.

[23] *Constitution of the Communist Party of the United States of America.* As an example we refer to the debate on the American Negro question (discussed in Chap. 17), which filled many pages in *Political Affairs,* 1946.

[24] Sidney and Beatrice Webb, *Soviet Communism: A New Civilization,* 3rd ed. (London, Longmans, Green & Company, 1947).

They point out that great freedom of debate exists where local conditions of work and similar problems are concerned, whereas the matters of higher policy are not supposed to be discussed among the lower ranks of the party.[25]

[25] Sir John Maynard, *Russia in Flux* (New York, The Macmillan Company, 1945), pp. 17, 361, 511. "On the lower planes of public affairs, a vigorous democratic system is actually in existence . . . the factory, the farm, the office, the mine are run under the perpetual criticism of the workers." p. 522.

19

The Selection of the Political Élite

THE SELECTION OF LEADERS

IF DEMOCRACY in a large community means government by representative officials and assemblies, the immense importance of choosing the right kind of people becomes immediately evident. The selection of a political élite of high quality is of course important in any system of government. But we are confronted with the paradox that in modern democracies this selection is achieved by competition, whereas in authoritarian régimes it is organized in a methodical way. Parties are not only the cadres from which the political élite is recruited—they are also the training grounds on which the qualities of the élite are developed. A hundred years ago Lorenz Stein thought that the working class would never be capable of ruling because its leaders lacked the experience of controlling man which, he believed, came only with the responsibilities of property ownership. Stein could not foresee that the labor movement itself, through labor parties, unions, and coöperative societies, would become a source and training ground from which numerous outstanding statesmen have come forth in our day. These distinguished leaders are only a very small part of the larger élite which is constantly created in the movement, from the union local upwards to the nationwide federations and parties.

The term *élite* should be taken in a neutral, technical sense; the quality of such a group can rarely be judged ob-

431

jectively, except by its ability to lead, to rule, and to stay in
power. In this sense even the most depraved and corrupt
ruling clique is an élite. Political parties serve most directly
as agencies for the training and selection of the leading
statesmen. Social movements contribute to the formation of
the political élite in various ways. Generally speaking, they
tend to bring to the fore large numbers of men and women
who have the ability to win the confidence of others, to guide
and lead, and to convert into action the sentiments, demands,
and desires of their supporters. We have pointed out (in
Chapter 13) that in every kind of social movement, even in
the most equalitarian-minded groups, a more or less enduring oligarchy will come into existence. This oligarchy is the
cadre from which individuals may advance into the political
élite of the entire society. If the movement consolidates
itself in a particular political party, and if this party attains
power, the leaders of the movement are likely to become
the leading statesmen. Or, if the movement remains independent from any particular political party, the parties may
offer political positions in the various branches of government to leading men in the movement in order to win the
support of its rank and file. Thus farmers' movements have
in various countries succeeded in placing high-ranking functionaries of coöperatives and other farmer organizations in
cabinet positions.[1] The impressive contributions of the labor
unions to the political élites in Western society have already
been mentioned.[2] The greater the freedom of association in
a country, the greater the variety of voluntary associations,

[1] For eastern Europe, see D. Tomasic, "Ideologies and the Structure of
Eastern European Society," *American Journal of Sociology,* Vol. LIII, No. 5
(March, 1950).

[2] The British case is obvious; less well known is the fact that Fritz Ebert,
the first President of the German Republic, was a trade union leader and
Social Democratic member of the National parliament. For the United
States, see C. Wright Mills, *The New Men of Power* (New York, Harcourt,
Brace & Company, 1948). Some United States Secretaries of Labor and
many of the State Secretaries of Labor came from the labor unions.

the more decentralized the organization, the larger will be the supply of individuals capable of holding positions of authority, responsibility, and leadership.

However, the unfolding of real political ability in the strict sense will occur in political parties. These alone are subject to tests of political success or failure. Trade union leaders, for example, may have been able to cope with opposition from among the rank and file and from rival leaders, but they are not faced with the task of winning support outside their union or outside the ranks of labor. This is the problem of the leaders of a labor party which is compelled to expand its membership and influence beyond the working class if it wants to hold power for any length of time. Therefore, the party leader has to develop a more comprehensive judgment of political affairs, and he will have to free himself of the narrow point of view of a particular movement and acquire a more statesmanlike view.

In Political Orders

Most methodical arrangements for the training and selection of a political élite have been made in the political orders, first, in the Communist Party of the U.S.S.R. and other Communist parties, later, and largely in imitation of the Communist model, by the Fascists and National-Socialists.[3]

The problem of selection of an élite is not the same in a totalitarian régime as in a democracy. In the first place, the leading statesman himself is selected in entirely different ways. In a democracy he is chosen through competition within and between political parties. In a régime with charismatic leadership, the supreme leader is regarded as a superior being, as the creator of the political order and not as a creature of the dominant party. The problem of finding

[3] For a good description, see: S. Neumann, *Permanent Revolution* (New York, London, Harper and Brothers, 1942), Chap. III; also A. Rossi, *A Communist Party in Action*, ed. and trans. by Willmoore Kendall (New Haven, Yale University Press, 1949).

a successor to the original leader cannot be solved by an institutionalized process; personal designation of the successor by the charismatic leader or a struggle for power within the higher party circle are the only ways in which a successor can be determined.[4]

In the Communist Party one would expect a more rational procedure; in Russia itself the problem has arisen only once, and it is significant for the post-revolutionary changes in the structure of the Bolshevist party that the man who controlled the organizational apparatus became the first successor of Lenin.

In parties with charismatic leadership the problem of training is limited to the level of lieutenants. The ways and means by which Fascists and National-Socialists sought to secure a steady supply of subleaders is well described by Neumann.[5] The most striking difference from democratic methods is the absence of *open* competition: the candidates for this kind of career were selected by party officials on various levels, which means that in the initial stages of the selection process the various factions within the party would try to get their favorites chosen.

The actual training of the future subleaders was done in party-controlled institutions: training camps, élite schools, and *Ordensburgen*.[6]

[4] Max Weber, *Theory of Economic and Social Organization*, especially Chap. III.

[5] Neumann, *op. cit.*, pp. 92 f.

[6] See "The Ordensburgen—Cradles of Leadership," *Facts in Review*, Vol. II, No. 36 (Sept. 2, 1940). This illustrated article in the official Nazi propaganda sheet for the United States of America conveys a good idea of the techniques employed in selecting and training. Although past history now, the program is interesting as an indication of Nazi mentality: "Heretofore...the training of political leaders in modern states had been left almost entirely to chance." Now it is going to be done in special institutions, the three *Ordensburgen*. Only young men who have actively participated in one or more of the various organizations of the party can be admitted to the *Ordensburgen*, which are the training centers for the *junker* or élite of the party. Perfect health, character, and moral stamina rather than intelligence and diligence are to be the prerequisites, since the training aims

In selecting new subleaders, the charismatic dictatorship is faced with a peculiar problem: on the one hand, the future leaders have to be trained and instructed in certain techniques of social control and administration. This can be done only in institutions or through institutional channels—a career has to be established, similar to that of a civil servant or an army officer. On the other hand, the future subleaders have to attain the confidence and favor of the supreme leader; they have to share to some extent in his charisma.

Thus, a rational method of selection is bound to compete with an irrational method (that is, irrational from the point of view of administrative efficiency). Concretely speaking, men belonging to the old guard may be given preference over late-comers, although the latter excelled in the training courses and camps.

In the Communist parties and in the Soviet political hierarchy more emphasis used to be placed upon intellectual training because of the great importance ascribed to a thorough acquaintance with the works of Marx, Engels, and Lenin. Since Stalin's rise to power, a kind of rather stale Marxist scholasticism seems to have developed with more emphasis on party discipline.

The methods of training and selection in the modern political orders have the common distinguishing feature of emphasizing loyalty and obedience to the order and its officers, and intolerance and ruthlessness against outside political adversaries as well as against skeptics and heretics within the very ranks of the political order. They also inculcate into the future political leaders a consciousness of superiority, an

---

mainly at the development of will-power and decision. Discipline permeates the whole program. Even "the digestion [sic] of lectures is not left to the students' arbitrary disposal, but it is assigned to special review periods under the alternative leadership of the candidates themselves."

Other élite schools of the Nazi régime were set up in former *Kadettenanstalten*, i.e., the institutions where the professional army officers had been trained under the imperial régime.

awareness of their partnership in the political élite, and consequently an attitude of arrogance towards all outsiders—that is, the rank and file of the citizens. They instill a habit of authoritative behavior in dealings with the lower ranks of the political order and with the unorganized populace. In many respects the type of leader which is thus formed resembles the professional army officer on the one hand and the militant religious fanatic on the other.

A peculiar trait in the Communist movement is the more or less institutional training which prominent leaders in all countries have received in the Soviet Union. The European party leaders Pieck, Ulbricht, Thorez, Tito, Anna Pauker, the late Georgi Dimitrov—to name only a few of the best known and of the most important—all spent years in the Soviet Union and some held positions in the Comintern before they assumed their present responsibilities.

This means that the Communist movement is led by men and women whose entire life has been a long and intensive political experience, harsh and often discouraging at the beginning, when most of them served long terms in prison, certainly strenuous when in exile in Russia, and in its total effect not likely to predispose these men to a conciliatory attitude in their dealings with the bourgeoisie and its political agents. On the other hand, these men are bound to be able politicians, much better informed about the areas in which they operate than many of their opposite numbers, and thoroughly trained in Communist strategy and tactics.

This kind of leadership training, while at first glance very intriguing because of its rationality, has its serious inherent weaknesses and pitfalls. At first it will attract men and women of great devotion to the goals of the movement, many of them idealists and original thinkers; gradually, as the movement gains power, and especially after it has established itself as an authoritarian régime, ambitious, power-desirous personalities will be attracted; the idealists will soon be outnumbered by the careerists. Simultaneously, the principle of absolute obedience and the repression of any independent and critical line of thought, will lead to a disintegration in the moral and intellectual caliber of the new generation of leaders. If the régime is permitted to operate undisturbed for a sufficiently long time, it is bound to deteriorate. In the case of the Hitler régime, the deterioration spread finally into the armed forces when political reliability and pliability became foremost prerequisites for promotion to high commanding positions.[7]

But even when the deterioration does not reach such extreme measures, the political order is in constant danger of developing into a spiritually and intellectually sterile power-apparatus which tends to become, for its members, an end in itself. Therefore, there is in the Communist movement, the great emphasis on the necessity of keeping in touch with the masses of the people, therefore there are also from time to time those mass expulsions which were discussed in another connection. (See Chapter 15.) The effect of such safeguards is bound to be rather limited and to become weaker in the course of time. If we may judge from the history of certain religious orders, any closed and authoritarian association is likely to become moribund through deterioration of the quality of its members.

[7] The Nazi case proves also the possibility of a moral, and to some extent intellectual, counter-selection under an authoritarian régime. The administrative and guard personnel in the concentration camps as well as at least the officers in the special detachments of the S.S.—those units which were used in the destruction of the Warsaw ghetto and in similar assignments—has quite obviously been an élite of sadistic and morally disoriented personalities. This result was achieved by a process of breaking-in, training, and sifting oriented by a set of values which was diametrically opposed to the Christian and Humanistic tradition. See Eugen Kogon, *Der S-S-Staat* (Stockholm, 1946), a comprehensive and detached sociological study of the Nazi concentration camps.

In Genuine Parties

The selection of political leaders through genuine political parties in a state whose government bases its claim to legitimacy upon tradition or upon rational grounds (legal authority)[8] follows quite different principles. Here it is based upon chance—as the authoritarians would say—or open competition for power between individuals within each party and also, of course, between the leaders of the various parties. The competition is open insofar as no citizen is excluded from entering upon a political career, provided he can find the time and the financial means required for the vocation of a politician. Nobody is compelled to go through a youth organization, through training camps and leader schools. Anyone can become an active politician as soon as he has reached the age at which one becomes eligible for office, or he can enter at a ripe age after more or less intensive experiences in other fields. And, what is equally important, an individual can retire from a political career voluntarily and without impairment for further activities in one's vocation or in a new field of activity where the experiences gained in political life may be considered an asset.

Under Parliamentary Government

However, there is, in each society, a characteristic or typical pattern to which the careers of prominent political leaders tend more or less to conform. In an attempt to systematize these patterns, we must first distinguish between the situation under a system of constitutional government in the narrow sense, where parliament can exercise only legislative and controlling functions, and the situation under parliamentary government where the majority party furnishes the personnel for the government or cabinet. The first system existed in

[8] Max Weber's "traditional" and "legal" authority; see *Theory of Social and Economic Organization,* Chaps. I, III, Sec. III.

Germany and some other European states until 1918, the second system developed in England slowly during the eighteenth and nineteenth centuries.[9] Parliamentary government was firmly established in France after 1871; it existed in Germany from 1918 to 1933, in Austria from 1918 to 1938, and is now the pattern in most of the Western democracies—except the United States of America.

According to the unwritten rules of parliamentary government in the United Kingdom, the cabinet must not only have the confidence of the majority in Parliament, but it must also consist of leading members of the majority party in the House of Commons, and these retain their seats in Parliament. This last point is extremely important, because it makes membership in Parliament the stepping stone, and the only one, to the position of a cabinet minister; at the same time, it gives every cabinet member a place to which he can retire if he should wish to resign from his government post, or if the party decides to make him resign, or if his party is ousted from power. The party thus becomes the agency through which the leading statesmen are selected and receive their training.

A government selected in the English way is not a government of specialists—whereas the imperial German government as a rule was composed of highly trained administrative experts—but it is a government composed of persons trained in the leadership of men and in the game of political struggle for influence, popular support, and power. These men are accustomed to making political decisions. And, last but not least, they are held responsible for the mistakes they may make: they pay for such mistakes with the loss of power and eventually with elimination from political prominence in

[9] According to K. B. Smellie, *A Hundred Years of English Government* (London, 1937), the process was much slower than usually assumed; he claims the final steps were made during the reign of Queen Victoria, certainly not before 1860.

their party. They are not shielded by the king or by their own leader; consequently they must be men who are ready to assume responsibility. This applies also to the opposition. The leaders of the opposition know that if they succeed in ousting a government—for example, by a temporary alliance with a minority in the majority party—they will have to form the new government out of their own ranks. However, they will resort to such tactics only if they are fairly sure that they are going to win the elections.[10] As long as they are not certain that they will be able to secure a majority in Parliament through the eventual dissolution of the present one and the election of a new one, they abstain from too rash or intransigent courses of action.

This mechanism of selection may not result in the production of political geniuses,[11] but it furnishes a good steady average, and it secures a high degree of continuity in the direction and content of policy—especially foreign policy. It also provides for succession in the ranks of leading statesmen so that the situation of a great statesman without an adequate successor—like Bismarck—can scarcely happen. It also makes the career of a parliamentarian attractive to gifted men with high ambitions.

The system of parliamentary government as it existed in Germany from 1918 to 1933 suffered not only from a lack of

[10] See A. Lawrence Lowell, *The Government of England* (New York, The Macmillan Company, 1926), Chaps. XVIII, XXIV. See also Smellie, *op. cit.*, pp. 75 ff. Smellie says, "Only slowly was the conception developed of the opposition as an alternative cabinet, prepared to take office when the one in power should fail." In 1864 this idea was still rejected by Disraeli.

[11] Erich Kauffman, *Zur Problematik des Volks-Willens* (Berlin and Leipzig, 1931) wrote in 1931: "The cry for the genius as a political leader [*nach der genialen Führerpersönlichkeit*] is a hysterical cry, a cry of impotence. Much is gained if the machinery of constitutional norms tends to bring men who have one or the other of the gifts of a leader into positions of responsibility and if these surround themselves with advisors and aids who can supply the rest [of the requirements]. This to be sure must be the aim in the handling of constitutional norms."

tradition [12] but also from the coming into the *Reichstag* of party bureaucrats and of representatives of particular interests (pressure groups) through the proportional representation system in combination with very large election districts in which the personal contact between candidate and voters was lost. Many of these delegates were not really political leaders, nor even politicians, but simply party workers of long standing or managers of businessmen's associations or trade union secretaries. The English system can not prevent the election to the House of Commons of men who represent particular interests, but by and large it tends to select the kind of politician who is capable of conducting himself as if he represented the entire nation and not only local or other particular interests. In addition to the factors already discussed, the growing influence of the central party offices on nominations, which has been mentioned in Chapter 14, contributes to this tendency.[13]

The French system favors to a greater extent than the English the selection of the type of delegate who considers himself primarily as the agent of the ruling groups in his election district, the servant of his voters. But, it can produce a type of politician who is the absolute ruler of his constituency.

---

[12] The rôle which had been assigned to the *Reichstag* under Bismarck's constitution and régime created among the progressive Liberals and the Socialists a tradition of negative criticism; among the Conservatives and among the largely conservative bureaucracy it created contempt for the opposition and a lack of understanding of the rôle of an opposition in a modern state. Thus the longing for a rule by a strong leader which helped the Nazis to gain power was quite in accord with the political tradition of the German upper classes. They tended to despise parties—any parties except their own.

[13] Herman Finer, *The Theory and Practice of Modern Government* (New York, Dial Press, Inc., 1934), pp. 247 f. Finer considers it "a fundamental defect of the French system" that "in France, local caucuses play a far larger part in selecting candidates than in England." Finer also mentions that in England the central offices manage to get the experts of their party nominated for "safe" seats; he claims that one-tenth of all seats contested by a party are likely to be reserved for such candidates.

The American System

No uniform mechanism for the training and selection of
leading statesmen exists in the United States of America. The
American system of presidential government lacks the essential elements of parliamentary government: a relatively
stable head of the state as the symbol of sovereignty and a
cabinet which can be dismissed or resign at any time when
majority support in parliament is failing. The President's office combines the offices of sovereign and chancellor (prime
minister) and is consequently in an intermediate position
between both.

The following facts should be taken into consideration as
affecting the selection of political leaders:

1. The President is never the complete master of his party
in Congress, because he can not force his party fellows into
line by appealing from an antagonistic Congress to the electorate. "He must persuade and cajole, he cannot afford to
threaten [with] a dissolution . . . he can do something with
patronage. . . ." [14] However, two-thirds of the senators are
largely beyond his power of control—they were elected before he came to office, and they can normally expect to remain in Congress long after the President's term has ended.
Behind and above Congress there looms the Supreme Court,
which may at any moment strike an act of Congress into
impotence. This again reduces the actual control of the
President over his party, or rather can make it ineffective on
crucial issues.

2. The President is not bound to select the cabinet members from the ranks of the United States senators of his party;
frequently the men chosen have not even had a leading position in the majority party. The Cabinet in the United States
therefore is not a team of old political friends who have

[14] Harold Laski, *The American Presidency* (New York, Viking Press,
Inc., 1948) pp. 56 f.

worked together for many years under the leadership of the President, as the men composing a British Cabinet have worked under the future prime minister. The Cabinet has no collective responsibility, and the individual Cabinet member has no great power in Congress. The Cabinet is really an advisory council to the President. Sometimes, the unofficial advisors to the President are more influential than the cabinet members.[15] Consequently, a post in the Cabinet is not an essential step in or the crown of a political career; it is not even of great significance for a politician's qualification as a candidate for the presidency.[16] The American politician can afford to decline a cabinet post without risking the finish of his political career. The United States cabinet post is merely an interlude in a career—not the final point.

3. There is no rule that the President (or Vice-President) should have been the leader of his party in Congress, although a few presidents and vice-presidents have been selected from the ranks of United States senators. In short, there is at present no established career by which a politician rises to the highest office in the federal government.[17]

Candidates for the presidency are frequently selected from the ranks of state governors as well as from outsiders. Although senators have been nominated and elected, it is safe to say that men who have a distinguished record in the Senate are not very likely to win the nomination just because their political views and actions are too well known and because they inevitably have antagonized certain blocs of

[15] *Ibid.*, pp. 74 ff.

[16] *Ibid.*, p. 88.

[17] This has not always been the case. Schattschneider, *op. cit.*, p. 152, points out that prior to the "fall of the congressional caucus" in 1824 "there was a recognized career leading to the presidency, and men were marked for the presidency well in advance.

"The power to nominate a party candidate for the presidency was firmly in the hands of the national party leaders. In fact, the president himself, acting through the national leaders . . . was usually able to bring about the nomination of his successor."

voters who could eventually be won over to support a candidate of less known stand.[18]

It is well known that the final choice, which is a result of compromises between the leaders of the party machines in the states, falls quite frequently on a man who is not at all a strong political leader with a long term of service in Congress and additional experience in Cabinet posts. Consequently, the location of actual political leadership tends to shift back and forth between the presidency and the Senate. If the President is a strong political personality, he will be the national leader of the party in power; if he is weak politically, the real leadership of national politics will lie with a group of senators. This introduces an element of chance and uncertainty into the process of political group will formation which obviously is a dangerous thing.

The President's rôle as party leader is not so definitely circumscribed as that of the English Prime Minister. In fact, the assumption of this rôle by the President except in time of emergency is a rather recent phenomenon, and each of the presidents since Theodore Roosevelt has had a different conception of it. Wilson, for instance, regarded himself as the leader of the Democratic Party in Congress, whereas Franklin D. Roosevelt thought of himself as the leader of the party in the country, using the method of direct appeal to his supporters among the voters—a method which had first been applied, on a small scale, by Theodore Roosevelt.[19]

The party leadership of the President is made precarious by the impossibility of enforcing strict discipline in the party. Also, it is precarious because, owing to the heterogeneous

[18] Charles A. Beard, *American Government and Politics,* 4 ed. (New York, The Macmillan Company, 1927), p. 174. "Men of marked power and leadership in the Senate are never chosen."

[19] *Ibid.,* pp. 72 f. Laski points out that political leadership of the President (not merely in his own party) has tremendously gained in importance since Theodore Roosevelt, even independent of the personality—that is, the *office* of the President has gained in significance.

composition of both parties, a president may have to seek the support of that wing of the opposition party which is closest to the wing in his own party from which he draws his main support.

The absence of a definite mechanism for the selection of the President and the Cabinet affects the quality of the men who aspire to a political career, especially to a seat in Congress. On the one hand, the office of a United States Senator is highly attractive for politically ambitious men. The great independence of a Senator within that large sphere of influence in which he is his own master [20] compensates for the fact that his chances to become a Cabinet member are slight and those of getting to the White House even slighter. Furthermore, a man of outstanding ability has a very good chance of actually becoming a leading statesman even if he remains within the Senate. This should and often does result in a high quality of senatorial personnel. On the other hand, since it is possible for a Senator to avoid the test of statesmanship by staying away from executive offices and since he can keep his seat by clever disposition of patronage, the Senate will always contain a number of people who are unqualified for responsible statesmanship. This applies even more generally to the House of Representatives. The over-all result seems to be that the average member of Congress develops a great skill in representing various and often diverse interests, that he becomes a master in the art of compromise, but that he rarely will be a man of strong political conviction and a leader of people. Other factors which tend to lower the quality of the personnel in the federal as well as the state legislatures are the requirement of local residence and the seniority rule in Congress. The former inevitably limits the choice of candidates; if an election district has among its residents but few of outstanding political talents, men of lesser

---

[20] Especially through senatorial courtesy: that is, the complete control over patronage in his own state, if he belongs to the President's party.

qualification must be elected; this provision on the other hand, tends to exclude from political careers a number of people from areas in which potential candidates of outstanding ability are numerous. It most likely also strengthens the tendency among legislators to regard themselves as agents of their local constituents rather than as representatives of the people at large.

Under the seniority rule in Congress, the chairman of a committee is always the majority party member with longest service. This arrangement may prevent the rise of senators or representatives of outstanding ability to the chairmanship of important committees and sometimes keeps mediocre men in these positions.

20

Conclusion

ON THE PREMISES OF PARTY GOVERNMENT

ANY KIND OF PARTY government presupposes the existence
of genuine political parties; it ceases to work if the parties
become mere pressure groups or political orders. A political
party is by definition a part of the larger political community;
it must therefore have a political action program which takes
into consideration all important questions of policy that are
live issues in the state; [1] it should be ready to assume responsibility; and it must respect the other parties not merely as
opponents and competitors but also as partners who share
certain basic political principles. One might say, genuine
parties should be in relation to each other like two football
teams: each of them certainly wants to win, but both have
also the common purpose of playing the game, and therefore
they are bound to observe certain rules and certain standards
of fairness. So-called parties which aim at a monopoly of
power for their own membership and intend to exclude the
opposition from participation in the formation of the political
common will are not true parties.

In modern democracy each party plays the game of politics
according to rules which they all acknowledge; the game is
a serious one, but the differences and conflicts between parties are never taken in deadly earnest; the antagonism be-

[1] Not merely land reform or monetary reform or limited goals of similar
kind.

447

tween parties is not supposed to transgress the limitations and restrictions of a true *agon* [2]—a competitive game. Under rules of parliamentary procedure individuals or groups who spoil the game by violating rules of order are subjected to various penalties (removal from the Chamber of the Legislature, suspension, temporary denial of right to speak, and so on) by the presiding officer of the Legislature.[3]

This relationship is possible because each of the teams acknowledges a higher aim than winning the game: namely, to keep the government functioning. This is the real meaning of the game, and the game can be played only if the parties are not so definitely opposed to one another that victory for the party becomes the primary aim. The system presupposes that the members of all parties are fundamentally united in a profound and strong sense of community, which enables them to place national unity above all party interests.

Although this conception of the party and party antagonism belongs to a very recent phase in the development of political institutions, it may be worth-while to trace it back into the archaic phases of society. We know the dualism of primitive society, where a tribe is split into two exogamic phratries that have different totems and where an antagonistic but "agonal" relationship exists between these two totemistic phratries.[4] We know, furthermore, that the two political parties of the Blues and the Reds (a symbolism still in use in military maneuvers) in Byzantium sprang from the clubs that contested at the races. They managed the races (*Ludi*) and were at the same time political organizations.[5]

Nobody who has watched a presidential or gubernatorial

[2] The Greek word *agon* means an athletic contest.

[3] A. Lawrence Lowell, *The Government of England* (New York: The Macmillan Company, 1926), Ch. XII on procedure in the House of Commons.

[4] J. Huizinga, *Homo Ludens; A Study of the Play-Element in Culture* (London, Routledge & Kegan Paul, Ltd., 1949), pp. 53 ff.

[5] *Ibid.*

campaign in the United States, from the pre-nomination con-
tests to the final election, can fail to recognize the sportive or
game element; the voters at least take it largely like a game
of chance, or like a match between various teams and cham-
pions; the very fact that wagers are made and that the prevalent odds are used (together with polls) in predicting the
chances of the contestants, is highly significant. The game,
however, may turn deadly earnest when the sociological
premises change. The great Dutch historian who was perhaps the first to point out the elements of play in British and
American party politics saw the danger. Writing in the days
of the imminent world domination by authoritarian political
orders, he made the following melancholic comments:

> More and more the sad conclusion forces itself upon us that the
> play-element in culture has been on the wane ever since the 18th cen-
> tury, when it was in full flower. Civilization today is no longer played,
> and even where it still seems to play it is false play—I had almost said,
> it plays false, so that it becomes increasingly difficult to tell where
> play ends and non-play begins. This is particularly true of politics.
>
> Not very long ago political life in parliamentary democratic form
> was full of unmistakable play-features. One of my pupils has recently
> worked up my observations on this subject into a thesis on parlia-
> mentary eloquence in France and England, showing how, ever since
> the end of the 18th century, debates in the House of Commons have
> been conducted very largely according to the rules of a game and in
> the true play-spirit. Personal rivalries are always at work, keeping up a
> continual match between the players whose object is to checkmate
> one another, but without prejudice to the interests of the country
> which they serve with all seriousness. The mood and manners of
> parliamentary democracy were, until recently, those of fair play both in
> England and in the countries that had adopted the English model
> with some felicity. The spirit of fellowship would allow the bitterest
> opponents a friendly chat even after the most virulent debate. It was
> in this style that the "Gentleman's Agreement" arose. . . . There can be
> no doubt that it is just this play-element that keeps parliamentary life
> healthy, at least in Great Britain, despite the abuse that has been lately
> heaped upon it. The elasticity of human relationships underlying the
> political machinery permits it to "play," thus easing tensions which
> would otherwise be unendurable or dangerous—for it is the decay of
> humor that kills. We need hardly add that this play-factor is present in
> the whole apparatus of elections.

In American politics it is even more evident. Long before the two-party system had reduced itself to two gigantic teams whose political differences were hardly discernible to an outsider, electioneering in America had developed into a kind of national sport. The presidential election of 1840 set the pace for all subsequent elections. . . . The emotionality of American politics lies deep in the origins of the American nation itself: Americans have ever remained true to the rough and tumble of pioneer life. There is a great deal that is endearing in American politics, something naïve and spontaneous for which we look in vain in the dragoonings and drillings, or worse, of the contemporary European scene.[6]

In the meantime, two of the game-spoiling political orders have succumbed to the combined forces of democratic, game-playing powers and the non-charismatic order of the Bolshevists.

The present-day Communists, like the fascistic political groups are not good sports from the point of view of party government. Because, for them, the essence of politics is the friend-foe relationship (a formulation invented by Carl Schmitt), instead of seeking to attain a compromise, they seek to annihilate the political adversary. Transferring the sociological pattern of international relations to the scene of domestic politics, these political orders deny the existence of a community between the adherents of different political creeds. No longer is the opposition regarded as acting presumably in good faith—it becomes the absolute enemy.

But even within the orbit of Western democracy, certain symptoms of a deep-seated inner crisis of party-government are discernible. The parliamentary system in its classical form was developed in England at a time when the old and the new ruling classes had settled most of their differences and had merged to a great extent by intermarriage and business connections.[7] There persisted the old antagonism between church and chapel, and that between the country squires and

[6] *Ibid.*, pp. 206-208.
[7] R. B. Smellie, *A Hundred Years of English Government* (London, 1937), pp. 67 ff.

their retainers on the one side and the merchant and manufacturing classes on the other side. The latter, in their non-conformist anti-ecclesiastic attitude, were supported by the high nobility of reformation origin which had enriched itself at the cost of the church. But there were no very fundamental differences of opinion with regard to the constitution or basic political institutions. Thus the parties were really factions within the ruling class of landed proprietors and industrial and commercial entrepreneurs. In such a situation, each party can be confident that the opposition party, if it should come to power by a shift in the party preferences of the voters, will not do anything which would seriously upset the established social and political order.[8]

The gradual extension of the franchise during the nineteenth century and the rise of the Labor Party in the twentieth century seemed to endanger this system.[9] For now a new class, opposed to the political dominance of land owners and capitalists, had entered the political arena and was sending into Parliament men who did not share the economic interests and political ideas of the ruling classes. In Italy, Germany, Spain, and other countries without a long experience of participation in political life by the broad masses of the people, an analogous situation had been or was soon to become the doom of constitutional government. In Great Britain, the system, in spite of Mosley's attempt to create a British Fascist party, survived the two severe crises of the depression of 1927–1933, and of the Second World War. The explanation may be found partly in the training and traditions of the political élite, including the leaders of the Labor Party. The same is true of the Scandinavian countries.

The system can function even where antagonistic social classes compete for political dominance, provided that all parties are agreed upon the necessity of preserving certain

[8] Lowell, *op. cit.*, Chap. XXIV.
[9] *Ibid.*, pp. 350 f.

basic political institutions (even at the price of postponement of ultimate political aims) and provided that the anti-democratic activists of various denominations can be kept out of the ranks of political leadership.

The integration of the many particular wills in the modern "great society" (Graham Wallas) into a united group-will depends in the last analysis on the existence of a general respect for compromise. This can spring only from a fundamental, deep-seated sense of community. It has been the good fortune of the British that they have developed and preserved this sense of community.

Readiness and willingness to compromise are not merely matters of expedience and tactics. There are, in political affairs, situations in which a good politician and an upright citizen should not compromise, but rather stick to convictions and principles. When we speak of the will to compromise which springs from a sense of community, we mean the willingness to sacrifice the pursuit of particular groups interests for the benefit of the common good, the willingness to see the good reasons in the antagonist's point of view and to search, together, for a solution acceptable to both parties. In this sense, the will to compromise and the respect for compromises agreed upon are essential for the formation of a common political will.

Throughout the nineteenth and twentieth centuries so far, the British ruling classes seem to have been more free from fear of the lower classes than any other European ruling class, and at the same time they have been more willing to let the leaders of the rising lower classes have a share in political responsibility. As a result, the lower social classes, especially labor, in Britain seem to have put more confidence in reform and adjustment than those in other large nations of Europe.[10]

[10] Smellie, op. cit., p. 353, observes that the underlying unity upon which the two-party system rested was endangered after the First World War. However, a new unity seemed to be developing between Conservatives and Labor, both agreeing that some kind of an economic plan had to be adopted.

In this respect, the political scene of Great Britain has much in common with that of the Scandinavian countries.

Another important factor in these countries was the broadening of the labor parties into real people's parties, whereas in Germany and Austria they remained essentially parties of the proletariat with an insecure fringe among the lower ranks of salaried workers and civil servants.[11]

Apart from the threat of class antagonism, there are certain tendencies in party structure which may turn out to be fatal for party government. We refer to those previously discussed tendencies which may impair the independence of individual members within the party. The very essence of democracy can be endangered if political parties are too elaborately organized. If the party, in becoming a big organization, has attracted a large body of permanent members who develop many ties with party-sponsored institutions, the leaders will manage to gain effective control over the members. In other words, the voter's freedom of choice between candidates or parties will be impaired. The high commands of each party, being able to count on certain blocs of voters, will become less and less willing to strike genuine compromises than if they had to compete with other parties for a large mass of independent voters.

One of the most astute critics of party government has expressed this idea as follows: an election can either result in genuine representation if it is meant to select the best men, or it can mean a mere appointment of agents for special interests; in this latter case the elected delegate is the dependent and subordinate employee of the electors. "As soon as permanent party organizations dominate as fixed, always present entities in parliament, the latter is no longer a representation of the people but a body of agents." [12]

This statement of a contemporary political scientist sounds

---

[11] Compare *ibid.*, p. 355.

[12] Carl Schmitt, *Verfassungslehre* (München und Leipzig, 1928), p. 219.

very much like the earlier liberal arguments against parties which we discussed in the beginning of this section. But it was not meant that way. A few years later, its author became a councilor of state for a modern dictator. Nevertheless, if we take the statement at its face value, it deserves serious consideration. Modern democracy is confronted with a dilemma: it cannot function, at least not in times of international tensions and crises, without a certain amount of discipline in the political parties—and yet one feels that party discipline ought not be carried too far. The voter should have the freedom to bolt from his party without fear of recrimination, and the elected representative of the people should have the freedom to vote according to his conviction—even against the majority of his party.

Seen in this light, a relative looseness of party ties, as it exists in the United States Congress and in the state legislatures, may in the long run prove to be a healthy condition.

SOCIAL MOVEMENTS AND THE SOCIAL ORDER

The rise of social movements in a society is a symptom of discontent with the existing social order. Political parties can come into existence, as we have seen, because of antagonism between groups of power-desiring people who, though not at all dissatisfied with the existing social order, want to occupy positions of control and remunerative public offices. Genuine social movements, as we have defined the concept, aim at changes in the social order. They arise therefore among people who are dissatisfied with the order that is in operation.[13]

Dissatisfaction with a social order arises when individuals no longer consider the values and norms on which the order

[13] The only exceptions are those movements which represent a reaction against the original movement—the conservative movements which profess to defend the status quo. Actually, these intend to hold up changes in the social structure which are already in the making, and *in this sense* they, too, want to change the present order by restoration of an older order.

is based to be the best or only possible values and norms. The agreement on social values and norms is the essence of social solidarity or of the sense of community. The sense of community is the foundation of any social order. Even certain social entities which come into existence through mere purposive or utilitarian motivations—like most purely contractual relations and associations—can not be maintained unless there is an underlying minimum sense of community among the partners. Otherwise the mutual confidence would be lacking which makes contractual relations possible and worthwhile. In the political field, a régime based solely upon fear is not a true social order; it is more like an armistice between hostile powers. A genuine social order is possible only where a set of values and a code of conduct are shared by the entire society. This does not mean that *all* values must be shared by every member of the society, nor that *all* norms must be valid for all members of the society. We know of very firmly established social systems—like the medieval Christian society or the old Hindu society—in which various status groups or ethnic and religious groups lived together, each adhering to its specific set of values and its particular code of conduct. A social order of this kind is possible if the *basic* values and the *fundamental* norms are shared by all groups and if the particular values and codes of each group are respected by those who do not recognize them as valid for themselves. This is what we mean by a fundamental sense of community or by *concord,* as we called it before.

From these premises it follows that a social movement which aims at a change in the social order may, under certain conditions, constitute a danger for the very existence of the social order, and we shall presently indicate what those conditions are. On the other hand, we also know that a society is not a static system; we know that external as well as immanent factors—such as an increase in population density—produce changes in the basic conditions of social life, and that codes of conduct and values will be affected by such changes.

In many cases adjustments of the value and norm systems as well as adjustments in social organization will be inevitable if the society is to survive at all. If the dominant minority in a society is unwilling to make the necessary adjustments, these will have to be achieved by concerted action of other groups—in other words, by a social movement. In this kind of situation, a social movement is the force which saves the society from destruction, although the dominant minority may not realize that at the time. This is probably one reason why it is so difficult to oppress permanently a movement whose aims are in harmony with *tendencies* of social change which are immanent in a given society. If repression is at all successful, it may result in a high degree of conformity of overt behavior and in the illusion of preserved or restored social solidarity.

Actually such repression will not extinguish the fire of discontent which smolders on under the surface, and the atmosphere of mutual distrust which is created will lead to further disintegration of the community. The experiences of the Nazi régime have shown this very clearly. While the Nazis achieved a high degree of conformity in behavior, they left, after their fall, the German nation in a state of disintegration, of mutual distrust and disunity worse than ever before.[14]

When a dominant minority resorts to repression (which it may do with the aid of a mass movement), it is usually a symptom of fear resulting from weakness. The very fact that a movement like that of the National Socialists was nursed along by certain groups in the economic, military, and political élite of the German nation because it promised restoration of national solidarity (the ethnic community of the people, or the *Volksgemeinschaft*), was symptomatic of the sense of weakness in those élite groups. By way of contrast, the British

[14] See R. Heberle, *From Democracy to Nazism* (Baton Rouge, Louisiana State University Press, 1945), p. 20.

and the Scandinavian nations were able to overcome and disperse similar movements before they had gained too much force. And this was achieved with a minimum of repression. These are nations in which the basic sense of community is very strong. Perhaps it is symptomatic that in the Swedish parliament the members are seated, not by parties, but in geographic order, according to the districts which they represent; if the leader of the Conservatives and the leader of the Social Democrats are both elected in different districts of Stockholm, they will occupy seats next to each other. The British institution of "His Majesty's opposition" is well known. Before the elections of 1950 the press carried a photograph showing the leaders of the three major parties—Winston Churchill, Mr. Attlee, and the leader of the Liberals, Mr. Davies—in attendance at a prayer meeting in St. Paul's Cathedral, sitting side by side in the front row, facing the high altar. This, we thought, was a most moving symbolization of the deep and strong sense of community among the British people.

In a society where there is this basic sense of community, the free and public expression of various and diverse opinions on public affairs is not regarded as a danger to the social order, as long as the various voices of public opinion respect one another and are willing to debate in sincerity with their opponents. Similarly, a variety of social movements can exist within a society without danger to social solidarity, provided that the members of these movements respect their opponents as fellow members of the larger community with whom they are willing to debate and to search for solutions which are acceptable to all. This is possible as long as political action—in the broadest sense—is regarded as a means and not as an end. Depending on how much a social movement comes to pursue its goals as if they represented ultimate values in themselves instead of means to higher ends, it will constitute a real and serious danger to the society. Thus the danger lies in the elevation of political goals to the rank and dignity of absolute, ultimate ends. It is, as a rule, not difficult to reach agreement on means, but ultimate ends are usually beyond rational discussion.

We may therefore say that social movements and political parties whose members do not claim to be in the possession of the absolute truth are no threat to the social order; they may be on the contrary a sign of vitality of a society. The intransigents, especially the totalitarian movements and their political orders, on the other hand, are bound to destroy the solidarity of a society because they are void of that sense of community which includes even the political opponent. But these movements, while they are led and supported in their beginnings only by small groups of fanatics or enthusiasts, (see Chapter 5), do not spring from nowhere. As we pointed out before, they have their causes in the conditions of a society, they are not only destroyers of a given social order, they are also symptoms of a disintegration which is quite independent from their actions. While any sensible statesman who believes in the existence of values that are of greater importance than political goals will curb such movements, it is not always possible to do this, or to do it successfully. Forcible repression is usually the least appropriate course of action. One has to cure the causes, not the symptoms. Movements of this sort arise when large masses of individuals begin to feel that under the existing social order, in particular under the existing economic and political institutions, they do not have a full stake in their society; they develop the idea that they are only *in* but not really *of* the society.

Those of the Western nations which enjoy a high degree of stability and solidarity in their social order have had political élites who knew how to prevent the spreading of such sentiments. Adequate and well-timed reforms in social institutions can take the wind out of the sails of a radical movement. Almost equally important is the rise of leaders of the discontented groups into the political élite. Again it must be emphasized that the latter policy cannot be applied in dealing with the leaders of totalitarian political orders, because they are not willing to play the game according to the rules of an integrated community.

Suggested Readings

~~~~~~

The following list of collateral readings contains only works in the English language. Most of the titles are quoted in the text or footnotes, but some which are not quoted have been added.

The list is arranged by parts; each title is listed only once, but it should be understood that many readings are relevant to more than one part.

The selections from the *Encyclopedia of the Social Sciences* are by no means complete; the student will find the Encyclopedia a most useful reference work.

For general orientation on the historical background we refer to William L. Langer's *Encyclopedia of World History,* a revised and modernized version of Ploetz's "Epitome" (Houghton Mifflin Company, 1949).

PART I

BECKER, Howard, *German Youth: Bond or Free* (New York, Oxford University Press, 1946).

BLUMER, Herbert, "Social Movements," *New Outline of Principles of Sociology,* A. M. Lee, ed. (New York, Barnes & Noble, Inc., 1946).

CHANDLER, Albert R., *The Clash of Political Ideals, A Source Book on Democracy, Communism, and the Totalitarian State,* 2nd ed. (New York, Appleton-Century-Crofts, Inc., 1949).

COKER, Francis W., *Recent Political Thought* (New York, Appleton-Century-Crofts, Inc., 1934).

DE RUGGIERO, G., "Liberalism," *Encyclopedia of the Social Sciences* (New York, The Macmillan Company, 1942).

ELLIOT, W. Y., *The Pragmatic Revolt in Politics* (New York, The Macmillan Company, 1928).

461

ENGELS, Friedrich, *Socialism, Utopian and Scientific*, E. Aveling, ed. (Chicago, Charles H. Kerr & Co., 1900); (New York, International Publishers Co., Inc., 1935); (London, George Allen & Unwin, Ltd., 1941).

GROSS, Felix, ed., *European Ideologies* (New York, Philosophical Lib., Inc., 1948).

HEIDEN, Konrad, *History of National Socialism* (New York, Alfred A. Knopf, Inc., 1935).

HITLER, ADOLF, *Mein Kampf* (New York, Reynal & Hitchcock, 1940).

HOBHOUSE, L. T., *Liberalism* (New York, Henry Holt & Company, Inc., 1911).

JASZI, Oscar, "Socialism," *Encyclopedia of the Social Sciences* (New York, The Macmillan Company, 1942).

KELSEN, Hans, *The Political Theory of Bolshevism* (Berkeley, University of California Press, 1949).

LAIDLER, Harry W., *Social-Economic Movements* (London, Routledge and K. Paul, 1949), also New York, Thomas Crowell, 1944.

LASKI, Harold J., "The Rise of Liberalism," *Encyclopedia of the Social Sciences* (New York, The Macmillan Company, 1942).

———, *The Rise of European Liberalism* (London, George Allen & Unwin Ltd., 1947).

LENIN, V. I., *State and Revolution* (New York, International Publishers Co., Inc., 1935); (Moscow, Foreign Languages Pub. House, 1949).

MARX, Karl, *A Contribution to the Critique of Political Economy*, trans. by N. I. Stone (New York, International Library Publishing Co., 1904).

———, and ENGELS, Friedrich, *Communist Manifesto* (many editions).

MEADOWS, Paul, "Theses on Social Movements," *Social Forces*, Vol. XXIV (May, 1946).

MICHELS, Roberto, *First Lectures in Political Sociology*, trans. with an introduction by Alfred de Grazia (Minneapolis, University of Minnesota Press, 1949).

PARES, Sir Bernard, *Russia* (New York, Mentor Books, the New American Library of World Literature, Inc., 1949).

SCHUMPETER, Joseph, *Capitalism, Socialism, and Democracy*, 2nd ed. (New York, Harper and Brothers, 1947).

SOMBART, Werner, *Socialism and the Social Movement*, trans. by M. Epstein (New York, E. P. Dutton and Co., Inc., 1909).

STALIN, Joseph, *Leninism* (New York, International Publishers Co., Inc., 1942).

ZIMMERN, Alfred, ed., *Modern Political Doctrines* (London, New York, Oxford University Press, 1939).

PART II

ABEL, Theodore F., *Why Hitler Came into Power* (New York, Prentice-Hall, Inc., 1938).

CANTRIL, Hadley, *The Psychology of Social Movements* (New York, John Wiley & Sons, Inc., 1941).

DE MAN, Hendrik, *The Psychology of Socialism*, trans. from 2nd German ed. by Eden & Cedar Paul (London, George Allen & Unwin, Ltd., 1928).

FROMM, Erich, *Escape from Freedom* (New York, Farrar & Rinehart, 1941).

GILBERT, G. M., *The Psychology of Dictatorship* (New York, The Ronald Press Company, 1950).

HOFFER, Eric, *The True Believer* (New York, Harper and Brothers, 1951).

LASSWELL, H. D., *Psychopathology and Politics* (Chicago, University of Chicago Press, 1934).

MACIVER, Robert M., "The Imputation of Motives," *American Journal of Sociology*, Vol. XLVI, No. 1 (July, 1940).

NEUMANN, Sigmund, "The Conflict of Generations in Contemporary Europe from Versailles to Munich," *Vital Speeches of the Day*, Vol. V., No. 20 (New York, City News Publishing Co., Aug. 1, 1939).

SPRANGER, Eduard, *Types of Men*, trans. by F. J. W. Pigors (Halle/Saale, M. Niemeyer, 1928).

WALLAS, Graham, *Human Nature in Politics* (New York, Alfred A. Knopf, Inc., 1921).

WEBER, Max, *The Theory of Social and Economic Organization*, trans. by A. M. Henderson and T. Parsons (New York, Oxford University Press, 1947), pp. 115 f.

PART III

ANDERSON, C. Arnold, "Agrarianism in Politics," J. S. Roucek, ed., *Twentieth Century Political Thought* (New York, Philosophical Lib., Inc., 1946).

BEARD, Charles A., *The Economic Basis of Politics*, 3rd ed. (New York, Alfred A. Knopf, Inc., 1945).

———, *An Economic Interpretation of the Constitution of the United States* (New York, The Macmillan Company, 1936).

BUCK, Solon J., *The Agrarian Crusade* (New Haven, Yale University Press, 1921).

BUNCHE, R. J., "The Negro in the Political Life of the United States," *Journal of Negro Education*, Vol. X (July, 1941).

CROSSER, Paul K., *Ideologies and American Labor* (New York, Oxford University Press, 1941).

EMERSON, Rupert, "An Analysis of Nationalism in Southeast Asia," *The Far Eastern Quarterly*, Vol. 5, No. 2 (Feb., 1946).

FARMER, Hallie M., "The Economic Background of Southern Populism," *South Atlantic Quarterly*, Vol. XXIX, 1930).

FINE, Nathan, *Labor and Farmer Parties in the United States, 1828-1928* (New York, Hanford Press, 1928).

HAYES, Carlton J. H., *The Historical Evolution of Modern Nationalism* (New York, Ray Long and Richard R. Smith, Inc., 1931).

JACOBY, Erich H., *Agrarian Unrest in Southeast Asia* (New York, Columbia University Press, 1949).

LASKI, Harold J., *The American Democracy* (New York, Viking Press, Inc., 1948).

NORTH, Cecil C., "Class Structure, Class Consciousness, and Party Alignment," *American Sociological Review*, Vol. 2 (June, 1937).

PARSONS, Talcott, "An Analytical Approach to the Theory of Social Stratification," *American Journal of Sociology*, Vol. 45 (May, 1940).

PERLMAN, Selig, *A Theory of the Labor Movement* (New York, The Macmillan Company, 1928).

RICE, Stuart Arthur, *Farmers and Workers in American Politics*, Columbia University Studies in History, Economics, and Public Law, V. 113, No. 2; Whole No. 253 (New York, Columbia University Press, 1924).

SPYKMAN, Nicholas J., "The Social Background of Asiatic Nationalism," *American Journal of Sociology*, Vol. XXXII (Nov., 1926).

TANNENBAUM, Frank, *A Philosophy of Labor* (New York, Alfred A. Knopf, Inc., 1951).

TAWNEY, R. H., *The British Labor Movement* (New Haven, Yale University Press, 1925).

TAYLOR, Carl C., and others, *Rural Life in the United States* (New York, Alfred A. Knopf, Inc., 1949), Chap. XXIX, "The Farmers' Movement and the Large Farmers Organizations."

TOMASIC, D., "Ideologies and the Structure of Eastern European Society," *American Journal of Sociology*, Vol. LIII, No. 5 (March, 1950).

TÖNNIES, Ferdinand, "Political Parties in Germany," *The Independent Review*, Vol. 3, p. 565 (Sept., 1904).

WEBER, Max, *From Max Weber: Essays in Sociology*, H. H. Gerth and C. Wright Mills, eds. (New York, Oxford University Press, 1946), Chap. VII, "Class, Status, Party."

PART IV

ANDERSON, Dewey, and DAVIDSON, Percy E., *Ballots and the Democratic Class Struggle* (Stanford, Calif., Stanford University Press, 1943).

BLUMER, Herbert, "Public Opinion and Public Opinion Polling," *American Sociological Review,* Vol. XIII, No. 5 (December, 1948).

CANTRIL, Hadley, *Gauging Public Opinion* (Princeton, Princeton University Press, 1944).

DODD, William E., "Social and Economic Background of Woodrow Wilson," *Journal of Political Economy,* Vol. 25 (1917).

GALLUP, G. H., *A Guide to Public Opinion Polls* (Princeton, Princeton University Press, 1948).

GOSNELL, Harold F., *Grass Roots Politics, National Voting Behavior of Typical States* (Washington, D.C., American Council on Public Affairs, 1942).

HEBERLE, Rudolf, *From Democracy to Nazism: A Regional Case Study on Political Parties in Germany* (Baton Rouge, Louisiana State University Press, 1945).

———, "The Ecology of Political Parties," *American Sociological Review,* Vol. 9 (August, 1944).

HOLCOMBE, Arthur N., *The Political Parties of Today* (New York, Harper and Brothers, 1924).

KEY, V. O., with the assistance of Alexander Heard, *Southern Politics, in State and Nation* (New York, Alfred A. Knopf, Inc., 1949).

LAZARSFELD, Paul F., BERELSON, Bernard, and GAUDET, Hazel, *The People's Choice,* 2nd ed. (New York, Columbia University Press, 1948).

LOOMIS, Charles P., and BEEGLE, Allan, "The Spread of German Nazism in Rural Areas," *American Sociological Review,* Vol. II, No. 6 (Dec., 1946).

OGBURN, W. F., and PETERSON, D., "Political Thought of Social Classes," *Political Science Quarterly,* Vol. 31 (June, 1916).

PAULLIN, Charles O., *Atlas of the Historical Geography of the United States,* John K. Wright, ed. (Published jointly by Carnegie Institute of Washington and American Geographical Society of New York, 1932).

RICE, Stuart, *Quantitative Methods in Politics* (New York, Alfred A. Knopf, Inc., 1928).

ROGERS, Lindsay, *The Pollsters; Public Opinion, Politics, and Democratic Leadership* (New York, Afred A. Knopf, Inc., 1949).

TINGSTEN, Herbert, *Political Behavior, Studies in Election Statistics,* Stockholm Economic Studies No. 7 (London, P. S. King & Son, Ltd., 1937).

PART V

BARBASH, Jack, *Labor Unions in Action* (New York, Harper and Brothers, 1948).

BEARD, Charles A., *American Government and Politics* (New York, The Macmillan Company, 1944).

Cousens, Theodore W., *Politics and Political Organizations in America* (New York, The Macmillan Company, 1942).

Ebon, Martin, *World Communism Today* (New York, McGraw-Hill Book Company, Inc., 1948).

Finer, Herman, *The Theory and Practice of Modern Government*, Rev. ed. (New York, Henry Holt & Company, Inc., 1949).

Gerth, Hans, "The Nazi Party: Its Leadership and Composition," *The American Journal of Sociology*, Vol. XLV (Jan., 1940).

Gosnell, Harold F., *Machine Politics, Chicago Model* (Chicago, University of Chicago Press, 1937).

———, "Parties, Political—Organization," *Encyclopedia of the Social Sciences* (New York, The Macmillan Company, 1942).

Key, V. O., *Politics, Parties, and Pressure Groups*, 2nd ed. (New York, Thomas Y. Crowell Company, 1947).

MacMahon, A. W., "Parties, Political; United States," *Encyclopedia of the Social Sciences* (New York, The Macmillan Company, 1942).

McGoldrich, J., "Clubs, Political," in *Encyclopedia of the Social Sciences* (New York, The Macmillan Company, 1942).

McHenry, Dean E., *His Majesty's Opposition, Structure and Problems of the British Labour Party 1931-1938* (Berkeley, California, University of California Press, 1940).

Michels, Robert, *Political Parties—A Sociological Study of the Oligarchic Tendencies of Modern Democracy*, trans. by Eden and Cedar Paul (Glencoe, Ill., The Free Press, 1949).

Neumann, Sigmund, *Permanent Revolution, The Total State in a World at War* (New York, London, Harper and Brothers, 1942).

Ostrogorski, M., *Democracy and the Organization of Political Parties*, trans. by Frederick Clark (New York, The Macmillan Company, 1908).

Pollock, James K., Jr., "British Party Organization," *Political Science Quarterly*, Vol. XLV, No. 2 (June, 1930).

———, "A Comparison of the American and British Party Systems," *Journal of the Royal Institute of International Affairs*, Vol. 9 (Mar., 1930).

———, "The German Party System," *American Political Science Review*, Vol. XXIII (Nov., 1929).

"The Report of the Royal Commission to investigate the facts relating to and the circumstances surrounding the communication, by public officials and other persons in positions of trust, of secret and confidential information to agents of a foreign power." (Ottawa, Controller of Stationery 1946, June 27, 1946).

Rosenberg, Arthur, "Socialist Parties," *Encyclopedia of the Social Sciences* (New York, The Macmillan Company, 1942).

Rossi, A., *A Communist Party in Action*, W. Kendall, ed. (New Haven, Yale University Press, 1949).

SAIT, Edward M., *American Parties and Elections,* 4th ed. (Penniman) (New York, Appleton-Century-Crofts, Inc., 1948).
SCHATTSCHNEIDER, E. E., *Party Government* (New York, Farrar & Rinehart, Inc., 1942).
"Trade Unions," *Encyclopedia of the Social Sciences* (New York, The Macmillan Company, 1942). See especially the articles on trade unions in England, Germany, France, and the Scandinavian countries.
WEBER, MAX, *The Theory of Social and Economic Organization,* trans. by A. M. Henderson and Talcott Parsons (New York, Oxford University Press, 1947), Chap. III, especially pp. 407 ff.

PART VI

BECKER, Frances B., "Lenin's Application of Marx's Theory of Revolutionary Tactics," *American Sociological Review,* Vol. II (June, 1937).
BRINTON, Crane, *The Anatomy of Revolution* (New York, W. W. Norton & Company, Inc., 1938).
BRISSENDEN, Paul F., "Industrial Workers of the World," *Encyclopedia of the Social Sciences* (New York, The Macmillan Company, 1942).
ELLIOTT, W. Y., "The Political Application of Romanticism," *Political Science Quarterly,* Vol. 39 (1924).
HUNT, R. N. Carew, *The Theory and Practice of Communism: An Introduction* (New York, The Macmillan Company, 1951).
KOHN, Hans, *Revolutions and Dictatorships* (Cambridge, Harvard University Press, 1941).
LENIN, V. I., "What Is to Be Done?" (1902), *Collected Works,* Vol. IV, book 2. Also (New York, International Publishers Co., Inc., 1929).
LORWIN, Lewis L., "Direct Action," *Encyclopedia of the Social Sciences* (New York, The Macmillan Company, 1942).
MAYNARD, Sir John, *Russia in Flux,* S. H. Guest, ed. (New York, The Macmillan Company, 1948).
MERTON, Robert K., "Unanticipated Consequences of Purposive Social Action," *American Sociological Review,* Vol I., No. 6 (Dec., 1936).
MEUSEL, Alfred, "Revolution and Counterrevolution," *Encyclopedia of the Social Sciences* (New York, The Macmillan Company, 1942).
NEUMANN, Sigmund, "The Structure and Strategy of Revolution: 1848 and 1948," *The Journal of Politics,* Vol. XI (Aug., 1949).
ROTHFELS, Hans, *The German Opposition to Hitler, An Appraisal,* The Humanist Library (Chicago, Henry Regnery Co., 1948).
The Strategy and Tactics of World Communism, Report of Subcommittee number 5, National and International Movements, Committee on Foreign Affairs, 80th Congress, 2nd session, House Document no. 619 (Washington, U.S. Government Printing Office, 1948).

TAYLOR, Carl C., "Notes on Some Theoretical Aspects of the Effect of Direct Action Farmers' Movements on Farmers' Organizations," *Social Forces,* Vol. XII, No. 3 (Mar. 1933).

TETREAU, E. D., "How to Study the Sociology of Direct Action Farmers' Movements," *Social Forces,* Vol. XII, No. 3 (Mar. 1933).

VERNADSKY, George, *A History of Russia,* new rev. ed. (New Haven, Yale University Press, 1949).

WAKELEY, Ray E., "How to Study the Effects of Direct Action Movements on Farm Organizations," *Social Forces,* Vol. XII, No. 3 (Mar. 1933).

PART VII

DOBLIN, Ernest M., and POHLY, Claire, "The Social Composition of the Nazi Leadership," *American Journal of Sociology,* Vol. LI, No. 1 (July, 1945).

HERMENS, Ferdinand A., "Democracy and Proportional Representation," *Public Policy Pamphlets* (1940).

LASKI, Harold J., *The American Presidency* (New York, Harper and Brothers, 1940).

LINDSAY, A. D., *The Essentials of Democracy* (Philadelphia, University of Pennsylvania Press, 1929).

LOWELL, A. Lawrence, *The Government of England* (New York, The Macmillan Company, 1926).

MILLS, C. Wright, and SCHNEIDER, Helen, *The New Men of Power: America's Labor Leaders* (New York, Harcourt, Brace & Company, Inc., 1948).

MOSCA, G., *The Ruling Class,* Livingston, ed. (New York, McGraw-Hill Book Company, Inc. 1939).

PALMER, Paul A., "Ferdinand Tönnies' Theory of Public Opinion," *Public Opinion Quarterly,* Vol. 2 (1938).

"The Presidency in Transition," *The Journal of Politics,* Vol. XI, No. 1 (Feb. 1949) (A special issue on the presidency).

ROGERS, Lindsay, *The American Senate* (New York, F. S. Crofts & Co., 1931).

SMELLIE, K. B., *A Hundred Years of English Government* (London, Gerald Duckworth & Co., Ltd., 1937).

WEBER, Max, "Politics as a Vocation," in Gerth and Mills, *From Max Weber: Essays in Sociology* (New York, Oxford University Press, 1946).

Index

Brissenden, 387, 466
Bruce, Harold R., 317
Bryce, James, 426
Buck, Solon J., 292, 462
Buelow-Kummerow, von, 58
Bulgaria, 332
Bunche, R. J., 462
Bund der Landwirte, 58, 292, 320
Burgess, J. Stewart, 3
Burke, Edmund, 10, 29, 45, 51, 52, 135
Burma, 145
Byzantium, 448

Cabinet,
  British, 443
  U. S. A., 442-444
Calhoun, John C., 415
California, 248
Canada spy case, 343, 344
Cannon, James P., 334
Cantril, Hadley, 3, 201, 462, 464
Capitalism, 33, 35, 49, 72
Capitalistic enterprise system, *see* Capitalism
Cash, W. J., 59, 185
Catholic Center Party, *see* Zentrumspartei
Caucus, 304, 425
Cavour, 120
Centers, Richard, 177
Central Office in British parties, 310, 311
Chafee, Zechariah, 364
Chamberlain, Joseph, 307
Chandler, Albert R., 385, 460
Change, Social, *see* Social change
Charisma, 288
Charismatic leader, 132, 136, 137, 288, 315, 433
Chartism, 378, 386
Chateaubriand, 51
Chicago, 260
China, 64, 332
Christensen, A., 101
Christian-Democratic Union, 166
Christian Trade Unions, 166
Civil rights, 46
Civil war, 120

Class, *see* Social class
Class consciousness, 7, 158
Class struggle, 75, 76, 77
Clausewitz, Karl von, 359, 360, 361
Cobban, Alfred, 167
Coker, Francis W., 53, 54, 460
Comintern (Communist International), 81, 436
Commons, John R., 179
Communism, 36, 63 f.
  future, 89
Communist League, 335
Communist Manifesto (Manifesto of the Communist Party), 25, 27, 71
Communist movement, 139, 334, 436
Communist Party, 65, 116, 147, 171, 276, 297, 433, 435
  in France, 329, 406
  in Germany, 165
  Lenin's concept of, 86, 350
  in Russia, *see* Bolsheviki
  in U. S. A., 302, 340, 346, 406, 429
Communistic communities, 70
Communists, 108, 116, 166, 171, 182, 450
Competition, 431, 433, 438, 448
Compromise, 452, 453
Conant, James B., 127
Confédération Générale du Travail, 329
Congress of Industrial Organizations (CIO), 182, 299-302
Congress of U. S. A., 442-446, 454
  committees of, 426
Conservateur, Le, 51
Conservatism, 37, 50
  American, 59; attitude in, 241-248
  British, 51, 53
  German (Prussian), 52, 53, 55 ff.
Conservative Party, 56, 57, 58, 135, 319, 321
Conservatives, 46, 170, 281
Constitutional government, 46
Constitutive ideas, 11, 13, 63
Consumers' coöperatives, 35, 175, 318
Correlation, coefficients of, 207, 226
Couch, W. T., 177
Counter-revolution, 30, 370, 372, 373, 403

Illegality, 338, 342
Illinois, 248
Immigrant groups, in U.S.A., 121, 147;
   see also Ethnic groups
India, 145
Indo-China, 145
Industrial Workers of the World (I.W.W.), 179
Infiltration, 292
Insecurity, economic, 243
Intellectuals, 83, 126, 127, 336
Intelligentsia, 83, 86, 372
Iowa, 243, 245, 248
Irish in U.S.A., 146
Italians in U.S.A., 147
Italy, 237, 332, 451

Jacoby, Erich H., 145, 463
Jack, T. H., 251
Jackson, James E., 396
Janet, Claudio, 305
Jaszi, Oscar, 461
Jefferson, 45
Jeffersonians, 60
Jesuits, 351-353
Jews, 126, 146
Jones, Claudia, 397
Jordan, Erich, 57, 136, 320
Jungvolk, 291
Junkers, 51, 55, 56
Jurkat, Ernst, 13

Kathedersocialisten, 67
Kaufmann, Erich, 423, 440
Kautsky, K., 85
Kelsen, Hans, 89, 417, 425, 461
Kendall, W., 424
Key, V. O., 254, 257, 258, 294, 464, 465
Kinneman, John A., 260
Knights of Labor, 179
Knights Templar, 351
Koch-Weser, Walter, 379
Kogon, Eugen, 437
Kohn, Hans, 466
Komsomol, 291
Konopszynski, L., 424

Krapotkin, 70
Krehbiel, Edward, 222
Kreuzzeitung, 57
Kulturlandschaft, 214, 215
Kuomintang, 332

Labor Movement, 35, 63, 80, 113, 174 f., 273, 431
Labor Party, British, 171, 291, 312, 451, 453;
   see also England
Labor unions, 35, 140, 175, 290, 329, 432
Labor's League for Political Education, 182, 299 f.
LaFollette, Robert M., 298
Laidler, Harry W., 3, 65, 68, 70, 147, 179, 381, 384, 461
Laissez-faire, 48
Lammenais, 51
Lassalle, 112
Laski, Harold J., 49, 181, 426, 427, 442, 444, 461, 463, 467
Lasswell, H. D., 103, 106, 112, 462
Latvians, 145
Lazarsfeld, Paul F., 202, 464
Leader, 132, 287, 403, 433, 436;
   see also Charisma
League for Industrial Democracy, 8
LeBon, Gustave, 97, 106
Lederer, Emil, 320, 401
Lenin, 25, 29, 79, 82-99, 139, 336-338, 339, 388, 397, 461, 466
Lennox, R., 51
Ley, 110
Liberal Association, 307
Liberal Party, in England, 281
Liberalism, 34, 38-50
   American, 45
   British, 39, 45
   German, 42
   Italian, 42
Liberals, 170
Liberty, 39, 55
Lindsay, A. D., 47, 413, 418, 467
Lithuanians, 145, 146
Litvinoff, Maxime, 116
Locke, 46
Lombroso, 106

INDEX

475

Neumann, Sigmund, 3, 288, 384,
433, 434, 462, 465, 466
Neurosis, 109
Nihilists, 384
Nilson, Sten Sparre, 208, 263
Nitzschke, Heinz, 4
Noetzel, Karl, 83
Nonpartisan League, 182, 241
Non-partisan policy, 292
Non-violent resistance, 385
Nordhoff, Charles, 70
North, Cecil C., 174, 463
North Dakota, 241, 243, 246, 247
Norway, 332

Office of Public Opinion Research,
197
Ogburn, W. F., 206, 216, 464
Ohio, 301
Oldenburg, 56
Oligarchy, 432
Oncken, H., 41, 44
Ordensburgen, 351, 434
Ostrogorski, M. S., 295, 305, 307,
313, 465
Owen, 70

Paine, Thomas, 46
Palmer, Paul A., 420, 467
Panel (interviewing), 202
Pares, Sir Bernard, 81, 461
Pareto, 26
Paris Commune, 85, 87
Park, Robert E., 3
Parker, Carleton, 387
Parliaments, 423, 451
of estates, 303
Parsons, Talcott, 463
Participation, 93, 94, 96
Parti Socialiste, 324
Party, Parties,
meanings of term, 274
membership, 317, 320
opinions about, 411-418
Pauker, Anna, 436
Paullin, 464
Pennsylvania, 248
People's Party, *see* Populism

Percy, William Alexander, 60
Perlman, S., 179, 463
Perón, 332
Personality, 100, 105, 111, 114
Pfautz, H. W., 152
Pieck, 436
Pietists, 57, 232
Planters, 59, 61, 185
Plato, 70
Pohly, Claire, 467
Poles, 146
Politburo, 349
Political Action Committee (CIO-
PAC), 182, 299-302
Political activists, 106, 115
Political "climate," 219, 265
Political clubs, 304, 305
Political parties, 9, 10, 11
American, 136
English, 135
Political type (of man), 103
Pollock, James K., 234, 310, 311,
465
Polls (opinion), 420
Pope, Liston, 177
Pope, Upham, 116
Populism, 187, 189, 240, 241, 256,
291
Portugal, 332
Posse, E. H., 121
Powell, Thomas Reed, 364
President of U.S.A., 442-446
Pressac, Pierre de, 219
Pressure group, 9, 292, 321
Prime Minister, 443, 444
Process, 9
Production, conditions, relationships,
74
Profit-principle, 33
Proletariat, 4, 72, 77
Propaganda, 31, 343
Property, 36, 55, 66, 431
abolition of, 78
Proportional representation, 282, 319,
424
Proudhon, 70
Prussia, 56
Psychoanalysis, 107
Public opinion, 201
Purges, 345, 404